PATHWAYS OF INFLUENCE

European Think Tanks and the Shaping of the European Union's Defensive Economic Policy toward China

XIN HUA

Carter & Co. Publishing

PATHWAYS OF INFLUENCE:

European Think Tanks and the Shaping of the European Union's Defensive Economic Policy Toward China

---

Published by
Carter & Co. Publishing
15601 60th Ave N
Plymouth, MN 55446
USA
www.carterandcopublishing.com

First published 2026

Library of Congress Control Number: 2026911356

ISBN: 978-1-970316-14-8 (paperback)

Book Page: https://www.carterandcopublishing.com/book?id=pathways-influence

Cataloging information is available from the Library of Congress.

Cover design by Min Peng
Edited by Brian Bin Li
Typeset by Dajishe Studio
Production management by Carter & Co. Publishing

Printed and bound in the United States of America

---

10 9 8 7 6 5 4 3 2 1

CONTENTS

Introduction

I. The EU's Strategic Reassessment and Structural Dilemmas under the Changing Circumstances 3

II. Strategic Drivers behind the EU's Formulation of Defensive Economic Policy toward China 23

III. The Outstanding Role of European Think Tanks in the EU's Decision-Making System 33

IV. Existing Literature on European and American Think Tanks 39

V. Research Approach and Structure 44

Chapter 1: Theoretical Frameworks for Explaining the Mechanisms of Think Tanks' Influence over Policymaking

I. Philosophical Ideas Underpinning Think Tanks' Policymaking Influence Mechanisms 53

II. Theoretical Paradigms for Explaining the Mechanisms of Think Tanks' Influence over Policymaking 59

III. Specific Analytical Perspectives and Explanatory Models for Think Tanks' Policymaking Influence Mechanisms 69

IV. Theoretical Framework for Explaining European Think Tanks' Influence over EU Policymaking: Integrating the "Field of Power" Perspective and the Multiple Streams Model 74

Chapter 2: The Overarching Mechanisms of European Think Tanks' Influence in the EU's Decision-Making System

I. Core Typologies of European Think Tanks 86

II. Specific Mechanisms of European Think Tanks' Influence over the EU's Decision-Making 95

III. Pathways of European Think Tanks' Influence in the EU's Decision-Making System: A Comparative Analysis with the U.S. Think Tanks 106

Chapter 3: The Strategic Dynamics Driving the EU's Formulation of Defensive Economic Policy toward China

I. The Contextual Factors Shaping the EU's China-related Decision-Making, 2008-2018 119

II. The EU's Situational Assessment and Strategic Cognition in Advancing Defensive Economic Decision-Making toward China 140

III. The Basic Architecture and Substantive Content of the EU's Defensive Economic Policy toward China 154

Chapter 4: EU-Level Think Tanks' Influence over the EU's Defensive Economic Policy toward China: A Case Study of the Brussels European and Global Economic Laboratory (Bruegel)

I. Existing Literature on the Study of EU-Level Think Tanks 163

II. The Rhythm and Effectiveness of Bruegel's Influence over the EU's Defensive Economic Policymaking toward China: A Comparison between Policy Advice Records and EU Official Policy Documents 172

III. Bruegel's Short-Term Influence over the EU's Defensive Economic Policy toward China: An Examination of the Meetings Convened by Bruegel 180

IV. Bruegel's Long-Term Indirect Influence over the EU's Defensive Economic Policy toward China: An Analysis of Its Participation in Inter-Think Tank Research Collaboration Platforms 186

V. Bruegel's Long-Term Direct Influence over the EU's Defensive Economic Policy toward China: An Analysis of the "Revolving Door" Mechanism 191

VI. Summary of Chapter 4 195

Chapter 5: German Think Tanks' Influence over the EU's Defensive Economic Policy toward China: A Case Study of the German Institute for International and Security Affairs (SWP)

I. Existing Literature on the Study of German Think Tanks 201

II. Efficacy and Rhythm of SWP' Influence over the EU's Defensive Economic Policymaking toward China: A Comparison Between Policy Advice Records and EU Official Policy Documents 206

III. SWP's Long-Term Indirect Influence over the EU's Defensive Economic Policy toward China: An Analysis of Research Projects and Inter-Think Tank Collaboration Platforms 212

VI. SWP's Long-Term Direct Influence over the EU's Defensive Economic Policy toward China: An Examination of the "Revolving Door" System 220

V. Summary of Chapter 5 224

Chapter 6: British Think Tanks' Influence over the EU's Defensive Economic Policy toward China: A Case Study of the Royal Institute of International Affairs (RIIA)

I. Existing Literature on British Think Tanks' Influence over Decision-Making ... 227

II. The "National Route" of British Think Tanks' Influence over EU Decision-Making 230

III. British Think Tanks and the European Think Tank System in the Context of Brexit 235

IV. RIIA's Influence over the EU's Defensive Economic Policy toward China: Comparing Policy Advice Records with EU Official Policy Documents 237

V. RIIA's Short-Term Influence: An Examination of Its Conferences 243

VI. RIIA's Long-Term Indirect Influence: Research Projects and Cooperation Platforms 248

VII. RIIA's Long-Term Direct Influence: Funding Sources and the "Revolving Door" Mechanism 252

VIII. Summary of Chapter 6 260

Conclusion

I. Sources of the Gap Between European and U.S. Think-Tank Systems 265

II. The Precise Positioning of European Think Tanks in the EU's Political Decision-Making System 270

III. Three Defining Features of the Mechanisms Through Which European Think Tanks Shape the EU's Defensive Economic Policy toward China 273

References

I. English Literature 279
II. Literature in Chinese (Including Translated Works) 308

Appendix I: List of Field Interviews with Experts of European Think Tanks

Appendix II: An Institutional Profile of the Brussels European and Global Economic Laboratory (Bruegel)

I. Institutional Overview 313
II. Internal Governance and Organizational Structure 317
III. Research Agenda and Institutional Output 321
IV. Achievements and Development Experience 330

Appendix III: An Institutional Profile of the German Institute for International and Security Affairs (SWP)

I. Institutional Overview 332
II. Internal Governance and Organizational Structure 335
III. Research Agenda and Institutional Output 339
IV. Achievements and Development Experience 345

Appendix IV: An Institutional Profile of the Royal Institute of International Affairs (RIIA)

I. Institutional Overview 348
II. Internal Governance and Organizational Structure 352
III. Research Agenda and Institutional Output 356
IV. Institutional Achievements 364

Index

List of Figures

Figure 1 of Introduction: EU's Future Political Trilemma in Pursuing European Economic and Technological Sovereignty. 22

Figure 1.1: Analytical Framework for Delineating the Position of Think Tanks within the EU Policymaking Structure and Process 78

Figure 2.1: Four Typological Categories of the European Think Tank System, Categorized by the Dual Analytical Dimensions of Specialization and Partisanship 88

Figure 2.2: 13 Modalities Through Which European Think Tanks Exert Influence over EU Decision-Making and Their Associated Typological Classification............ 98

Figure 2.3: The Position of U.S. Think Tanks in the U.S. Political Decision-Making System 108

Figure 2.4: Overall Roadmap of the Brussels Route and National Route for European Think Tanks' Influence over EU Decision-Making 113

Figure 2.5: Operational Mechanisms of European Think Tanks' Influence over EU Decision-Making via the Brussels Route 116

Figure 3.1: Monthly Changes of the Surpluses of the EU, Germany, and France in their Goods Trade with the United States, January 2016-April 2017 (Unit: US$ million) 131

Figure 3.2: Monthly Changes in the Growth Rates of the Surpluses of the EU, Germany, and France in their Goods Trade with the United States, February 2016-April 2017 (%) 132

Figure 3.3: The Relative Positions of China, Japan, the United States, and the EU in the Global Economic System (2010-2017) 136

Figure 6.1: Pyramid Structure of the UK Foreign Policymaking System 232

Figure 6.2: The Pathways of the "National Route" for British Think Tanks to Influence EU Decision-Making 234

Appendix Figure 1: Funding Structure of Bruegel (2022) 320

Appendix Figure 2: Organizational Structure of the Executive Board of SWP (2023) 337

Appendix Figure 3: Allocation of Federal Government Funding and Composition of External Funding Sources of SWP (2022) 339

Appendix Figure 4: Funding Structure of the Royal Institute of International Affairs (2022) 356

List of Tables

Table 1.1: Analytical Framework for Delineating the Position of Think Tanks in the EU Policymaking Structure and Process 57

Table 2.1: Types and Characteristics of Think Tank Conferences 102

Table 2.2: Analysis of Typological Characteristics of Think Tank Publications 104

Table 2.3: The Hierarchical Position of European Think Tanks in the EU's Decision-Making System 109

Table 3.1: The Status of Major Populist Parties in Selected European Countries (2016-2018) 124

Table 3.2: A Comparison of the Average Annual GDP Growth Rates of China and the Group of Seven Countries (2008-2015).. 135

Table 3.3: Changes in the Shares of Global GDP Held by China and the Group of Seven Countries (2008-2015) 135

Table 3.4: Three Stages in the Responses of the European Union Decision-Making System to the Belt and Road Initiative 146

Table 3.5: The Structure and Content of the EU's Defensive Economic Policy toward China 156

Table 4.1: Comparative Timelines of Bruegel's Policy Recommendations and EU Official Policy Documents on the EU's Defensive Economic Policy toward China (February 2006-September 2018) 175

Table 4.2: Statistics on Meetings Convened by Bruegel Directly Related to EU-China Relations and the EU's Economic Policy toward China (December 2011-June 2018) 181

Table 4.3: Think Tank Collaboration Platforms Involving Bruegel in EU Economic Decision-Making on China (2016-2018) 188

Table 4.4: Bruegel's "Revolving Door": A Statistical Overview (as of September 30, 2018) 192

Table 5.1: Comparative Timelines of SWP's Policy Recommendations and EU Official Policy Documents on the Twelve Key Points of EU Defensive Economic Policy toward China (February 2006-July 2018) 208

Table 5.2: Research Projects Hosted or Participated in by SWP Related to EU Economic Policy toward China (September 2015-September 2018) 214

Table 5.3: Composition of the Research Team of the SWP-Led Project "Elements of German Foreign and Security Policy in a Changing World" (Autumn 2012-End of 2013) 216

Table 5.4: Inter-Think-Tank Collaborative Platforms Involving SWP with Potential Influence over the EU's Economic Policy toward China 219

Table 5.5: Analysis of the Revolving-Door Structure of SWP Personnel (as of the End of September 2018) 222

Table 6.1: Comparison of Timings and Formats of the RIIA's Policy Advice and the EU's Policy Documents on Twelve Key Points of EU's Defensive Economic Policy toward China (December 2005-September 2018) 239

Table 6.2: Statistics on Meetings Convened by RIIA on Issues Directly Related to EU-China Relations and the EU's Economic Policy toward China (November 2006-June 2018) 244

Table 6.3: Research Projects Operated by RIIA Directly Related to EU–China Relations (Early 2014–September 2018) 250

Table 6.4: Think Tank Collaboration Platforms Involving RIIA in EU Economic Decision-Making on China (early 2016–September 2018) 251

Table 6.5: Overview of Funding Sources for Research at the RIIA (2014-2017) 254

Table 6.6: Analysis of the Revolving-Door Structure of RIIA Personnel (as of the End of September 2018) 257

Appendix Table 1: Linkages between Priority Research Projects (2023–2024) and Traditional Policy Areas at Bruegel 328

Appendix Table 2: Distribution of RIIA Research Staff by Field and Position, 2023 (Unit: Number of People) 357

Introduction

Economic relationships, often described as the ballast of China-U.S. relations, actually carry even greater significance in China-European Union (EU) relations. Considerable geographical distance apart and the EU's peripheral role in the Asia-Pacific strategic-security architecture mean that while China and the EU harbor no overtly conflicting strategic interests, they also lack a compelling imperative for maintaining sustained, high-intensity strategic engagement. Rather, the stability, continuity, and incremental development of their relations are fundamentally underpinned by an intricate network of mutual economic interests. The centrality of economic considerations in the EU's strategic calculus vis-à-vis China is conspicuously evidenced in its official policy discourse. The European Commission's policy paper *Elements for a New EU Strategy on China*, promulgated on June 22, 2016, dedicates the bulk of its substantive content to detailing China-EU economic relations and the overarching principles of EU economic policy toward China.[①] Similarly, the *Joint Statement of the 20th EU-China Summit* on July 16, 2018 enumerates 44 key points, with 25 or over half of its substantive provisions directly addressing economic relations,[②] the very fact of which underscores the structural importance of economic interaction in the China-EU relationship. Nevertheless, the macro-structure and operational dynamics of China-EU economic relations are subject to a complex array of influential factors: they are conditioned not only by the overarching constraints inherent in the global economic system and the international strategic-security order, but are also profoundly shaped by the respective domestic strategic environments, internal trajectories of economic development, and processes of societal transformation within China and the EU, as well as by the respective orientations and intentions of their foreign economic policies.

---

① European Commission, Joint Communication to the European Parliament and the Council, Elements for a New EU Strategy on China, JOIN (2016) 30 final, Brussels, June 22, 2016.

② Council of the European Union, Joint Statement of the 20th EU-China Summit. July 16, 2018.

The 2008 global financial crisis precipitated a seismic transformation in the structural architecture and operational rhythm of the world economy and, by extension, the international strategic-security system, causing a consequential shift in the trajectory of China-EU relations and the EU's policy orientation toward China. In the ensuing decade after 2008, the EU faced a series of external and internal disruptions. Externally, turmoil in the Middle East and North Africa arising from the 2011 Arab Spring and the 2014-2015 Ukraine crisis exacerbated a progressive fragmentation of the EU's peripheral strategic-security environment. Concurrently, the multilateral trading system represented by the World Trade Organization—along with the broader architecture of global governance—encountered mounting resistance and even signs of erosion. Internally, the economic dividends generated by the dual processes of post-Cold War economic globalization and European regional integration had been largely exhausted, while the inherent socio-political contradictions entered a phase of intense eruption. This facilitated the dramatic entry of once-marginal populist political forces into the mainstream of politics and, in several instances, even swept them to power. Against this backdrop of compounded internal and external pressures, the EU has, since roughly 2011-2012, met with successive crises that have shaken the normative foundations of its long-cherished system of values, including economic globalization, regional integration, left-liberalism, and cultural pluralism. Faced with such multifaceted predicaments, EU decision-makers are compelled to reassess and revamp their policy frameworks. In this context, the EU's strategic considerations and policy orientations toward China have undergone a profound shift. A particularly notable trend is the gradual expansion, refinement, and institutionalization of the EU's "defensive" economic policy toward China. Currently, this evolving policy architecture spans multiple domains from trade, investment, and industry to technology transfer, intellectual property protection, and other areas. It is gradually exerting a formative influence not merely on the fundamental outlook of China-EU economic relations but also on the prospective developmental trajectory of the broader bilateral strategic partnership. Consequently, it is of considerable academic and practical significance to analyze and elucidate the role and influence of European think tanks—as pivotal societal actors of the European polity—in the formulation and steering of the EU's "defensive" economic policy toward China. Such research carries profound implications well beyond the policy realm.

I. The EU's Strategic Reassessment and Structural Dilemmas under the Changing Circumstances

In the decade following the outbreak of the 2008 global financial crisis, dramatic shifts in Europe's internal and external circumstances forced its political elites and the EU decision-makers to constantly revise their strategic perceptions and repeatedly adjust the agendasetting, policy preferences, focal concerns, and decision-making pathways of the EU's external strategies and specific policies. Yet, certain inherent structural features of the EU's institutional framework invariably impede its decision-making process, creating much oscillation and uncertainty in the European integration process.

1.1 The EU's Overall Assessment of the Changing Circumstances since the 2008 Global Financial Crisis

In adapting to shifting macro situations and evolving strategic intentions, the EU leadership's overarching perceptions, strategic positioning, fundamental attitudes, and policy formulations regarding China have undergone substantial change. Europe's changing internal and external landscapes can be broadly categorized into three dimensions.

First, the course of economic globalization and the liberal international order that have defined the international system since the end of the Cold War are encountering significant setbacks and entering a phase of pronounced turbulence. This structural shift compels the EU to fundamentally reassess its strategic outlook and redefine its policy intentions. Both the contemporary multilateral trading system and global governance architecture are currently experiencing systemic crises, with populist forces establishing a visible presence in mainstream Western politics. Meanwhile, deepening societal cracks in both Europe and the United States have generated formidable resistance to globalization. Confronted with these challenges, the EU's new leadership has increasingly downplayed its self-perceived image as a "normative power", shifting its focus instead toward building genuine and substantive "sovereignty" for the European integration process per se. This strategic pivot aims to bolster the EU's internal decision-making authority and enhance its capacity to respond more effectively to global crises.

On the one hand, the subsequent eruptions of the global financial crisis and the Euro area crisis between 2008 and 2010 came as a proverbial "Pandora's Box", unleashing profound and destabilizing change across the global economic spectrum and the international politic arena. The period from 2016 to 2017 witnessed a series of consequential events, most notably the UK's referendum on EU membership ("Brexit"), the election of Donald Trump as President of the United States, and the accelerating entry of populist political movements into the mainstream of Western politics. All these precipitated dramatic realignments in the internal political fabrics of both the United States and Europe. These internal shifts, in turn, exerted a profound influence on their external economic relations. International commercial frictions have intensified markedly, the global governance framework has been significantly undermined by sustained skepticism and contestation from the United States, and the positive momentum of economic globalization has effectively stalled, with clear signs of regression in multiple domains.

On the other hand, the Western strategic studies community has engaged in more intensive and critical scrutiny of the inherent flaws and distributional consequences of the globalization process and the liberal international order, revealing a deepening crisis of the existing system. Comparatively speaking, EU policymakers and scholars alike—partly because of their more deeply ingrained ideological commitment to globalization and liberal internationalism—are limited in their response to and analysis of these macro shifts in the international strategic scene. American scholars and policymakers, however, have shown greater sensitivity to these shifts. In light of major breakthroughs in cutting-edge technology, the rapid rise of emerging economies and the quiet emergence of populist forces in the United States and Europe since 2010, American scholars have come to realize that the well-established globalization process and liberal international order since the end of the Cold War might fall into turmoil, with various forces in the international strategic space already kickstarting a new round of reorganization.[①] In the wake of the ongoing seismic events, this critical discourse in American academia has intensified in both frequency and stridency after 2016-2017. Influential scholars such as economist Dani Rodrik and international relations

---

① Between 2010 and 2012, American economists such as Dani Rodrik and Joseph Stiglitz, as well as strategists like Michael D. Swaine and John J. Mearsheimer already criticized economic globalization and the liberal international order, arguing that they would face a severe crisis and predicting the evolution of strategic competition between China and the United States. Representative works on this topic can be found in: Joseph E. Stiglitz, *The Price of Inequality: How Today's Divided Society Endangers Our Future*, New York: W. W. Norton & Company, 2012, pp. 1-19.

theorist John J. Mearsheimer have gone so far as to publicly question the long-term viability of the U.S.-led liberal international order established after the Cold War,[①] which resonates well with some European intellectuals.

The profound turbulence in the international configuration, amplified by this pervasive current of rigorous criticism and sober reflection on globalization, has profoundly unsettled the leadership of the EU and its member states. This has prompted a fundamental and necessary reconsideration of the modalities and pathways for advancing the European integration process in a global environment increasingly hostile to the assumptions of hyper-globalization. Emerging from the evolving policy trajectories of the European Commission under the leaderships of Jean-Claude Juncker and Ursula von der Leyen in recent years is a clear line of deliberate intellectual progression: from the repeated emphasis on the urgent necessity of European solidarity in 2017[②] to vocal advocacy for the construction of what is called European Sovereignty in 2018, culminating in the focused conceptual elaboration of European economic and technological sovereignty between 2019 and 2020. This evolution in the strategic posture of the EU's political elites, shaped by the vicissitudes of the global macro-environment, reflects a crystallizing consensus on a core strategic premise that

① John Mearsheimer, *The Great Delusion: Liberal Dreams and International Realities*, New Haven and London: Yale University Press, 2018, pp. 211-227; "Bound to Fail: The Rise and Fall of the Liberal International Order", *International Security*, Vol. 43, No. 4, Spring 2019, pp. 7-50; Dani Rodrik, *The Globalization Paradox: Why Global Markets, States, and Democracy Can't Coexist*, Oxford, UK and New York: Oxford University Press, 2011, pp. 184-231; *Straight Talk on Trade: Ideas for a Sane World Economy*, Princeton, U.S. and Oxford, UK: Princeton University Press, 2018, pp. 139-158.

② Following the inauguration of Donald Trump as President of the United States in 2017, populist and Eurosceptic political forces across Europe were significantly emboldened. Capitalizing on the shifting transatlantic political climate, these movements rapidly entered the mainstream political arena through parliamentary elections in several major European states, including France, Netherlands, the United Kingdom, and Germany. The EU leadership reacted with considerable alarm and perceived the development as exerting substantial political pressure upon the existing institutional and normative foundations of European integration. In response, EU institutions subsequently issued a series of major policy documents outlining strategic reflections on the future trajectory of European integration. These documents uniformly stress the necessity for the member states to strengthen cohesion at the EU level and to safeguard the long-term direction of the European integration project through enhanced political unity and coordinated institutional action. Representative policy documents include: European Council President Donald Tusk's Letter to 27 Heads of EU Member States, January 31, 2017; European Commission, *White Paper on the Future of Europe: Reflections and Scenarios for the EU 27 by 2025*, Brussels, March 1, 2017.

geopolitics, driven by the renewed strategic competition among major powers, has forcefully reasserted itself as a central feature of international relations. In response, the EU must actively assert the subjectivity and proactivity of the European integration framework and decisively strengthen its internal cohesion and operational capacity.

Second, as for bilateral and multilateral relations between the EU and extraregional major powers, intensified trilateral competition among China, the United States, and the EU has placed unprecedented pressure on EU decision-makers. The EU senses that growing China-U.S. strategic competition is shaping the fundamental architecture of the future international strategic order, with the possible emergence of a new "bipolar structure", yet it cannot predict the pace or trajectory of this evolution process. The simultaneous escalation of U.S.-EU tensions and China-EU rivalry has put the EU in an awkward strategic dilemma, forcing it to perform a precarious balancing act. Given the high uncertainty of China-U.S.-EU trilateral competition, the EU has shown a marked tendency to sway between the two major powers, adopting a form of strategic opportunism of hedging its bets, while at the same time seeking to minimize structural dependence—economic or strategic—on either side. To achieve this goal, the EU has concluded that it must consolidate and expand its internal integration framework to enable Europe to speak with one voice and act with a unified stance. Accordingly, it has resolved to pursue EU Strategic Autonomy and deepen the construction of European Sovereignty, while adopting a more protectionist posture in foreign trade and investment policy.

When it comes to the anticipated China-U.S. strategic competition, European political elites and academics have, in comparative terms, responded much more slowly than their American counterparts. In fact, following China's emergence as the world's second-largest economy in 2010, U.S. policymakers and strategic analysts begun to anticipate the possibility of a global-scale strategic rivalry between China and the United States.① During

① Representative works in the U.S. strategic studies community that first offered systematic analyses of the prospects for strategic competition between China and the United States can be found in the following publications: Alastair Iain Johnston and Robert S. Ross (Eds.), *Engaging China: The Management of an Emerging Power*, London and New York: Routledge, 1999, pp. 279-302. After China emerged as the world's second-largest economy, only second to the United States, a number of influential works produced within the American strategic studies and academic communities further examined this issue; representative contributions in this body of literature include the following: Michael D. Swaine (Ed.), *America's Challenge: Engaging a Rising China in the Twenty-First Century*, Washington, D.C.: Carnegie Endowment for International Peace, the second term of the Obama administration, senior U.S. officials explicitly emphasized the need to manage competition with China.① American scholars, drawing upon the analytical framework of Power Transition Theory, systemically examined a wide range of scenarios in which China might challenge the U.S.-led international order.② By contrast, it was not until the publication in 2016 of two key EU strategic documents—*Elements for a New EU Strategy on China* and *A Global Strategy for the European Union's Foreign and Security Policy*—that the EU formally acknowledged the intensification of China-U.S.-EU competition. Despite this, it then continued to place considerable emphasis on the prospects for cooperation among major global actors. After the United States launched a trade war against China in March 2018, the EU firstly adopted a posture of strategic free-riding, seeking to leverage U.S. trade sanctions as an indirect means of exerting pressure on China,③ while simultaneously accelerating its own decision-making process to explicitly pursue

2011, pp. 337-386.

① During the second term of the Obama administration, policymakers in Washington became increasingly concerned about the possible emergence of comprehensive strategic competition between China and the United States, and consequently adopted a more vigilant posture toward China. This shift in policy perception and strategic assessment was clearly reflected in the National Security Strategy, released by the U.S. government in February 2015.

② The American strategic studies and academic communities have approached the future trajectory of China-U.S. relations from the analytical perspective of Power Transition Theory; representative works adopting this theoretical framework include: Michael D. Swaine (Ed.), *America's Challenge: Engaging a Rising China in the Twenty-First Century*, Washington, D.C.: Carnegie Endowment for International Peace, 2011, pp. 230-232; G. John Ikenberry, *Liberal Leviathan: The Origins, Crisis, and Transformation of the American World Order*, Princeton, U.A. and Oxford, UK: Princeton University Press, 2011, pp. 58-60; Ashley J. Tellis, *Balancing without Containment: An American Strategy for Managing China*, Washington, D.C.: Carnegie Endowment for International Peace, 2014, pp. 14-16; Stephen G. Brooks and William C. Wohlforth, "The Rise and Fall of the Great Powers in the Twenty-First Century: China's Rise and the Fate of America's Global Position", *International Security*, Vol. 40, No. 3, Winter 2015/2016, pp. 7-53.

③ In 2018, the EU issued or officially implemented multiple regulations and policy documents aimed at significantly strengthening its trade protection and investment screening mechanisms against China. It also released a policy document *Connecting Europe and Asia* that intended to compete with China's Belt and Road Initiative. This can be seen from: Regulation (EU) 2018/825 of the European Parliament and of the Council of May 30, 2018, *Official Journal of the European Union*, L 143/1, June 7, 2018; European Parliament, "EU Framework for FDI Screening", Briefing on EU Legislation in Progress, July 12, 2018; European Commission, *Connecting Europe and Asia: Building Blocks for an EU Strategy*, JOIN (2018) 31 final, Brussels, September 19, 2018.

"defensive" external economic policies with China as the target. Nevertheless, the EU still did not accord sufficient analytical centrality to the structural implications of China-U. S. strategic competition. It was only from the second half of 2018 onward, as transatlantic tensions deepened and China-U.S. trade confrontation intensified, that EU decision-makers and the European strategic studies community began to engage in sustained and systematic debate regarding the global ramifications of China-U.S. rivalry, increasingly converging on the view that the EU should reinforce European Sovereignty, maintain a calibrated distance from both China and the United States, and avoid being compelled into a binary strategic alignment. For example, the German Institute for International and Security Affairs (SWP) has argued that European Sovereignty should serve as the basis for exercising some form of supranational geopolitics,[①] while Ursula von der Leyen has emphasized that, if Europe is to become a "global player not a global playground", it must accelerate the construction of EU-level sovereignty in the economic and technological domains.[②] It should be noted, however, that while the transformation of strategic cognition among European political elites has proceeded relatively slowly, a wide range of actors within the broader European political system—particularly those embedded in European civil society, including think tanks, interest groups, non-governmental organizations, and epistemic communities—have, since the onset of the 2008 global financial crisis, engaged in continuous and often contentious debates concerning the direction and pace of European integration, as well as the overarching orientation and specific configuration of the EU's external strategy. Through these ongoing discursive and analytical processes, their perceptions of China-EU relations and the general trajectory of EU policy toward China have undergone gradual yet cumulative change, thereby exerting a subtle but consequential influence on the ways in which European political elites conceptualize China and articulate policy discourse.

At the same time, the deterioration of transatlantic relations since 2016-2017, coupled with the intensification of China-EU competition, has compelled the EU to confront, in parallel, strategic pressures from both the United States and China. On the one hand, following the inauguration of the first Trump administration in 2017, tensions between

① Barbara Lippert and Volker Perthes eds., "Strategic Rivalry between United States and China: Causes, Trajectories, and Implications for Europe", SWP Research Papers, Berlin, SWP, April 20, 2020, pp. 2, 10, 52-54.

② European Commission, Keynote Speech by Commission President von der Leyen at the BusinessEurope Day 2020, Brussels, March 5, 2020.

the United States and the EU have become more contentious across multiple domains—from bilateral economic relations and global governance to strategic security. Bilateral trade disputes involving tariffs have persisted, largely remaining unabated even during the COVID-19 pandemic, while competition in advanced technology and high-end manufacturing has intensified. After withdrawing from the *Paris Agreement*, a cornerstone of the global climate governance framework prized by the EU, the United States has proactively sought to undermine the authority of the World Trade Organization (WTO), an institution the EU is committed to upholding. Concurrently, Washington demonstrated a diminishing willingness to bear the burdens of European security and defense, a stance epitomized by the Trump administration's June 2020 announcement of its intent to withdraw a significant portion of U.S. troops from Germany. Furthermore, the United States unilaterally withdrew from the *Joint Comprehensive Plan of Action*, more commonly known as "the Iran nuclear deal", in which the EU had invested considerable diplomatic effort to establish and preserve. These cumulative developments have put substantial and multifaceted pressure on the EU.

On the other hand, the competitive—and increasingly adversarial—dimension of contemporary China-EU economic relations has continued to intensify. This trend manifests in several key areas: 1) As China's position within global value chains has gradually ascended, technological and industrial development gaps between China and Europe have narrowed. Enterprises on both sides are consequently engaged in ever fiercer competition for greater international market share and for leadership in advanced technologies and high-end manufacturing. A prime example is the global high-speed rail sector: following the rapid expansion of China Railway Rolling Stock Corporation (CRRC) in the international market since 2015-2016, the French and German governments pushed in early 2019 for a merger between Alstom and Siemens, aiming to create a European industrial champion to compete with CRRC.[①] Similarly, competition between Huawei and European telecommunications firms for dominance in 5G network markets has escalated significantly; 2) China maintains a substantial trade surplus with the EU, even as certain industrial sectors in the EU have contracted, leading to greater European dependence on Chinese industrial supply chains; and 3) competition between Chinese and European firms in third-country markets—such as those

① European Political Strategy Center, "EU Industrial Policy After Siemens-Alstom: Finding a New Balance between Openness and Protection", March 18, 2019.

in Latin America, Africa, and Russia—has grown increasingly intense.① In light of these developments, European think tanks, scholars and EU policymakers are more inclined to frame China as the EU's systemic rival and economic competitor at the global level.② In sum, concurrent dual competitive pressure from the two great powers of the United States and China have convinced the EU of the necessity to leverage the conceptions of Economic Sovereignty and Technological Sovereignty. This approach entails centralizing greater resources and decision-making authority to enable more robust state intervention in the economy, thus giving the EU leverage to effectively counter the challenges posed by both Washington and Beijing.

Third, key social actors within the EU—particularly European business and industrial interest groups—have also advocated for a reinforcement of EU-level decision-making authority to better navigate a transformed global landscape. Faced with intensifying China-EU economic competition, escalating U.S.-EU trade frictions, and the Trump administration's more aggressive economic nationalist policies, European business circles have in recent years encountered mounting competitive pressure in international commerce. This has galvanized their support for the EU's pursuit of Economic and Technological Sovereignty, spurring strong demands for the Union to formulate a more assertive industrial strategy, revamp its competition policy framework on internal mergers and acquisitions, and provide upgraded support for European firms. The overarching aim is to dismantle institutional barriers within Europe that impede technological research and development and industrial upgrading, thus enabling European industries to adapt to the new realities of international competition. These increasingly emphatic appeals from the business community have become a strong impetus behind the European Commission's related policy initiatives.

For example, in early January 2019, the Federation of German Industries (Bundesverband der Deutschen Industrie, BDI), one of Germany's largest and most influential industrial associations, argued in a position paper that China engages in "systemic competition" with Europe. Consequently, it urged the EU to bolster "internal solidarity" and adopt more robust policies in the domains of trade and investment.③ Similarly,

① Alicia Garcia-Herrero et al., "EU-China Trade and Investment Relations in Challenging Times", Policy Department for External Relations, the European Parliament, May 25, 2020, P. 7.

② Ibid, P. 17. European Parliament Briefing, "EU-China Relations: Taking Stock after 2020 EU-China Summit", June 30, 2020, pp. 4-7.

③ Federation of German Industries (BDI), "Partner and Systemic Competitor: How Do We Deal with China's

BusinessEurope, the most prominent EU-level business federation which predominantly represents manufacturing interests, has issued over a dozen position papers, research reports, and policy briefs since the beginning of 2019. These documents call upon EU leadership to undertake "strategic action" to fortify "European Economic and Technological Sovereignty," to ensure that "the EU speaks with one voice" on the global stage, and to pursue "More Europe"—meaning deeper integration—particularly in the policy domain shaped by the COVID-19 pandemic.① In December 2019, the European Round Table for Industry (ERT), another major Brussels-based industry group, submitted recommendations containing similar arguments to the von der Leyen Commission.② It is evident, therefore, that business and industrial interest groups operating at the EU level and in major member states have, since 2016, engaged in increasingly intensive deliberations regarding the necessity and feasibility of the EU strengthening its "defensive" external economic policies. This sustained discourse has generated a potent ideational and advocacy environment, which has in turn put significant pressure on, and provided impetus for, the European Commission under the leaderships of Jean-Claude Juncker and Ursula von der Leyen to progressively advance policy decisions in this strategic direction.

1.2 Shifts in the EU's Theoretical Framework and Ideological System for Responding to the Changing Circumstances

Political elites and strategic research circles in Europe have long attached pivotal importance to theoretical construction, stressing the need to interpret and analyze rapidly

State-Controlled Economy?", Policy Paper on China, January 2019, pp. 11-12, 19.

① Regarding the composition of the members of BusinessEurope in Brussels, please refer to Xin Hua, "The Interest Groups' Influence Mechanisms on the Policymaking in the U.S.-EU Trade Negotiations: A Comparative Study of the U.S. Chamber of Commerce and the BusinessEurope", *Chinese Journal of European Studies*, 2018, 36(06), pp. 56-82+6. Since the second half of 2019, BusinessEurope in Brussels has produced a substantial number of policy memoranda and advisory reports urging the decision-making institutions of the EU to adopt a more coherent industrial policy and strengthen European Sovereignty. Among these advisory materials, the most representative one is a research report submitted directly to EU policymakers: BusinessEurope, *Prosperity, People, Planet: Three Pillars for the European Union Agenda in 2019-2024*, November 2019, P. 5; BusinessEurope, *The EU and China: Addressing the Systemic Challenge, A Comprehensive EU Strategy to Rebalance the Relationship with China*, January 16, 2020, pp. 43-46, 149.

② European Round Table for Industry, *Turning Global Challenges into Opportunities: A Chance for Europe to Lead*, December 9, 2019, P. 16.

changing domestic and international situations through rigorous theoretical frameworks, with the hope of understanding and responding to structural shifts through concise yet thorough conceptual systems. At different stages of contextual evolution, the European strategic research community and academia have engaged in successive rounds of theoretical inquiry and debate, while European political elites have continuously adjusted their theoretical preferences and positional stances in line with shifts in domestic political power configurations and focal social contradictions. As a result, the theoretical frameworks and conceptual systems that guide EU policymaking practice have remained in a constant state of flux. Broadly speaking, three strands of theoretical debate have, to a considerable extent, shaped the strategic perceptions, policy orientations, and institutional architecture of the EU's decision-making circles in responding to changing circumstances. Meanwhile, the ongoing transformation of Europe's general internal and external context, along with shifts in its political and social ecosystems, has once again prompted EU decision-makers and European political elites to revise their theoretical leanings and overarching conceptual frameworks, so as to properly address new issues and dynamics in policy practice.

First, the long-standing intellectual contestation between the liberalist theories that call for an open international order grounded in complex interdependence and the traditional geopolitical theories centered on great-power competition has consistently structured European political elites' strategic perceptions at the macro level. However, the contemporary slowdown of economic globalization, setbacks to European regional integration, and the EU's exposure to overlapping internal and external crises have pushed European political elites to gradually return to geostrategic theory and re-embrace the perspective of power politics.

In practice, whenever geopolitics driven by great-power rivalry dominated the international order, European scholars tended to emphasize Europe's awkward position in the rivalry among global powers, called for the consolidation of internal strength within the European integration framework, and advocated the construction of "supranational sovereignty", while decision-makers of the European Community (EC) and the EU paid greater attention to Economic and Technological Sovereignty. By contrast, when economic globalization fostered an open international society, theorists supporting the liberal international order generated extensive research on the EU as a Normative and Civilian

Power, foregrounding its soft power attributes and encouraging the EU to project its values and regulatory frameworks outward with considerable confidence. Under such conditions, reference to European Sovereignty receded, giving way instead to a more assertive articulation of Europe's normative commitments.

The geopolitical standoff of the Cold War, defined by U.S.-Soviet confrontation, spawned a body of scholarly literature exploring how Western European nation-states could safeguard their strategic and economic autonomy, laying the intellectual foundation for early theories of European integration.① Influenced by these ideas, Western European states initiated integration through the European Coal and Steel Community and the Common Agricultural Policy, transferring limited economic sovereignty to the supranational level of the European Community and endowing it with initial supranational characteristics. In the post-Cold War era, neoliberalism prevailed, and the United States worked to build a multilateral trading system and a global governance architecture aimed at establishing universal rules and norms. In this context, academic works on the EU as a normative power within the liberal international order proliferated,② prompting the EU to deepen the European

---

① Early literature on the institutional architecture and future development direction of European integration, focusing on expectations for the prospect of European unification within the Cold War structure, proposed visions or institutional designs for constructing a future European political integration framework characterized by supranational and federalism features. Therefore, the initial design of the architecture and evolutionary direction of European integration was based on strategic and security considerations and political purposes, rather than economic calculations. Representative works on this topic include: Ernst B. Hass, *The Uniting of Europe: Political, Social, and Economic Forces 1950-1957*, Stanford of California, U.S.: Stanford University Press, 1958, pp. 32-58, 213-317. For a summary of the intellectual trends and literature from this period advocating for a Federal Europe, see: Michael Burgess, *Federalism and European Union: The Building of Europe, 1950-2000*, London and New York: Routledge, 2000, pp. 23-54.

② Representative works commenting on and providing recommendations for the EU's normative power and soft power in this period include: Andrew Moravcsik, "Preferences and Power in the European Community: A Liberal Intergovernmental Approach", *Journal of Common Market Studies*, Vol 31, No. 4, December 1993, pp. 473-524; Beate Kohler-Koch, "The Evolution and Transformation of European Governance", in Beate Kohler-Koch and Rainer Eising (Eds.), *The Transformation of Governance in the European Union*, London and New York: Routledge, 1999, pp. 13-34; John Peterson, "The Santer Era: the European Commission in Normative, Historical and Theoretical Perspective", *Journal of European Public Policy*, Vol. 6, No. 1, 1999, pp. 46-65; Ian Manners, "The Constitutive Nature of Values, Images and Principles in the European Union", in Sonia Lucarelli and Ian Manners (Eds.), *Values and Principles in European Union Foreign Policy*, London and New York: Routledge, 2006, pp. 19-41.

Single Market and Economic and Monetary Union (EMU) while actively promoting its values and regulations globally. From 2008 to 2010, the global financial crisis and the Euro area crisis laid bare the accumulated contradictions of the neoliberal international order. The EU's neighborhood became geopolitically fragmented amid the Arab Spring and the Ukraine crisis, while the rise of emerging economies intensified China-U.S. strategic competition. In response, European academia and the strategic research community have resumed intensive discussions on the features of power politics and geopolitics, revisited Power Transition Theory concerning major power rivalry, and explained in growing detail the necessity of building European Sovereignty amid evolving China-U.S. competition.[①] These classical geopolitical perspectives are clearly reflected in the policy documents and public statements of the European Commission under the leaderships of Jean-Claude Juncker and Ursula von der Leyen, which consistently emphasize European Sovereignty, Strategic Autonomy, and European Economic and Technological Sovereignty.

Second, the enduring debate between the theories of economic and technological nationalism and the theory of economic globalization has continuously shaped the EU's external economic policy trajectory. Mounting pressure from ongoing internal and external shifts has pushed EU decision-makers to adopt an increasingly explicit stance of economic and technological nationalism in framing and managing external economic relations.

The doctrine of economic and technological nationalism advocates robust intervention by an exclusive sovereign authority, with the aim of freeing the sovereign system from dependence on foreign economies and external actors, and maximizing the sovereign entity's economic growth and technological advancement through autonomous strategic choices. Economic nationalism emerged in the early 19th century, when the United States and Western Europe engaged in international strategic competition driven by divergent paces of industrialization. Its systematic intellectual framework was later summarized in the writings

① Representative recommendations that elaborate on the necessity of strengthening European sovereignty against the geostrategic backdrop of China-U.S. rivalry, based on an assessment of theories of great-power competition and power transition, include: Alicia Garcia Herrero, "Europe in the Midst of China-U.S. Strategic Economic Competition: What Are the European Union's Options?", Working Paper, Bruegel, April 8, 2019; Maria Demertzis et al., "A Strategic Agenda for the New EU Leadership: Memo to the Presidents of the European Commission, Council and Parliament", Bruegel, June 13, 2019; Barbara Lippert and Volker Perthes (Eds.), "Strategic Rivalry between United States and China: Causes, Trajectories, and Implications for Europe", SWP Research Papers, Berlin, SWP, April 20, 2020.

of German scholar Friedrich List from the 1830s to 1840s.① Since then, periods of major restructuring in the world economy and resultant international competition intensification have been accompanied by heated debates over economic nationalism. The concept of technological nationalism emerged in the late 19th century among late-industrializing states pursuing technological and industrial catch-up strategies. It evolved along a broadly similar trajectory to that of economic nationalism, but places greater emphasis on the need for the sovereign authority to achieve autonomy in cutting-edge technologies and high-end industries.② At its core, the theory of economic and technological nationalism entails the political and strategic design of industrial policy and the implementation of trade protection, placing it in close intellectual proximity to paradigms such as trade protectionism,③ import substitution strategy,④ strategic trade policy,⑤ and the developmental state.⑥ It emerged as a prominent intellectual current three times: between the two World Wars, from the late 1960s

① For a detailed account of Friedrich List's ideological system of economic nationalism, see: Friedrich List, *The National System of Political Economy*, Sampson S. Lloyd trans., New York: Longmans, Green, and Co., 1909, pp. 159-263.

② Literature on the conceptual framework of technological nationalism in the late 19th century: Richard J. Samuels, *"Rich Nation, Strong Army": National Security and the Technological Transformation of Japan*, Ithaca and London: Cornell University Press, 1996, pp. 33-78. Systematic discussions on the theory of technological nationalism since the end of the Cold War: Sylvia Ostry and Richard R. Nelson, *Techno-Nationalism and Techno-Globalism: Conflict and Cooperation*, Washington, D. C.: The Brookings Institution, 1995, pp. 60-62.

③ Representative works on the political economy theory of trade protectionism, see: Jagdish Bhagwati, *Protectionism*, WANG Shihua et al. (trans.), Beijing: China Renmin University Press, 2013, pp. 37-96.

④ Representative discussions on the theory and policy practice of the import-substitution strategy, see: Javier A. Reyes and W. Charles Sawyer, *Latin American Economic Development*, 2nd edition, London: Routledge, 2015.

⑤ The essence of strategic trade policy lies in industrial policy implemented for external strategic competition; representative works include: Paul R. Krugman, *Strategic Trade Policy and the New International Economics*, Cambridge, Massachusetts, U.S. The MIT Press, pp. 1-46.

⑥ The developmental state refers to a national economic decision-making and operational system in which the government maximizes economic growth through industrial policy planning guided by economic nationalism. The earliest work to propose this concept is: Chalmers A. Johnson, MITI and the Japanese Miracle: The Growth of Industrial Policy, 1925-1975, Stanford, California: Stanford University Press, 1982, pp. 35-82. Subsequently, American scholars used the terms "hidden developmental state" and "developmental network state" to refer to the official economic decision-making system of the United States that implements industrial policy driven by economic nationalism, and "developmental bureaucratic state" to denote Japan's economic decision-making and operational system. For specific discussions, see: Fred Block, "Swimming against the Current: The Rise of a Hidden Developmental State in the United States", *Politics & Society*, Vol. 36, No. 2, June 2008, pp. 169-206.

to the mid-1970s, and in the mid-1980s.① The theory of economic globalization, by contrast, is closely associated with the neoliberalist theory of interdependence that has emerged since the 1970s, which posits widespread interdependence among national economies in the industrial age, and holds that the globalization of markets and production value chains enhances global economic efficiency and drives rapid global wealth growth.

This theoretical tension is conspicuously mirrored in the policy discourses of the European Community (EC) and the European Union (EU) in the form of an ideological contest between "Fortress Europe" and "Global Europe."② As European integration deepens, the supranational institutions of the European Community and the EU have gradually assumed economic decision-making powers previously reserved for nation-states. As a result, economic and technological nationalism—traditionally a national-level phenomenon—has evolved into a supranational-level one that covers the whole region of the European Union and is imbued with Fortress Europe overtones, also referred to as "supranational economic patriotism".③ Over the seven decades since the establishment of the

① Representative works on the ideas and policy practices of European economic nationalism from the 1950s to the 1980s: Jean-Jacques Servan-Schreiber, *The American Challenge*, Harmondsworth: Penguin, 1969; Christian Grabas and Alexander Nützenadel (Eds.), *Industrial Policy in Europe after 1945: Wealth, Power and Economic Development in the Cold War*, Houndmills, UK and New York: Palgrave Macmillan, 2014, pp. 13-186; Yves Meny and Vincent Wright (Eds.), *The Politics of Steel: Western Europe and the Steel Industry in the Crisis Years (1974-1984)*, Berlin: Walter de Gruyter & Co., 1986. Representative works on the theories of technological nationalism and technological sovereignty in the 1970s and 1980s: Steven Globerman, "Canadian Science Policy and Technological Sovereignty", *Canadian Public Policy*, Vol. 4, No. 1, Winter 1978, pp. 34-45; Maurice Charland, "Technological Nationalism", *Canadian Journal of Political and Social Theory*, Vol. 10, No. 1-2, 1986, pp. 196-220; Robert B. Reich, "The Rise of Techno-Nationalism", *The Atlantic Monthly*, May 1987, pp. 62-69.

② Fortress Europe refers to an exclusionary policy framework in the European integration architecture targeting actors outside Europe, encompassing the common external tariffs and non-tariff barriers of the European Single Market, Common European Asylum System, and *European integrated border management*. In the field of EU external economic policy, Fortress Europe denotes the industrial policies and trade protection measures implemented by the EU for the purpose of external economic competition. Representative works include: Brian T. Hanson, "What Happens to Fortress Europe? External Trade Policy Liberalization in the European Union", *International Organization*, Vol. 52, No. 1, 1998, pp. 55-85; Alasdair R. Young, "The Incidental Fortress: The Single European Market and World Trade", *Journal of Common Market Studies*, Vol. 42, No. 2, 2004, pp. 393-414. Global Europe refers to the trade and investment liberalization policies pursued by the EU in response to the trend of economic globalization. The term was officially adopted in the EU's 2006 trade strategy document.

③ Representative theoretical elaborations on the supranational EU-level regional economic nationalism, see:

European Coal and Steel Community, whenever the European integration framework faced disadvantages in economic and technological competition with the United States, Japan, or emerging economies, the ideology of economic and technological nationalism would exert a strong pull on EC and EU decision-makers. The policy framework of European economic and technological sovereignty vigorously pursued by the current von der Leyen Commission emphasizes the EU's autonomous control over economic decision-making and critical technological research and development, seeking to reduce dependence on extra-regional products and technologies, and aiming to secure the EU's global leadership in cutting-edge technologies and advanced industries.① It thus bears the distinct hallmarks of a supranational form of European regional economic and technological nationalism.

Third, the persistent contest between the state interventionism, which is aimed at enhancing economic competitiveness, and the market fundamentalism, which advocates laissez-faire governance, has continuously shaped the specific institutional design of the EU's external economic policy, constraining agenda-setting and the tempo of decision-making in the management of external economic relations. Since the 2008 financial crisis, as neoliberal economic theory continues to face mounting criticism and skepticism, EU decision-makers have gradually gravitated toward state interventionism, actively strengthening oversight across all sectors of the European economy. In particular, they have been intensifying administrative intervention and policy guidance in technological and industrial fields to shape the EU's strategic competition with external powers.

In fact, right from the founding of the European Coal and Steel Community in the early 1950s, Western Europe already lagged behind the United States in terms of labor productivity and economic growth. From that point to the present, whenever major technological breakthroughs in the United States accelerated the widening of the transatlantic gap in industry and technology, EC and EU decision-makers would experience recurring bouts of competitiveness anxiety, while European academia and the strategic research community have produced a wealth of policy proposals and scholarly works

---

Ben Clift and Cornelia Woll, "Economic Patriotism: Reinventing Control over Open Markets", *Journal of European Public Policy*, Vol. 19, No. 3, April 2012, pp. 307-323.

① European Commission, *A New Industrial Strategy for Europe*, COM (2020) 102 final, Brussels, March 10, 2020; European Commission President von der Leyen, Keynote Speech at the BusinessEurope Day 2020, Brussels, March 5, 2020.

pushing for the elevation of state interventionism to the EU level in the form of regional interventionism.[①] When the pace of divergence in transatlantic competitiveness slowed—as in the early 1990s following the collapse of the Soviet Union and the end of the bipolar structure—the EU, influenced by mainstream transatlantic economic thought, tilted more strongly toward market fundamentalism, promoting liberalization of the European Single Market and external trade. Although the transfer of decision-making power in industrial and technological policy—directly linked to economic competitiveness—from member states to the EC has proceeded more slowly than in the sectors of agriculture, trade, and monetary policy, the EC and EU have persistently adopted a wide range of industrial policy instruments. They have sought to harness European integration and the Europeanization of member states to gradually centralize industrial and technological decision-making at the EU level, and through strengthened supranational authority, to implement EU-wide regional interventionist policies to boost European economic competitiveness and secure Europe's economic lead in global industrial and technological competition.

Over the decade following the 2008 global financial crisis, the U.S.-Europe gap has widened further in emerging strategic technologies and industries, including artificial intelligence, quantum computing, information and communications, and big data applications—as well as in overall economic competitiveness.[②] In February 2014, the

---

① In the mid-to-late 1960s, technological breakthroughs and industrial upgrading in the U.S. semiconductor and aerospace sectors plunged Europe into its first major crisis. French scholar Jean-Jacques Servan-Schreiber published a dedicated book elaborating on the American challenge, which sent profound shockwaves through the decision-making circles of the European Community. In response, the EC embarked on formulating vertical industrial policies and promoting collaborative technological R&D project plans among its member states. This marks the first documented instance of competitive anxiety among decision-makers within the European integration framework, as well as the EC's first systematic implementation of regional interventionism. For details on the specific process. See: Laurent Warlouzet, "Towards a European Industrial Policy? The European Economic Community (EEC) Debates, 1957-1975", in Christian Grabas and Alexander Nützenadel (Eds.), *Industrial Policy in Europe after 1945: Wealth, Power and Economic Development in the Cold War*, Houndmills, UK and New York: Palgrave Macmillan, 2014, pp. 213-235. Subsequently, in the mid-1980s and the period 1999-2005, the European Community (later the European Union) experienced two more waves of competitive anxiety. Centering on the core concerns of competitiveness, it formulated and implemented a series of industrial policies and technological R&D projects.

② European think tanks have produced numerous elaborations and policy recommendations on U.S.-Europe gaps in emerging strategic technology sectors. See: Ulrike Franke, "Harnessing Artificial Intelligence", European Council on Foreign Relations, July 2019; Dalia Marin, "Europe Needs a DARPA", Bruegel, February 14, 2020.

Europe 2020 Competitiveness Report launched by the World Economic Forum in Davos noted that the gaps between the EU and the United States in average income levels and labor productivity had expanded in the five years after the financial crisis.[①] In August 2019, a research report published by the Sant'Anna School of Advanced Studies in Pisa, Italy, found that between 2008 and 2018, total factor productivity (a key indicator of technology-driven growth) contracted in the EU (excluding Central and Eastern European countries), while it continued to grow in the United States.[②] In early 2020, the market capitalization of Apple Inc., a single American high-tech firm, exceeded the combined market capitalization of the 30 leading German companies listed on the DAX index.[③] These trends signal an accelerating divergence in technological progress between the United States and Europe. Confronted with this severe situation, EU decision-makers have experienced a renewed surge in competitiveness anxiety.[④] Consequently, the core of the von der Leyen Commission's policy framework for European economic and technological sovereignty lies in competitiveness-related industrial and technological sectors, with priority decision-making agendas focused on supranational EU industrial policy, embodying a clear commitment to EU regional interventionism.

---

① World Economic Forum, "The Europe 2020 Competitiveness Report: Building a More Competitive Europe", February, 2014, pp. 4-6.

② Randolph Luca Bruno et al., "Determinants of Productivity Gap in the European Union: A Multilevel Perspective", Institute of Economics Scuola Superiore Sant'Anna, August 2019.

③ "The Apple Effect: Germany Fears Being Left Behind by Big Tech", Financial Times, January 28, 2020, https://www.ft.com/content/6f69433a-40f0-11ea-a047-eae9bd51ceba, accessed June 1, 2020.

④ During the period from 2018 to 2019, EU decision-makers and the European strategic research community experienced the latest wave of competitive anxiety. They recognized that Europe was not only falling behind the United States in the R&D of emerging technologies such as AI and the advancement of related industries, but also facing challenges from emerging economies like China. Against this backdrop, a surge of literature and policy proposals emerged, focusing on assessing the EU's economic competitiveness and offering countermeasures. Representative works include: Andrea Renda, "Artificial Intelligence: Ethics, Governance and Policy Challenges", Task Force Report, Center for European Policy Studies, Brussels, February 2019; Maria Demertzis and Guntram Wolff (Eds.), "Braver, Greener, Fairer: Memos to the EU Leadership, 2019-2024", Bruegel, July 2019; Ulrike Franke and Paola Sartori, "Machine Politics: Europe and the AI Revolution", Policy Brief, European Council on Foreign Relations, July 2019; Michael Servoz, "The Future of Work? Work of the Future: on How Artificial Intelligence, Robotics and Automation are Transforming Jobs", European Commission Report, May, 2019; European Parliament, "How to Tackle Challenges in a Future-Oriented EU Industry Strategy?", 2 volumes, June 14, 2019. These are research reports that are all over 100 pages long.

Since early 2017, the Trump administration has forcefully pursued a policy mix of national mercantilism, economic nationalism, and trade protectionism, deliberately seeking to dismantle the existing multilateral trading system and global governance architecture. This has triggered a backlash against globalization, a re-emergence of the Kindleberger Trap, and a crisis derived from insufficient international public goods such as global governance and international institutions, raising the risk of renewed disorder in the world economy and international politics. Against this backdrop, the EU has increasingly turned to the theoretical lenses of classical power politics and geopolitics, adopting a supranational form of economic and technological nationalism, and structuring its policy agenda around an interventionist governance model. In the process, EU decision-makers are gradually transforming the theoretical foundations and conceptual systems that guide their policymaking practice.

1.3 Strategic Dilemmas Confronting the EU in Advancing Its Policy Agenda

Shifting internal and external circumstances over the past decade have compelled the EU to revamp its internal and external policies on an ongoing basis, most notably by progressively strengthening a defensive protectionist policy architecture in its external relations. At the same time, however, the EU has confronted profound strategic dilemmas in advancing its external decision-making process. As early as 2011, American scholar Dani Rodrik observed that the post-Cold War wave of globalization faced a Political Trilemma: economic globalization, the sovereign nation-state system, and the rights of conventional liberal democracy could not coexist in tandem—only two of the three could be sustained at any given time. Rodrik argued that the continued advancement of globalization could follow one of two paths: either political elites of nation-states are required to abide by the specific set of macroeconomic policies enshrined in the Washington Consensus to achieve the fullest possible liberalization of trade and capital flows, a course that would inevitably erode mass democratic rights centered on equity; or national-level democratic politics is integrated into the framework of global governance to preserve democratic entitlements, yet the supranational character of global governance structures would unavoidably compromise the institutional integrity of the nation-state. If both the sovereign integrity of the nation-state and popular democratic rights were to be upheld simultaneously, the process of globalization would have to be kept within bounds.[①] Rodrik predicted that the EU would eventually fall prey to a similar predicament. His prophecy has been fully vindicated. Between 2008 and 2010, the EU was battered by the global financial crisis and the Euro area crisis, which shook the foundational structure of the Eurozone and sharpened divisions among its member states. From 2015 onward, the Union was struck by a cascade of overlapping crises: the refugee surge, terrorist attacks, Brexit, and the rise of populist and Eurosceptic political forces. The repeated setbacks to European integration in the post-2008 decade offered conclusive proof of his forecast. The evolution and development of the EU are thus trapped in the trilemma illustrated in Figure 1.

As Figure 1 shows, the EU faces a political trilemma in which any two of the following three dynamics can coexist, yet the combination of all three remains structurally incompatible: the process of European integration, the European system of nation-states, and the institutional system of popular democratic rights in Europe cannot coexist together. This dilemma not only severely disrupts the consolidation of the EU's internal institutional framework but also continuously shapes the orientations and pathways of its external decision-making. Specifically, for European integration to proceed further, the EU must deepen the integration of its internal institutional structures and strengthen its supranational decision-making authority. This requires not only asserting the EU's subjectivity in the realm of economic diplomacy but also rolling out a unified industrial strategy for the whole EU, and advancing research and development of cutting-edge technologies and the upgrading of advanced manufacturing on a pan-European scale. Such an undertaking entails intervention and regulation in the more microeconomic and foundational layers of the European economy, which may give rise to multiple lines of tension: on the one hand, EU decision-makers and member states will have to negotiate a more detailed and granular division of competences, risking intensified contestation over the allocation of sovereignty; on the other hand, the EU will inevitably reinforce supranational centralization in the governance of the European Single Market, the screening of inward foreign investment, the monetary policy, and the EU-level taxation and public finance. This means that the already widely criticized Brussels bureaucracy may intervene more intrusively and precisely in the daily lives and social welfare provisions of European citizens, stoking public resentment toward

① Dani Rodrik, *The Globalization Paradox: Why Global Markets, States, and Democracy Can't Coexist*, Oxford, UK and New York: Oxford University Press, 2011, pp. 232.

supranational governance. The fierce backlash among the Greek public and even sections of its political elite against the EU and Germany in the wake of the 2011 Greek debt crisis—when Brussels and Berlin intervened in Greek fiscal policy and imposed austerity measures—stands as a stark illustration. The recent rise of populism and Euroscepticism, which have entered the European political mainstream through elections at both the EU and national levels, demonstrates that the constraints imposed by European integration on the national sovereignty of member states, along with the neglect of grassroots popular interests by pro-integration political elites, have triggered deep social fault lines across Europe. Correspondingly, EU decision-makers—once staunch advocates of economic globalization and trade liberalization—are forced to reflect on the negative externalities of globalization and regional integration and to respond to popular grievances channeled by populist and Eurosceptic forces, leading to a step-by-step tightening of defensive policy toward China. In short, the interplay and contestation among European grassroots citizens, national political elites, and EU decision-makers will largely determine the pace of the EU's internal and external policy adjustment.

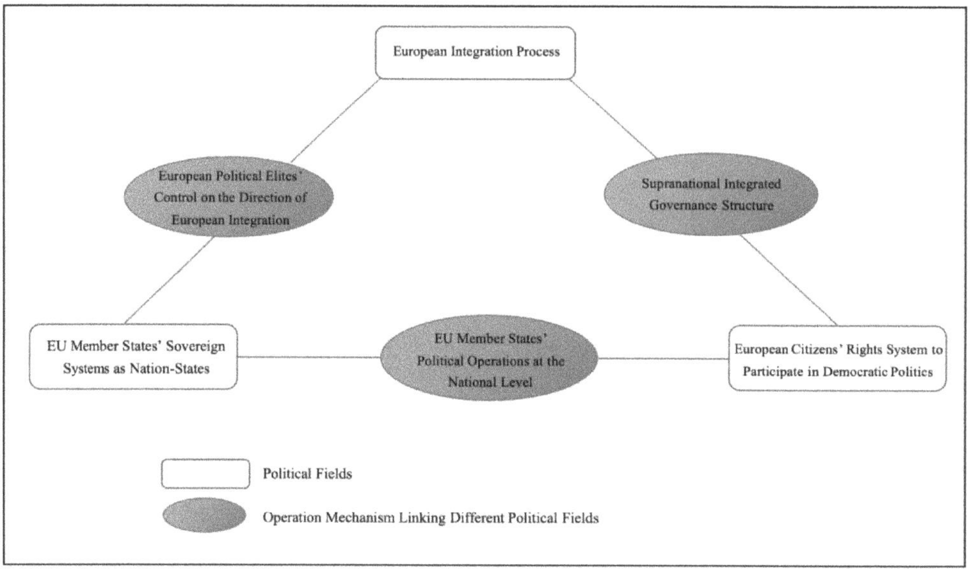

Figure 1 of Introduction: EU's Future Political Trilemma in Pursuing European Economic and Technological Sovereignty.

Source: Illustrated by the author

II. Strategic Drivers behind the EU's Formulation of Defensive Economic Policy toward China

In the context of ever-deepening globalization, the economic operation of any country relies on the cross-border movement of productive factors and key resources. As a result, the pace and scale of international trade, cross-border investment, and exchange rate movements directly affect the market size, price level, and profit-making potential of specific industries and sectors in the country, which in turn shape its structural attributes as well as the growth and stability of its macroeconomy. On the other hand, the inflow of foreign goods and capital, together with the associated transfer of key technologies, subtly transforms the corporate governance and industrial structures of the host country, alters the position of its enterprises and industries in the globally integrated value chains according to the division of labor, and ultimately influences the country's comprehensive national strength, as well as its standing in the world economic system. To address this complex interplay, decision-makers in advanced economies have gradually formulated the concept and system of Defensive Trade Policy, also known as Trade Defense Policy. As cross-border flows of production factors become more complex, trade relations based on the cross-border movement of goods are no longer the sole pillar of international economic relations. The original system of Defensive Trade Policy has gradually expanded into investment, industry, and other domains, forming an integrated policy framework that spans multiple sectors and levels and is upgraded into a system of Defensive External Economic Policy.[①]

Defensive External Economic Policy refers to a cross-cutting policy framework covering trade, investment, industry, and other areas, formulated by a country's decision-

① Defensive Trade Policy first emerged in American scholars' discussions on Strategic Trade Policy and should be regarded as a subset of the latter. In essence, it refers to a comprehensive policy framework of trade protectionism. For further details, see Paul Krugman (Ed.), *Strategic Trade Policy and the New International Economics*, Cambridge, Massachusetts: MIT Press, 1998, pp. 269. While the EU occasionally uses the term Defensive Trade Policy in policy documents, it more frequently adopts expressions such as Trade Defense Policy or Trade Defense Instruments. Since 2016-2017, building on the consolidation and enhancement of its existing Trade Defense Policy, the EU has successively formulated policy frameworks in areas including investment, industrial policy, technology transfer, and intellectual property protection. These frameworks aim to restrict foreign goods and capital, safeguard domestic output, employment, and intellectual property rights, and when integrated with the Trade Defense Policy, form a complex and systematic policy architecture. This book collectively refers to this integrated architecture as Defensive External Economic Policy.

makers to safeguard the stable operation of the national economy and, further, to protect national economic security and social stability. It employs a combination of tools including economic legislation, public investment, government subsidy, and intelligence monitoring to restrict or block the inflow of foreign goods, screen and vet incoming foreign capital, adjust domestic industrial structures, and regulate technology transactions and transfers in the country. Its purpose is to prevent foreign goods and capital from undermining domestic macroeconomic stability, to stop cross-border flows of production factors and economic resources from hindering national economic growth, and to prevent distortions in the direction of national economic development, industrial upgrading, and technological progress. Thus, Defensive External Economic Policy is closely associated with the concept of economic security. It represents a comprehensive and strategic policy framework devised by a country's decision-makers based on their strategic evaluation of the international situation and external economic relations.[①]

2.1 The EU's Basic Perceptions and Strategic Calculus on China

Since the 2008 global financial crisis, especially after the EU was hit by multiple internal and external crises from 2015 to 2016, the EU's decision-making elites have shown a gradual yet discernible shift in its overall perception of the contemporary global economic system and the international strategic-security landscape, coupled with a major recalibration of its China-EU policy orientation. It is precisely in this evolving cognitive and strategic context that the EU has persistently advanced the formulation and implementation of a set of "defensive" economic policies directed at China. The EU's strategic calculations may be summarized in several interrelated dimensions.

First, the EU increasingly holds the view that it has suffered disproportionate losses in the process of economic globalization, whereas China has grabbed what is perceived as unfair gains—an assessment that, in more colloquial terms, reflects a belief within European circles of policymakers and political elites that Europe has paid the price while China has reaped the benefits. In the wake of the 2008 global financial crisis and the 2010-2011 Euro area crisis, the European economy has experienced a prolonged period of stagnation,

① Lei Jiasu (Ed.), *National Economic Security: Theories and Analysis Method*, Beijing: Tsinghua University Press, 2011, pp. 217-220.

accompanied by intensifying internal structural contradictions. Against this backdrop, the EU has come to perceive itself as occupying a relatively disadvantaged position in the distribution of gains generated by globalization, having suffered significant relative losses that have, in turn, contributed to a marked decline in its standing in the global economic hierarchy. Consequently, although the EU continues, at the level of official discourse, to affirm its commitment to globalization, it has in practice engaged in a critical reassessment of the asymmetrical distributional outcomes associated with globalization, while actively seeking to establish alternative policy frameworks capable of redressing these imbalances.[①] The persistence of a substantial trade surplus in China's favor in bilateral trade, coupled with the pronounced divergence in economic growth rates between the two sides, has further accentuated the EU's increasingly negative evaluation of China-EU economic relations, leading to a growing consensus among EU policymakers that more robust and targeted measures are required to rectify the perceived structural asymmetry in bilateral economic ties.

Second, while the EU has officially adopted an accommodating stance on China's Belt and Road Initiative (BRI), it actually harbors a considerable degree of strategic caution, skepticism, and even resistance, holding a comparatively negative view of the 17+1 Cooperation Framework (which had been called the 16+1 Cooperation Framework before April 2019) involving Central and Eastern European countries. Although EU institutions have refrained from issuing explicit public repudiations of these initiatives, significant underlying concerns persist among European policymakers, who fear that the 17+1 Cooperation Framework may contribute to intra-European fragmentation by exacerbating divisions between Western Europe and Central and Eastern Europe, thus undermining the cohesion of the Union. Moreover, the advancement of the BRI in Europe—particularly Chinese investment, under its framework, in sectors such as transport infrastructure, energy, telecommunications, and advanced manufacturing—is perceived as potentially weakening the EU's economic decision-making authority and posing latent risks to European economic security. Driven by such concerns, the EU has deemed it necessary to develop a set of precautionary and restrictive policy instruments designed to counter what is framed as a potential threat posed by China to the EU's economic security.

① European Commission, Reflection Paper on Harnessing Globalization, COM (2017) 240, May 10, 2017.

Analysts in European think tanks have explicitly noted that one of the underlying strategic rationales behind the EU's 2018 *Connecting Europe and Asia – Building Blocks for an EU Strategy* was to establish a framework capable of competing with China's BRI and of contesting influence in regions such as Central Asia, the Middle East, and North Africa.① From this perspective, the BRI is interpreted not merely as an economic development initiative but as a geostrategic instrument aimed at expanding China's political influence. Given that the Middle East and North Africa constitute regions of immediate strategic relevance to the EU, China's growing presence there has inevitably caused unease in the European policy circles. Similarly, investment activities undertaken by Chinese enterprises under the BRI framework—such as the acquisition and operation of port infrastructure in countries including Greece and Belgium—have deepened European concerns over strategic dependency and control over critical infrastructure.② At the same time, some analysts have emphasized that European responses are not uniformly restrictive, noting, for instance, that while full ownership of strategic assets—as in the case of the Port of Piraeus—may trigger resistance, minority equity participation in port investments, such as COSCO's involvement in Rotterdam, has been viewed more favorably by the Netherlands.③ Overall, European think tank experts tend to suggest that, provided that concrete synergies can be identified between the BRI and the EU Strategy on Connecting Europe and Asia at the level of specific projects, the EU remains open to selective cooperation, even as its underlying precautionary stance is likely to persist over the long term.

Third, the EU's decision-making elites have expressed growing dissatisfaction with the current state of China-EU relations, contending that China has failed adequately to understand or accommodate the EU's core interests, and has increasingly articulated critical assessments of bilateral economic interactions. In the view of the EU, Chinese companies, particularly state-owned enterprises, which benefit from substantial state support and

① This view was discussed during interviews and fieldwork conducted in Europe by Sven Biscop of the Egmont (Belgium Royal Institute for International Relations), and Frans-Paul van der Putten and Maaike Okano-Heijmans of the Clingendael Institute (Netherlands Institute of International Relations) in April 2019.

② This point was mentioned by Chinese scholar Hu Weinian of the Centre for European Policy Studies during fieldwork in Brussels in June 2019.

③ This opinion was discussed with Frans-Paul van der Putten of the Clingendael Institute during fieldwork in The Hague, Netherlands, April 2019.

intervention, have expanded exports and investment into Europe in ways that are perceived as exploiting the openness of the EU market, engaging in what is characterized as unfair competition, and, in some instances, constituting forms of social dumping that undermine European economic interests.[①] In response to these concerns, the EU has, since early 2017, not only declined to grant China Market Economy Status (MES)[②] but has also introduced a series of new regulatory and policy instruments aimed at constraining Chinese exports and investment in the European market. Notably, the European Commission's framework for a Foreign Direct Investment (FDI) screening mechanism issued on September 13, 2017, and the revised EU anti-dumping regulations officially adopted on December 19, 2017, both contain provisions with clear restrictive implications for China.[③] Furthermore, on December 20, 2017, the European Commission released *Commission Staff Working Document on Significant Distortions in the Economy of the People's Republic of China for the Purposes of Trade Defense Investigations*, an unprecedented report exceeding 450 pages in length, which has served as a detailed analytical foundation for the formulation and implementation of the EU's defensive economic policies toward China.[④] At the core of the EU's policy demands in China-EU relations are several key principles and concerns, including the Reciprocity Principle in market access, the establishment of a level playing field for European enterprises operating in China, the perceived monopolistic role of Chinese state-owned enterprises, and issues related to technology transfer and the protection of intellectual property rights. Analysts in European think tanks have cautioned that, should China fail to respond constructively to these core concerns, the EU's policy stance toward China is likely

---

① Monika Kiss, *Understanding Social Dumping*, Briefing of the European Parliament Research Service, March 2017.

② EU Commissioner for Trade Cecilia Malmstrom, "A Progressive Trade Policy in a Protectionist Age", Speech in EESC Plenary Session, Brussels, March 29, 2017; "Europe's Progressive Trade Policy", Speech at the European Business Summit, Brussels, May 22, 2017; "Trade in a Protectionist World", Speech at the Lunch hosted by the Friedrich Naumann Foundation, Hamburg, May 23, 2017.

③ European Commission, Proposal for a Regulation of the European Parliament and of the Council Establishing a Framework for Screening of Foreign Direct Investments into the European Union, SWD (2017) 297 Final, COM (2017) 487 Final, 2017/0224 (COD), Brussels, September 13, 2017.

④ European Commission, Commission Staff Working Document on Significant Distortions in the Economy of the People's Republic of China for the Purposes of Trade Defense Investigations, SWD (2017), 483 Final/2, Brussels, December 20, 2017.

to become progressively more assertive.

Finally, under the cumulative influence of the foregoing strategic considerations, European political elites have undergone a significant shift in their overall perception and evaluation of China's economic and political system, which has, in turn, led to a fundamental recalibration of the EU's strategic positioning of China-EU relations. The EU no longer regards China as a strategic cooperative partner in the full and original sense of the term, but instead conceptualizes China simultaneously as a negotiating partner, an economic competitor, and a systemic rival.① In this process, European political elites and the strategic studies community have, to an increasing extent, been influenced by prevailing analytical frameworks in the United States, often attributing difficulties in advancing China-EU relations to structural incompatibilities between China's political economy and the market-based system endorsed by the EU. Accordingly, the EU's analytical perspective and policy approach toward China have undergone a marked transformation. Although the EU continues, at the level of official rhetoric, to avoid explicit alignment in the context of China-U.S. strategic rivalry, in practice it has often adopted a strategy of indirect alignment, effectively allowing the United States to take the lead in confronting China while positioning itself in a more supplementary role. Despite the absence of explicit acknowledgment, there is a notable degree of convergence between EU and U.S. assessments of China's economic system and external economic practices, as reflected in the EU's increasing adoption of similar discourse, attitudes and policy orientations.②

In other words, the EU's strategic approach toward China has undergone a profound shift, with China-EU relations increasingly being conceptualized, in implicit terms, as a relationship that is neither fully adversarial nor genuinely cooperative. While the EU continues to refrain from overtly choosing sides between China and the United States, a pattern of coordination among the United States, Japan, and the EU in confronting China is gradually taking shape. The evolution of European political elites' strategic cognition and baseline assessments of China has prompted a comprehensive reassessment of bilateral economic relations, leading to the step-by-step strengthening of the EU's defensive economic policy framework toward China, particularly in the domain of trade protection.

---

① European Commission, "EU-China: A Strategic Outlook", March 12, 2019, pp. 1.

② This opinion was referred to by Frans-Paul van der Putten of the Clingendael Institute in April 2019.

Although Chinese foreign direct investment accounts for only a relatively small share of total inward FDI into the EU, the EU and its key member states such as Germany increasingly perceive China as posing an immediate and significant challenge in strategic high-technology sectors. Consequently, since 2017, the EU has progressively tightened its FDI screening mechanisms with regard to China. Guided by the overarching concept of European Economic Sovereignty, the European Commission under the leadership of von der Leyen has further strengthened regulatory control over mergers and acquisitions involving Chinese firms.[①] Concurrently, the EU, along with member states such as Germany and the Netherlands, has been actively considering the development of more comprehensive and refined industrial and technological policy frameworks, with the objective of ensuring that Europe maintains a competitive position in the global race for frontier technologies and strategic industries, and avoids falling behind both the United States and China.

2.2 The EU's Basic Orientations in China-EU Relations

As the EU's fundamental perceptions of and strategic calculus regarding China undergo significant shifts, its overarching policy orientation toward managing China-EU relations is correspondingly being recalibrated along several key dimensions.

First, in order to enhance its own decision-making authority and strengthen its agency vis-à-vis external actors, the EU has demonstrated a growing propensity to draw sharper conceptual distinctions between the Self and the Other. Consequently, as the EU has progressively consolidated its internal institutional architecture following the Brexit Referendum in 2016—while simultaneously reinforcing its decision-making authority and advancing the construction of EU-led European Sovereignty—it has also moved toward adopting a more critical and, at times, overtly negative stance toward China's foundational economic and social systems. This shift has recalibrated the strategic positioning of China-EU relations and deliberately widened the gap between the two sides. In fact, since Juncker assumed office in 2014, the European Commission had already begun to adjust the EU's conceptualization of China-EU relations, no longer treating China as a strategic cooperative partner in the full sense of the term. This shift was reflected in a series of policy actions:

① European Commission, Guidance to the Member States concerning foreign direct investment and free movement of capital from third countries, and the protection of Europe's strategic assets, ahead of the application of Regulation (EU) 2019/452 (FDI Screening Regulation), C (2020) 1981 final, Brussels, March 25, 2020.

the refusal to grant MES to China at the end of 2016, the release of the document on significant distortions in the economy of China in late 2017, and the publication of the *EU-China: A Strategic Outlook* in March 2019. After von der Leyen took office, the European Commission has notably refrained from using the term strategic partnership to describe China-EU relations, instead repeatedly emphasizing China's status as a systemic rival.[①] These signs indicate that the EU's new leadership increasingly perceives China not as a cooperative partner, but as a potential source of disruption to Europe's economic stability and normative order. Currently, the competitive and confrontational nature of China-EU relations has become a priority consideration for EU policymakers. In future, the European Commission led by von der Leyen is likely, on the one hand, to accelerate the formulation of new industrial policies, reform existing competition policy frameworks, foster the emergence of European corporate champions, and intensify intervention in industrial upgrading processes to prevent China from overtaking Europe in key sectors. On the other hand, it is almost certain to strengthen policy instruments targeting China in areas such as trade protection, investment screening, and intellectual property rights enforcement. For instance, shortly after the COVID-19 pandemic broke out in March 2020, the European Commission issued *Guidance to the Member States concerning Foreign Direct Investment and Free Movement of Capital from Third Countries and the Protection of Europe's Strategic Assets, ahead of the Application of Regulation,*[②] which was followed by the publication on June 17 of the *White Paper on Leveling the Playing Field as regards Foreign Subsidies*[③]-both of

① During von der Leyen's first term as President of the European Commission, both the European Commissioner for Trade, Phil Hogan, and the High Representative for Foreign Affairs and Security Policy, Josep Borrell, explicitly expressed their alignment with the characterization of China as a systemic rival. See: European Commission, Speech by Commissioner Phil Hogan at the Publication of BusinessEurope's Strategy Paper on the EU-China Economic Relations, Brussels, January 20, 2020; Josep Borrell, "Trust and Reciprocity: The Necessary Ingredients for EU-China Cooperation", Le Monde, May 15, 2020. Regarding the meaning of this positioning, see: European Parliament Briefing, EU-China Relations: Taking Stock after the 2020 EU-China Summit, June 30, 2020.

② European Commission, Guidance to the Member States concerning Foreign Direct Investment and Free Movement of Capital from Third Countries, and the Protection of Europe's Strategic Assets, ahead of the Application of Regulation (EU) 2019/452 (FDI Screening Regulation), C (2020) 1981 final, Brussels, March 25, 2020.

③ *White Paper on Leveling the Playing Field as regards Foreign Subsidies*, COM (2020) 253 final, Brussels, June 17, 2020.

which contained provisions widely interpreted as targeting China. These measures should be understood as an inherent part of the broader policy trajectory pursued by both Juncker and von der Leyen since 2017-2018, centered on the construction of European Sovereignty and the reinforcement of the EU's internal institutional capacity.

Second, as policymakers and the strategic studies community in the United States have progressively escalated their confrontational posture toward China, and as China-U.S. strategic rivalry has emerged as a defining structural feature shaping the global order, the EU is likely to continue pursuing a hedging strategy between China and the United States, seeking to preserve strategic flexibility and maneuverability. Accordingly, EU decision-making in relation to China will increasingly differentiate across issue areas and policy domains, adopting distinct positions vis-à-vis China and the United States depending on the sector in question. In the financial domain, the EU is expected to intensify efforts to enhance the international role of the euro and counter U.S. dollar hegemony. In the field of strategic security, it will seek to develop the EU's Defense Technological and Industrial Base (EDTIB) to offset the influence of the U.S.-led transatlantic security architecture. In both of these domains, the EU may, to some extent, leverage China's substantial economic weight by expanding economic and financial cooperation with China as a means of signaling and balancing against the United States. By contrast, in the areas of trade and investment, the EU is likely to coordinate more closely with the United States, maintaining the existing trilateral consultation mechanism among the United States, Japan, and the EU at the ministerial level.[①] It will utilize U.S. pressure on China—particularly in the context of trade disputes—to secure institutional, regulatory, and policy concessions from Beijing, thereby securing indirect benefits from U.S.-China tensions. In this sense, the EU's approach toward China is likely to become increasingly opportunistic and transactional in strategic terms.

Third, although the EU's competitiveness anxiety has historically been framed primarily in relation to the United States, the intensification of China-EU competition, together with

① Since December 2017, senior trade officials from the United States, Japan, and the EU periodically convened trilateral meetings and issued joint statements addressing Unfair Trade Practices. These meetings, while not explicitly naming China, evolved into a regular mechanism for U.S.-Japan-EU trilateral coordination to put pressure on China for trade-related issues. The European Union actively took part in this framework since 2018, with the most recent trilateral meeting held online on November 30, 2021. Since then, this coordination became irregular and informal.

China's rapid advancements in frontier technologies and advanced manufacturing sectors in recent years, has led the EU to increasingly perceive China as a significant challenger in the technological and industrial domains. Moreover, the COVID-19 pandemic has amplified ongoing debates within EU decision-making circles and the European strategic studies community regarding the need to reduce dependence on Chinese supply chains,[①] thereby further accelerating discussions on supply chain diversification and strategic adjustment. As the EU continues to refine its agenda for European Sovereignty and advance the project of European Strategic Autonomy, it may seek to encourage European firms to relocate portions of their capital and production chains away from China, while simultaneously engaging in more cautious and competitive bilateral interactions with China in industrial and technological fields. Notably, the High Representative of the Union for Foreign Affairs and Security Policy, Josep Borrell, issued on April 30, 2020 a policy brief through the European Council on Foreign Relations (ECFR), and published on May 15 commentaries in several major European media outlets, repeatedly emphasizing the necessity for Europe to "reduce dependence on China" and achieve "supply chain diversification", while calling for stronger EU-level leadership in these areas.[②] Similarly, in a report released on May 13, 2020, Andrew Small of the ECFR explicitly stated that the EU's strategies across industrial policy, digital technology, and connectivity are all geared toward a single objective: "The EU's industrial, connectivity, and digital strategies are infused with the perceived need to compete with China more effectively.", calling on "European political leaders.... many of them expected competition, and even rivalry, with China, to proceed under a cloak of civility."[③] These

---

① Around the time of the signing of the "Phase One" U.S.-China trade agreement in early 2020, discussions urging Europe to reduce its supply chain dependency on China were already surfacing in Brussels-based think tank circles. Since the outbreak of the COVID-19 pandemic, deliberations on this issue have intensified among EU policymakers and the strategic research community. Representative perspectives from European strategic research institutes include: Alicia Garcia-Herrero, "Companies Must Move Supply Chains further from China", Bruegel, February 28, 2020. Andrew Small, *The Meaning of Systemic Rivalry: Europe and China beyond the Pandemic*, Policy Brief, European Council on Foreign Relations, May 2020.

② Josep Borrell, "The Post-Coronavirus World is Already Here", Policy Brief, European Council on Foreign Relations, April 2020; "Trust and Reciprocity: The Necessary Ingredients for EU-China Cooperation", Op-eds, *the Irish Times*, May 15, 2020.

③ Andrew Small, *The Meaning of Systemic Rivalry: Europe and China beyond the Pandemic*, Policy Brief, European Council on Foreign Relations, May 2020, pp. 5.

assessments suggest that, as the EU deepens the adjustment of its internal and external policy frameworks, bilateral competition between China and the EU in technological and industrial domains is likely to intensify further.

Since the adoption on 22 June 2016 of the Joint Communication to the European Parliament and the Council *Elements for a New EU Strategy on China*, the EU has not only maintained close scrutiny and systematic evaluation of China-EU economic relations, but has also successively introduced a wide array of new policy instruments and regulatory measures. It has established a comprehensive system across multiple domains, including trade, investment, industrial policy, technology transfer, and intellectual property protection, aimed at restricting, monitoring, screening, and vetting Chinese exports to and investment in the European market. Taken together, these measures constitute a broad, complex, and highly structured policy architecture governing the EU's external economic relations with China. In order to develop an analytically robust understanding of the decision-making logic and operational mechanisms underpinning this policy system, it is essential to examine in detail the structural characteristics of the EU's decision-making framework and identify the key actors capable of exerting influence over EU economic policymaking toward China. Among the various actors shaping the EU's China policy, one category stands out as particularly pivotal: European think tanks. They exert substantial influence over the EU's strategic cognition of China-EU economic relations and contribute significantly to the construction of ideational frameworks through which EU decision-makers interpret China-related issues. Without a systematic and in-depth analysis of the mechanisms through which European think tanks shape EU economic decision-making vis-à-vis China, it would be extremely difficult to explain the structure and processes of EU policymaking on China-related issues, identify the underlying drivers and patterns of the EU's economic policy toward China, or make reliable projections about the future evolving trajectory of the EU's China policy.

III. The Outstanding Role of European Think Tanks in the EU's Decision-Making System

The EU is arguably the most institutionally complex international organization in the world today. Its decision-making architecture encompasses the European Council, the Council of the European Union, the European Commission, and the European Parliament, forming a hierarchically overlapping and procedurally complex system. Unlike the institutional structure of a typical nation-state grounded in Representative Democracy, the EU grants its citizens no direct electoral power over most of its core institutions beyond the European Parliament, nor has it succeeded in fostering a deeply internalized and widely shared sense of a unified European identity. More fundamentally, the EU embodies a hybrid polity that simultaneously exhibits marked supranational and inter-state attributes. Its establishment and operational logic have historically reflected, to a considerable degree, the abstract ideals of European political elites, while lacking robust mechanisms for effectively aggregating and channeling popular preferences upward, thus giving rise, since its formal founding in 1993, to the enduring problem of a democratic deficit. At the same time, as the process of European integration continues to gain traction and the organizational scope of the EU constantly expands, economic and social development across Europe has been expedited, albeit with additional transaction costs on grassroots economic and social operations. This has rendered the provision and acquisition of public goods more complex than in representative democratic nation-states such as the United States, while constraining the natural diversification of public goods demand shaped by Europe's diverse socio-cultural backgrounds.

Since the outbreak of the 2010-2011 sovereign debt crisis, particularly with the intensification of both internal and external challenges facing the EU, an increasing proportion of European citizens have shifted to Euroscepticism, voicing dissatisfaction with and resistance to the Union's supranational outlook. Driven by such sentiments, the 2016-2017 period saw the rapid rise of radical populist parties opposing European integration. By capitalizing on electoral participation in national parliamentary and presidential contests, these parties entered mainstream politics with considerable momentum, further exacerbating the EU's democratic deficit.[①] The sources of public discontent may be traced to two principal factors. First, the supranational nature of the EU is underpinned by a meta-narrative imbued with political correctness, to which EU decision-makers have remained strongly committed. This has hindered their ability to accurately and responsively capture the specific interests and grievances of grassroots constituencies, resulting in their failure to connect

① Eelco Harteveld et al., "Blaming Brussels? The Impact of the Refugee Crisis on Attitudes towards the EU and National Politics", *Journal of Common Market Studies*, 2018, Vol. 56, No. 1, pp. 157-177 with realities on the ground.[①] Despite longstanding efforts to promote a system of multilevel governance, persistent multiple decision-making tiers and a highly complex institutional architecture have kept EU institutions and European societies structurally apart, leading to inadequate communication channels and, in certain instances, a marked divergence between elite perceptions and public sentiment—as evidenced in the EU's handling of the refugee crisis. Second, the EU's supranational system has progressively accumulated resources and authority from the member-state system, giving rise to what is widely perceived as a Leviathan that is only partially accountable to national governments, while continuously seeking to expand its own power. This dynamic has fostered a perception among segments of the European public that they are being governed by Brussels bureaucracy detached from their national sovereignty and cultural frameworks, which in turn intensifies alienation and resentment. Further exacerbated by the accumulated contradictions of globalization and regional integration, these tensions have entered a phase of intense eruption in recent years. Radical populist movements have capitalized on this trend to advance their Eurosceptic discourse, fueling popular distrust toward the elite-driven supranational system of the EU.[②]

Across Europe, political parties, chambers of commerce, industry associations, trade unions, professional organizations, and a wide spectrum of other interest groups have transcended national boundaries to form pan-European pressure groups. Together with EU-level media, think tanks, academic institutions, and advocacy networks, they collectively form a European-level civil society that exerts a subtle yet profound influence on the EU's external policymaking. In light of the persistent and, in some respects, deepening democratic deficit, the EU—more so than typical representative democratic nation-states—has come to place considerable emphasis on the role of civil society in its macro-level political decision-making system, relying extensively on EU-level pressure groups and associated

---

① A survey report, published on June 15, 2017 by the U.S.-based public opinion polling organization, the Pew Research Center, revealed the following findings among respondents in ten EU member states (Greece, Sweden, Italy, Spain, Hungary, Poland, the United Kingdom, France, Germany, and the Netherlands). On average, 74 percent of respondents in each country believed that matters concerning immigration and refugees should be controlled by their national governments and addressed outside the EU policy framework. Furthermore, 51 percent of respondents held the view that the authority to conduct foreign trade negotiations should also rest with their national governments. http://www.pewglobal.org/2017/06/15/eu-back-in-favor-but-brussels-handling-of-economy-and-refugees-still-questioned/, accessed September 14, 2018.

② Michael Birnbaum, "7 Reasons Why Some Europeans Hate the E.U.", *The Washing Post*, June 25, 2016.

organizations to facilitate interaction between policymakers and public opinion. EU decision-makers perceive such actors, including pressure groups, think tanks, and advocacy organizations, as key organizational forms of Organized Civil Society, and have deliberately established institutional frameworks of Participatory Democracy, where the involvement of these actors in the EU decision-making process has been formalized and routinized, effectively integrating them into the governance architecture of the Union. Consequently, the influence exerted by EU-level pressure groups and civil society actors on EU policymaking is, in many respects, more substantial than the influence of domestic civil society structures within individual member states on their respective national decision-making processes.

Within the European civil society system, the politics of pressure groups—encompassing institutionalized interactions and strategic contestations among political parties, interest groups, think tanks, media organizations, and decision-making elites—has evolved into a central operational modality of the EU's Multilevel Governance Mechanism. In this context, think tanks, as relatively independent public policy research institutions, function as crucial channels and platforms through which European pressure groups articulate their interests and exert influence upon EU decision-makers. British political expert Bill Coxall characterizes think tanks as a distinct category of pressure group,[①] while American political scientist Thomas A. Birkland identifies think tanks, alongside political parties, interest groups, and the media, as one of the four principal types of non-governmental actors influencing public policy.[②] In practice, think tanks have increasingly assumed the role of an external brain for policymakers, being regarded, alongside the legislative, executive, judicial, and media powers, as a fifth force shaping political decision-making. Compared with the think tank system in the United States, the European think tank landscape has evolved into a complex dual-level and quadrilateral structure, comprising think tanks operating both at the EU level—often referred to as Brussels-based think tanks—and at the level of major member states such as the United Kingdom and Germany, particularly in the domain of foreign policy. Through elaborate networks of communication and interaction with the highest decision-making bodies at both EU and member-state levels,

---

① Bill Coxall, *Pressure Groups in British Politics*, London: Pearson Education Limited, 2001, pp. 74-76.

② Thomas A. Birkland, *An Introduction to the Policy Process: Theories, Concepts, and Models of Public Policy Making*, 3rd edition, New York: M. E. Sharpe, 2011, pp. 142-146.

these think tanks collectively form a dynamic and adaptive mechanism that increasingly shapes—and, in certain respects, constrains—the processes of policymaking in the EU across economic, social, and foreign policy domains.

From the perspective of power structure and interest distribution within the European political system, think tanks are key actors in the EU's Interest Representation and its Multilevel Governance. They maintain extensive channels of information exchange and resource interaction with various components of the EU's political decision-making apparatus, thus influencing the relative balance of power among different actors, while simultaneously functioning as an autonomous force within the system itself. From the vantage point of ideational construction and decision-making process, think tanks form integral components of "Epistemic Community",[①] "Policy Community",[②] and "Policy Networks"[③] at both the EU level and within major European states. They are proactively involved in the conception and construction of policy paradigms, value orientations, and cognitive frameworks through which EU decision-makers interpret specific issue areas, shape situational assessments, and structure agenda-setting processes, ultimately influencing

---

① Representative works that analyze the influence of European think tanks from the perspective of the Epistemic Community include: Heidi Ullrich, "European Union Think Tanks: Generating Ideas, Analysis and Debate", in Diane Stone and Andrew Denham (Eds.), *Think Tank Traditions: Policy Research and the Politics of Ideas*, New York: Manchester University Press, 2004; Lorenzo Allio, *The Role of Brussels-based Think Tanks in the EU Decision-Making Process*, a Thesis for the Degree of Master of European Studies, College of Europe, May 2002. In addition, a number of studies examining the role of Epistemic Community in shaping the EU leadership's decision-making ideas and policy paradigms in specific policy domains also make reference to the role played by European think tanks; such discussions can be found in various works, including: Mari'a K. Davis Cross, *Security Integration in Europe: How Knowledge-Based Networks Are Transforming the European Union*, Ann Arbor: University of Michigan Press, 2011.

② Representative studies that interpret the position of European think tanks within the EU political system from the perspective of the Policy Community include: Simon Nichelson, *EU Think Tanks in Brussels: Policy-Making Roles, Functions and Influence*, a Thesis for the Degree of Master of European Politics and Policies, Katholieke Universiteit Leuven, 2009.

③ Representative works that examine the relationship between European think tanks and political decision-making structures from the analytical perspective of Policy Networks include: Tanja A. Borzel, "What's So Special About Policy Networks: An Exploration of the Concept and Its Usefulness in Studying European Governance", *European Integration Online Papers*, Vol. 1 (1997), No. 016, August 25, 1997; John Turnpenny et al., "Mapping Actors involved in Climate Change Policy Networks in the UK", Tyndall Center for Climate Change Research, Working Paper 66, January 2005.

the pace, sequencing, and trajectory of EU policymaking (Hall, 1992; Allio, 2002; Ullrich, 2004; Teichler, 2007; Cross, 2011). Overall, think tanks exert a subtle yet significant influence on EU decision-making, particularly in the domains of foreign and security policy. A systematic analysis of this influence can contribute to a more precise theoretical understanding of the mechanisms through which think tanks shape policy outcomes, as well as to a clearer conceptualization of the relationship between European think tanks and the EU decision-making system. It is precisely in this analytical endeavor that the theoretical contribution of the present study resides.

Given the pivotal role of European think tanks in the EU's decision-making structures and processes, the absence of a systematic synthesis and rigorous conceptualization of the mechanisms through which they influence EU policymaking would render it extremely difficult to accurately grasp the essential characteristics and operational logic of EU decision-making, particularly with respect to the formulation of economic policy toward China. Moreover, since the beginning of 2015, the EU has entered a period of heightened turbulence marked by multiple overlapping and sequential crises, including the Euro area crisis, terrorist attacks, Brexit, and influx of large-scale refugees. Collectively, these crises make EU decision-making processes more complex, volatile, and nonlinear, while simultaneously activating and amplifying the policy advisory functions of European think tanks, further highlighting their influence on EU policymaking. Indeed, the EU's evolving assessment of its position in the globalizing world economy, its evaluation of China's fundamental economic system and the nature of China-EU relations, and its interpretation of the strategic implications of initiatives such as the BRI and the 17+1 Cooperation Framework can, upon closer examination, be traced back to the conceptual framework, analytical paradigm, and discourse system developed by European think tanks.[①] From this perspective, European think tanks play a subtle yet consequential role in shaping how EU decision-makers identify policy issues and frame policy agendas. Accordingly, a systematic investigation into the position of think tanks within the EU's external decision-making system, the identification of specific stages and mechanisms through which they influence EU economic policymaking toward China, and a detailed analysis of the timing, modalities, pathways, and effectiveness

① Garima Mohan, *Europe's Response to the Belt and Road Initiative*, Policy Brief of the German Marshall Fund of the United States, No. 014, 2018.

of such influence, are essential for elucidating the structural characteristics and dynamic mechanisms underlying the EU's policy framework toward China, particularly its defensive economic policy regime. This endeavor carries both significant academic value and important practical implications.

IV. Existing Literature on European and American Think Tanks

Internationally, research on think tanks has been most extensive and systematical in the United States and Canada, where a comparatively rich corpus of comprehensive and empirical research has been amassed.[①] Since January 2007, the Think Tanks and Civil Societies Program (TTCSP) directed by James G. McGann at the University of Pennsylvania has undertaken a long-term research initiative devoted to evaluating and ranking think tanks worldwide. The annual *Global Go To Think Tank Index Report* produced by this program provides a comprehensive statistical overview of the geographical distribution and numerical scale of think tanks across regions and countries, while also assessing and ranking their research quality. This ranking system, to date, remains the only globally recognized framework for evaluating think tanks. However, despite its considerable international visibility and influence, it has also attracted some substantial methodological and conceptual criticism in the academic community.[②] Existing literature indicates that, since the 1990s,

① Monographs on research by American think tanks include: James G. McGann, *Global Think Tanks: Policy Networks and Governance*, London: Routledge, 2001, *Think Tanks and Policy Advice in the United States: Academics, Advisors, and Advocates*, New York: Routledge, 2007, *Tanks, Politics, and Public Policy*, Northampton: Edward Elgar Publishing Inc., 2005; Murray Weidenbaum, *The Competition of Ideas: The World of Washington Think Tanks*, New Brunswick: Transaction Publishers, 2009; Donald E. Abelson, *A Capital Idea: Think Tanks and US Foreign Policy*, Montreal: McGill-Queen's University Press, 2006, *Do Think Tanks Matter? Assessing the Impact of Public Policy Institute*, London: McGill-Queen's University Press, 2002; Diane Stone & Andrew Denham, *Think Tank Traditions: Policy Research and the Politics of Ideas*, Manchester: Manchester University Press, 2004; Andrew Rich, *Think Tanks, Public Policy, and the Politics of Expertise*, Cambridge: Cambridge University Press, 2004; James Allen Smith, *The Idea Brokers: Think Tanks and the Rise of the New Policy Elite*, New York: The Free Press, 1991.

② During the author's field interviews with European think tanks conducted in 2013-2014, several leading figures from Brussels-based think tanks expressed reservations regarding the rankings contained in the *Global Go To Think Tank Index* compiled by James G. McGann. For instance, Fabian Zuleeg, Chief Executive of the scholars in the United States and Canada have produced roughly 12 monographs devoted to the study of think tanks, but the overwhelming majority of these works focus primarily on the American think tank system, examining its operational mechanisms, institutional characteristics, and policy influence in the U.S. political context. The core contributions of this body of scholarship can be summarized in the following several principal respects.

First, a number of studies have offered comprehensive and systematic accounts of the overall structure of the American think tank ecosystem, providing detailed comparative analyses of internal institutional features such as the typological distribution of think tanks, their organizational structures, personnel composition, operational mechanisms, and funding sources. Some scholars have even undertaken spatial analyses of foreign policy think tanks in Washington, D.C., carefully mapping their geographical distribution patterns and demonstrating, from a spatial and institutional perspective, the close proximity and structural interconnections between the well-known "K Street" cluster of think tanks and the centers of legislative and executive power in the U.S. government (Weidenbaum, 2009). Scholars have also adopted different classificatory criteria and terminologies to propose a variety of typologies for categorizing American think tanks. Nevertheless, most researchers have highlighted one key differentiating dimension: the extent to which think tanks exhibit identifiable ideological orientations or political value commitments. Think tanks with pronounced ideological leanings are often treated as a distinct category and are widely considered to maintain close relationships with competitive lobbying and policy advice activities in the American political system, thereby exercising significant influence on partisan politics and presidential election campaigns (Weidenbaum, 2009; Abelson, 2002, 2006; Smith, 1991).①

European Policy Centre, as well as Jan Techau, then Director of Carnegie Europe, the European branch of the Carnegie Endowment for International Peace, both indicated that they did not fully endorse the rankings presented in the report. Similarly, in April 2016, when the author conversed with Pascal Abb and Patrick Köllner, scholars affiliated with the German Institute of Global and Area Studies, they also expressed many reservations about the rankings in the report.

① Murray Weidenbaum, *The Competition of Ideas: The World of Washington Think Tanks*, New Brunswick: Transaction Publishers, 2009, pp. 9-36; Donald E. Abelson, *Do Think Tanks Matter? Assessing the Impact of Public Policy Institute,* London: McGill-Queen's University Press, 2002, pp. 17-48; *A Capital Idea: Think Tanks and U.S. Foreign Policy*, Montreal: McGill-Queen's University Press, 2006, pp. 225-232; Martin J. Smith, "From Policy Community to Issue Networks: Salmonella Eggs and the New Politics Food", *Public Administration*, Vol.

Second, scholars have devoted considerable attention to analyzing the mechanisms through which American think tanks exert influence on public policy, as well as to evaluating the magnitude and effectiveness of such influence. Researchers have approached this question from multiple angles: some have measured the frequency and timing of media appearances by prominent think tanks to gauge their agenda-setting capacity in the public sphere (Abelson, 2006)①; others have tracked the participation of think tank experts in congressional hearings (Abelson, 2002; Smith, 1991)②; and still others have catalogued the themes and frequency of speeches delivered by senior officials from executive departments at Washington-based think tanks (Weidenbaum, 2009)③. Besides, a number of scholars have adopted a case-study approach to look at specific cases of think tank influence on the policy process, with a particular focus on the RAND Corporation and the Council on Foreign Relations (CFR)④. Despite these diverse methodological efforts, however, most researchers ultimately converge on one similar conclusion: while think tanks undeniably play a role in the American policymaking process, the precise magnitude and causal mechanisms of their influence remain difficult to measure with precision, largely because policymaking itself

69, Summer 1991, pp. 235-255.

① Donald E. Abelson, *A Capital Idea: Think Tanks and US Foreign Policy*, Montreal: McGill-Queen's University Press, 2006, pp: 234-242.

② Donald E. Abelson, *Do Think Tanks Matter? Assessing the Impact of Public Policy Institute,* London: McGill-Queen's University Press, 2002, pp. 17-48; *A Capital Idea: Think Tanks and U.S. Foreign Policy*, Montreal: McGill-Queen's University Press, 2006, pp. 225-232; Martin J. Smith, "From Policy Community to Issue Networks: Salmonella Eggs and the New Politics Food", *Public Administration*, Vol. 69, Summer 1991, pp. 235-255.

③ Murray Weidenbaum, *The Competition of Ideas: The World of Washington Think Tanks*, New Brunswick: Transaction Publishers, 2009, pp. 122-231.

④ Alex Abella, *Soldiers of Reason: The RAND Corporation and the Rise of the American Empire*, New York and London: Harcourt, Inc., 2008; Jean-Loup Samaan, *The Reconfiguration of Strategic Studies in the United States*, Renuka George trans., New York: Palgrave Macmillan, 2012; Laurence H. Shoup and William Minter, *Imperial Brain Trust: The Council on Foreign Relations and United States Foreign Policy*, New York and London: Monthly Review Press, 1977; Laurence H. Shoup, *Wall Street's Think Tank: The Council on Foreign Relations and the Empire of Neoliberal Geopolitics, 1976-2014*, New York: Monthly Review Press, 2015; Roberts D. Schulzinger, *The Wise Men of Foreign Affairs: The History of the Council on Foreign Relations*, New York: Columbia University Press, 1984; Inderjeet Parmer, *Think Tanks and Power in Foreign Policy: A Comparative Study of the Role and Influence of the Council on Foreign Relations and the Royal Institute of International Affairs, 1939-1945*, New York: Palgrave Macmillan, 2004.

remains a highly complex black box in which multiple actors and institutional dynamics interact.①

Third, several scholars have proposed innovative theoretical perspectives for conceptualizing the position and operational logic of think tanks in the American political system. For instance, in the early 1990s, some researchers advanced the influential notion that the American think tank system operates within a highly competitive "Market Place of Ideas", in which think tanks function as "Idea Brokers", mediating between intellectual production and policy demand. This conceptual framework has since been widely adopted in think tank studies across different regional and national contexts (Smith, 1991).② In another line of scholarship, researchers have, drawing upon foundational concepts from political philosophy such as public sphere, social space, and field of power, proposed the theoretical lens of US think tanks as the central space within the field of power, offering an accurate account of the relationship between think tanks and other components of the U.S. political system (Medvetz, 2012).③

Taken together, existing literature on American think tanks is both extensive and methodologically diverse, encompassing a wide range of theoretical approaches and empirical materials. Its analytical sophistication, empirical depth, and documentary comprehensiveness have reached a comparatively high level of maturity. In contrast, scholarly research devoted specifically to European think tanks remains limited. Existing English-language literature does not appear to include monographs dedicated exclusively to the systematic study of European think tanks; rather, relevant discussions are scattered across journal articles and edited volumes.④ Moreover, the available data on European think

---

① Donald E. Abelson, "Old World, New World: The Evolution and Influence of Foreign Affairs Think Tanks", *International Affairs*, the Royal Institute of International Affairs, 2014, Vol. 90: 1 (2014), pp. 125-142; *A Capital Idea: Think Tanks and US Foreign Policy*, Montreal: McGill-Queen's University Press, 2006, *Do Think Tanks Matter? Assessing the Impact of Public Policy Institute*, London: McGill-Queen's University Press, 2002.

② James Allen Smith, *The Idea Brokers: Think Tanks and the Rise of the New Policy Elite*, New York: The Free Press, 1991.

③ Thomas Medvetz, *Think Tanks in America*, Chicago: University of Chicago Press, 2012.

④ Among the currently available literature on the study of European think tanks, most scholarly research tends to concentrate on 3 principal categories of think tanks, namely those operating at the EU level, in the U.K., and in Germany. In light of this pattern in the literature, Chapters 4, 5, and 6 of this book will respectively undertake a more detailed and systematic review of the relevant scholarly works concerning these three types of think tanks are often fragmentary and insufficiently systematic. Nevertheless, European think tanks have been indeed mentioned in a small number of English-language studies addressing the institutional structure of the EU political system and the functioning of EU decision-making processes. Some of these works approach the issue from the perspective of European pressure group, the EU's Interest Representation, and its system of Multilevel Governance, focusing on the institutional configurations and operational dynamics formed by the interaction of interest groups, advocacy organizations, lobbying bodies, and other actors across different levels of governance. Within this analytical framework, European think tanks are generally conceptualized as actors belonging to civil society in the institutional architecture of Participatory Democracy at the EU level.[①] Among such works, the studies of British scholar Justin Greenwood provide one of the more systematic and comprehensive overviews of supranational interest-group politics within the EU. While acknowledging the existence and role of European think tanks in this broader ecosystem, his work only mentions them in passing and does not develop into a sustained analytical inquiry.[②] Other studies have adopted the perspective of epistemic community or policy community involved in shaping EU policy paradigms, focusing on particular decision-making domains such as European security policy, and identifying certain European think tanks as components of these communities.[③] Overall, while existing English-language scholarship does acknowledge the presence of think tanks in the EU policy environment, it generally does so only in passing, and systematic studies specifically devoted to analyzing the mechanisms through which European think tanks influence EU policymaking remain notably scarce.

---

tanks, so as to provide a comprehensive survey of the research landscape associated with each category.

① Alex Warleigh and Jenny Faribrass (Eds.), *Influence and Interests in the European Union: the New Politics of Persuasion and Advocacy*, London: Taylor & Francis Group, 2003; Institute for European Studies (IES) of Vrije Universiteit Brussel, *The European Commission and Interest Groups: Towards a Deliberative Interpretation of Stakeholder Involvement in EU Policy Making*, Brussels: Brussels University Press, 2008; Jan Beyers, Rainer Eising and William A. Maloney (Eds.), *Interest Group Politics in Europe: Lessons from EU Studies and Comparative Politics*, London: Routledge, 2010; Michele Knodt, Christine Quittkat and Justin Greenwood (Eds.), *Functional and Territorial Interest Representation in the EU*, London: Routledge, 2012.

② Justin Greenwood, *Interest Representation in the European Union*, Hampshire: Palgrave Macmillan, 2011.

③ Mari'a K. and Davis Cross, *Security Integration in Europe: How Knowledge-Based Networks Are Transforming the European Union*, Ann Arbor: University of Michigan Press, 2011; Falk Daviter, *Policy Framing in the European Union*, Hampshire: Palgrave Macmillan, 2011.

Since the early 2000s, Chinese academic research on Western think tanks has also grown steadily, producing a number of scholarly works; however, the overwhelming majority of these studies likewise concentrate on the United States. Among Chinese-language publications on Western think tanks since 1981, approximately 67 percent of the academic articles focus on American think tanks, while many others provide general descriptive overviews of foreign think tanks. Only a handful of articles published in major Chinese academic journals examine European think tanks in a more specialized manner, and these typically focus on analyzing European think tanks' research agendas concerning China.[①] Monographs in Chinese on the subject are almost entirely devoted to the American think tank system, with only a few exceptions: one edited volume published in 2004 offers a relatively detailed overview of the national distribution and research areas of European think tanks; another monograph presents a comparative analysis of European and American think tanks; and a further study examines the influence of European think tanks on the EU's Middle East policy.[②] Nonetheless, Chinese-language scholarship that systematically investigates the influence of European think tanks on EU decision-making remains extremely limited, and studies that integrate the analytical frameworks of EU pressure group politics, European think tanks, and the EU's defensive economic policy toward China are, to the best of current knowledge, virtually nonexistent.

V. Research Approach and Structure

This book takes as its principal object of analysis three major types of European think tanks, namely, EU think tanks (commonly referred to in the literature as "Brussels-based think tanks"), German think tanks, and British think tanks. This book also uses the

① Fang Lexian, "Recent Tendencies in European Think Tanks' Perceptions of China: A Case Study of the European Council on Foreign Relations", *Forum of World Economics & Politics*, 2012(01), pp. 95-104; PAN Zhongqi, "The latest developments of European think tanks and their research on China", *Contemporary International Relations*, 2010(10), pp. 8-14+20; WANG Yan, "The Role of European Think Tanks in the Formulation of the EU's China Policy", *Chinese Journal of European Studies*, 2009, 27(02), pp. 92-104+161.

② China Institutes of Contemporary International Relations, *European Think-Tanks and their Studies on China*, Beijing: Current Affairs Press; Chu Ming, *Comparative Study of American and European Think Tanks*, Beijing: China Social Sciences Press, 2013; Xin Hua, *European Think Tanks' Influence on EU's Policy Making Towards the Middle East*, Beijing: Social Sciences Academic Press, 2017.

EU's defensive economic policy toward China as the specific policy lens through which to observe and assess the influence of think tanks on political decision-making.[①] By integrating a theoretically robust analytical framework with systematic empirical data analysis, the study within this book evaluates the effects, tempo, pathways, and modes through which European think tanks exert influence upon EU policy decisions, with the broader objective of constructing a theoretically rigorous and empirically grounded account of think-tank influence in the European policymaking process. More specifically, the analysis proceeds along several interrelated lines of inquiry.

First, this book surveys and synthesizes the principal theoretical paradigms, analytical perspectives, and explanatory models that existing studies have adopted to account for the policy influence of think tanks, interest groups, and other actors in civil society, on which basis, it further constructs an analytical framework suitable for explaining the influence of European think tanks on EU decision-making. Existing studies have drawn upon a range of theoretical paradigms, including elitism, pluralism, institutionalism, and neo-Gramscian approaches, and in the process, have developed a number of conceptual perspectives, such as the "Central Space of the Four-Dimensional Power Field", "Epistemic Community", "Policy Community", "Policy Network", "Discourse Coalition", and "Advocacy Coalition". Additionally, scholars have proposed several dynamic explanatory models, including the Hallstadius Model, Comprehensive Influence Model, Four-Factor Model of Think-Tank Influence, Multiple-Policy-Stream Framework, and Punctuated Equilibrium Model, all of which provide valuable theoretical support for analyzing the interaction between policy knowledge and political decision-making.

Building upon these foundations, the study within this book employs key concepts derived from political philosophy and analytical tools developed in public policy analysis to construct an explanatory framework tailored to the European context. More specifically, drawing upon the theoretical traditions of pluralism and institutionalism, this study elaborates on Jürgen Habermas's concept of public sphere along with Pierre Bourdieu's

① The defensive economic policy toward China referred to here encompass the European Union's fundamental policy positioning, overall strategic framework, and long-term policy orientation toward China, as well as the specific policy instruments adopted by the EU in four key domains, including trade, investment, industrial policy, technology transfer, and intellectual property protection. A detailed exposition of the substantive content and institutional configuration of these policy frameworks is provided in Table 3.5 of Chapter 3 of this book.

notion of field in social life. On this basis, it formulates the analytical concept of a three-layered field of social space. In this conceptual structure, the perspective of the "Central Space of Power Field" is combined with John Kingdon's "Multiple-Policy-Stream Model" to construct a synthetic theoretical framework. Within this framework, European think tanks are conceptualized as occupying a central position situated between four major domains—politics, media, academia, and the economic-financial sector—in the broader "power field" of the EU decision-making system. Their policy-influencing activities are interpreted primarily as part of the policy stream and the politics stream in the EU decision-making process. By examining the static interactive structure linking European think tanks with these four domains of the EU power field, and by analyzing the roles they play in the dynamic convergence of multiple decision streams and the opening of policy windows (also termed as decision-making window, referring to specific time when great changes occur in the policymaking process.), this study seeks to reveal the essential characteristics of think-tank influence in EU policymaking.

Second, based on a systematic mapping of the overall structure of the European think-tank system, this book categorizes and synthesizes the various operational modes through which European think tanks influence political decision-making, and identifies the specific components of EU and member-state decision structures that are affected by each mode of influence, thereby outlining the general mechanisms through which European think tanks shape policy outcomes at both the EU and national levels. According to the intensity and duration of influence, the operational instruments employed by European think tanks are classified into four major categories (i.e. short-term indirect influence, short-term direct influence, long-term indirect influence, and long-term direct influence), comprising thirteen distinct modes of influence in total. Previous research has observed that organizations in European civil society can influence EU policy through two principal channels, commonly referred to as the Brussels route and the national route (also termed as the member-state route). Building upon this insight, the present study analytically breaks down the decision-making structures of both the EU and its member states, and examines how each of the twelve influence modes employed by European think tanks interacts with specific components of these two levels of governance. Through this analysis, the book constructs a comprehensive map of the mechanisms through which European think tanks influence

EU policy via both the Brussels route and the national route, with the aim of presenting a systematic and coherent picture of the overall process.

Third, this study selects three specific think tanks as representative cases corresponding to the aforementioned three categories of European think tanks, and focuses on three critical moments when policy windows open in the EU decision-making process concerning defensive economic policies toward China. At each of these junctures, the study examines the major policy adjustments made by the EU and analyzes the effects, tempo, pathways, and modes through which the selected think tanks influenced these policy changes, thus revealing the positions and roles of these think tanks in the interactive relationships of the EU power field and the dynamic evolution of multiple streams. Drawing upon data from the *Global Go To Think Tank Index Report* compiled by James G. McGann of the University of Pennsylvania, this study comprehensively examines rankings in three major areas: general research capacity, external economic policy research, and foreign and security policy research. Next, this study selects the most highly ranked and widely recognized think tank from each of the three categories under examination: the Brussels European and Global Economic Laboratory (Bruegel), a Brussels-based EU-level think tank; the German Institute for International and Security Affairs (SWP) in Berlin; and the Royal Institute of International Affairs (Chatham House) in London. These three institutions are treated as principal cases of observation, while the EU's defensive economic policies toward China serve as the focal policy domain for the case studies.

This book identifies three critical junctures at which policy windows opened and prompted the EU to make significant adjustment to its strategic perceptions and overall policy orientation toward China: 1) the period from February to May, 2012. In the aftermath of the 2009-2010 Euro area crisis, Europe's economy remained mired in prolonged stagnation, characterized by high unemployment and mounting social tensions. Under these circumstances, the EU began actively considering the formulation of new defensive economic policies, and initiated consultation with relevant stakeholders to safeguard internal production and employment; 2) the period from February to July, 2016. In Europe, Brexit severely destabilized the EU's existing normative framework and institutional architecture, while the rapid rise of radical populist forces across Europe stoked widespread grassroots dissatisfaction with globalization and regional integration. Consequently, the EU was compelled to respond more explicitly to domestic demands for stronger trade and industrial protection. At the same time, externally, imports of steel products into the EU peaked, while Article 15 of China's WTO Accession Protocol connected to the "market economy status" of China was approaching expiration. Faced with these simultaneous internal and external pressures, the EU reactivated its policymaking process, reviving the concept of managing globalization and initiating intensive discussions on the establishment of new trade defense instruments; and 3) the period from February to May, 2017. The acquisition of German "Kuka Robotics" by a Chinese company in early 2017 triggered widespread debate across Europe and heightened public concern. In February 2017, the economy ministers of Germany, France, and Italy jointly wrote to the European Commission, calling for the establishment of an EU foreign direct investment screening mechanism, catalyzing a Europe-wide debate on the necessity to strengthen defensive trade and investment policies directed at China. As a consequence, beginning in September 2017, the EU started to formulate a comprehensive policy framework encompassing trade, investment, industrial policy, technology transfer, and intellectual property protection. Focusing on these three key moments of policy adjustment, this book examines the EU's major policy recalibrations concerning defensive economic policies toward China, and looks at the roles played by the three selected think tanks in shaping these developments.

Fourth, this book evaluates the policy influence of these three think tanks from four analytical perspectives: 1) comparative textual analysis between the policy recommendations made by the think tanks and the formulations of relevant EU policy documents, in order to assess the effect and tempo of think tank influence on specific decision points; 2) analysis of the structural characteristics of conferences and policy forums organized by the think tanks, which serves to evaluate the mechanisms through which think tanks exert short-term direct influence on decision-makers; 3) examination of research programs and think tank collaboration networks, through which their long-term indirect influence on policy agendas and policy communities can be assessed; 4) investigation of personnel linkages established through the revolving door mechanism between think tanks and the political, economic-financial, academic, and media sections of the power field, which helps reveal channels of long-term direct influence. The influence of think tanks on political decision-making has long been one of the most widely discussed and practically significant issues in think-tank research. Yet, because political decision-making systems are inherently complex and constantly evolving, the accurate measurement of think-tank influence has proven notoriously difficult. British scholar Diane Stone has argued that think tanks can only be regarded as a cog wheel in the larger machinery of governance, making further quantitative assessment of their influence extremely challenging.① Similarly, Canadian scholar Donald E. Abelson suggests that it is more appropriate to discuss the relevance of think tanks in policymaking processes than to attempt to measure their exact degree of influence.② By contrast, James G. McGann contends that think tanks exert a particularly clear influence during the early stages of the policymaking process, especially in problem definition and agenda setting.③ This book maintains that although the influence of think tanks cannot be measured with numerical precision, systematic observation of think-tank activities along the four analytical dimensions outlined above can nonetheless yield a detailed understanding of the mechanisms and effects through which European think tanks influence EU policy decisions. These four analytical perspectives therefore make up the principal methodological approach adopted in the present study.

This book consists of 6 chapters. Chapter 1, corresponding to the first analytical perspective outlined above, develops the theoretical framework for explaining think-tank influence. Chapter 2 focuses on the second analytical perspective and provides a detailed description of the operational mechanisms through which European think tanks influence EU decision-making. Chapter 3 offers a systematic overview of the specific policy domain under examination, namely, the EU's defensive economic policies toward China, which lays the groundwork for the subsequent analysis of think-tank influence in this area. Chapters 4, 5 and 6, corresponding to the third and fourth analytical perspectives, present detailed case studies of Bruegel, SWP, and Chatham House as representative examples of EU, German, and British think tanks respectively, examining in depth the mechanisms and effects through

① Diane Stone, "Public Policy Analysis and Think Tanks", in Frank Fischer, Gerald J. Miller and Mara S. Sidney (Eds.), *Handbook of Public Policy Analysis: Theory, Politics and Methods*, Boca Raton of Florida: CRC Press of Taylor & Francis Group, 2007, pp. 145.

② Donald E. Abelson, *Do Think Tanks Matter? Assessing the Impact of Public Institutes*, Montreal: McGill-Queen's University Press, 2002, pp. 165.

③ James G. McGann, *Think Tanks and Policy Advice in the United States: Academics, Advisors and Advocates*, New York: Routledge, 2007, pp. 52.

which each of these institutions has influenced the principal policy frameworks underpinning the EU's defensive economic policies toward China. Through these case studies, this book aims to illuminate the position and role of European think tanks in the EU's decision-making system concerning China-related policies, thus contributing to a more systematic understanding of the relationship between think tanks and policymaking in the EU.

Chapter 1: Theoretical Frameworks for Explaining the Mechanisms of Think Tanks' Influence over Policymaking

It is widely acknowledged that think tanks, defined as the "external brains" that provide specialized information and advisory services to political decision-makers, first emerged in the 1920s as an outward extension of what Max Weber termed the "rationalization" trend of the state's bureaucratic administrative system. At the end of the 19th century, Weber argued that the highly efficient, sophisticated, and complex administrative bureaucratic system operating within the context of a capitalist market economy would emerge as the primary organizational form for political decision-making in modern states, owing to its technical superiority in skillfully applying specialized expertise in the rational policymaking process. He further maintained that, alongside the increasing refinement of professional specialization, decision-makers in the bureaucratic system would come to comprise impersonal experts in command of specialized professional knowledge[①], while also identifying an emerging trend of the "state capitalist transformation" of universities.[②] With the advent of the 20th century, however, economic and social activities became unprecedentedly complex, rapidly outstripping the capacity of even the most sophisticated bureaucratic administrative apparatus to control. Contemporary policymaking agendas are characterized by their intricate, dynamic, and constantly evolving nature, involving a multiplicity of competing stakeholder interests, vast volumes of disparate information, and highly technical insights drawn from an array of deeply specialized professional fields with

① Max Weber, *Economy and Society: An Outline of Interpretive Sociology*, Chapter III, The Types of Legitimate Domination, Chapter IX, Political Communities, Guenther Roth and Claus Wittich (Eds.), Berkeley: University of California Press, 1978, P. 225, pp. 973-975.

② Max Weber, *Academic and Politics*, in *The Collected Works of Max Weber*, Vol. 1, trans. Qian Yongxiang et al., Guilin: Guangxi Normal University Press, 2004, p. 157.

fine divisions of labor. Under these circumstances, even the most seasoned expert decision-makers, who possess decades of hands-on experience navigating complex policy landscapes and command extensive specialized knowledge in their respective domains, find it difficult to handle the policymaking tasks before them, constantly overstretched to keep up. The unfolding challenges are simply beyond the reach of the broader cohort of political decision-makers. This hard reality has generated a demand for "external brains" across both the policymaking space and wider society.

Against this backdrop, a range of organizations and institutions outside the formal bureaucratic system began to draw on their specialized expertise and academic resources to provide policy analysis, policy option selection, and related advisory services, fulfilling part of the peripheral functions of rationalized decision-making as envisioned by Weber.

In the first decade of the 20th century, Britain's military expansion and capital export reached their historical apex, which tasked the British policymaking establishment with an unprecedented complex array of affairs spanning the entire globe. Overwhelmed by the scale and scope of these responsibilities, the British government established a series of advisory committees with quasi-think tank characteristics, recruiting scholars and experts from outside the formal administrative bureaucracy to provide specialized advisory services.[①] During the same period in the United States, unprecedented social challenges—including widening wealth inequality and financial turbulence—exacerbated social contradictions, generating a massive societal demand for rigorous intellectual output. The progressive movement championed by the nation's intellectual community produced a transformative influence, while large-scale corporate philanthropy surged. The convergence of these two powerful trends gave birth to iconic institutions such as the Brookings Institution, which was famously described as "a university without students".[②] It was in this historical and institutional context that the think tank—a type of modern professional policy research institution dedicated to delivering high-quality decision-making advisory services, formally

---

① Political and Economic Planning (PEP), *Advisory Committees in British Government, A PEP Report*, London: George Allen and Unwin Ltd., 1960.

② James G. McGann, *Think Tanks and Policy Advice in the United States: Academics, Advisors, and Advocates*, New York: Routledge, 2007, pp. 8-10; Donald E. Abelson, *A Capital Idea: Think Tanks and US Foreign Policy*, Montreal: McGill-Queen's University Press, 2006, pp. 63-64. *Do Think Tanks Matter? Assessing the Impact of Public Policy Institute*, London: McGill-Queen's University Press, 2002, pp. 89-90.

came into being.

I. Philosophical Ideas Underpinning Think Tanks' Policymaking Influence Mechanisms

While genuinely institutionalized think tanks have a history of less than a century, their status, role, and influence in modern political decision-making systems have expanded at a remarkable pace. Theoretical inquiries into the relationship between think tanks and political decision-makers can draw profound insights and analytical foundations from a series of core propositions in modern philosophical theory. Jürgen Habermas categorized the relationship between political decision-makers and technical experts in modern states into three distinct models.[①]

1) The Decisionistic Model: Under this model, political decision-makers exercise coercive state power to govern all domains of society, selectively drawing on the findings of scientific research to advance their own interests. Within this framework, specialized academic research plays almost no role in the policymaking process and exerts negligible influence on the general public—a model Habermas identified as prevalent in traditional structures of government operation.

2) The Technocratic Model: In this model, technical experts leverage their specialized knowledge to influence, and even shape every stage of the policymaking process, to the extent that they significantly constrain, and in some cases direct the outcomes of political decision-making. When intractable, unprecedented new issues emerge on the political agenda, diverse political actors, lacking sufficient knowledge, expertise, and intellectual frameworks to understand and respond to these novel challenges, urgently seek information, guidance, and analytical clarity from experts in command of relevant specialized knowledge. Over time, these expert communities and networks gain pivotal influence over the course and direction of political operations.[②]

① Jürgen Habermas, *Knowledge and Human Interests*, trans. Jeremy J. Shapiro, Boston: Beacon Press, 1966, pp. 43-64; *Toward a Rational Society: Student Protest, Science, and Politics*, trans. Jeremy J. Shapiro, Boston: Beacon Press, 1971; "Verwissenshcaftlichte Politik und offentliche Meinung", in Jürgen Habermas (Ed.), *Technik und Wissenschaft als 'Ideologie'*, Frankfurt: Suhrkamp Verlag, 1976, pp. 120-145.

② Some researchers refer to the small circles of experts and scholars in this context as the "nerve centers"

3) The Pragmatic Model: This model is defined by institutionalized communication and consultation between political decision-makers and technical elites, who jointly steer and direct the political decision-making process. In this system, there is no rigid hierarchical structure of domination and subordination between the scientific research community and the political decision-making establishment, a feature that has led contemporary researchers to regard this model as the closest approximation to the ideal normative framework of "governance".① Habermas's three-model typology, alongside his seminal concept of the Public Sphere, centers its analytical focus on the relationship between specialized knowledge and the political system, laying the foundational theoretical groundwork for contemporary scholarship on governance.

While Habermas did not explicitly address think tanks in his original formulation, he did identify the unique relational dynamic between the bureaucratic system and scientific advisory institutions, arguing that specialized expertise has the capacity to shape political decision-making and influence structures of power.② Pierre Bourdieu similarly argued that intellectuals form an integral component of the ruling class, exerting a profound influence on the conceptual and ideological framing of rulers' perceptions and priorities.③ The three relational models between technical experts and decision-makers articulated by Habermas demonstrate that the position of technical experts in the shifting political decision-making system in accordance with economic and social development trends, as well as changes in the structure of political power. In many instances, technical experts themselves act as architects of the balance of political forces within a given system. Variations in the relative power balance between technical experts and rulers in command of coercive political power shape the intensity and operational model of their relationship, which in turn exerts an influence on the typology, substantive content, and implementation timeline of the policies that are ultimately formulated. Building on these insights, subsequent researchers

---

of the political decision-making process. (See: FFreiburghaus, D. and W. Zimmermann, *Wie wird Forschung politisch relevant?* Bern: Haupt, 1985, P. 35.)

① Pierre, J. and B. G. Peters, *Governance, Politics, and the State*, New York: St Martin's Press, 2000, P. 25.

② Jürgen Habermas, *Technology and Science as "Ideology"*, trans. Li Li and Guo Guanyi, Shanghai: Xuelin Press, 1999, pp. 106-109.

③ Pierre Bourdieu, *Cultural Capital and Social Alchemy: Interviews with Bourdieu*, trans. Bao Yaming, Shanghai: Shanghai People's Publishing House, 1997, pp. 79-82.

have further divided the second model identified by Habermas into two distinct types: the first is the Administrative Technocratic Model, in which the administrative bureaucracy retains ultimate decision-making authority and control over the pace and direction of the policymaking process, while technical experts exert a decisive influence over the development of policy options and the detailed substantive content of policy design. The second is the Scientific Technocratic Model, in which the entire policymaking system is fundamentally directed and dominated by technical experts. In terms of policy design and substantive decision-making content, both models lead to demonstrably distinct outcomes.[①]

To more precisely analyze the position of specialized knowledge, advisory services, and research institutions in the political decision-making system, existing scholarly literature has widely adopted and elaborated on the concepts of "Social Space" and "Field" first developed by French sociologist Pierre Bourdieu, constructing a theoretical framework for empirical analysis. Bourdieu argued that the overall structure of interactive relations between all actors in a society constitutes a "social space", and that within this space, diverse actors, drawing on social capital at their disposal, engage in a continuous process of communication and exchange, forming distinct network systems that form the various "fields" in the broader social space.[②] He further advanced the seminal proposition regarding the relationship between the "field of cultural production" and the "field of power", arguing that the field of cultural production is situated within the field of power, yet occupies a dominated position (Bourdieu, 1985).[③] Bourdieu's conceptualization of social space in fact shares profound conceptual affinities with Habermas's concept of public sphere, as both frameworks emphasize the stable structural formations constructed through the exchange of resources and information between diverse social actors[④]. Bourdieu placed particular analytical

① Fritz Sager, "Habermas' Models of Decisionism, Technocracy and Pragmatism in Times of Governance: The Relationship of Public Administration, Politics and Science in the Alcohol Prevention Policies of the Swiss Member States", *Public Administration*, Vol. 85, No. 2, 2007, pp. 429-447.

② David Swartz, *Culture and Power: The Sociology of Pierre Bourdieu*, trans. Ju Wei (Shanghai: Shanghai Translation Publishing House, 2006), p. 136; Pierre Bourdieu and Loic J. D. Wacquant, *An Invitation to Reflexive Sociology*, Chicago: University of Chicago Press, 1992.

③ Pierre Bourdieu, *Cultural Capital and Social Alchemy: Interviews with Bourdieu*, trans. Bao Yaming, Shanghai: Shanghai People's Publishing House, 1997.

④ Jürgen Habermas, *The Structural Transformation of the Public Sphere*, trans. Cao Weidong et al., Shanghai: Xuelin Press, 1990, pp. 32-35.

emphasis on the relational dynamic between the field of cultural production and the field of power in the social space, reiterating that the former occupies a subordinated position within the latter①. This proposition provides the critical theoretical foundation for explicating the inherent structural characteristics of the "Research-Policy Nexus" between specialized research and political decision-making, and by extension, for systematically analyzing the policymaking influence of think tanks.

Building on Bourdieu's foundational concepts of social space and field, existing scholarly literature has developed a diverse array of theoretical paradigms and analytical perspectives, applying them to the empirical observation of the influence exerted by think tank-style specialized research and advisory institutions on political decision-making. This study, building on a systematic review and synthesis of these theoretical paradigms and research perspectives, develops a conceptual framework of the three-tiered field structure in the social space, which is subsequently applied to examine and define the precise position of European think tanks in the EU's political system and its member states. This study posits that, when think tanks are taken as the central analytical focus, the social space formed by the EU political system can be divided into three concentric layers extending from the inner core to the outer periphery, with each layer constituting a distinct field. This three-tiered field structure, extending from the inner to the outer layer, provides a clear and systematic framework for defining the relational dynamic between European think tanks and the EU political system. The specific characteristics of each tier within the three-tiered field structure of the social space are detailed in Table 1.1.

In this three-tiered field structure of the social space shown in Table 1.1, the inner layer consists of a micro-level, concrete "organizational field" collectively formed by all European think tanks. In other words, this field comprises a relatively stable network of diverse types of think tank organizations, which engage in continuous competition and collaboration to generate innovative insights, perspectives, conceptual frameworks, and ideas, thereby constructing a Knowledge Regime that serves the needs of the wider society. The interaction between this knowledge regime and political decision-makers in turn forms what is widely called the "market place of ideas".

① Pierre Bourdieu, *Cultural Capital and Social Alchemy: Interviews with Bourdieu*, trans. Bao Yaming, Shanghai: Shanghai People's Publishing House, 1997, pp. 79-82.

The outer layer of this social space features the broader macro-level field of power, which is jointly constituted through exchanges of resources and information between the think tank system and the four domains of politics, the economy, academia, and the media. American think tank scholar Thomas Medvetz argues that think tanks occupy a central position in this field of power, thereby constituting a distinctive think tank space, which may also be understood as an interstitial field situated between these four domains. The boundaries between the space and field formed by the think tank system and the four domains of the Field of Power are perpetually shifting, never fixed or static.① Put in a different way, the think tank space located at the center of the field of power continually draws on resources from these four domains and exhibits certain characteristics associated with each of them.

Table 1.1: Analytical Framework for Delineating the Position of Think Tanks in the EU Policymaking Structure and Process

Characteristic / Dimension	Inner Layer Space	Middle Layer Space	Outer Layer Space
Spatial Form	Organizational Field	Force Field	Field of Power
Spatial Structure	An Epistemic Community composed of a diverse array of think tank-type institutions	A composite of dynamic, mutually constitutive relational dynamics between the Organizational Field formed by the think tank system and the Field of Power constituted by the macro-level political system	A system of power operations constituted by four interlocking domains: political, financial, academic, and media, with the think tank system occupying the Central Space in this system
Core Constituent Elements	Think tanks, in-house research units of bureaucratic institutions with think tank functions, interest groups, lobbying firms, and advocacy groups	Attractive and repulsive forces that facilitate or impede proximity between the think tank system and the policymaking system, constituted by the interactive relations between a range of actors within the social space	The political, financial, academic, and media domains, alongside the think tank system situated at the intersection of these four domains
Internal Interactive Mechanism	A Knowledge Regime formed through stable competitive and collaborative relations between diverse think tank-type institutions	A Dual Dynamics mechanism formed through the exchange of scarce resources between the think tank system and the bureaucratic apparatus and central authority of political decision-making	A dynamic mechanism formed through the continuous exchange of resources and information between think tanks and the four core domains of the Field of Power, positioning the think tank system as the Central Space in the Field of Power

Source: Compiled by the author.

① Thomas Medvetz, *Think Tanks in America*, Chicago: University of Chicago Press, 2012, pp. 36-39, P. 116.

Between the inner and outer layers lies an intermediate space, namely, the force field, which arises from exchanges between the think tank system and the four domains of the field of power discussed above. A central feature of this force field is the coexistence of forces of attraction and repulsion: the former draw think tanks closer to these four domains, especially the political sphere and its decision-making apparatus, while the latter constrain such proximity. Attraction is expressed through cooperation between think tanks and senior decision-makers based on the exchange of scarce resources. On the one hand, think tanks provide policymakers with knowledge, ideas, and cognitive frames distilled from vast and rapidly changing flows of information, thus serving as an external source of policy expertise. On the other hand, decision-makers at the center of power continuously articulate specific demands that shape the priorities and research orientations of think tanks. This interaction gives rise to a dual dynamic.[①]

Simultaneously, however, the specialized insights, knowledge, and conceptual frameworks required by senior decision-makers are never monopolized by a single think tank. Intense competition exists between individual think tanks, while media, universities, diverse lobbying groups, and commercial consulting firms all perform the same function of delivering specialized information to decision-makers, placing them in direct competition with think tanks. This competitive environment constrains the extent to which any particular think tank can move closer to the decision-making system, thereby generating the "repulsive force" in the force field. The interaction between attraction and repulsion may at times produce a state of relative equilibrium, analogous to the concept of equilibrium in economics, yet this balance is perpetually dynamic and shifting, determining the operational trajectory and strategic behavior of think tanks over time.

---

① American political scientist Samuel Workman, in his study of the collaborative and interactive relationship between the U.S. Congress and the central administrative bureaucracy, proposed the concept of "Dual Dynamics". He utilizes this term to characterize the interplay between the U.S. Congress, which wields decision-making authority, and the administrative bureaucracy, which possesses specialized technical information. In reality, the administrative bureaucracy is far from omniscient; a significant portion of the information used by contemporary U.S. power centers for policymaking is supplied by think tanks, the media, and academia. Consequently, this article contends that the "Dual Dynamics" framework may also be effectively applied to depict the collaborative relationship between think tanks and the decision-making system. (For a detailed discussion of "Dual Dynamics," see Samuel Workman, *The Dynamics of Bureaucracy in the U.S. Government: How Congress and Federal Agencies Process Information and Solve Problems*, Cambridge: Cambridge University Press, 2015, pp. 1-25.

In summary, as Europe's long-standing representative democracy reaches a highly developed level, the three-tiered field structure of the social space outlined above has correspondingly evolved into a highly complex, sophisticated system that forms the foundational architecture shaping the policymaking influence mechanisms of European think tanks. This study therefore proceeds from the perspective of the above three-tiered fields to observe the position and role of three specific European think tanks in each field, and further synthesizes a theoretical picture with empirical precision to explain the mechanisms through which these three think tanks exert influence on the EU's economic policymaking toward China.

II. Theoretical Paradigms for Explaining the Mechanisms of Think Tanks' Influence over Policymaking

Within the scholarly fields of political science and public policy research, the influence exerted on policymaking by social actors including think tanks and interest groups has long been a subject of intensive, sustained scholarly inquiry. Since the 1950s, scholars in the United States and Europe, particularly in the former, have closely examined, through detailed empirical observations, of the position and role of diverse types of social actors in political systems, continuously advancing competing theoretical paradigms to explain their behavior and influence. As political practice in the United States and Europe has evolved, a series of enduring debates have emerged among these theoretical paradigms. A systematic review and synthesis of these debates will no doubt offer important theoretical guidance for understanding the influence of think tanks on policymaking. Building on a comparative synthesis of these theoretical paradigms, this book develops an analytical framework that provides the conceptual foundation for the subsequent analysis.

2.1 Debates over the Macro Distribution of Political Power: Elite Theory vs. Pluralist Theory

Drawing on political practices in the United States and Europe during the 1950s and 1960s, researchers have sought to delineate the macro-level distribution of political forces shaping policymaking, assessing the position and policymaking influence of diverse types of social actors in this broader structural landscape. This inquiry has given rise to the sustained debate between elite theory and pluralist theory①, and subsequently to the development of the two-level game analytical perspective. As early as the founding of the United States, James Madison identified the inherent tendency of diverse social groups in commercially and industrially advanced societies to form factions and associations. While this natural inclination can support the advancement of the rights and interests of diverse segments of society, Madison warned that powerful groups in command of disproportionate resources could exert oppressive dominance over other groups, a conceptual tension widely referred to as the "Madisonian Dilemma".② In the aftermath of World War II, the United States and Europe experienced more than two decades of sustained, rapid economic growth, which saw the increasing activism of diverse interest groups, think tanks, and non-governmental organizations, alongside the intensification of political lobbying activities by different social constituencies. Motivated by the intellectual project of resolving the Madisonian Dilemma, American scholars advanced the two theoretical frameworks of elite theory and pluralist theory during the 1950s and 1960s. The former argues that societal elites, with their inherent advantages in terms of wealth, social connections, and organizational resources, effectively influence, and in many cases control, the decision-making activities of the political system. The latter, by contrast, posits that competition between diverse social groups is the primary force that shapes and drives the policymaking process. With the rise of economic globalization and the increasing frequency of U.S. international economic negotiations during the 1980s, scholars further developed the concept of two-level game③ to explicate the structural characteristics of domestic interest bargaining within the context of international

---

① For key classical sources on "Elite Theory", see: Charles Wright Mills, *The Power Elite*, New York: Oxford University Press, 1956; Elmer E. Schattschnider, *The Semi-Sovereign People: A Realist's View of Democracy in America*, New York: Holt, Rinehart and Winston, 1960; George William Domhoff, *The Power Elite and the State: How Policy is Made in America*, New York: Aldine de Gruyter, 1990, *Who Rules America? Power, Politics, and Social Change*, 5th edition, New York: McGraw Hill, 2006; Godfrey Hodgson, "The Establishment", *Foreign Policy*, No. 10, Spring 1973, pp. 3-40; Murray Milner, Jr., *Elites: A General Model*, Cambridge, UK: Polity Press, 2015. For key classical sources on "Pluralist Theory", see: David B. Truman, *The Governmental Process: Political Interests and Public Opinion*, New York: Alfred A. Knopf, 1951; Frank Fischer, *Technocracy and the Politics of Experience*, Newbury Park, CA: Sage Publications, 1990; Steven Lukes, *Power: A Radical View*, 2nd edition, New York: Palgrave MacMillan, 2004.

② *The Federalist Papers*, New York: New American Library, 1961, pp. 77-84.

③ Robert D. Putnam, "Diplomacy and Domestic Politics: The Logic of Two-level Games", *International Organization*, Vol. 42, No. 3, Summer 1988, pp. 427-460.

economic negotiations.

Sharing inherent logical connections, these theoretical paradigms and concepts are all grounded in the analysis of power distribution structures to explain mechanisms of interest representation. While the bulk of scholarly work on elite theory and pluralist theory does not specifically elaborate on the unique role and mechanisms through which think tanks—as a distinct organizational form—influence policymaking, they nevertheless situate think tanks within the broader macro-level competition among diverse social groups vying for influence over political leadership. These frameworks explicate the behavioral characteristics of think tanks, which leverage their unique form of social capital, specialized professional knowledge and data to influence decision-makers and engage in interactive strategic bargaining with other types of social actors. The two theoretical paradigms offer distinct analytical perspectives and substantive arguments regarding the position and role of think tanks, as a unique type of social actors, in the macro space of political power distribution.

The elite theory explanation of the mechanisms through which think tanks influence political decision-making first appeared in the works of American political scientist Charles Wright Mills.[①] Theorists of this school argue that even in the American social system, which is often saliently characterized by its diverse and complex distribution of political forces, the trajectory of political decision-making is ultimately determined by a small cohort of societal elites. They conceptualize think tanks as an integral component of a top-down policymaking system, which provides decision-making elites with academically grounded discursive frameworks, theoretical perspectives, and ideological architectures to justify and legitimate their policy decisions.

In other words, decision-making elites frequently draw on the specialized analytical work of think tanks to articulate coherent, evidence-based justifications for their pre-existing policy preferences. Elite theory therefore argues that think tanks, through their professional and academic authority, exert a powerful influence on the policymaking process, to the extent that they constrain and even shape the cognitive frameworks, policy preferences, and discursive strategies of decision-makers.[②] A key limitation of this theoretical school,

① Charles Wright Mills, *The Power Elite*, New York: Oxford University Press, 1967, P. 23.

② George William Domhoff and Thomas R. Dye, (Eds.), *Power Elites and Organizations*, London: Sage Publications, 1987; Thomas R. Dye, *Top Down Policymaking*, New York: Chatham House Publishers, 2000. Laurence H. Sharp and William Minter, *Imperial Brain Trust: The Council on Foreign Relations and United* however, is that it fails to clearly explicate how think tanks translate their connections to other components of the policymaking system into tangible influence, with relatively limited scholarly attention paid to the ontological status of think tanks themselves. Critics of this framework therefore argue that its explanation of think tank influence mechanisms is static, overly mechanistic, and linear, and fails to account for the dynamic interaction between think tanks and other social forces.

In contrast to elite theory, pluralist theory emphasizes the pluralistic nature of the social structure of forces influencing the policymaking system. It posits that multiple forces within the social structure compete with one another in a decentralized and constantly shifting configuration, with each seeking to exert greater influence over decision-makers than its counterparts. Within this framework, think tanks are regarded as merely one among many such forces, largely indistinguishable from interest groups, lobbying groups, and advocacy organizations, and exerting only limited influence over specific stages of the policymaking process. A core limitation of pluralist theory lies in its primary focus on the stage of open competition among various forces after the policymaking process has been initiated, while neglecting the less visible stages prior to its formal onset, such as agenda-setting. Consequently, critics of this paradigm often argue that, while it helps explain the direct influence of think tanks on the policymaking process, it fails to account for their indirect influence.[①] Since the beginning of the 21st century, as scholarly understandings of the cognitive mechanisms of decision-making become more refined and sophisticated, the analytical appeal of the pluralist perspective for researchers has diminished accordingly.

States Foreign Policy, New York: Monthly Review Press, 1977; James Allen Smith, *The Idea Brokers: Think Tanks and the Rise of the New Policy Elite*, New York: Maxwell Macmillan International, 1991.

① Steven Lukes, *Power: A Radical View*, 2nd edition, New York: Palgrave MacMillan, 2004; Frank Fischer, *Technocracy and the Politics of Experience*, Newbury Park, CA: Sage Publications, 1990; David B. Truman, *The Governmental Process: Political Interests and Public Opinion*, New York: Alfred A. Knopf, 1951. Donald E. Abelson, "From Policy Research to Political Advocacy: The Changing Role of Think Tanks in American Politics", *Canadian Review of American Studies* 25, No. 1: 93-126; *Do Think Tanks Matter: Assessing the Impact of Public Policy Institutes*, Montreal: McGill-Queen's University Press, 2002.

2.2 Debates over the Tension Between Objective Context and Policymaking Cognitive Rationality: Institutionalism vs. Constructivism

From the 1960s onward, under the influence of the "behavioral revolution" in the social sciences, scholars directed growing analytical attention to the tension between the objective system of material context and the cognitive rationality of policymaking, conducting research from this analytical perspective and sparking the debate between institutionalism and constructivism.① The former argues that the objective system of the material environment imposes rigid, deterministic constraints and shapes effects on the agenda-setting, operational pace, and path selection of political decision-making. The latter, by contrast, explicates the mechanisms through which decision-makers' own ideational systems, cognitive heuristics, and subjective preferences filter and process external influences, as well as how these factors constrain and guide decision-makers' cognitive processes of situational assessment and policy selection. The debate between these two theoretical schools has driven the continuous evolution of research methodologies in the existing scholarly literature on social actors including think tanks and interest groups. From the mid-1980s onward, scholars in the United States and Europe, drawing on the Institutionalist perspective, advanced the dichotomy between Inside Lobbying and Outside Lobbying, providing a more accurate framework for explicating the specific tactics and pathways through which social actors such as think tanks exert influence on policymaking.②

Institutionalist theory holds that the structure and functions of institutions constrain

---

① Major literature analyzing foreign policy decision-making mechanisms and the European integration process from the perspective of institutionalism include: Theodore J. Lowi, "American Business, Public Policy, Case-Studies, and Political Theory", *World Politics*, Spring, 1964, pp. 677-715; Paul Pierson, "The Path to European Integration: A Historical Institutionalist Analysis", *Comparative Political Studies*, Vol. 29, No. 2, April 1996, pp. 123-163; Henry Farrell and Adrienne Heritier, "A Rationalist-Institutionalist Explanation of Endogenous Regional Integration", *Journal of European Public Policy*, Vol. 12, No. 2, April 2005, pp. 273-290. Key classical works on Constructivism include: Robert Jervis, *Perception and Misperception in International Politics*, Princeton, U.S.: Princeton University Press, 1976; Alexander Wendt, *Social Theory of International Politics*, Cambridge, UK: Cambridge University Press, 1999; Jeffrey T. Checkel, "The Constructive Turn in International Relations Theory", *World Politics*, Vol. 50, Issue 02, January 1998, pp. 324-348.

② Works examining the behavioral modes and process features of Inside Lobbying and Outside Lobbying include: Kay Lehman Schlozman and John T. Tierney, *Organized Interests and American Democracy*, New York: Harpers and Row, 1986; Ken Kollman, *Outside Lobbying: Public Opinion and Interest Group Strategies*, Princeton, N.J.: Princeton University Press, 1998, the behavior of actors within the system. Think tanks are seen as important actors that help shape the structure of the policymaking system and influence its processes. Accordingly, any attempt to clarify the influence of think tanks on decision-making must begin with an analysis of the institutional configuration of the policymaking system. Since the operation of institutions relies on the enforcement of external authority, Institutionalist theory directs its analytical focus toward the constraining and shaping effects of objective material structures of power distribution and operational logic on actors involved in the policymaking process. Scholars of this school further argue that think tanks form an integral component of the "epistemic community" of policymaking, participating in the shaping of political agendas, influencing the formation of policy, supporting the implementation of policy, and engaging with every stage of the decision-making process, thus exerting substantial influence on policy outcomes.[①] This theoretical approach, however, fails to clearly explicate the mechanisms through which think tanks influence the structure of social forces beyond the formal political decision-making system (such as the academic community and public opinion). As a result, some scholars have criticized it for offering an overly narrow account of think tank influence, focusing primarily on their academic and professional expertise while neglecting their broader social embeddedness.

In contrast to institutionalism, constructivism directs its primary analytical focus toward the influence of ideational systems on decision-makers' perceptions of strategic contexts and assessments of policy options, rather than the constraining effects of material power structures and systems on policy intentions. It therefore centers its analysis on the ideational, cognitive, and discursive dimensions of policymaking. Scholarly work adopting a constructivist lens has made detailed observations of the role played by social actors including think tanks and interest groups in constructing the ideational and discursive frameworks that shape decision-makers' understanding of strategic contexts and policy choices. Existing literature, however, lacks a sufficiently granular, mechanistic analysis of the specific operational dynamics of this construction process, alongside a relative paucity

① Donald T. Critchlow, *The Brookings Institution, 1916-1952: Expertise and the Public Interest in a Democratic Society*, Dekalb: Northern Illinois Press, 1985; Robert D. Schulzinger, *The Wise Men of Foreign Affairs: The History of the Council on Foreign Relations*, New York: Columbia University Press, 1984; Ronald N. Jacoby and Eleanor Townsley, *The Space of Opinion: Media Intellectuals and the Public Sphere*, New York: Oxford University Press, 2011.

of detailed empirical case studies, meaning that its empirical depth and analytical precision remain areas for further scholarly development.

2.3 Paradigmatic Debates Along the Temporal Dimension: Competing Schools of Policy Process Theory

Politics and public policymaking are inherently ongoing and dynamic processes. Accordingly, many scholars have focused on the policymaking process as it unfolds over time, analyzing its patterns from a temporal perspective and examining how it is shaped by the interaction of various political forces. This line of inquiry has given rise to distinct strands of policy process theory, including the "multiple policy streams framework"① and the "punctuated equilibrium model".② Each of these theoretical approaches focuses on dividing the policymaking process into distinct stages, examining how different political forces and social factors influence decision-making at each stage, and identifying the critical junctures at which profound structural changes in policy outcomes occur. A core analytical focus of these frameworks is the identification of temporal junctures that drive profound structural shifts in policy, known as "policy windows". These theories intensively analyze the patterns of change in the political system during these policy windows, delineate the strategic bargaining between different types of political forces in the process, and explicate the endogenous dynamic mechanisms that restore equilibrium to the policymaking process after the windows are closed. In doing so, they provide a critical, dynamic, temporally grounded theoretical framework for analyzing and understanding the mechanisms of think tanks' influence on policymaking.

The multiple policy streams framework, for example, argues that even in highly specialized public policy domains such as transportation and energy, the policymaking process is defined by continuous strategic bargaining between diverse political forces. These bargaining dynamics can be categorized into three distinct streams that progress in parallel over time: the politics stream, which encompasses the strategic bargaining between

① The seminal work on Multiple Policy Streams theory is: John W. Kingdon, *Agenda, Alternatives, and Public Policies*, 2nd edition, New York: Addison-Wesley Educational Publishers Inc., 2003.

② Literature providing a systematic account of Punctuated Equilibrium theory includes: Frank R. Baumgartner and Bryan D. Jones, *Agendas and Instability in American Politics*, 2nd edition, Chicago, Illinois: University of Chicago Press, 2009.

competing political forces; the policy stream, which operates at the administrative and decision-making level; and the problem stream, which addresses society's response to urgent, high-stakes societal challenges. Under normal circumstances, these three streams proceed independently in parallel, each following its own internal rhythm and logic. However, when a major, urgent societal crisis triggers widespread social upheaval or systemic shock, placing intense pressure on the policymaking establishment to respond with decisive action, a policy window opens. At this critical juncture, the three streams converge, driving profound, transformative changes to existing policy. The punctuated equilibrium model, by contrast, argues that for the most part of the administrative policymaking process, the political decision-making establishment operates in a state of stable equilibrium, adhering to its established principles and exhibiting inherent inertia and slow responsiveness to emerging issues and trends, with no significant shift in the policy direction. During rare, exceptional moments, however, the intervention of sudden, unforeseen external factors can rapidly disrupt this pre-existing equilibrium. In an extremely compressed time frame, the cognitive frameworks of the political decision-making establishment undergo radical change, leading to the rapid introduction of a suite of major new policy initiatives. Both the Multiple Policy Streams and Punctuated Equilibrium theories provide a robust temporal theoretical architecture for research into the policymaking influence of think tanks.

2.4 Paradigmatic Debates Along the Spatial Dimension of the Political Decision-Making System: Contention among Structuralist Perspectives

The policymaking operation of any political entity is invariably characterized by a complex, multi-layered architecture of hierarchies and pathways, and only through a granular dissection of this "labyrinth" of policymaking architecture is it possible to reveal the root causes and mechanisms through which different actors exert influence on policy outcomes. Existing scholarly literature broadly adopts three distinct theoretical paradigms and perspectives to dissect the architecture, hierarchies, and operational pathways of the policymaking system, with the goal of explicating the mechanisms through which social actors influence policymaking.

First, scholars analyze the mechanics of strategic interaction between three interlocking levels: domestic social actors, the domestic political decision-making establishment, and foreign actors. Building on the seminal two-level game concept first developed by American scholars, European researchers have advanced the three-level game① and synthesized two-level game② perspectives to explain the influence of European think tanks and interest groups on the EU's external economic negotiation decision-making at the "supranational" level.

Second, drawing on the resource dependence theory from management studies, scholars have adopted a resource exchange paradigm to examine the interactive dynamics through which social actors and the political decision-making establishment exchange information, resources, and authority. American scholars have advanced analytical perspectives including venue-shopping③ and legislative subsidy④, while European researchers have developed the theory of "access goods and access points⑤, which are exchanged for opportunities to gain entry into the policymaking system. This body of work synthesizes the logic of informational lobbying⑥, further advancing the concept of opportunity structures that shape influence over EU decision-making.⑦

Third, European scholars have examined the position of interest groups in the EU' s

① Helmut Hubel, "The EU's Three-Level Game in Dealing with Neighbors", *European Foreign Affairs Review*, Volume 3, No. 9, 2004, pp. 347-362.

② Alasdair R. Young and John Peterson, *Parochial Global Europe: 21st Century Trade Politics*, Oxford, UK: Oxford University Press, 2014, pp. 23-47.

③ Sarah B. Pralle, "Venue Shopping, Political Strategy, and Policy Change: The Internationalization of Canadian Forest Advocacy", *International Public Policy*, Vol. 3, No. 23, pp. 233-260. Frank R. Baumgartner and Bryan D. Jones, *Agendas and Instability in American Politics*, 2nd edition, Chicago and London: University of Chicago Press, pp. 1-39.

④ Richard L. Hall and Alan V. Deardorff, "Lobbying as Legislative Subsidy", *American Political Science Review*, Vol. 100, No. 1, February 2006, pp. 69-84.

⑤ Pieter Bouwen, "Exchanging Access Goods for Access: A Comparative Study of Business Lobbying in the European Union Institutions", *European Journal of Political Research*, Vol. 43, 2004, pp. 337-369.

⑥ Patrick Bernhagen, *The Political Power of Business: Structure and Information in Public Policymaking*, London and New York: Routledge, 2007, pp. 24-53; Heike Kluver, *Lobbying in the European Union: Interest Groups, Lobbying Coalitions, and Policy Change*, Oxford, UK: Oxford University Press, 2013, pp. 93-130, "Informational Lobbying in the European Union: The Effect of Organizational Characteristics", *West European Politics*, Vol. 35, No. 3, 2012, pp. 491-510; Adam William Chalmer, "Trading Information for Access: Informational Lobbying Strategies and Interest Group Access to the European Union", *Journal of European Public Policy*, Vol, 20, No. 1, January 2013, pp. 39-58.

⑦ Sebastiaan Princen and Bart Kerremans, "Opportunity Structures in the EU Multi-Level System", *West European Politics*, Vol. 31, No. 6, 2009, pp. 1129-1146.

multi-level governance system, exploring the lobbying models of think tanks and interest groups, as well as their influence on EU decision-making, along two interconnected dimensions: the process of "integration" at the EU level and the course of "Europeanization" at the member state level.① The structuralist perspective has been widely adopted and applied by scholars in the United States and Europe, owing to its granular, precise description of the direction and pathways of power operation and resource flow in political systems.

Structuralist research, which focuses on the EU political decision-making, has sparked far-reaching debate between Neo-functionalism and Inter-governmentalism.② The former argues that the European Community and the EU would ultimately evolve into a fully supranational system, with unified decision-making over trade and other policy domains that transcends the nation-state level. The latter, by contrast, contends that the operation of the European Community and the EU is fundamentally the product of negotiation and cooperation between sovereign states to advance shared interests, with national governments playing a dominant role in EU decision-making. Building on this debate, scholars have advanced the concept of the "synthesized sets of two-level game"③, which conceptualizes the interest structure of the EU's external economic negotiations as comprising four layers of relations of opposition: between the EU and its external counterparts; between the European Commission and the Council of the European Union; between the EU and its member state governments; and between member state governments and their domestic interest groups. These layers are integrated into two interlocking two-level game frameworks, thus providing

① Rainer Eising, "Multilevel Governance and Business Interests in the European Union", *Governance: An International Journal of Policy, Administration, and Institutions*, Vol. 17, No. 2, April 2004, pp. 211-245. Andreas Dur and Gemma Mateo, "Who Lobbies the European Union? National Interest Groups in a Multilevel Polity", *Journal of European Public Policy*, Vol. 19, No. 7, 2012, pp. 969-987, "The Europeanization of Interest Groups: Group Type, Resources and Policy Area", *European Union Politics*, Vol. 15, No. 4, 2014, pp. 572-594; Matia Vannoni, "Explaining the Variation in the Europeanization of Business: An Institutionalist Theory", *Journal of European Public Policy*, Vol. 22, No. 10, 2015, pp. 1467-1488.

② Ernst Haas, "International Integration: The European and Universal Process", *International Organization*, Vol. 15, No.3, 1961, pp. 366-392; L. N. Lindberg and S. A. Scheingold, *Europe's Would-be Polity*, Englewood Cliffs of New Jersey: Prentice-Hall, 1970; Stanley Hoffmann, "Obstinate or Obsolete? The Fate of the Nation-State and the Case of Western Europe", *Daedalus*, Vol. 95, No. 3, 1966, pp. 862-915; A. S. Milard, *The European Rescue of Nation State*, London: Routledge, 2000.

③ Alasdair R. Young and John Peterson, *Parochial Global Europe: 21st Century Trade Politics*, Oxford, UK: Oxford University Press, 2014, pp. 40-43.

a more sophisticated analytical framework for understanding the role of interest groups in the EU's external economic decision-making.

2.5 Paradigmatic Research from a Critical Perspective on Discourse and Ideational Systems: Neo-Gramscism

Neo-Gramscian theorists, proceeding from a critique of elite cultural hegemony in advanced capitalist societies, tend to downplay the professional and academic attributes of think tanks. Instead, they emphasize the role of think tanks in helping the ruling elites reproduce non-coercive power relations across different social groups, thereby underscoring their function as "gatekeepers" of the existing social order. In this view, think tanks are seen as one among many organizations in civil society that contribute to the establishment and maintenance of non-coercive power relations among social groups. By providing discourses that legitimate decision-making, they serve as gatekeepers of advanced capitalist social formations. Think tanks are accordingly viewed as wielding powerful and long-term influence insofar as they disseminate the ideas and discourses that sustain cultural hegemony.[①] This theoretical framework, however, is limited to advancing a systemic critique, failing to clearly explicate the specific structural architecture of cultural hegemony in advanced capitalist societies, as well as the precise mechanisms through which think tanks produce and disseminate discourses that legitimate policy decisions. Because of this, critics argue that the theory overemphasizes the ideological orientation of think tanks, while neglecting the sort of commitment to independence and professional rigor that defines the operation of many prominent think tanks.

III. Specific Analytical Perspectives and Explanatory Models for Think Tanks' Policymaking Influence Mechanisms

While policymaking inherently encompasses a complex interactive architecture and dynamic rule-based procedures, it is ultimately a cognitive process occurring in the minds of

① Charles Murray, "The Coming White Underclass", *Wall Street Journal*, October 29, 1993; Inderjeet Parmar, "Institutes of International Affairs: Their Roles in Foreign Policy Making, Opinion Mobilization, and Unofficial Diplomacy", in Diane Stone (Ed.), *Think Tank Traditions: Policy Research and the Politics of Ideas*, Manchester: Manchester University Press, 2004.

decision-makers, characterized by a significant degree of opacity and unpredictability. While researchers can deconstruct the policymaking system into its constituent parts and identify the diverse range of influencing factors, it remains exceptionally difficult to definitively demonstrate the specific pathways and mechanisms through which these factors exert influence on decision-makers. For this reason, researchers often refer to the policymaking system as the "policymaking black box". This challenge is particularly pronounced in the study of think tanks, as their relationship with the policymaking system is highly complex and dynamic, making the analysis of relevant data and information especially difficult. In addition, some think tanks deliberately withhold information about their activities. As a result, the assessment of think tanks' influence on decision-making has long been contested and remains difficult to develop in depth.

Building on the multiple core theoretical paradigms outlined above, scholars seeking to reveal the structural characteristics and evolutionary dynamics of think tanks' influence mechanisms have advanced a diverse array of specific theoretical perspectives and explanatory models from both the macro and meso levels of the social and political system. These frameworks, grounded in detailed case study analysis of the relationship between think tanks and the policymaking system, provide the foundational theoretical architecture for analyzing the policymaking influence of think tanks, drawing on both the structural distribution of political power and the construction of policymaking ideational systems.

3.1 Specific Theoretical Perspectives for Explicating Think Tanks' Policymaking Influence Mechanisms

1) The perspective of the central space within a four-dimensional field of power. Building on Bourdieu's seminal proposition regarding the relationship between the field of cultural production and the field of power, alongside Habermas's concept of public sphere, American scholar Thomas Medvetz conceptualizes the political decision-making system as a composite field of power constituted by four interlocking domains: politics, finance, media, and academia. He frames the think tank system as a distinctive central space situated at the very heart of this field of power, positioning think tanks as a critical hub for the flow of policy-relevant information and resources, which engage in institutionalized information exchange and resource interaction with each of the four domains of the field of power,

thus wielding influence across all four spheres.① He argues that the think tank system is characterized by a high degree of elasticity, expanding and contracting in response to shifting contextual conditions, a feature that accurately reflects the adaptive, dynamic nature of American think tanks, which continuously adjust their functions and strategies in response to intense competition within the Market Place of Ideas. Medvetz's pioneering concept of the central space has had a profound and lasting influence on subsequent think tank scholarship.

2) The perspectives of epistemic communities, policy communities, and policy networks. Existing literature on epistemic communities suggests that knowledge elites, including think tank researchers, may form interconnected communities based on shared professional expertise and common normative and principled commitments. Through the production and diffusion of specialized knowledge, rather than direct participation in political bargaining, such communities help shape how decision-makers understand particular policy issues.② Building on the concept of the epistemic community, some theoretical approaches further contend that different actors sharing an interest in a particular policy domain or issue may form relatively stable networks through flows of information and exchanges of resources. A well-known example is the "iron triangle" linking interest groups, Congress, and the administrative bureaucracy in the United States. Such networks tend to operate according to shared rules and engage in regular debate over common policy concerns, thereby generating certain consensual views. Within these networks, think tanks are seen as actors that influence decision-making through the provision of professional knowledge and thus constitute a particular type of pressure group.③

---

① Thomas Medvetz, *Think Tanks in Ame*rica, Chicago: University of Chicago Press, 2012.

② Thomas Teichler, "Think Tanks as an Epistemic Community: The Case of European Armaments Cooperation", Paper presented at the annual meeting of the International Studies Association 48th Annual Convention, Chicago, Illinois, 2007; Peter M. Hass, "Epistemic Communities and International Policy Coordination", *International Organization*, Vol. 46, No. 1 (Winter 1992), pp. 1-35.

③ F. Gregory Hayden, *Policymaking Network of the Iron-Triangle Sub-government for Licensing Hazardous Waste Facilities*, Faculty Publications, University of Nebraska, June 2002; S. Wilks and M. Wright (Eds.), *Comparative Government-Industry Relations: Western Europe, United States, and Japan*, Oxford: Clarendon Press, 1987; T. Lowi, *The End of Liberalism*, New York: Norton Publisher, 1969; R. A. W. Rhodes, *Understanding Governance: Policy Networks, Governance, Reflexivity and Accountability*, Buckingham: Open University Press; M. J. Smith, "From Policy Community to Issue Networks: Salmonella in Eggs and the New Politics of Food", *Public Administration*, 69 (summer), pp. 234-255.

3) The perspectives of advocacy coalitions and discourse coalitions. These perspectives maintain that social groups possessing specialized expertise often seek to shape decision-makers' understandings through lobbying, thus advancing their interests and articulating their policy preferences. Studies of think tank orientations sometimes draw on these two perspectives.①

4) The perspective of think tanks as mediators of paradigm shift. This perspective holds that when decision-makers find that the policy instruments available within an existing paradigm are no longer capable of resolving a crisis, they may begin to reconsider their understanding of the situation, along with their underlying ideologies, values, and knowledge structures, and may thus become more receptive to paradigm change. In such circumstances, think tanks, as intermediaries between political decision-makers and the outside world, can contribute to the reshaping of policy paradigms by providing new concepts and discourses. In the early 1990s, several British scholars examined the shift in the UK government's macroeconomic policy paradigm from Keynesianism to neoliberalism, or monetarism, highlighting the role of social forces, including think tanks and the media, in the reconstruction of decision-makers' ideas and cognitive frameworks. These studies stand as classic contributions to the literature on the role of think tanks in paradigm shift.②

3.2 Three Core Models for Analyzing Think Tanks' Policymaking Influence

In the scholarly practice of analyzing think tanks' influence on policymaking, researchers have developed the following three models, which remain valuable analytical tools and conceptual frameworks for dissecting the specific pathways through which think tanks exert influence on policymaking:

1) The Holsti Model: American political scientist Kalevi Jaakko Holsti argues that influence over foreign policy is shaped by four core variables: the overall capabilities and relevance of resources of the state, the mutual needs of two states for one another, the level of technical expertise commanded by foreign policy decision-making actors, and the degree

---

① Paul A. Sabatier and Christopher M. Weible, The Advocacy Coalition Framework: Innovations and Clarifications, in Paul A. Sabatier, *Theories of the Policy Process*, London: Westview Press, 2007.

② Hugh Pemberton, *Policy Learning and British Governance in the 1960s*, Hampshire: Palgrave Macmillan, 2004, P. 283; Peter A. Hall, "Policy Paradigms, Social Learning, and the State: The Case of Economic Policy Making in Britain", *Comparative Politics*, April 1993, Vol. 25, pp. 275-296.

of responsiveness of one actor to the demands of another. Integrating these four variables, Holsti constructs a model that explicates the mechanisms through which influence over foreign policy is generated. The core logic of the model is as follows: for actors A and B, and event X, if B makes no response to A's demand and completes event X independently, A is deemed to have no influence over B. If B responds to A's demand to varying degrees, this demonstrates that A exerts corresponding levels of influence over B. The sum total of the resources under A's control, B's need for A, and B's degree of responsiveness to A collectively determines the likelihood of success of A's attempts to exert diplomatic influence over B. While this model is notably concise and intuitive, making it applicable to the analysis of less complex social structures, its core limitation is that it can only assess immediate, direct forms of influence, while being unable to capture indirect, latent, and long-term forms of influence. While Holsti recognizes that the volume of resources at the disposal of foreign policy actors is not directly equivalent to their influence, and places significant emphasis on the concepts of "relevance of resources" and "responsiveness of the affected actor", he nevertheless provides relatively limited elaboration on the specific operational mechanisms through which actors exert influence.①

2) The Holistic Model: American political scientist Hugh Heclo pioneered the seminal concept of the Issue Network. He contends that, while the operational scope of the political decision-making system includes semi-autonomous systems of interest exchange and hidden forms of interest group politics such as the "iron triangle," certain far-reaching issues draw multiple stakeholders into the process, giving rise to complex networks. In these networks, actors engage in frequent interaction, characterized by ongoing exchanges of resources, information, and interests. As a result, each actor exerts a continuous and shifting influence on others, particularly on decision-makers. Consequently, the influence of such networks can only be understood in a holistic manner, in terms of their overall patterns of operation and their impact on the evolution of decision-making on particular issues.② Building on the concept of issue networks, scholars have developed a "holistic influence" model, which divides the policymaking system into centers (sub-governments) and a broader periphery (the

① K. J. Holsti, *International Politics: A Framework for Analysis*, Englewood Cliffs of New Jersey: Prentice-Hall, 1988, pp. 142-142.

② Hugh Heclo, "Issue Networks and the Executive Establishment", in Anthony King (Ed.), *The New American Political System*, Washington D.C.: The American Enterprise Institute, 1978.

general public). The model suggests that between the periphery and the decision-making center, expertise clusters-composed of diverse sources of specialized knowledge-emerge and exert a combined influence on the perceptions and behaviors of decision-makers.① A key limitation of this model is that it captures only the basic functioning of the decision-making system and is poorly equipped to delineate its internal and external layers, as well as the interrelationships and internal structures of the various groups that shape decision-making.

3) The four-indicator model of think tank influence. Proposed by James G. McGann, this model holds that think tank influence can be disaggregated into four components. The first is the resource dimension, including funding sources, human resources, networks, and the think tank's reputation. The second is the output dimension, referring to books, articles, reports, and other forms of publication produced by the think tank. The third is the external service dimension, which captures the extent of the think tank's engagement with the media and government officials. The fourth is the impact dimension, referring to the extent to which the think tank's research outputs are adopted by the media and government.② While these four indicators provide a broad overview of a think tank's external influence, they remain difficult to quantify and operationalize in a consistent, rigorous manner for empirical analysis.

IV. Theoretical Framework for Explaining European Think Tanks' Influence over EU Policymaking: Integrating the "Field of Power" Perspective and the Multiple Streams Model

The paradigms, perspectives, and models outlined above provide a systematic set of theoretical tools for the study of think tank influence, and existing literature in this field has offers a certain degree of theoretical depth. However, when it comes to analyzing the mechanisms through which think tanks influence specific political decision-making

① Volker Schneider, "Hugh Heclo, 'Issue Networks and the Executive Establishment'", in Martin Lodge et al. (Eds.), *The Oxford Handbook of Classics in Public Policy and Administration*, Oxford, UK: Oxford University Press, 2015, pp. 372-382.

② James G. McGann, *Think Tanks and Policy Advice in the United States: Academics, Advisors, and Advocates*, New York: Routledge, 2007 systems, the existing literature still lacks the necessary analytical accuracy. In particular, it remains insufficiently precise, both structurally and empirically, with regard to the internal hierarchical relations within specific political systems, the concrete ways in which think tanks exert influence on decision-making systems, and the specific sites and operational stages at which such systems are affected by think tank influence. In light of these limitations, this book develops an analytical framework for the study of think tank influence by focusing on the mechanisms through which European think tanks influence the EU's external policymaking. It examines, as detailed case studies, the activities through which three of the most representative think tanks at the EU level, in Germany, and in the United Kingdom (UK) exert influence on the EU's decision-making toward China. In so doing, it seeks to provide a clearer and more precise theoretical picture of this type of research in relation to a specific empirical issue.

Among the existing literature, the theoretical paradigms and perspectives outlined above constitute a conceptual point of departure for research on the relationship between think tanks and policymaking. Specifically, the perspective of the central space within the field of power offers the clearest account of the position of think tanks in the policymaking system. These paradigms and perspectives, however, are relatively static in character and fail to clearly explain the evolving process of interaction between think tanks and decision-makers. In addition, although scholars have proposed several models for explaining think tanks' influence on policymaking, these models are difficult to apply to empirical analysis. Owing to the opacity of the "policymaking black box," the influence of think tanks on decision-making is difficult to identify and measure with precision. As a result, existing literature often remains limited in both theoretical depth and empirical precision. To bridge the gap, this book proceeds from elite theory and institutionalism, and combines John Kingdon's multiple streams model with the perspective of the central space in the field of power in order to construct a general analytical framework for explaining how European think tanks influence EU decision-making.

4.1 John Kingdon's Multiple Streams Model for Agenda-Setting

Harold Dwight Lasswell was the first scholar to propose that general policymaking activities could be divided into seven sequential stages, from information collection through to impact evaluation.[①] Influenced by the burgeoning methodological revolutions of scientism and behavioralism in the 1950s and 1960s, Lasswell's seven-stage theory of the policy process provided a clear, intuitive, temporally grounded analytical framework for subsequent research into policymaking mechanisms, despite limitations in terms of its mechanistic and linear conceptualization of the policymaking operational logic.[②] Building on and refining Lasswell's theory, existing scholarly literature generally divides the policymaking process into five sequential stages: agenda-setting, policy formulation, policy selection, policy implementation, and policy evaluation and review. This stage-based theory of policymaking, however, remains overly broad and generalized. John W. Kingdon therefore developed the Multiple Streams model of agenda-setting, which offers a more refined explanation of how the policymaking process is set in motion.[③]

Kingdon argued that policymaking activities are inherently complex, unpredictable, and non-linear, rather than strictly rational, ordered processes that can be neatly divided into discrete sequential stages. Building on the Garbage Can Model[④] of organizational choice developed by Johan P. Olsen, Kingdon posited that the diverse forces influencing policymaking converge into three distinct streams: politics, policy, and problem. These streams progress independently in parallel under normal circumstances, forming a complex, unstructured system in which diverse policy issues rise and fall in prominence, without necessarily being translated into concrete policy outcomes. This pre-agenda state is referred to as the Policy Primeval Soup. On occasion, shifts in the broader macro context lead decision-makers to prioritize and address specific issues, at which point the three streams converge, enabling the issue to enter the formal policymaking agenda and be translated into explicit policy outcomes. Kingdon termed this transformative juncture the Policy Window, which triggers the convergence of the three streams. He identified two primary scenarios

---

① H. D. Lasswell, *The Decision Process: Seven Categories of Functional Analysis*, College Park: University of Maryland Press, 1956.

② Werner Jann and Kai Wegrich, "Theories of the Policy Cycle", in Frank Fischer et al. (Eds.), *Handbook of Public Policy Analysis: Theory, Politics, and Methods*, Boston and London: CRC Press, Taylor & Francis Group, 2007, pp. 43-47.

③ John W. Kingdon, *Agenda, Alternatives, and Public Policies*, New York: Longman, 2007.

④ Michael D. Cohen, James G. March, and Johan P. Olsen, "A Garbage Can Model of Organizational Choice", *Administrative Science Quarterly*, Vol. 17, No. 1 (March 1972), pp. 1-25.

that lead to the opening of a "policy window": a major transformative shift within the politics stream, or a sudden, urgent intensification of a specific problem within the problem stream. In other words, Policy Windows open in response to either a major reconfiguration of the structure of political forces, or a sudden, disruptive event that triggers acute systemic instability.① According to this model, by capturing the opening of a policy window and examining the role and influence of specific actors at the moment when the three streams converge within the window, researchers can effectively explicate the mechanisms through which these actors influence the policymaking process.

4.2 An Integrated Analytical Framework Combining the Multiple Streams Model and the Field of Power Perspective

Although the EU decision-making system is highly complex, it can likewise be understood as a "field of power" composed of politics, business and finance, academia, and the media, with European think tanks occupying the "central space" in this field and serving as a hub for the circulation of information and resources that shape decision-making. Policy-related activities that unfold in this field of power resemble what Kingdon describes as the disorderly and diffuse state of the "policy primeval soup": the political, policy, and problem streams flow separately over time, while the field of power as a whole remains in a condition of relative equilibrium.

If profound changes occur in any of the three streams—for example, if a crisis suddenly erupts in the problem stream and sharply disrupts the internal or external environment of decision-makers, if the distribution of forces in the political stream is reconfigured and new political actors come to power, or if decision-makers in the policy stream recognize the seriousness of a particular issue and decide to initiate the policymaking process—then the equilibrium of the field of power begins to break down. At such a moment, a policy window opens, the three streams converge, and a given issue enters the EU decision-making process, gradually developing into EU policy. Once that policy is implemented and the situation gradually stabilizes, the three streams separate once again and continue to move forward independently, while the field of power across the four domains returns to a state of relative balance. This dynamic process is illustrated in Figure 1.1.

① John W. Kingdon, *Agenda, Alternatives, and Public Policies*, New York: Longman, 2007, pp. 168-169.

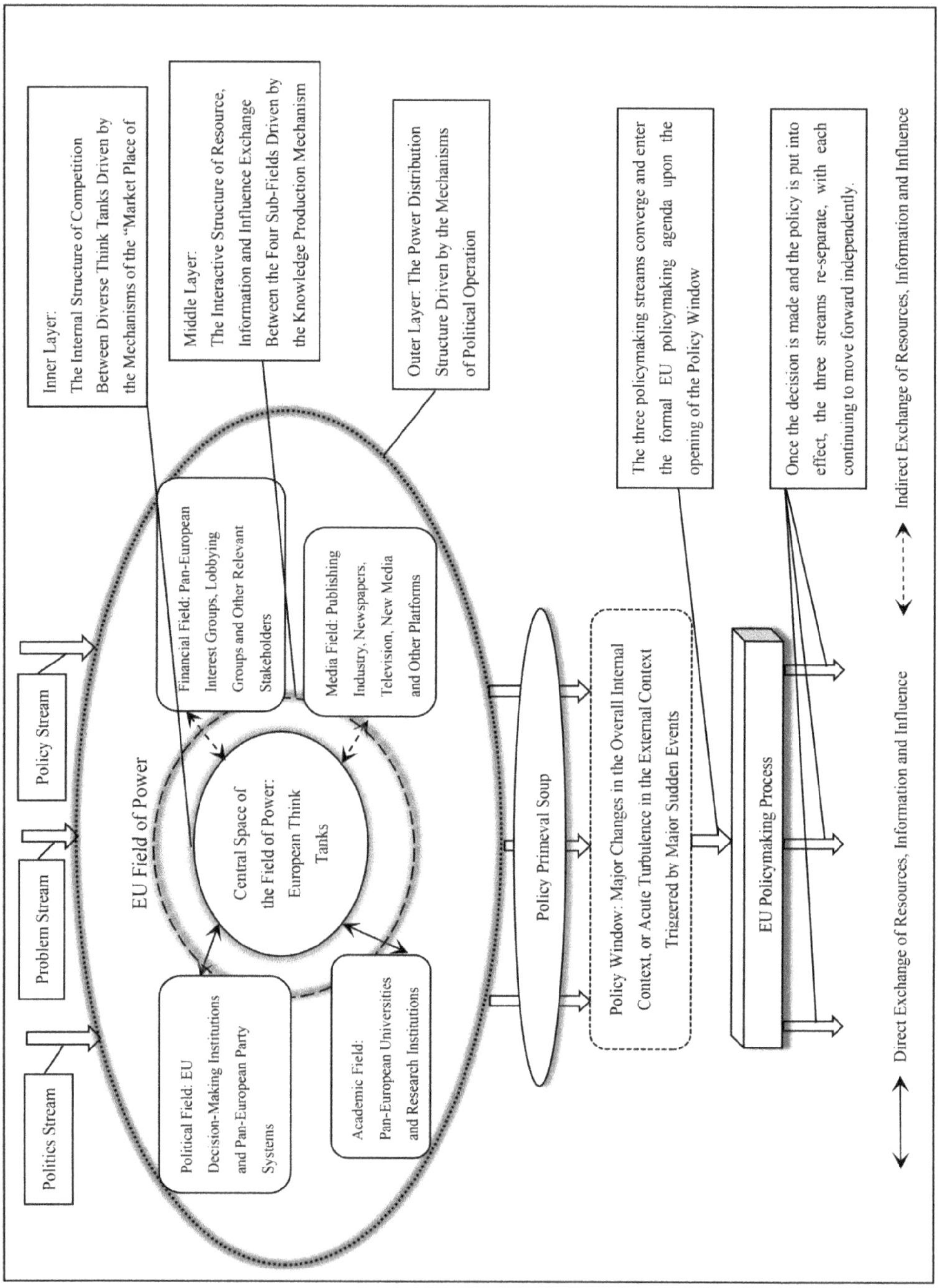

Figure 1.1: Analytical Framework for Delineating the Position of Think Tanks within the EU Policymaking Structure and Process

Source: Developed and illustrated by the author

Within the domain of EU external policymaking, actors that influence decision-making outcomes include the EU's decision-making institutions (the Council of the European Union, the European Council, the European Parliament, and the European Commission), the governments of EU member states, and a diverse array of non-governmental actors at the pan-European level, including interest groups, lobbying firms, advocacy organizations, and think tanks. Applying Kingdon's model to conduct a granular examination of the three policymaking streams reveals the following core dynamics: 1) The politics stream of EU decision-making encompasses the evolutionary trajectory of the balance of power between the diverse actors involved in the process. Within this stream, the Council of the European Union holds ultimate decision-making authority over EU policy, and therefore occupies the core, central position. 2) The policy stream encompasses the process of policy debate and the development of policy proposals by diverse actors, within which stakeholders seek to articulate their interests and policy preferences, with the goal of influencing the agenda-setting and policy orientation of the EU's external decision-making. In this stream, actors in command of specialized policy expertise, most notably EU-level think tanks, occupy the central position. 3) The problem stream encompasses the interactive processes through which diverse actors continuously monitor, assess, and frame issues related to the EU's external decision-making, including the EU's position in the international system, the international security environment, and the EU's security strategy. Within this stream, the European Commission and the European External Action Service, which are directly responsible for the day-to-day implementation and operation of the EU's external policy, have the most immediate, comprehensive, and up-to-date access to the factual realities of the EU's external relations, and therefore occupy the central position in the problem stream.

4.3 Three Policy Windows for the EU's Defensive Economic Policymaking Toward China

To study the mechanisms through which European think tanks influence the EU's external decision-making, it is essential to identify the policy windows that trigger the convergence of the three streams of the field of power. It is at the juncture when the three streams converge through the opening of a policy window that the intensity of the EU decision-making institutions' policymaking activities and the frequency of their interaction with external stakeholders increase dramatically. It is during these critical moments that the think tanks within the EU system, as specialized providers of decision-making advisory services, are able to exert the maximum degree of influence on policy outcomes.

Scholars generally categorize the policy windows articulated by John Kingdon into three distinct types. The first consists of windows that emerge within the politics stream, generally triggered by major shifts in the internal distribution of power. When new political forces assume control of the policymaking process, they often implement profound overhauls of the existing policy agenda in accordance with their own political beliefs and strategic cognitive frameworks, diverting the policymaking process from its pre-existing trajectory. The convergence of the three streams triggered by this type of windows is widely referred to as the "ideational coupling mechanism".① The second type comprises windows that emerge within the problem stream, most often triggered by an unforeseen crisis. Crises generate acute systemic shocks to the previously stable internal and external environment, putting sudden, intense pressure on decision-makers and forcing them to initiate the policymaking process and engage in intensive deliberation over response options. The convergence of the three policymaking streams triggered by this type of windows is referred to as the "consequential coupling mechanism".② The third type encompasses windows that emerge within the policy stream. On occasion, specific institutions and decision-makers in the policymaking establishment recognize the severity of a particular issue, proactively initiate policy deliberation, and kickstart the policymaking process, driving the convergence of the three streams. This dynamic is referred to as the "delegative coupling mechanism".③

A detailed examination of the policymaking process of the EU's defensive economic policy toward China reveals three distinct policy windows, which align precisely with the typology outlined above:

1) The February-May 2012 window: In late 2009, the Greek sovereign debt crisis broke out, sending shockwaves across Europe and undermining the foundational stability of the Eurozone's financial system. In the first half of 2010, the Greek debt crisis dominated

---

① Nikolaos Zahariadis, *Ambiguity and Choice in Public Policy: Political Manipulation in Democratic Societies*, Washington, D.C.: Georgetown University Press, 2003, P. 72.

② Ibid, P. 72.

③ Robert Ackill, Adrian Kay, and Nikolaos Zahariadis, "Ambiguity, Multiple Streams, and EU Policy", *Journal of European Public Policy*, Vol. 20, Issue 6, 2013, pp. 871-887.

media headlines, while Portugal, Ireland, Italy, Greece, and Spain (collectively referred to by the acronym "PIIGS") faced severe crises stemming from their massive public sector debt liabilities, becoming the defining focal point of the European sovereign debt crisis. Between 2010 and early 2012, as the European sovereign debt crisis continued to unfold, the European economy entered a period of sustained recession and long-term stagnation. Under these circumstances, the EU was forced to consider the adoption of proactive protectionist measures, seeking to boost domestic output and employment through restrictions on external imports to stimulate economic growth. Starting in early 2012, European think tanks and the European Commission released a series of intensive evaluation reports exploring the feasibility of developing and implementing defensive economic policies, most notably trade protection measures. In response, the European Commission launched a public consultation process in 2012 to solicit stakeholder views, while simultaneously introducing accompanying industrial policy measures and considering the formulation of corresponding investment policy frameworks.[①] On May 10, 2012, the Directorate-General for Trade of the European Commission held a high-level meeting, formally initiating the policymaking process.[②] Owing to internal disagreements, the more stringent anti-dumping and anti-subsidy (AD/AS) policies tabled in the process were ultimately dropped, with the EU only introducing new regulations to consolidate its tariff system.[③] This window was opened through the proactive actions of the European Commission in response to persistent economic stagnation and therefore falls into the third type outlined above. The convergence of the three streams in this case can be interpreted as a delegative coupling mechanism within the policy stream.

2) The February-July 2016 window: During the first half of 2016, a series of landmark events that would shape the trajectory of European society and politics unfolded

---

① European Commissioner for Trade Karel De Gucht, *A Trade Defense System for Today's Global Economy*, Speech at the High-Level Conference on Modernization of Trade Defense Instruments, Brussels, May 10, 2012; European Commission, *A Stronger European Industry for Growth and Economic Recovery*, SWD (2012) 299 Final, COM (2012) 582 Final, Brussels, October 10, 2012.

② European Commission, News Archive, High-Level Conference: Modernization of Trade Defense Instruments, May 10, 2012.

③ Regulation (EU) No. 978/2012 of the European Parliament and of the Council of 25 October 2012 Applying a Scheme of Generalized Tariff Preferences and Repealing Council Regulation (EC) No. 732/2008, *Official Journal of the European Union*, October 31, 2012.

in rapid succession, delivering a profound shock to the pre-existing policy intentions of the EU decision-making establishment and forcing the EU to continuously re-evaluate and fundamentally adjust its policy framework. Within the EU, the Brexit referendum in the UK, which unfolded from early 2016 through to the referendum on June 24, accelerated the rise of populist forces across Europe. The result of the referendum, in which a majority of voters supported leaving the EU, further emboldened anti-globalization and Euroskeptic political forces opposed to regional integration. The decision of the UK, a major European economy, to leave the EU represented a profound crisis that severely undermined the EU's value system and operational architecture. This development exposed the intense public discontent with globalization and regional integration among significant segments of the European public, placing intense pressure on the EU to respond more explicitly to the interests and demands of these voters, including through partial accommodation of their calls for stronger protection of trade, investment, and domestic industry. Externally, the volume of steel products imported into the EU from external sources reached record highs in the first half of 2016, triggering significant upheaval in the EU's domestic steel industry and exacerbating social tensions. Simultaneously, the impending expiration of Paragraph 15 of *Protocol on The Accession of The People's Republic of China*, which addressed the issue of China's market economy status, sparked intense debate within the EU decision-making establishment and wider European society, forcing the EU to formulate a formal response. On July 20, 2016, the European Commission held a debate on whether to substantially tighten its anti-dumping policy toward China, formally setting off the policymaking process. During the second half of 2016, deliberation and policymaking activity related to the EU's defensive trade policy increased markedly. This policy window, which emerged in the first half of 2016, was triggered by major changes in the EU's internal and external environment and as such, it falls into the second type of windows outlined above, representing a consequential coupling mechanism driven by crisis within the problem stream.

3) The January-May 2017 window: Between late 2016 and the first half of 2017, parliamentary and presidential elections were held in Austria, the Netherlands, Hungary, and France, further elevating the prominence of Euroskeptic radical populist parties in the European political landscape. Simultaneously, the acquisition of European high-end manufacturing enterprises by Chinese firms sparked intense discussion across Europe.

In early 2017, the acquisition of the German robotics firm KUKA AG by China's Midea Group triggered widespread doubt and criticism from European media and the general public, making it a major turning point in China-EU economic relations.① In February 2017, the economic ministers of Germany, France, and Italy sent a joint letter to the European Commission, calling for the establishment of an EU-level investment screening framework. From March 10 to 20, 2017, the European Parliament moved forward with draft position papers calling for the strengthening of trade anti-dumping and anti-subsidy mechanisms and the establishment of an investment screening mechanism, drawing wide support from parliamentary groups across the political spectrum for stronger protective mechanisms against external investment. On May 10, 2017, the European Commission released the policy paper *Reflection Paper on Harnessing Globalisation*, launching a formal policy debate and setting the policymaking process in motion. Between September and December 2017, the EU rolled out a concentrated wave of policies and regulations, imposing stricter rules and measures of restriction, monitoring, screening, and prevention across such areas as trade, investment, industry, technology transfer, and intellectual property protection, thereby establishing a multi-sectoral regulatory framework. The policy window that opened between January and May 2017 was triggered by the KUKA acquisition move at the beginning of the year and the joint letter sent in February by the economic ministers of Germany, France, and Italy. As these ministers were members of the Council in the EU institutional system and may therefore be regarded as part of the EU decision-making leadership, this window likewise falls into the third type outlined above, namely, a delegative coupling mechanism initiated proactively by decision-makers within the policy stream.

The release of *Commission Staff Working Document on Significant Distortions in The Economy of The People's Republic of China for The Purposes of Trade Defence Investigations* by the Juncker Commission on December 20, 2017 marked the beginning of a profound shift in the EU's overall strategic approach and policy intentions toward China. From early 2018 onward, the Juncker and von der Leyen Commissions have introduced in succession increasingly stringent, detailed, and systematic regulations, progressively

① During the author's field research in Europe from October 15 to 25, 2017, this point was highlighted by scholars from several European think tanks, including Claudia Schmucker of the German Council on Foreign Relations (DGAP), Hanns Günther Hilpert of the German Institute for International and Security Affairs (SWP), and Sven Biscop of the Egmont – Royal Institute for International Relations.

strengthening the EU's anti-dumping and anti-subsidy trade protection mechanisms and investment screening framework targeting China. The publication of the *EU-China-A strategic outlook* in March 2019 signaled a fundamental shift in the EU's general strategic perception of China. The EU decision-making process that led to these three policy windows—that is, the process through which the EU assessed its economic relationship with China and formulated its external economic policy from early 2012 to the end of 2017—contained an evolutionary dynamic in which the EU's agenda-setting, assessment of circumstances, and even strategic intentions underwent a fundamental overhaul under the immense pressure of dramatic internal and external changes and the successive shocks of multiple crises.

Therefore, by sorting through and analyzing the various activities through which European think tanks influenced EU decision-making during the three policy windows outlined above, it becomes possible to trace the rhythms and fluctuations through which the EU's defensive economic policymaking toward China has moved forward, enabling serious effort to reflect on the broader changes in the configuration of political forces within and beyond the EU, and to depict the development of the EU decision-making leadership's strategic perceptions and policy intentions in this regard. Such an analysis makes it possible not only to identify the structural characteristics of the EU's decision-making mechanisms on China-related issues, but also to put together the operational features through which the different components of the EU's field of power interact with and constrain one another, thereby highlighting the underlying logic with which the European think tank system, as the central space in this field of power, exerts influence. Accordingly, in examining and explaining the mechanisms behind European think tanks' influence on the EU's defensive economic policymaking toward China, this book focuses in particular on the interactive characteristics of the relationship between the EU's decision-making leadership and European think tanks as it unfolds when the above three types of policy windows open.

Chapter 2: The Overarching Mechanisms of European Think Tanks' Influence in the EU's Decision-Making System

Contemporary European think tanks have evolved into a sophisticated two-tier, four-actor interactive structure, featuring a systemic framework defined by reciprocal influence and sustained, high-frequency engagement between two distinct cohorts of think tanks that operate respectively at the EU level and within EU member states, and two core sets of decision-making authorities, namely the institutional decision-making apparatus of the EU and the national governments of its member states. In this overarching structural framework, think tanks based in EU member states occupy a uniquely distinctive position by virtue of their dual institutional identity: they offer not only tailored public policy advisory services to their respective national governments, but also specialized policy research and consultancy to the EU's decision-making bodies, while simultaneously bringing the policy preferences of national capitals into the EU's legislative and policymaking processes, thus integrating themselves as indispensable constituent elements of the EU's broader decision-making system. British political scientist Justin Greenwood, in his seminal work on EU interest intermediation, categorizes nine distinct types of interest groups that seek to influence and shape EU decision-making processes. Among these categories, think tanks are identified as a prominent and influential form of pressure group, positioned alongside business and industrial interest groups, trade union organizations, advocacy groups, and major transnational corporations. According to his empirical statistical analysis, European think tanks account for approximately 3.5 percent of the total number of organized interest groups operating across the EU.[①] Actors participating in and seeking to exert influence on EU decision-making activities are extraordinarily diverse and multifaceted, encompassing

① Justin Greenwood, *Interest Representation in the European Union*, Hampshire: Palgrave Macmillan, 2011, P. 10.

not only the long-established array of interest groups, lobbying firms, public relations and consultancy agencies, and large-scale transnational corporations that have long occupied a central role in the EU's traditional interest representation system, but also a rapidly expanding cohort of emerging civil society organizations including non-governmental organizations (NGOs) and advocacy groups, all of which have coalesced to form a highly intricate and interconnected policy community within which the aforementioned two-tier, four-actor think tank system becomes a core and structurally significant component. Against this analytical backdrop, it follows that delineating the precise structural position of the think tank system within the EU's multifaceted policy community, and unpacking the overarching mechanisms through which think tanks based in EU member states exert tangible influence over EU decision-making processes, constitute the essential foundational prerequisite for conducting detailed, granular empirical analyses in the rest of this book. That said, the EU itself is characterized by an unwieldy institutional architecture, a sprawling and multifaceted systemic framework, a highly convoluted and multi-layered decision-making structure, and notoriously protracted, circuitous, and often opaque operational and legislative processes. As a direct consequence of this institutional complexity, the operational trajectories of any actor seeking to exert influence over policy outcomes and transmit specific political or policy demands into the EU system are frequently subsumed and obscured by the multiple, rapidly evolving, and parallel streams of EU decision-making that advance continuously through the Union's institutional machinery. For this reason, any attempt to navigate the labyrinthine complexity of the EU's decision-making system must, as a critical first step, set out a clear and systematic categorization of the European think tank system, alongside a comprehensive delineation of the core modalities, tactics, and instruments through which these think tanks exert their influence over EU policy and decision-making.

I. Core Typologies of European Think Tanks

Given a rapidly evolving global landscape which is characterized by unprecedented information circulation and dissemination, and the constantly shifting and increasingly diverse demands placed by policymakers on high-quality policy advisory and research services, coupled with the unique reality that the European continent encompasses an extraordinarily diverse array of cultural traditions, multi-layered and heterogeneous economic systems, and multi-dimensional political and institutional architectures, the European think tank ecosystem is invariably marked by exceptional complexity, heterogeneity, and organizational diversity. Against this contextual backdrop, this chapter posits that the core typologies of European think tanks can be systematically categorized using the two-dimensional analytical framework set out below, a framework that enables a comprehensive mapping of the broad landscape, structural characteristics, and institutional architecture of the European think tank system.

1.1 A Typological Categorization in Two Analytical Dimensions: Specialization and Partisanship

The dimension of specialization refers to the degree of thematic, geographic, and sectoral granularity and focus that a think tank applies to its research agenda and analytical outputs: a think tank is deemed to have a high level of specialization if it maintains a sustained, long-term research focus on specific geographic regions or individual countries, or if it concentrates its analytical work consistently on well-defined thematic policy areas such as foreign policy, external economic policy, or other specialized issue-specific domains; by contrast, a think tank with a lower level of specialization is understood to have a broad, comprehensive, and cross-cutting research mandate spanning multiple policy areas and geographic regions. This specialization dimension thus serves as the core analytical axis through which to identify the professional division of labor, core research competencies, and distinctive analytical strengths of individual think tanks in the broader European ecosystem.

The second analytical dimension, namely partisanship, encompasses two interrelated core components that together define a think tank's institutional positioning. The first component centers on the degree of institutional independence of a think tank in relation to its funding sources and the day-to-day governance and operation of its research activities: a think tank is classified as lacking institutional independence if it relies on an overly narrow, concentrated set of funding channels, and if its research agenda and analytical outputs are demonstrably subject to the direction, control, or influence of specific external institutional or corporate actors. The second component relates to the presence of explicit normative and ideological value judgments in the research findings, analytical outputs, and public interventions that a think tank advances in the context of policy debates and decision-making advisory processes. Taken together, these two components of the partisanship dimension enable the systematic positioning of any given think tank along the political spectrum, from left to right, and from radical or extremist ideological positioning to moderate, centrist, and politically neutral institutional stances. Based on these two interlocking analytical dimensions of specialization and partisanship, contemporary European think tanks can be systematically classified into four distinct typological categories, as shown in Figure 2.1 below.

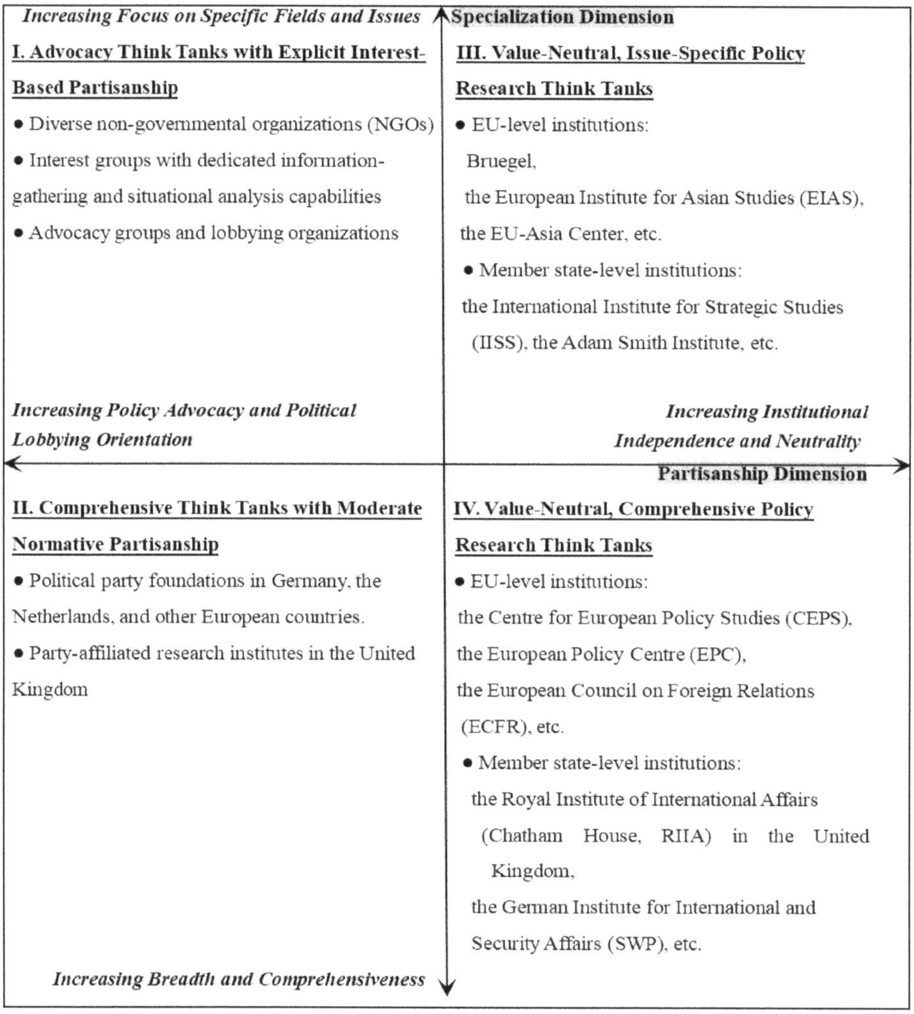

Figure 2.1: Four Typological Categories of the European Think Tank System, Categorized by the Dual Analytical Dimensions of Specialization and Partisanship

Source: Compiled by the author

To develop a comprehensive, holistic understanding of the European think tank system, it is necessary to examine each of these four typological categories in systematic detail, with a specific focus on unpacking their internal organizational and compositional structures, as well as their core operational characteristics, institutional mandates, and modes of engagement with the EU's decision-making processes.

First, we look at the category of think tanks characterized by a high level of specialization but a low level of partisanship. This category includes a number of prominent Brussels-based think tanks, often referred to collectively as the "Brussels think tank community", such as Bruegel, which maintains a specialized research focus on European economic conditions and EU economic policymaking; the EU-Asia Center, the European Institute for Asian Studies (EIAS), and the European Centre for International Political Economy (ECIPE), all of which concentrate their analytical work on specialized thematic and geographic areas related to Asia and EU-Asia relations. This typological group also includes a range of leading specialized research institutes beyond Brussels, including the European Union Institute for Security Studies (EUISS), the EU's official in-house think tank based in Paris; the Stockholm International Peace Research Institute (SIPRI) in Sweden; the Centre for Military Studies (CMS) at the University of Copenhagen in Denmark; and the International Institute for Strategic Studies (IISS) in the United Kingdom, a world-leading institute specializing in security strategy, defense policy, and geopolitical analysis. Think tanks of this category are typically described as "small, focused, specialized, and deeply authoritative", a characterization that reflects their strong academic orientation and rigorous research standards, as they concentrate their analytical work exclusively on a single academic discipline or policy domain, or maintain a sustained, long-term research focus on a specific geographic region or individual country. Leveraging their deep academic expertise, decades of accumulated empirical data and contextual research, and their active, consistent participation in high-level policy debates on breaking current events and core decision-making priorities within the EU system, these think tanks have built enduring, well-established reputations and authoritative standing among the EU decision-making circles in Brussels, as well as across the broader EU policy community as a whole. Beyond their core research and advisory functions, these specialized think tanks also play a pivotal role in supporting the EU to implement institutionalized public diplomacy and Track II diplomacy initiatives with regions and countries beyond Europe's borders. The EU-Asia Center, for example, has played a central and well-documented role in the EU's Track II diplomatic engagement with Japan. As a direct result of their specialized expertise, deep contextual knowledge, and established credibility in the EU policy circles, these think tanks fulfil an irreplaceable and uniquely influential role in shaping the agenda-setting process within specific, well-defined domains of EU policy and decision-making.

The second typological category encompasses think tanks with both a high level of specialization and a high level of partisanship. Organizations of this category are typically social entities that integrate robust, specialized research capabilities into their core institutional mandates, and they include a wide array of NGOs, interest groups with dedicated in-house capacities for systematic information gathering and contextual political and economic analysis, as well as a broad range of advocacy groups and formal lobbying organizations. Prominent examples of organizations of this category include the International Crisis Group (ICG), which maintains a major operational presence in Brussels; Transparency International (TI) and the European Stability Initiative (ESI), both of which are headquartered in Germany; and Amnesty International (AI), which has its global headquarters in the United Kingdom. In addition to these leading organizations, research institutes established by Europe-wide chambers of commerce, industry associations, and trade union federations also fall squarely into this typological category, as do certain public relations consultancy firms and specialist lobbying companies that possess and exercise research and analytical capabilities aligned with those of formal think tanks. Organizations of this category are characterized by their active, vocal, and consistent participation in highly contentious and polarized public policy debates, a feature that means their work tends to carry a far more pronounced orientation of political lobbying and policy advice, while exhibiting a more limited formal academic orientation compared to the highly specialized, low-partisanship think tanks discussed above. Despite their reduced academic focus, however, these organizations maintain unparalleled, close-up access to the most urgent and pressing policy demands and interest claims of specific social groups and constituencies, while conducting long-term, systematic monitoring and tracking of the most acute and contentious points of conflict and tension among different social groups in specific policy domains. In addition to such core monitoring and analytical work, these organizations also provide comprehensive, granular baseline data and detailed, evidence-based information to underpin and inform political debates between different societal stakeholders, and in many cases, they engage directly in targeted political lobbying activities and explicit policy advice initiatives directed at the core decision-making institutions of the EU. As a result of their deep embeddedness into societal constituencies and their constant engagement with the shifting dynamics of EU and national political processes, these organizations are extraordinarily sensitive to shifts and realignments in the structure of political forces in the EU and its member states, effectively functioning as a reliable and immediate barometer of political change and evolving political dynamics across the EU system. Furthermore, in order to influence and shape public discourse, build public momentum for their policy priorities, and secure discursive power in public and policy debates in the context of their policy advice and political lobbying activities, these organizations systematically develop and maintain formalized, institutionalized relationships with media outlets and journalistic platforms, making them the most media-engaged and media-connected category of think tanks across the entire four-part typology.

The third typological category consists of think tanks with a low level of specialization but a high level of partisanship, a group that is dominated by the political party foundations of Germany and the Netherlands, as well as the party-affiliated research institutes based in the United Kingdom. High-profile examples of organizations of this category include the Konrad Adenauer Foundation (KAS), which is affiliated with Germany's center-right Christian Democratic Union, and the Friedrich Ebert Foundation (FES), which is linked to Germany's center-left Social Democratic Party, the two dominant mainstream political parties in the German political space. Additional prominent examples include the Centre for Policy Studies (CPS), which is closely aligned with the UK's Conservative Party, and the Fabian Society, the long-standing socialist think tank affiliated with the UK's Labor Party. Think tanks of this category are defined by their explicit and well-documented party political affiliations and clearly articulated ideological positions, and while they tend to exert relatively limited direct structural influence over the formal EU legislative and decision-making processes, they do place significant strategic emphasis on fulfilling the role of a structured "communication platform" that facilitates dialogue and engagement between different political forces, societal stakeholders, and interest groups across the European political landscape. These organizations conduct the highest volume of convening activity among all four think tank categories, with an exceptionally high frequency of events including academic seminars, high-level policy forums, expert roundtables, and targeted research projects that they fund and support. They maintain a highly active and visible presence in political activities at the EU level, particularly in the party group politics that structure the work and decision-making of the European Parliament. The political party foundations of Germany and the Netherlands fulfil a dual set of core functions: on the one hand, they operate within their respective national political systems as influential forums for structured political debate, ideological deliberation, and the development of party policy positions, while on the other hand, they maintain permanent offices in Brussels, through which they actively participate in party political activities at the EU level and engage directly with the political party groups within the European Parliament. Simultaneously, these foundations also operate an extensive network of representative offices across every major geographic region of the world, through which they deliver a wide range of academic seminars, societal exchange programs, and structured political debate initiatives, all of which are designed and implemented in alignment with the ideological principles, normative values, and political priorities of the political parties they represent. Through this multi-layered, transnational operational structure, these party foundations have emerged as a uniquely distinctive category of actors in the EU's broader political system, exerting tangible influence over the core stages of the EU policy cycle, including the critical phases of problem identification, agenda-setting, and the formulation and selection of policy alternatives.

The fourth and final typological category comprises think tanks characterized by both a low level of specialization and a low level of partisanship, a group that consists overwhelmingly of comprehensive, academically rigorous foreign policy research institutes with broad, cross-cutting research mandates and established reputations for high-quality, non-partisan policy analysis work. Leading examples of organizations of this category operating at the EU level include the Centre for European Policy Studies (CEPS), the European Policy Centre (EPC), and the European Council on Foreign Relations (ECFR), while prominent national-level institutes of this group include the Royal Institute of International Affairs (Chatham House) in the United Kingdom, the German Institute for International and Security Affairs (SWP), the French Institute of International Relations

(IFRI), the Institute for International Political Studies (ISPI) in Italy, and the Netherlands Institute of International Relations (Clingendael). Foreign policy as a policy domain is defined by its exceptionally high degree of specialization, multifaceted and cross-cutting complexity, and extreme time sensitivity, all of which place significant demands on the institutional capacity of any governing body to develop and implement informed, evidence-based foreign policy decisions. The EU, however, is significantly constrained in this regard by its unwieldy institutional architecture, its highly bureaucratic and convoluted operational and legislative procedures, and the fragmented nature of its foreign policy decision-making structures, which together mean that it faces substantial structural challenges in acquiring the specialized technical expertise and accurate, real-time information required for effective foreign policy decision-making, as well as in conducting continuous, real-time monitoring of rapidly evolving developments in the international system beyond Europe's borders and producing accurate, forward-looking predictive analysis of emerging global trends and geopolitical shifts. As a direct consequence of these structural institutional constraints, the EU relies heavily on the "external brain" function fulfilled by these comprehensive, non-partisan think tanks, which provide the EU's decision-making bodies with the specialized expertise, real-time analysis, and forward-looking strategic insight that the Union's own institutional structures are often unable to generate internally in a timely and comprehensive manner.

1.2 Typological Categorization Based on Variations in Think Tanks' Research Areas and Strategies

The first category consists of comprehensive foreign policy think tanks. Think tanks of this category conduct intensive, cross-cutting research across the full spectrum of foreign policy-related domains, including general foreign policy formulation, international economic policy, and strategic and security policy. Prominent and representative examples of this typology include the Center for Strategic and International Studies (CSIS) in the United States, the Royal Institute of International Affairs (Chatham House) in the United Kingdom, and the German Institute for International and Security Affairs (SWP). The second category encompasses think tanks specializing in strategic and security studies, which focus on macro-level strategic research in the fields of national defense, military affairs, and security policy, with a core analytical emphasis on monitoring the external strategic security environment and evaluating external threats to domestic and regional security. Think tanks of this category can be further subdivided into two sub-groups: the first comprises think tanks dedicated to macro-level strategic research, exemplified by the International Institute for Strategic Studies (IISS) in London, while the second includes think tanks specializing in targeted defense and military affairs research, such as the Royal United Services Institute (RUSI). The third category consists of think tanks specializing in international economic affairs research, which conduct sustained, long-term tracking of economic interactions between major global economies, alongside systematic observation and analysis of shifts within the global multilateral economic system and the architecture of global economic governance. Think tanks of this category can also be further divided into two clear subcategories: the first includes think tanks focused on International Political Economy (IPE) issues such as international development, foreign assistance, and global economic governance, with the German Development Institute (DIE) and the Institute of Development Studies (IDS) in the United Kingdom as their prominent examples, while the second encompasses think tanks that conduct specialized research in defined technical fields including international trade, international finance, and international commercial law, such as the Institute of Economic Affairs (IEA) and the Center for Economic Policy Research (CEPR) in the United Kingdom.

Think tanks specializing in international affairs vary considerably in their preferred research strategies, which in turn leads to distinct characteristics and unique value in the policy advice they provide to policymakers. In general, scholars and practitioners can combine micro and macro analytical frameworks with the qualitative and quantitative methodological to map out four distinct preference-based typologies of research strategies for international affairs analysis. The first typology combines a micro-level analytical perspective with quantitative methodological approaches, which forms a strategy that is preferentially adopted by most think tanks conducting specialized research in defined fields such as international trade and finance, placing a premium on granular empirical details and quantifiable data in their analytical work. The second typology integrates a micro-level analytical perspective with qualitative methodological approaches, which constitutes a strategy that is favored by think tanks specializing in defense and military affairs research, which typically focus their analytical work on specific weapons systems, military service branches, and geographic regions of strategic interest. The third research strategy combines a macro-level analytical perspective with quantitative methodological approaches, which makes up a framework that is most commonly utilized by think tanks concentrating their research on core IPE issues. The fourth and final research strategy links a macro-level analytical perspective with qualitative methodological approaches, which becomes a mode of analysis that is most frequently deployed by think tanks specializing in strategic and security studies. As a quintessential example of a comprehensive foreign policy think tank, the Royal Institute of International Affairs (Chatham House) demonstrates no pronounced preference for any single one of the four aforementioned research strategies, and instead flexibly selects and deploys the appropriate analytical framework based on the specific characteristics of the issue under examination and the unique requirements of each individual research case.

An analysis of publicly available research outputs and scholarly literature on China studies produced by leading European and American think tanks shows that Category III and Category IV think tanks, as identified and outlined in Figure 2.1, maintain a notably higher level of sustained focus on China-related issues relative to other typological groups. Several Category III institutions are exclusively dedicated to specialized research on China or East Asia more broadly, and the degree of influence they exert over the formulation of U.S.-China and EU-China policies is widely and formally recognized in both the transatlantic think tank community and the senior official decision-making circles of the United States and the EU, with prominent examples including the EU-Asia Center in Brussels and the Mercator Institute for China Studies (MERICS) in Berlin. Category IV think tanks, by contrast, are defined by their broad, comprehensive research mandates, and almost all maintain dedicated, permanent research teams focused specifically on China or East Asia issues, which allows them to sustain consistent, long-term analytical attention to political, economic, and strategic developments inside China and its evolving role in the international system.

II. Specific Mechanisms of European Think Tanks' Influence over the EU's Decision-Making

In the policy debates and broader public discourse of any given decision-making system, multiple actors consistently coexist and engage in structured competition to secure both substantive influence and discursive power. For this reason, the sustained interaction between think tanks, the underlying structures of political authority, and formal decision-making systems is widely recognized as a core component of the "Marketplace for Ideas",① a framework that has led scholars and practitioners to characterize think tanks as "the Idea Brokers".② The ability of a think tank to secure a proactive position and competitive advantage within this Marketplace for Ideas depends, to a predominant extent, on the specific modalities and tactics it deploys to exert influence over senior decision-makers. While existing scholarly literature has undertaken partial analysis and descriptive elaboration of the tactics and modalities through which think tanks shape policy outcomes, no comprehensive or systematic categorization of these tools has been produced to date. This gap means that a more granular, detailed classification of the specific modalities of think tank influence, alongside their associated typologies and core characteristics, is both necessary and analytically valuable for deepening understanding of think tank behavior in policy systems.

2.1 Overarching Categorization of the Modalities and Typologies of European Think Tanks' Influence over Decision-Making

This chapter argues that, based on the structural characteristics and interactive dynamics between European think tanks and the EU's decision-making system, the modalities through which European think tanks exert influence over EU policymaking can be classified into 13 distinct forms as outlined in Figure 2.2. Furthermore, this chapter develops a coordinate framework organized around two core dimensions: the intensity of influence that each modality exerts over EU decision-making, and the duration of such influence. Using this

① British philosophers John Milton and John Stuart Mill were the first to systematically elaborate on the concept of the "Marketplace for Ideas", a theoretical framework that is regularly and widely employed by think tank scholars to characterize the dynamic operational structure of policy debates and broader public discourse.

② James Allen Smith was the first scholar to systematically articulate the concept of "the Idea Brokers", deploying this analytical framework to explain the evolutionary trajectory and structural characteristics of the mechanisms through which U.S. think tanks exert influence over the decision-making processes of the U.S. government. For a full elaboration of this conceptual development, see James Allen Smith, *The Idea Brokers: Think Tanks and the Rise of the New Policy Elite*, New York: Macmillan Inc., 1991. This concept was subsequently expanded, refined, and further contextualized by scholars specializing in European think tanks, with one foundational scholarly contribution being Simon James's book "*The Idea Brokers: The Impact of Think Tanks on British Government*", *Public Administration*, Vol. 71, No. 4, Winter 1993.

framework, these 13 modalities are grouped into four distinct typological categories: short-term direct modalities, short-term indirect modalities, long-term direct modalities, and long-term indirect modalities. This classification framework clearly illustrates the core characteristics of each individual influence modality, as well as the structural and functional relationships between different modalities.

Across different political institutional systems and decision-making environments, individual think tanks prefer and adopt specific tactics and modalities to shape policy outcomes, and they also rely on distinct causal pathways even when deploying the same influence modality. For example, in the political systems of the United States and the United Kingdom, the national legislature holds considerable authority to constrain, and even finalize, foreign policy decisions. This dynamic is particularly pronounced in the United States, where the agenda-setting, policy alternative selection, and final decision-making for major military operations and external economic affairs are all subject to congressional oversight and approval. As a result, think tanks in these systems place an extremely high value on participation in congressional hearings, which they view as a critical modality to directly engage with and influence senior decision-makers. Scholarly work by McGann and Abelson also identifies the frequency of a think tank's testimony before the U.S. Congress as a key quantitative metric for evaluating the institution's policy influence. In the EU system, by contrast, the European Parliament holds significantly less decision-making authority and constraining power relative to the Council of the European Union and the European Commission in the domains of foreign affairs, security policy, and external economic affairs. This gap is especially evident in the core stages of the policy cycle, including agenda-setting and policy alternative selection, where the European Parliament's influence is far more limited than that of the U.S. or UK legislatures relative to their respective national executive branches. The European Parliament also hosts fewer formal hearings compared to the legislative bodies of the United States and the United Kingdom. For these reasons, European think tanks do not view testimony before European Parliament hearings as a high-impact modality for influencing EU decision-making. Instead, they place far greater strategic emphasis on convening high-level forums that invite officials from the relevant directorates-general of the European Commission to participate and engage directly with researchers and stakeholders.

Figure 2.2: 13 Modalities Through Which European Think Tanks Exert Influence over EU Decision-Making and Their Associated Typological Classification

Source: Compiled by the author

2.2 Categorization of the Typologies and Core Characteristics of Think Tank Conferences and Publications

Among the wide range of modalities through which think tanks exert influence over policy outcomes, two broad categories consistently generate extensive, well-documented archival records, which in turn provide detailed, verifiable evidence for observing and analyzing the mechanisms of think tank influence over decision-making. These two categories are respectively think tank conferences, which correspond to Modalities I, III, and IV, and think tank publications, which correspond to Modalities V, VI, and X as shown in Figure 2.2.

Think tank conferences function in practice as short-term structured platforms for research exchange and stakeholder engagement, and as such, they represent a core institutional format through which think tanks, acting as a central nodal space in the field of power, connect the four core constituent components of that field: political authorities, financial and business communities, academic and research institutions, and media organizations. Within the structured setting of a think tank conference, these four components of the field of power can engage in direct, face-to-face information exchange and resource sharing. More critically, think tank conferences with active participation from senior decision-makers often feature diverse stakeholders from across civil society who can directly covey their interest claims and policy preferences to the decision-making apparatus, while also engaging in targeted political advocacy. Simultaneously, senior decision-makers can directly articulate their thinking on high-priority policy issues, their planned structure for the policy agenda, and their intended direction for specific policy frameworks to a broad cross-section of societal stakeholders. For these reasons, think tank conferences have effectively emerged as one of the core operational hubs of the political decision-making system, and they can vividly and concretely reflect the operational characteristics of the interest representation mechanisms embedded into a given political decision-making structure.

Think tank publications, by contrast, cannot dynamically and comprehensively reflect the processes and characteristics of political decision-making and interest representation in the same real-time, interactive manner as think tank conferences do. However, their fixed, formal written format means that they can indirectly reveal the analytical perspective, ideological framework, discursive structure, and intellectual approach that a think tank adopts when it examines a specific policy issue. These publications can also be systematically compared with official policy documents produced by decision-making authorities to empirically verify and measure the extent of a think tank's policy influence. For these reasons, a more granular classification of think tank conferences and publications, alongside a systematic delineation of their typological characteristics, can significantly help scholars better map the causal pathways and structural dynamics of the mechanisms through which think tanks exert influence over policy outcomes.

This chapter classifies the conferences hosted by the three core think tanks examined in this book into six distinct typologies, and summarizes their core characteristics in Table 2.1. As outlined in Table 2.1, all think tank conferences can be grouped into the following categories, organized in descending order of representativeness and level of formality:

First, high-level forums. This typology of conferences has the largest scale, longest duration, highest number of keynote speakers, and broadest geographic and institutional diversity among participants. Generally, these events attract elite participants from all four core components of the field of power, including political authorities, media organizations, financial and business communities, and academic institutions. Leading figures from these sectors deliver formal keynote addresses, including opening remarks, thematic research presentations, and closing summary statements, or moderate structured panel discussions during the events. The core themes of high-level forums focus on complex, high-profile issues in international economics and politics that attract widespread attention from across societal sectors, and these overarching themes are typically broken down into several targeted sub-themes for deeper discussion. These events usually last at least one full day, with many high-level forums running for two to three consecutive days. They are typically structured into five to six sequential plenary sessions, or multiple parallel breakout panels focused on specialized sub-themes, and feature a minimum of ten formal keynote or panel speakers. These events almost always include active participation from senior decision-makers from the EU or the national government where the host think tank is based. For these reasons, high-level forums serve as a critical connection point between the four core domains of the field of power, and they represent a high-impact modality through which think tanks exert short-term direct influence over the EU's decision-making authorities.

Second, lectures and research findings launch events. A standard lecture event typically features only two core guest participants: a lead keynote speaker and a moderator, with an additional discussant included in some formats. These events are structured around a single, clearly defined central figure, namely the keynote speaker, who is typically a prominent figure from the think tank community or a senior member of the decision-making apparatus. Through formal presentation, the keynote speaker may share critical updates on emerging developments in the decision-making apparatus, or articulate the policy preferences and interest claims of a specific societal group. Research findings launch events have a slightly more complex format than standard lecture events, and typically feature four to five core guest participants. The primary purpose of this typology of events is to disseminate information to the public following the completion of a think tank research project and the publication of its associated research report or other outputs, or following the release of a new scholarly monograph by an affiliated researcher. During these events, organizers outline the core theme of the research project, elaborate on its key findings and analytical arguments, and engage in structured discussion and exchange with the audience regarding the major conclusions, real-world policy relevance, and academic value of the work. Such events are designed to disseminate research findings to a broad public audience, and as a result, they attract participants from a wide range of institutional and sectoral backgrounds.

Third, thematic symposia, which include two primary formats: large-scale academic symposia and small, focused thematic workshops, alongside flexible variants such as policy breakfast briefings. This typology of events typically focuses intensive discussion on a single, narrowly defined specific issue in current affairs or policy research, and is characterized by a high degree of technical specialization and thematic focus. Participants are almost exclusively expert researchers and academics from think tanks and university institutions who specialize in the relevant issue area, and they attend with the goal of reaching a defined degree of analytical consensus or developing a deeper, more nuanced understanding of the issue through structured discussion and interactive exchange. Structured thematic panel discussions and moderated question-and-answer sessions form the core operational format of these events.

Fourth, closed-door meetings. This typology of events represents the most closely connected format through which think tanks engage directly with senior political decision-making authorities. These events operate on an invitation-only basis, with no public access to the content of their discussions, and only partial public disclosure of the list of keynote speakers and participants. Speakers and participants regularly include senior decision-making officials with direct policy authority, as well as their designated official representatives. For these reasons, closed-door meetings have the highest degree of direct influence over policy outcomes of all think tank conference typologies.

Table 2.1: Types and Characteristics of Think Tank Conferences

Conference Characteristic \ Type of Conference		I.High-Level Forum	II.Lecture Event	III. Research Findings Launch Event	IV.Large-Scale Academic Symposium	V.Small Focused Thematic Workshop	VI. Closed-Door Meeting
Conference Representativeness (distribution of the professional backgrounds and institutional affiliations of keynote speakers and attendees)		Extremely Broad	Relatively Broad	Relatively Broad	Relatively Concentrated	Relatively Concentrated	Highly Concentrated
Thematic Focus of the Conference (targeted relevance, professional specialization, and technical precision of conference discussion content)		Low	Moderate	Relatively High	Relatively High	Very High	Very High in Most Cases
Level of Formality of Conference (recognition as a high-profile networking platform across sectors)		Exceptionally Formal	Highly Formal	Formal	Formal	Relatively Formal	Informal
Level of Institutionalization of Conference (regularity of scheduling, dedicated funding, and fixed venue support)		Generally High	Generally Low	Variable	Generally High	Generally High	Variable
Level of Operational Integration of Conference (degree of alignment with research projects, collaborative platforms, and inter-think tank research networks)		Moderate	Moderate	Relatively High	Relatively High	Relatively High	Variable
Conference Scale	Number of Keynote and Remarks Speakers	Relatively Large (10-40)	Relatively Small (2-3)	Relatively Small (2-5)	Moderate (10-20)	Relatively Small (5-10)	Variable
	Number of Discussants and Audience Members	Relatively Large (50-100)	Relatively Large (50-100)	Moderate (30-50)	Variable	Relatively Small (20-30)	No Audience
Conference Duration		1-2 Days	0.5 Days	1-2 Days	1-2 Days	0.5 Days	0.5-1 Days
Level of Participation from the Four Core Components of the *Field of Power*	**Political Decision-Making Authorities**	High	Generally Low	Generally Low	Relatively High	Relatively Low	Variable
	Business and Financial Community	High	Generally Low	Generally Low	Generally Moderate	Relatively Low	Minimal
	Academic Circles	High	Relatively High	Relatively High	Relatively High	Relatively High	Moderate
	Media Sector	High	Moderate	Moderate	Moderate	Moderate	Variable

Source: Compiled by the author

Think tanks produce an extensive and diverse array of publications in substantial annual volume. While a think tank cannot guarantee a large readership for every individual publication it releases, these written outputs nevertheless represent the most consistent and effective formal medium for shaping and disseminating its public identity and institutional brand. For this reason, think tanks consistently distribute a wide range of publications to both senior decision-makers and the general public. This chapter classifies all publications produced by the three core think tanks examined in this book into eight distinct typologies, organized in ascending order of length, and summarizes their core characteristics in Table 2.2. As outlined in Table 2.2, media commentary represents the think tank publication with the shortest length, highest time sensitivity, and broadest reach is media commentary. It consists of rapid analytical remarks made by think tank experts in response to breaking current events and high-profile policy issues. Because this category of publication delivers strong communicative impact and significantly elevate a think tank's public visibility and influence among the general population, U.S. and UK think tanks highly conscious of brand awareness typically impose formal requirements on their full-time researchers regarding the frequency of their media appearances, and track and compile annual statistical metrics on the institution's overall media exposure. Media commentary, however, is limited in the depth and technical precision of its analysis of policy issues. For this reason, as demonstrated in later sections of this book, the most numerous category of think tank publications, and the format that maintains the closest conceptual, discursive, and substantive alignment with official policy documents produced by decision-makers, consists of research reports and working papers. The volume, publication frequency, and sustained output of research reports and working papers focused on a specific policy issue directly reflect the depth of a think tank's research on that topic, the cadence of its engagement with senior decision-makers on the issue, and ultimately the degree of discursive power the institution holds in that specific policy domain.

Table 2.2: Analysis of Typological Characteristics of Think Tank Publications

Type	Length	Dissemination Channels and Scope	Thematic Features & Time Horizon	Validity Period of Research Findings
Media Comments (Blog Comments)	Very short (approx. 1 page)	Media channels targeting the general public, with a wide reach	Focus on specific short-term issues	Short
Policy Briefs / Briefing Notes	Short (approx. 2 pages)	Specialized channels for influencing senior decision-makers	Mostly specific short-term issues	Short
Conference Speeches and Presentations	Short (1-2 pages)	Variable	Variable	Variable
Decision-making Advisory Reports & Thematic Research Reports (commissioned reports, briefing papers)	Medium (2-5 pages)	Specialized channels for influencing senior decision-makers	Mostly urgent, specific short-term issues	Short
Working Paper	Medium to long (5-10 pages)	Variable	Mostly specific medium-term issues	Medium
Research Papers / Program Research Reports (research papers, program papers)	Long (10-200 pages)	Variable	Mostly medium-term specific issues or abstract propositions	Medium
Edited Conference or Project Volumes (edited collections of papers)	Very long (50-200 pages)	Channels for influencing high-level decision-making and academic dissemination channels	Mostly abstract propositions requiring medium-to-long term observation	Long
Academic Papers and Monographs	Very long (20-200 pages)	Academic dissemination channels	Propositions with theoretical significance requiring medium-to-long term observation	Long

Source: Compiled by the author

The relative effectiveness of the different modalities through which think tanks exert influence varies significantly across the distinct stages of an advancing policy stream. As articulated by prominent public policy scholar John W. Kingdon, there are two core scenarios in which a policy window opens. The first scenario occurs when a major structural shift takes place in the balance of forces in the political stream, representing a development that typically unfolds after a long period of incremental evolutionary change in the broader political landscape. Actors in the policy stream, including think tanks, media outlets, and academic institutions, regularly conduct sustained long-term monitoring of emerging trends and engage in ongoing policy debate well before formal policy shifts occur, thus exerting a gradual, underlying influence on decision-makers in the period leading up to the opening of the policy window. In this scenario, think tanks are able to seize the strategic initiative by developing and advancing pioneering, forward-looking policy proposals, and exert a proactive, anticipatory influence over the direction of policy change. Furthermore, their indirect modalities of influence, particularly the publication of written outputs including newsletters, policy briefs, and research reports, can have a particularly profound impact on decision-makers, as these formats allow for the systematic, comprehensive, and detailed elaboration of policy recommendations and the design of concrete policy alternatives.

The second scenario in which a policy window opens is when a major unforeseen crisis or emergency event breaks out. In this context, the rapid and dramatic shift in circumstances takes all actors by surprise. Decision-makers in the political stream have access to sophisticated intelligence systems, a complex bureaucratic administrative apparatus, and extensive resources that can be deployed for emergency response at a moment's notice. This allows them to mount a rapid response, make major policy adjustment within a compressed timeframe, and even establish an all-new policy framework in response to the crisis. Think tanks, academic institutions, and other actors in the policy stream, by contrast, cannot anticipate the event or seize the strategic initiative in advance, and are rarely able to make a more rapid or definitive response than senior political decision-makers. These actors can, however, conduct a critical review and systematic assessment of the policy changes that have already been enacted, and put forward complementary and extended policy recommendations to refine and strengthen the official response. In this scenario, the rapid and volatile shift in circumstances places decision-makers under extreme policy pressure, creating an urgent and immediate demand for concise, targeted, and rapidly delivered information and policy recommendations. For this reason, face-to-face engagement between think tanks and decision-makers, including convening high-level forums, participating in hearings, debates, and small focused discussion sessions hosted by decision-making authorities, becomes the most impactful and consequential modality through which think tanks can exert influence over policy outcomes.①

① During interviews conducted by the author with a number of think tanks in the second half of 2013 and the first half of 2014, leading officials of these institutions—including Jan Techau, Director of Carnegie Europe, and Hanns Günter Hilpert from the German Institute for International and Security Affairs (Stiftung Wissenschaft

III. Pathways of European Think Tanks' Influence in the EU's Decision-Making System: A Comparative Analysis with the U.S. Think Tanks

The political decision-making systems of the United States and the EU possess distinct and defining structural characteristics of their own. The United States operates as a nation-state under a system of representative democracy, while the EU functions as a supranational international organizational structure. These fundamental institutional differences mean that the pathways and modalities through which think tanks exert influence in each system also differ substantially. Existing scholarly literature contains extensive, in-depth analysis of U.S. think tanks and their role in domestic policymaking. For this reason, a comparative analysis of the structural position of European and U.S. think tanks in their respective decision-making systems, alongside the structural architecture of the pathways through which they exert influence, delivers two core analytical benefits. First, it facilitates a deeper understanding of the fundamental differences in the structural characteristics and operational mechanisms of the U.S. and EU decision-making systems. Second, it provides a clearer, more granular delineation of the unique structural position and functional role of European think tanks in the EU's decision-making apparatus.

3.1 The Position and Role of U.S. Think Tanks in the U.S. Foreign Policy Decision-Making System

While the U.S. political system is defined by pluralistic competition across a wide range of actors, authority over U.S. foreign policy—particularly external economic policy—remains heavily concentrated in the executive branch. This concentration of authority stems from the fact that foreign policy combines a high degree of technical specialization with inherent strategic significance, as decisions in this domain can have a profound and nuanced impact on the long-term fundamental national interests of the United States.

und Politik, SWP)—noted to the author that think tanks are incapable of predicting crises, nor can they provide technical assistance to political decision-makers when the latter are urgently addressing specific issues in the midst of a crisis. Instead, think tanks are positioned to offer decision-makers long-term, strategic policy recommendations, and to support them in conducting macro-level, strategic retrospectives in the aftermath of a crisis.

The congressional legislative branch retains the ability to exercise substantial authority through bill sponsorship, oversight, and regulatory checks on executive action. Interest groups, media outlets, and think tanks can also wield meaningful influence during the problem identification and agenda-setting stages of the policy cycle, where they play a role in initiating policy debate and providing concrete policy recommendations. During the subsequent stages of the decision-making process, however, including situational assessment and policy option selection, the central executive branch—particularly the President and his senior White House staff—exercise dominant authority. The decision-making principles, analytical frameworks, and discursive structures of these senior executive actors largely shape the substantive content and overall direction of policy outcomes. In this system, there is a pronounced and clearly defined core-periphery stratification between political elites and the general public in the foreign policy decision-making process.

U.S. scholars typically divide the U.S. public and foreign policy decision-making system into three concentric layers: an inner layer, a middle layer, and an outer layer. This chapter, by contrast, subdivides the system into eight distinct hierarchical layers, as illustrated in the figure below. This chapter argues that Layers I and II, which control core political authority and hold primary responsibility for public and foreign policy decision-making, should be classified as the Core Layer. Layers III and IV, whose actors participate in the distribution of political authority and make partial policy decisions, constitute the Central Layer. Layers V through VII, whose actors do not participate in the direct distribution of political authority but can exert measurable influence over policy outcomes, form the Semi-Peripheral Layer. Finally, Layer VIII consists of the general public, whose members neither participate directly in the distribution of political authority nor exert measurable influence over formal policy outcomes. Within this hierarchical framework, think tanks are situated in Layer VII, placing them within the Semi-Peripheral Layer, as they do not participate in the direct distribution of political authority but can exert significant and measurable influence over policy outcomes.

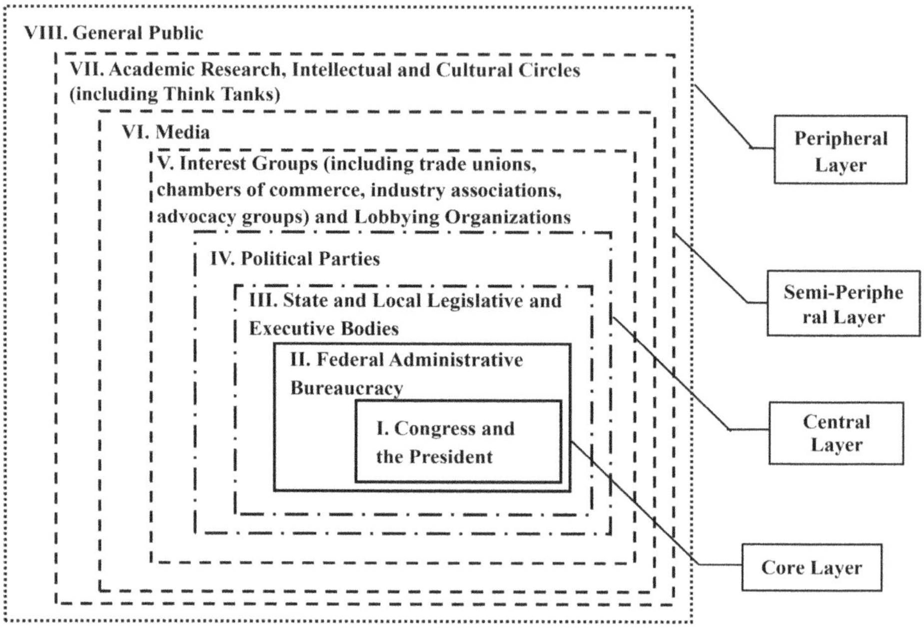

Figure 2.3: The Position of U.S. Think Tanks in the U.S. Political Decision-Making System
Source: Compiled by the author

3.2 The Overall Position of European Think Tanks in the EU's Foreign Policy Decision-Making System and the Overarching Pathways of Their Influence

The EU is an organization with supranational characteristics, constructed by European political elites in accordance with abstract conceptual frameworks, rather than a typical representative democratic structure of a nation-state. Its official decision-making architecture can be divided into at least three concentric components from core to periphery: 1) the three core decision-making bodies of the EU's institutional triad, namely the European Parliament, the Council of the European Union and the European Council, and the European Commission; 2) institutions that participate in decision-making and policy implementation in specific specialized domains of EU policy, including the European Central Bank (ECB), European Bank for Reconstruction and Development (EBRD), European External Action Service (EEAS), and Court of Justice of the European Union (CJEU); and 3) peripheral official EU bodies that exert influence over decision-making, such as the European

Economic and Social Committee (EESC) and European Committee of the Regions (CoR). Within such a convoluted institutional architecture, the EU's decision-making processes and pathways are inevitably less hierarchically structured or clearly delineated than those of the national governments of its member states, thus effectively forming a complex policy labyrinth. To ensure that its decisions are firmly grounded in popular will, the EU has established a multi-level governance structure that encompasses the subnational, national member state, and supranational European integration levels, while advancing its operational functions through institutionalized engagement and interaction with organized civil society. This institutional design has made the EU's decision-making system even more complex and dynamically variable. Table 2.3 delineates the hierarchical position of European think tanks in the EU's decision-making system, and reveals, through this framework, the operational mechanisms of multi-level governance and interest representation embedded within the EU's decision-making apparatus.

Table 2.3: The Hierarchical Position of European Think Tanks in the EU's Decision-Making System

Analysis of Stakeholder Level	Most active and principal stakeholders	Primary modes of activity
EU Decision-Making Level	• National leadership and government departments of member states • Europe-wide interest groups • **Think tank**s at the EU and member state levels • Europe-wide political advocacy organizations • Political groups of the European Parliament	1. Transmission of interest demands 2. Debate on specific policy issues 3. Construction of policy discourse and narratives
Europe-wide Civil Society Level	○ Europe-wide interest groups (i.e. "umbrella groups and peak groups") ○ **Think tanks** and university research institutions at the EU and member state levels ○ Europe-wide political advocacy organizations ○ Europe-wide political parties (Europarties) formed by national political parties of member states	1. Construction of policy discourse and narratives 2. Debate on specific policy issues
Member State Level	• Political parties and parliamentary groups in member state legislatures • Interest groups (including pressure groups and lobbying groups) • **Think tanks** and university research institutions of member states • Non-profit, non-governmental civic advocacy organizations	1. Transmission of interest demands 2. Construction of policy discourse and narratives 3. Debate on specific policy issues
Sub-National Level	○ Sub-national regional branches of political parties ○ Sub-national regional organizations of interest groups	Transmission of interest demands
Grassroots Society Level	• General public	Transmission of interest demands

Source: Compiled by the author

With regard to the essential characteristics of the EU's decision-making mechanisms, there has long been a theoretical debate between two core paradigms: neo-functionalism and intergovernmentalism.① The former paradigm holds that EU decision-making is essentially about the regulation and management of affairs, which falls into the scope of national sovereignty by supranational authorities, while the latter argues that the operation of the EU is the product of inter-state negotiation and compromise, and as such, invariably reflects the intentions and policy preferences of decision-makers in sovereign member states. The structural hierarchy of the EU's refugee policy developed in response to the European migration crisis demonstrates the empirical validity of both the neo-functionalist and intergovernmentalism theoretical paradigms, as the EU concurrently possesses the characteristics of both a supranational entity and an inter-state organization. All policies formulated by the EU can be categorized into levels ranging from the supranational to the subnational. Broadly speaking, policy architectures operating at the supranational level advance in a sustained, relatively stable rhythm, even if the decision-making and implementation process is relatively slow. In contrast, policy architectures operating at the inter-state level are more constrained by member states' calculations of interest distribution and the strength of their willingness to cooperate, which means that not only is their progress slow, but the rhythm of their policy formulation and operation is also extremely unstable, marked by frequent disputes, impasses, dramatic fluctuations, and high levels of uncertainty.

In general terms, the pathways through which European think tanks exert influence over EU decision-making can be broadly divided into two core routes: the National Route (which is also called "the member-state route"), and the Brussels Route. The overall operation of these pathways within the political systems of the EU and its member states is illustrated in Figure 2.4. These two routes are utilized not only by European think tanks to transmit influence to the EU, but also by the full range of European advocacy groups, NGOs, interest groups, lobbying firms, and public relations consultancies seeking to exert their own influence over EU decision-making. For this reason, these two routes delineate the primary

① Ernst Haas, "International Integration: The European and Universal Process", *International Organization*, Vol. 15, No. 3, 1961, pp. 366-392; L. N. Lindberg and S. A. Scheingold, *Europe's Would-be Polity*, Englewood Cliffs of New Jersey: Prentice-Hall, 1970; Stanley Hoffmann, "Obstinate or Obsolete? The Fate of the Nation-State and the Case of Western Europe", *Daedalus*, Vol. 95, No. 3, 1966, pp. 862-915; A. S. Milard, *The European Rescue of Nation State*, London: Routledge, 2000 contours of influence transmission in the labyrinth of the EU's decision-making architecture.

As illustrated in Figure 2.4, the National Route refers to the mechanism through which think tanks in EU member states can leverage their home country's specific decision-making advisory and interest articulation mechanisms to pass on their institutional positions, analytical perspectives, and policy preferences to the national government's decision-making authorities. This process shapes the position, stance, and behavioral patterns of the member state when it participates in the intergovernmental meetings of the European Council and the Council of the European Union, and in turn influences ultimate EU policy outcomes. The Brussels Route, by contrast, refers to the mechanism through which think tanks exert direct influence over EU decision-making by leveraging the existing institutional architecture of the EU's multi-level governance system, through Europe-wide communication and engagement platforms, including the epistemic communities that underpin EU decision-making. Specifically, the Brussels Route encompasses several core operational modalities. First, think tanks can participate in the full range of advisory and dialogue mechanisms hosted by the EU's core and peripheral decision-making bodies, such as joining the Social Dialogue mechanism of the European Economic and Social Committee (EESC), which is the EU's peripheral consultative body, or participating in the Public Consultation mechanisms launched by the European Commission for major policy decision issues, thereby shaping EU policy outcomes through these formal institutional channels. Second, think tanks can exert direct influence over EU decision-making through the EU-level interest representation system, by leveraging Europe-wide federated organizations or operational networks collectively established by civil society groups including interest groups and advocacy organizations from EU member states.

These two routes exhibit measurable differences in multiple dimensions, including the timeline and effectiveness of influence generation, and the operational costs associated with deployment. By leveraging the Brussels Route, through close engagement and direct observation of the EU's official decision-making bodies and Europe-wide think tank collaboration networks, European think tanks can exert direct and regular influence over the EU's day-to-day decision-making activities, particularly during the core stages of the policy cycle such as problem identification and agenda-setting, delivering relatively rapid and tangible policy impacts. By contrast, the National Route requires the transmission of preferences, demands, and normative frameworks through the member state government via mechanisms including the summits of the European Council and the meetings of the Council of the European Union. This creates a circuitous and lengthy pathway for influence, with an additional layer of intermediation through the national member state government, which means that influence generation takes significantly longer, delivers slower results, and in some cases, produces only limited tangible impact. That said, effective operation of the Brussels Route requires long-term monitoring and in-depth understanding of the unique structural architecture of the EU's decision-making labyrinth, as well as timely and precise insight into the rhythm and latest developments of EU political decision-making, which often requires the permanent placement of staff in Brussels. These requirements create substantial barriers for many member state think tanks. In other words, the knowledge reserves, accumulated experience, and financial support required to deploy each of the two routes are fundamentally different. As a result of these structural differences, think tanks operating at different levels show varying preferences for the two routes across different policy domains and issue areas.

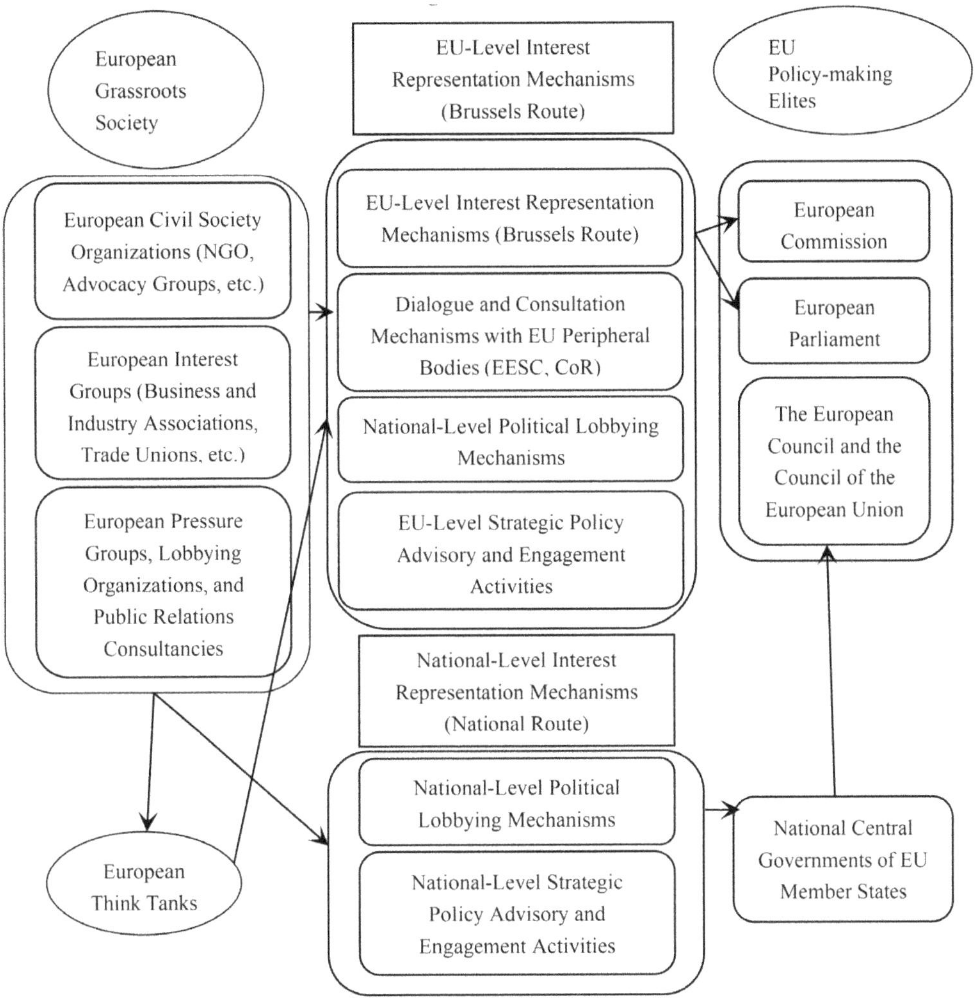

Figure 2.4: Overall Roadmap of the Brussels Route and National Route for European Think Tanks' Influence over EU Decision-Making

Source: Compiled by the author

Most EU-level think tanks are headquartered in Brussels, which gives them unparalleled ease of access for taking the Brussels Route. The European Policy Centre (EPC), for example, had its offices located directly across the street from the headquarters of the European Commission, just one Schuman Roundabout away from the Council of the European Union and the European External Action Service, in 2014. This enabled the EPC to easily engage in face-to-face interaction with EU decision-making officials with only a short walk. The Schuman Roundabout in Brussels and its surrounding streets, most notably Rue de la Loi, host a dense concentration of these think tanks, in a dynamic analogous to K Street in Washington, D.C., the capital of the United States. EU-level think tanks, however, focus their research exclusively on EU policy issues and European regional affairs, and their research domains and thematic priorities are often significantly detached from the decision-making focus of the national governments of EU member states. This means that they rarely have the opportunity to deploy the National Route, and instead almost exclusively utilize the Brussels Route, concentrating all of their institutional resources on engagement with the EU's decision-making authorities.

Think tanks based in EU member states are generally not headquartered in Brussels, but rather in major cities in their home countries, thus keeping them geographically and operationally distant from the EU's core decision-making bodies. Effective deployment of the Brussels Route requires not only the establishment of a permanent office in Brussels, but also the development of a specialized team to navigate the unfamiliar decision-making labyrinth of the EU and Europe-wide think tank networks. While this route can deliver relatively direct and tangible influence outcomes, it also incurs substantial operational costs. On the other hand, member state think tanks are far more familiar with their home country's interest representation mechanisms and the operational architecture of national political decision-making, and maintain more extensive connections with domestic decision-makers and civil society stakeholders. Deployment of the National Route, while requiring a longer timeline for influence generation and inevitably causing slower result delivery, is a familiar, low-barrier operational model with significantly lower associated costs. For these reasons, member state think tanks often tend to utilize the National Route for policy domains and interest claims that do not attract widespread attention and intensive debate across Europe, or to exert influence through the EU-level organizational channels of other types of actors including interest groups. When it comes to policy domains and issues with Europe-wide relevance, such as the EU's external economic negotiations, foreign and security policy architecture, and refugee and migration policy, by contrast, these member state think tanks are inclined to place far greater strategic emphasis on deployment of the Brussels Route. In addition, the position of the member state itself in the EU's decision-making system also shapes the attitude of its think tanks toward the two routes. Germany, for example, occupies a dominant position in the decision-making process for many major EU policy issues, and German think tanks accordingly place significant emphasis on the Brussels Route. The United Kingdom, by contrast, only assumes a relatively peripheral position in the EU, and many prominent UK think tanks, including the Royal Institute of International Affairs (Chatham House), therefore place limited emphasis on the Brussels Route. They maintain no permanent offices in Brussels, with minimal participation in Europe-wide think tank collaboration networks.

3.3 Specific Pathways Through Which European Think Tanks Exert Influence over EU Decision-Making via Diverse Modalities

To clearly delineate the operational trajectory of the Brussels Route in the labyrinth of EU decision-making, this chapter links the 13 modalities of European think tank influence over EU decision-making as categorized in Figure 2.2, to the specific targets and audiences of influence transmission within the EU's decision-making system via the Brussels Route. It conducts a one-to-one corresponding analysis of these linkages, and develops a comprehensive map of the overall operational mechanisms of the Brussels Route as illustrated in Figure 2.5. As the map shows, different influence tactics and modalities act on distinct components of the EU's policy community, and impact different parts of the EU's core decision-making bodies through specific mechanisms embedded into this community.

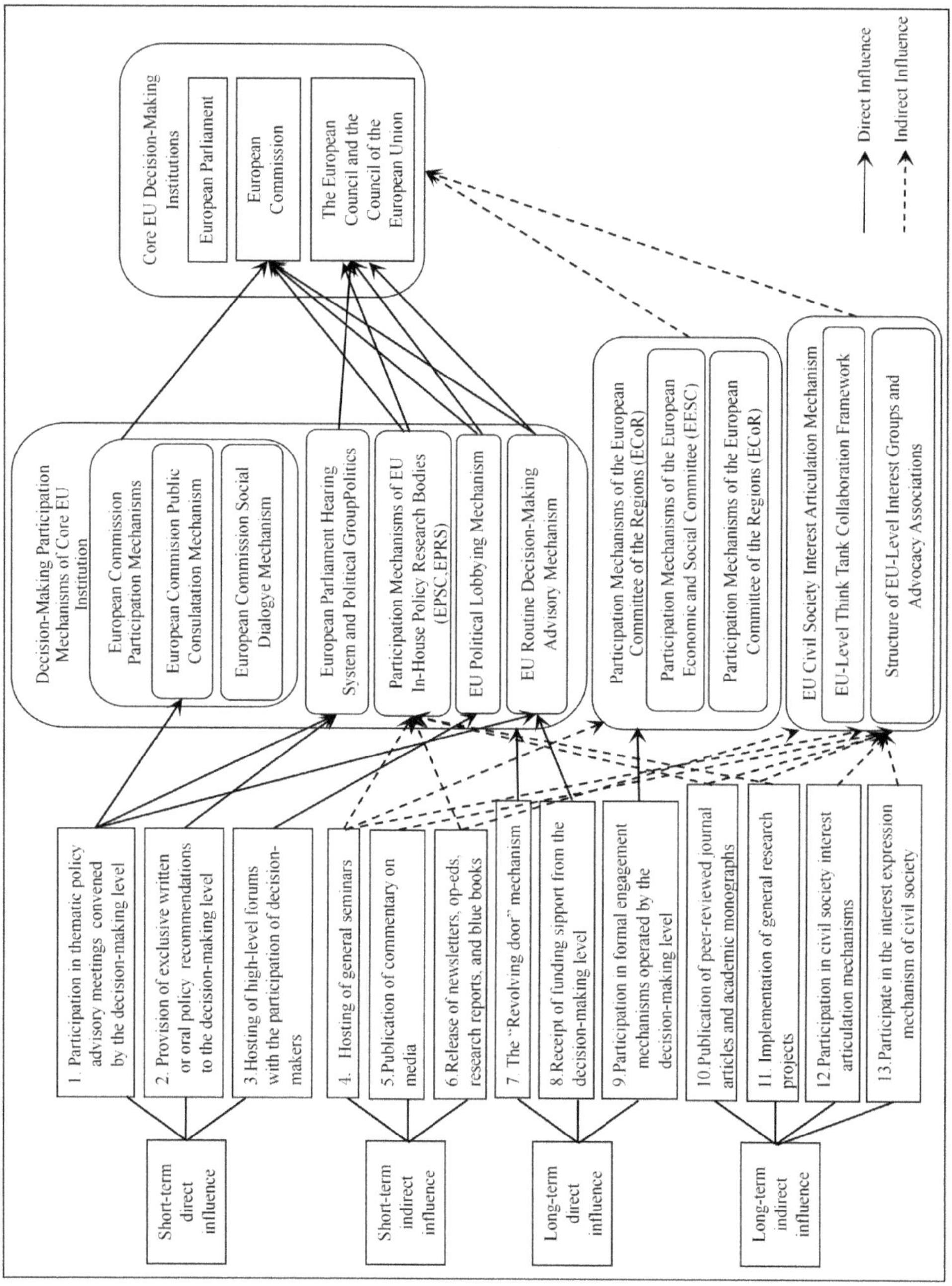

Figure 2.5: Operational Mechanisms of European Think Tanks' Influence over EU Decision-Making via the Brussels Route

Source: Compiled and created by the author

As illustrated in Figure 2.5, a one-to-one corresponding analysis of the 13 modalities of European think tank influence over EU decision-making as categorized in Figure 2.2, when aligned with the various components of the operational mechanisms of the Brussels Route, reveals the overall structural architecture of the pathways through which European think tanks, including both the so-called Brussels think tanks at the EU level and national member state think tanks, exert influence over EU decision-making. Within this structure, different influence tactics and modalities act on distinct components of the EU's policy community, and exert their influence on different parts of the EU's core decision-making bodies through specific mechanisms embedded into this community. The ultimate target of influence for think tanks operating via the Brussels Route is the European Commission and the European Parliament, the two core bodies in the EU's institutional triad, with the European Commission's relevant directorates-general as the primary focus. The Council of the European Union, by contrast, remains largely outside of this operational mechanism, as it possesses no formal institutional architecture for direct engagement with EU-level organized civil society. In practice, the Council of the European Union is subject to direct influence from the national governments of member states, and as such, remains the ultimate target of the National Route. That said, the National Route operates through the layer of the member state's interest representation mechanisms and national political decision-making architecture, and the specific operational structures of political decision-making may vary significantly, and in some cases dramatically, across individual member states. This structural variation means that it is impossible to develop a universally applicable operational mechanism map for the National Route. In Chapter 6 of this study, based on a detailed analysis of the UK's political decision-making architecture, this book presents a structural roadmap of the operational mechanisms of the National Route for UK think tanks before the UK's actual exit from the EU in 2020, and elucidates the precise nature and function of the National Route.

Chapter 3: The Strategic Dynamics Driving the EU's Formulation of Defensive Economic Policy toward China

At a relatively early stage, the EU's decision-making elites had already developed a clear inclination toward constructing a more systematic and comprehensive framework of economic policy toward China. While continuing to seek commercial benefits from trade and investment relations with China, the EU also moved gradually to refine a set of trade-protectionist and economic-nationalist policy instruments directed at China. In the first half of 2012, at a time when the European economy remained mired in persistent stagnation, the EU's decision-making body launched deliberations on this issue and considered a comprehensive revision and substantial updating of the existing policy framework toward China. Owing, however, to internal resistance and controversy, only part of the envisaged measures was formally adopted.

Between 2016 and 2018, under the successive shocks of a series of internal and external crises—including Brexit, the refugee influx, terrorist attacks, and the arrival of the Trump administration—the EU's decision-making leadership steadily sped up its policy process toward China and began to establish a detailed and systematic "defensive" economic policy framework spanning trade, investment, industry, technology transfer, and intellectual property protection. This process laid the groundwork for the publication of the *EU-China Strategic Outlook* in March 2019.

The EU's ability, between 2016 and 2018, to gradually complete its institutional build-up and establish a layered and relatively coherent "defensive" economic policy framework toward China was attributable not only to profound changes in the broader internal and external environment, but also to the gradual shift of the EU's own situational assessments and strategic perceptions. To accurately capture the defining characteristics of EU decision-making in this domain, it is essential to pay close attention to the internal and external contexts that shape its policy choices, carefully examine the EU's situational assessments and strategic perceptions, and, on that basis, systematically outline the structure and core components of its "defensive" economic policy framework toward China.

In short, such an inquiry requires tracing the direction and pace of the internal and external changes that shaped EU decision-making, so as to identify the interactive mechanisms through which contextual change drives the decision-making process.

I. The Contextual Factors Shaping the EU's China-related Decision-Making, 2008-2018

Between the 2008 global financial crisis and the full onset of the Trump administration's trade war and strategic competition with China in 2018, the EU went through profound structural changes in both its internal political landscape and its external strategic environment. These changes were accompanied by significant shifts in the EU's relations with China and the United States, while trilateral geopolitical competition among them intensified as evolving power balances were entwined with the rise of industries linked to "emerging disruptive technologies." Collectively, these developments reoriented the EU's assessment of its strategic environment and its broader strategic perceptions, prompting adjustment-and in some respects, a revamping-of its economic policy framework toward China.

1.1 Dramatic Shifts in the EU's Internal Political Landscape

The 2008 global financial crisis and the 2009-2010 European sovereign debt crisis exacerbated Europe-wide public discontent with both globalization and the EU-led process of regional integration. Particularly after 2014-2015, as Europe was successively confronted with terrorist attacks, the refugee influx, and Brexit, European societies became increasingly polarized, while populist forces-on both the left and the right-gained momentum, leading to profound shifts in the European political landscape.

Donald Trump's election as President of the United States in November 2016 further emboldened these populist currents. Populist parties gradually entered mainstream politics, with some even seizing power through elections. This trend spread from countries on the geographic and political peripheries of Europe—such as Norway and Finland in Northern

Europe, Poland and Hungary in Central and Eastern Europe, Greece in Southeastern Europe, and non-EU Switzerland—toward the core states of Central and Western Europe, particularly those at the heartland of the EU and the euro area, including France, Germany, the Netherlands, and Italy.

Between the first half of 2017 and the end of 2018, three core EU member states-the Netherlands, France, and Germany-held parliamentary elections. In all the cases, populist parties that were previously excluded from mainstream politics, such as the Dutch Party for Freedom, France's National Front, and Germany's Alternative for Germany, secured substantial vote shares and emerged as major parliamentary forces (see Table 3.1). The most dramatic shift, however, occurred in Italy. Following the parliamentary elections of March 2018, two major populist parties that strongly opposed European integration and advocated withdrawal from both the EU and the euro area—the League and the Five Star Movement—won 50.1 percent of the seats in the Chamber of Deputies and 49.8 percent in the Senate, effectively resetting the direction of Italian politics and marking an unprecedented change of the Italian political landscape.

During the decade from 2008 to 2018, populist parties came out of the political wasteland and gained prominence, emerging from the fringes of the political establishment to enter the mainstream of European politics. This trend signaled both Europe's deepening internal crisis and the EU's mounting challenges, which became visible in the following ways.

First, intensifying social fragmentation and political polarization in the EU, which gave rise to three prominent layers of structural contradiction. In the decade from 2008 to 2018, the wave of accelerating globalization since the breakup of the Soviet Union in 1991 and the collapse of the bipolar international system met with successive setbacks. Meanwhile, the dividends generated by technological innovation and globalization-fueled economic growth were largely exhausted, while the accumulated tensions of this phase of globalization reached a breaking point. In this decade, three major layers of contradiction-all rooted in globalization-emerged in Europe's social structure and political architecture, collectively defining the basic spectrum of European populist politics.

The first layer of contradiction arose from the sharp widening of wealth disparities, manifesting as a conflict between domestic elites and grassroots populations, or, in other words, between establishment and anti-establishment forces. Domestic elites, generally well-educated and capable of participating in the international division of labor, accrued substantial wealth and often wielded significant political influence, aligning themselves with the dominant liberal and pluralist ideologies. By contrast, grassroots populations, largely composed of blue-collar workers and small proprietors facing unstable employment and precarious incomes, experienced relative impoverishment as a consequence of globalization and were in a disadvantaged position in both political and discursive arenas, which gave them incentives to embrace populist ideologies. The second layer of contradiction consisted of the complex ethno-cultural and religious tensions between domestic grassroots populations and incoming migrant communities. While some migrants were able to integrate into the elite hierarchy, the majority engaged in low-skilled labor and thus occupied positions similar to those of domestic grassroots groups, which subjected them to employment instability and economic insecurity. These tensions were further exacerbated by differences in lifestyles, cultural values, and psychological dispositions, which in turn led to cultural and religious antagonisms. The third layer of contradiction reflected the resistance and hostility of domestic actors toward external elite forces that promote globalization and regional integration. While domestic elites broadly supported globalization and regional integration, a minority-including segments of the traditional manufacturing business community and elites committed to preserving national cultural values-aligned with grassroots populations in opposing the rapid expansion of globalization and regional integration. Together, they stood opposite those external forces driving these processes, particularly supranational structures such as the EU and their international elite backers.

Domestic actors who perceive their interests as adversely affected in these three layers of contradiction are the social base of European populist parties. Those who emphasize the first layer of contradiction tend to support left-wing populist parties and ideologies, while those who stress the second layer are more likely to back right-wing populism. However, both left- and right-wing populist forces exhibit little divergence in their perceptions of the third layer of contradiction.

Second, growing public opinion support for the incorporation of populist parties into mainstream politic across Europe. As the three layers of contradiction generated by globalization progressively gained traction, rising populism would still emerge as a salient trend in European politics even in the absence of Brexit or the election of Donald Trump. On November 24, 2016, the *Economist* released the results of a public opinion survey which it conducted through interviews across 25 countries (comprising all G20 members except EU states, along with Sweden, Peru, Israel, Poland, Belgium, and Hungary) between September 23 and October 7, 2016,①. According to the survey, 60% of respondents believed that their countries were on the wrong track, while only 40% considered their countries to be developing in the right direction. In 14 countries, including 10 European countries, the proportion of respondents holding the former view was higher than 60%. In these countries, respondents identified unemployment, income inequality, healthcare provision, and immigration as their primary concerns, all of which were directly linked to the three layers of contradiction outlined above. In particular, in France, Germany, and the United Kingdom, approximately 90%, over 70%, and around 60% of the respondents, respectively believed that their countries were on the wrong path. This survey gave a clear picture of widespread dissatisfaction in the European publics, which effectively provided fertile ground for the rise of populist politics.

In Italy, public discontent was especially pronounced, marked by a sweeping wave of public disillusionment with the EU. Since 2014-2015, multiple major EU policy measures-including mandatory refugee quotas, the imposition of fiscal austerity policies on Italy, and euro area monetary policies largely shaped by Germany-have provoked strong public resentment in Italy. Many Italians believe that countries like Germany have leveraged the single European currency and rigid common monetary policies, along with their technological advantages and economies of scale in medium- to high-end manufacturing, to export large volumes of industrial goods to Italy and generate substantial trade surpluses. Their perception is that Italy has incurred considerable losses from euro area membership while Germany has disproportionately benefited. As early as March 2016, the European polling firm Ipsos reported that the proportion of Italians expressing confidence in the EU declined from 73% in 2010 to 54% in 2014, and further to 40% in 2016.② On February 28,

① "What the World Worries About: Though Populism is Rife, the Causes Vary from Country to Country," the Economist, November 24, 2016, https://www.economist.com/graphic-detail/2016/11/24/what-the-world-worries-about, accessed on March 29, 2026.

② ANSA English, "How Italy 'Fell out of Love' with EU", Ansa Editorial, March 17th, 2016. https://www.ansa.it/english/news/politics/2016/03/17/how-italy-fell-out-of-love-with-eu-ft_1e699d00-b105-4931-b45d-

2018, the European public opinion platform Eupinions projected that if a referendum on EU membership were then held in Italy, only 56% of respondents would vote in favor of remaining in the Union. While these figures may not be entirely precise, they nonetheless reflected a profound shift in the Italian public's prevalent attitude toward the EU.①

Third, consolidated populism foothold in mainstream European politics. This makes populist forces an important and increasingly influential player in shaping both EU-level and member state political decision-making. In fact, as early as around 2010, scholars already begun to anticipate the rise of populist forces-particularly right-wing populism-in Western Europe. Between 2010 and 2011, Matthew Goodwin of the University of Nottingham conducted a year-long study of extremist populist parties in Europe. Commissioned by the Royal Institute of International Affairs (Chatham House), the study culminated in a report published in September 2011, which argued that "populist extremists in Europe have moved from the margins into the mainstream," predicting the continual expansion of populist parties over the coming decades, which would profoundly shape a whole generation of European youth. Subsequent developments in European populism after 2011 have largely borne out this prediction.②

While establishment elites and political leaders in Europe have repeatedly emphasized that populism should not be accommodated in mainstream politics, populist forces have nonetheless become firmly embedded within it, emerging as a formidable and unavoidable political force. Given that most European countries operate under parliamentary systems, within the short span from early 2017 to the end of 2018, populist parties in core EU and euro area countries entered mainstream politics through parliamentary elections, becoming important actors at multiple levels of legislative bodies-from national to local-and playing a key role in shaping dominant political discourse and influencing agenda-setting at both national and EU levels. Even where excluded from coalition governments by establishment

---

dc788793cd77.html, accessed March 27, 2026.

① Catherine E. de Vries and Isabell Hoffmann, "Dissatisfied and Disenchanted: How Italians View European and National Politics", Eupinions Brief, February 28, 2018, https://eupinions.eu/de/text/dissatisfied-and-disenchanted, accessed on March 27, 2026.

② Mathew Goodwin, Right Response: Understanding and Countering Populist Extremism in Europe, A Chatham House Report, London: Chatham House (The Royal Institute of International Affairs), September 2011, pp. 12-22.

elites, these parties still managed to steadily move closer to executive power. Following Brexit and the election of Donald Trump in 2016-2017, populist parties had their greatest impact in Italy, where the League and the Five Star Movement not only controlled parliament in 2018 but also assumed executive authority and entered government. By comparison, populist influence was weaker in Germany, yet even there, the radical populist Alternative for Germany secured 13.3% of seats in the Bundestag in 2018, becoming the third largest party. The rise of populist parties thus signifies the quiet intensification of a crisis capable of profoundly challenging the existing order of the EU. In the 2019 and 2025 elections to the European Parliament, radical right-wing populist parties further increased their share of seats, continuing to expand their influence.

Table 3.1: The Status of Major Populist Parties in Selected European Countries (2016-2018)

Attribute / Country	**Name of Populist Party**	**Party Leader**	**Political Ideological Affiliation**	**The Party's Reaction to the Election of Donald Trump**	**Position of the Party in the National Political System after the Most Recent General Election before the End of 2018**
Germany	Alternative for Germany (AfD)	Frauke Petry	Radical right-wing; anti-immigration; strongly nationalist	The party believed that it shared certain ideological affinities with Trump.	Following the German federal election of October 2017, the party obtained 13.3% of the seats in the Bundestag, becoming the third largest party in parliament.
France	National Front (FN), renamed National Rally on June 1, 2018	Marine Le Pen	Radical right-wing; anti-immigration; anti-EU; anti-globalization	"Trump's victory has brought hope to those who have become disillusioned with globalization."	In the two rounds of the French presidential election in April-May 2017, party leader Le Pen received the second highest number of votes, only behind the eventual winner Emmanuel Macron. This brought the party close to the position of being the second largest political force. In the new National Assembly elected in June 2017, the party's influence somewhat declined, securing 8 seats, but it remained one of the country's major political parties.
United Kingdom	UK Independence Party (UKIP)	Nigel Farage and Gerard Batten	Radical right-wing; anti-immigration; anti-EU	Farage was the first European politician to visit Trump after the results of the U.S. presidential election were announced.	After the 2016 referendum on the United Kingdom's withdrawal from the EU, the party gradually receded from the center of British politics; following the 2017 UK general election, it held no seats in the House of Commons.

Country \ Attribute	Name of Populist Party	Party Leader	Political Ideological Affiliation	The Party's Reaction to the Election of Donald Trump	Position of the Party in the National Political System after the Most Recent General Election before the End of 2018
The Netherlands	Party for Freedom (PVV)	Geert Wilders	Radical right-wing	"People have grown tired of politicians who turn a deaf ear to the concerns of ordinary citizens."	After the Dutch parliamentary election of March 2017, the party secured 13.1% of the seats in the House of Representatives, becoming the second largest party in the Dutch parliament.
Austria	Freedom Party of Austria (FPÖ)	Norbert Hofer	Radical right-wing	Expressed support	After the Austrian parliamentary election of October 2017, the party obtained 28.4% of the seats, becoming the third largest party in parliament.
Italy	Five Star Movement	Beppe Grillo	Radical left-wing	Expressed support	After the Italian parliamentary election of March 2018, the party secured 32.68% of the seats in the Chamber of Deputies, becoming the largest party in Italy
Spain	Unidos Podemos	Pablo Iglesias	Radical left-wing	Expressed support	After the Spanish parliamentary election of 2016, the party obtained 21.15% of the seats in the Congress of Deputies and 8.6% of the seats in the Senate, becoming the third largest political party in Spain.

Source: Compiled by the author

1.2 The United States' Retreat from the International Multilateral Trading System and the Architecture of Global Economic Governance

At the very outset of its first term in office, the Trump administration moved to repudiate and disparage the international multilateral trading system-represented most prominently by the World Trade Organization (WTO), as well as the broader architecture of global economic governance, while simultaneously setting in motion a policy framework grounded in economic nationalism, state mercantilism, and trade protectionism, and relying on unilateral economic statecraft to advance U.S. demands and safeguard U.S. national interests. The external economic policy of the first Trump administration embodied several core elements, which profoundly shaped the EU's assessment of the future global economic trajectory.

First, it sought to deny the authority of the WTO, hollow out its rule-based system, and advance the doctrine of "America First." Trump and his first-term governing team deliberately endeavored to weaken the authority of the WTO's regulatory framework, particularly the legitimacy of its dispute settlement mechanism, while reinforcing the exclusive sovereignty of the U.S. government in the conduct of external economic affairs-especially in the domains of trade and investment-in order to lay the groundwork for the implementation of more assertive protectionist measures. *The 2017 Trade Policy Agenda of the President of the United States*, issued by the Office of the United States Trade Representative in March 2017, explicitly asserted that WTO decisions do not exert direct binding force upon the United States; that WTO rules are to be deemed invalid whenever they conflict with U.S. law or diminish rights previously enjoyed by the United States; and that rulings concerning trade disputes between the United States and other countries will not be honored if the U.S. Congress considers them to contravene domestic law or undermine national interests. The document further declared that "the Trump Administration will aggressively defend American sovereignty over matters of trade policy".[①] This constituted a highly significant signal, indicating that whereas the Obama administration had sought to circumvent the WTO framework indirectly through initiatives such as the Trans-Pacific Partnership and the Transatlantic Trade and Investment Partnership, the Trump administration would, in its external economic policymaking, openly and forcefully challenge the authority of the WTO while advancing a doctrine centered on the primacy of U.S. interests. The *2018 Trade Policy Agenda*, released in March 2018, went further by accusing the WTO not only of failing to discipline certain "market-distorting" economies, but also of enabling such economies to obtain "unfair advantages" relative to market-oriented states such as the United States. In addition, it alleged that these countries exploited the WTO framework to create market barriers, engage in dumping and subsidization, and pursue "other market-distorting practices," thereby inflicting serious harm upon U.S. interests.[②]

Second, the administration significantly intensified the United States' trade

① Office of the United States Trade Representative, *2017 Trade Policy Agenda and the 2016 Annual Report of the President of the United States on the Trade Agreements Program*, pp. 1-14.

② Office of the United States Trade Representative, *2018 Trade Policy Agenda and the 2017 Annual Report of the President of the United States on the Trade Agreements Program*, pp. 37-60.

protectionist policy apparatus, adopting a hardline stance even toward its allies. The first Trump administration devoted substantial administrative resources to constructing a more comprehensive and tightly coordinated protectionist policy system, with the aim of minimizing the impact of imported goods on domestic sectors such as agriculture and labor-intensive large-scale manufacturing, while simultaneously encouraging the repatriation of investment to the United States. Adopting forceful language, *The 2017 Trade Policy Agenda* emphatically discussed U.S. legal instruments, including anti-dumping and countervailing duty measures, which were designed to counter "unfair trade". It underscored the administration's intention to make extensive use of the broad authorities granted under Sections 201 and 301 of the Trade Act of 1974 in an effort to impose strong retaliatory measures against foreign products and trade practices deemed "unfair" by the Trump administration. The document unequivocally stated that the administration would not "turn a blind eye" to unfair trade practices that harm ordinary Americans "for the sake of hypothetical geopolitical advantages." This position implied that even close U.S. allies—such as Japan, South Korea, and Canada—could find themselves in opposition to the United States as a consequence of its uncompromising protectionist policies. In early June 2018, the United States formally imposed punitive tariffs on steel and aluminum imports from the EU.

Third, the administration exerted pressure on other countries to reduce economic intervention and conform to U.S.-defined principles of "fair trade." The first Trump administration pressed foreign governments to meet U.S. demands in areas including exchange rate policy, export subsidies, the role of state-owned enterprises, market access for U.S. firms, and technical regulatory regimes governing trade. *The 2017 Trade Policy Agenda* criticized, albeit without explicitly naming them, both Japan and the EU, arguing that Japan had been reluctant to open certain sectors—such as agriculture—to U.S. exports, while the EU had stubbornly adhered to its complex system of technical standards and regulatory frameworks, refusing to align them with U.S. rules, thus constituting "unfair trade practices.". The document pledged to adopt robust measures to address these issues. During his meeting with Canadian Prime Minister Justin Trudeau on February 13, 2017, Trump emphasized the need to establish a durable "level playing field" in bilateral economic relations—a formulation that had previously been employed by the Obama administration primarily in criticizing countries unwilling to grant full market access and national treatment to U.S. investors, but rarely applied to Western strategic allies. The early use of such rhetoric by the Trump administration toward allies such as Japan, the EU, and Canada signaled the beginning of preparations for broader trade confrontations. In June 2018, the administration formally initiated the imposition of high tariffs targeting the EU, particularly on steel, aluminum, and automobiles, setting off an unprecedented shock to transatlantic economic relations.

Fourth, the United States sought to replace the existing global multilateral trading system with U.S.-led, small-group bilateral or plurilateral arrangements. The first Trump administration expressed a strong desire to dismantle the existing multilateral trading order and to reconstruct regional and interregional frameworks of economic integration and international cooperation—particularly in the domains of trade and investment-by substituting, to the greatest extent possible, U.S.-dominated and exclusionary bilateral or limited multilateral mechanisms for the WTO-centered system, in a bid to address what it perceived as the structurally disadvantageous position of the United States, characterized by persistent capital outflows and trade deficits. Immediately upon taking office in 2017, Trump announced the United States' withdrawal from the Trans-Pacific Partnership, and in 2018 concluded the United States-Mexico-Canada Agreement (USMCA) with Canada and Mexico, replacing the North American Free Trade Agreement that had been in force since 1994. It altered the previously more open and preferential access granted to neighboring economies. From the summer of 2017 onward, the Trump administration instructed the Office of the United States Trade Representative and the Department of Commerce to conduct investigations in preparation for trade sanctions against major global economies, including China and the EU. On July 2, 2018, the administration further drafted *The Fair and Reciprocal Tariff Act*, which would grant the president sweeping authority to unilaterally set tariff levels, with the explicit aim of circumventing and effectively hollowing out the institutional role of the World Trade Organization.

1.3 The Deterioration of Transatlantic Relations

On March 17-18, 2017, German Chancellor Angela Merkel visited the United States, with the expectation of easing transatlantic tensions and preserving the existing framework of U.S.-EU relations. However, the visit not only failed to achieve its intended purpose, but also exposed profound divergences between the two sides. Merkel's visit thus marked a turning point of considerable symbolic and substantive significance, as transatlantic relations shifted from a superficially harmonious alliance to an increasingly conflictual and adversarial configuration. In fact, since the United Kingdom initiated the Brexit process in late June 2016, the balance of power between the United States and Europe had already begun to tilt progressively in favor of the former, with Europe becoming increasingly disadvantaged relative to the United States across economic and strategic-security domains. Meanwhile, the first Trump administration's growing hostility toward Europe further accelerated the widening and deepening of transatlantic fissures after early 2017. More specifically, the deterioration of U.S.-EU relations manifested itself in several key aspects.

First, the rift between the United States and Europe in the realm of strategic security deepened continuously. In the security domain, the U.S. attitude toward the North Atlantic Treaty Organization—the cornerstone of the transatlantic security alliance—shifted from what had previously been near-unconditional support and maintenance to a more conditional and qualified endorsement, constituting an unprecedented shift that signaled a substantial downgrading of Europe's position within the U.S. global security architecture, while simultaneously deepening the sense of strategic unease among the highest decision-making circles in the EU, as well as in France and Germany. At the outset of Merkel's March 2017 visit, European actors—from political leadership to business communities and broader society—had widely hoped to hear a firm commitment from President Trump in support of NATO; yet his statements proved deeply disappointing to the European side. During the joint meeting on March 17, 2017, although Trump expressed nominal support for NATO, he explicitly emphasized that certain member states had failed to meet their defense spending obligations, claiming that they had "owed a lot of money for many years" and that this situation was "unfair to the United States," further stating bluntly that "countries that owe money must pay." While Trump did not elaborate in detail, the severity of his language was highly unusual.①

On March 16, 2017, the day before Trump met Merkel, the U.S. administration released the federal budget proposal for Fiscal Year 2018, which increased defense spending

① The White House, Remarks, Joint Press Conference with President Trump and German Chancellor Merkel, March 17, 2017.

by $54 billion, an approximately ten percent rise compared to 2017. The juxtaposition of a substantial increase in U.S. military expenditure with explicit demands for greater financial contributions from European NATO members signaled two developments highly unfavorable to Europe in the evolving geopolitical landscape: on the one hand, Europe was becoming progressively less important to U.S. strategic priorities, as the Trump administration, from 2017 onward, reoriented its global security focus toward the Asia-Pacific region—particularly areas adjacent to China's southeastern coastline—while steadily reducing the allocation of military resources to Europe; on the other hand, following the outbreak of the Ukraine crisis in 2014, the geopolitical environment to Europe's east had become increasingly fragmented and unstable, generating persistent anxiety among EU member states, which initially expected the Trump administration to adopt a firm stance toward Russia, only to find instead that it showed little inclination to constrain Russia for the sake of European strategic interests and, on the contrary, engaged in frequent contacts that raised concerns about potential compromises at Europe's expense, further exacerbating the deterioration of Europe's surrounding strategic environment. The matter became more complicated when Trump announced in May 2018 the withdrawal of the United States from the Joint Comprehensive Plan of Action—an agreement highly valued by the EU—, and later, in mid-July 2020, proposed the withdrawal of a significant number of U.S. troops stationed in Germany, developments that collectively deepened mutual distrust across the Atlantic.

Second, contradictions and antagonisms between the United States and Europe in the economic domain also worsened. In the trade and investment domains, after Trump took office in 2017 onward, it became increasingly unlikely that transatlantic economic cooperation would deepen or that the existing frameworks governing trade, finance, and investment would head for further liberalization. Indeed, the severity of U.S. protectionist measures directed at Europe was, in certain aspects, comparable to those applied to Mexico and China. During his meeting with Merkel on March 17, 2017, Trump did not explicitly announce the termination of negotiations on the Transatlantic Trade and Investment Partnership, but he did sharply criticize the North American Free Trade Agreement—characterizing it as "a disaster" for the United States—and expressed dissatisfaction with Germany's use of free trade arrangements to develop its manufacturing sector, which he associated with persistent U.S. trade deficits. The following day, at the first G20 meeting of finance ministers and central bank governors held in Baden, Germany, U.S. Treasury Secretary Steven Mnuchin, newly appointed by the Trump administration, made clear his opposition to trade liberalization. At his insistence, the meeting's joint communiqué dropped the phrase "oppose all forms of protectionism" and replaced it with a sentence emphasizing that trade should more directly serve domestic economic interests, which was an unprecedented shift in the history of G20 declarations. Throughout Trump's first term, the United States and the EU hovered on the brink of a trade war, with further disputes arising in June 2020 over digital taxation.

As illustrated in Figures 3.2 and 3.3, from early 2016 through mid-2017, the EU consistently maintained a substantial surplus in goods trade with the United States, with Germany accounting for nearly half of the EU's total surplus. Moreover, the scale of these surpluses exhibited minimal fluctuation, generally varying by no more than 0.4-0.5 percentage points. France's surplus with the United States was significantly smaller and somewhat more variable, though even its fluctuations remained within a range of approximately 1.5-1.6 percentage points and displayed clear cyclical patterns. These data show that, at least in the domain of goods trade, Europe enjoyed a pronounced surplus relative to the United States, reflecting a structurally imbalanced transatlantic trade relationship that persisted up to the beginning of Trump's second term in early 2025.

Figure 3.1: Monthly Changes of the Surpluses of the EU, Germany, and France in their Goods Trade with the United States, January 2016-April 2017 (Unit: US$ million)

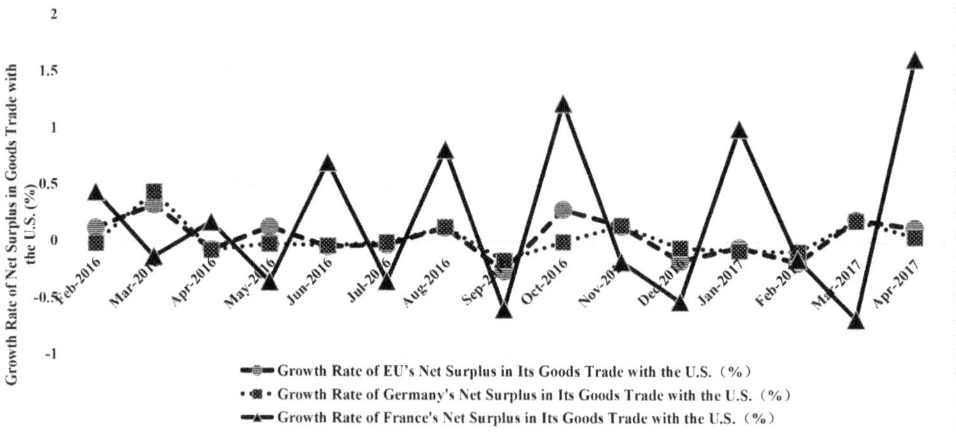

Figure 3.2: Monthly Changes in the Growth Rates of the Surpluses of the EU, Germany, and France in their Goods Trade with the United States, February 2016-April 2017 (%)

Source: Compiled and calculated by the author based on statistical data provided by the United States Census Bureau

Confronted with such pronounced imbalances in transatlantic trade, Trump, from the outset of his presidency in 2017, sought to decisively alter the status quo and disrupt the established trade relationships between the United States and the EU, as well as between the United States and key member states such as Germany and France. He deliberately pushed negotiations on the Transatlantic Trade and Investment Partnership into a stalemate, effectively freezing the process and allowing it to lapse without formal termination. At the same time, under his direction, U.S. trade authorities adopted increasingly stringent measures to restrict European exports to the United States, while sharply criticizing what they characterized as excessive EU regulatory constraints on bilateral trade, causing persistent friction in U.S.-EU relations. Between 2017 and 2018, the United States International Trade Commission initiated and adjudicated a total of 36 anti-dumping and countervailing duty cases, of which eight involved firms from EU member states, accounting for more than one-fifth of the total. From early March 2017 through the end of September 2018, U.S. industry groups submitted an increasing number of petitions to the Commission requesting investigations into specific products, of which 25 were accepted or were in the filing process, including five involving EU firms, again approximately one-fifth of the total. Notably, during the same period, the European Commission was conducting 27 anti-dumping and countervailing investigations, of which 22 involved Chinese firms and 18 were directed exclusively at China, while none targeted U.S. companies, forming a stark contrast.

In the domains of technology and industry, the rise of "emerging disruptive technologies" since 2010, along with the rapid expansion of associated sectors, gave rise to a new round of transatlantic competition. Following Trump's inauguration in 2017, the U.S. government mobilized substantial administrative resources to vigorously pursue vertical industrial policies aimed at attracting European manufacturing capital to the United States in order to stimulate domestic industrial development, while the EU, in turn, issued a wide array of policy documents seeking to advance high-end manufacturing through industrial policy instruments. At the same time, both sides sought to establish leadership over the standards and regulatory frameworks governing emerging technologies and advanced manufacturing, with the United States relying primarily on material capabilities, whereas the EU aimed to leverage its so-called "normative power"—often conceptualized as the "Brussels Effect"[①]—to externalize its regulatory standards. Intensifying competition further strengthened the EU's determination to pursue "industrial autonomy." In the domain of global governance, the Trump administration's intention to abandon the World Trade Organization and dismantle the multilateral trading system favored by the EU further exacerbated bilateral tensions.

Third, mainstream political elites in the United States and Europe have increasingly diverged in the realm of political ideology, with their differences continuing to deepen. Both sides have advanced evolving interpretations of core Western values—such as freedom, democracy, and human rights—yet the gap between their respective understandings has widened considerably, extending even to differences in modes of thinking and discursive frameworks. The March 2017 meeting between Trump and Merkel not only brought their disagreements over the refugee issue into the open, but also revealed profound conceptual divergences between U.S. and European political elites. Trump's discursive framework and cognitive approach align more closely with traditional American right-wing conservatism, viewing freedom and rights as concrete and conditional rather than abstract and universally applicable, and emphasizing that genuine freedom must be grounded in maximal respect

① See Anu Bradford, *The Brussels Effect: How the European Union Rules the World*, New York: Oxford University Press, 2020, pp. 47-90.

for market-based institutions. Although he did not articulate an explicit doctrinal position on cultural pluralism, his consistent rhetoric suggests a pronounced skepticism toward it, as evidenced by his willingness, during his March 2017 meeting with Merkel, to state explicitly—contrary to mainstream U.S. media discourse—that "immigration is a privilege, not a right".① By contrast, the political elites of the EU and its major member states, particularly France and Germany, continue to operate within the intellectual framework of European left-liberal multiculturalism, emphasizing abstract and universal rights. Trump's open support for radical populist parties in Europe, his disparagement of the EU's liberal principles, and his overtly dismissive attitude toward Europe's mainstream political elites have all contributed to the intensification of transatlantic antagonism.

1.4 Changes in the Relative Positions of China and the EU in the Global Distribution of Economic and Political Power

In 2009, Javier Solana de Madariaga, then serving as the High Representative for the Common Foreign and Security Policy of the European Union, issued an evaluative report which, despite being released more than a year after the outbreak of the global financial crisis and in the early stages of the European sovereign debt crisis, still reflected a relatively optimistic assessment of the EU's internal conditions, security environment, and international standing. The report not only characterized the EU as an "anchor of stability," asserting that "the EU's enlargement has spread democracy and prosperity," and that "our neighborhood policy establishes a solid framework for relations with partners to the east and south," but also advanced the claim that "the European Union must lead a renewal of multilateral order at the global level".②

However, as Europe's economic stagnation persisted and the sovereign debt crisis continued to unfold, the optimistic assessment of the EU's decision-making elites was soon found to be untenable. According to statistical data compiled by the International Monetary Fund, the relative position of the EU—and of its major member states—in the global economy has experienced a steady decline. As shown in Table 3.2, between 2008 and 2015,

① https://www.youtube.com/watch?v=54bsLlWRcEc, accessed March 27, 2026.

② The General Secretariat of the Council of European Union, Report on the Implementation of the European Security Strategy: Providing Security in a Changing World, 2009.

the average annual GDP growth rates of the EU's three principal economies—the United Kingdom, France, and Germany—were not only significantly lower than that of China, but also lagged behind those of Canada and the United States.

Table 3.2: A Comparison of the Average Annual GDP Growth Rates of China and the Group of Seven Countries (2008-2015)

Country	China	Canada	The United States	The United Kingdom	Germany	France	Japan	Italy
Average Annual GDP Growth Rate, 2008-2015	8.56%	1.485%	1.2%	0.91%	0.87%	0.43%	0.154%	−1.05%

Source: Compiled and calculated by the author based on data provided by the International Monetary Fund

Table 3.3 further indicates that, during the period from 2008 to 2015, the declining shares of global economic output by France and Germany—the core economies of the EU—were significantly more pronounced than those of the United States and Canada. In fact, shortly after the establishment of the euro area, the EU's then 15 member states, taken as a whole, surpassed the United States in terms of aggregate economic output in 2003, becoming the largest economic entity in the world. However, under the dual shocks of the global financial crisis and the sovereign debt crisis, Europe's economic contraction and stagnation proved more severe than that of the United States, and its subsequent recovery was correspondingly slower. From 2015 onward, the United States once again overtook the EU in annual gross domestic product, thus reclaiming its position as the world's largest economy.

Table 3.3: Changes in the Shares of Global GDP Held by China and the Group of Seven Countries (2008-2015)

Country	China	The United States	Canada	The United Kingdom	France	Germany	Italy	Japan
Change in Each Country's Share of Global GDP	Increased by 7%	Increased by 1.26%	Decreased by 0.33%	Decreased by 0.51%	Decreased by 1.3%	Decreased by 1.37%	Decreased by 2.48%	Decreased by 2%

Source: Calculated and compiled by the author based on data released by the International Monetary Fund in April 2016

At the very time when the EU economy remained trapped in persistent sluggishness, China's economy continued to sustain rapid growth. While the relative position of the

EU and its principal economies—such as the United Kingdom, France, and Germany—in the global economic system continued to decline, the Chinese economy rose swiftly and markedly. Following the initiation of market-oriented reforms in 1992, China maintained double-digit GDP growth throughout the latter half of the 1990s, attracting widespread global attention. After China's accession to the World Trade Organization in 2001, and up until the outbreak of the global financial crisis in 2008, its annual GDP growth rate remained consistently at around 10 percent. In 2010, China surpassed Japan to become the world's second largest economy. Consequently, the notion of the "rise of China" emerged as a focal topic of intense discussion among policymakers and strategic research communities worldwide. The continuous shift in the relative positions of China and the EU in the global economic order thus produced a striking contrast.

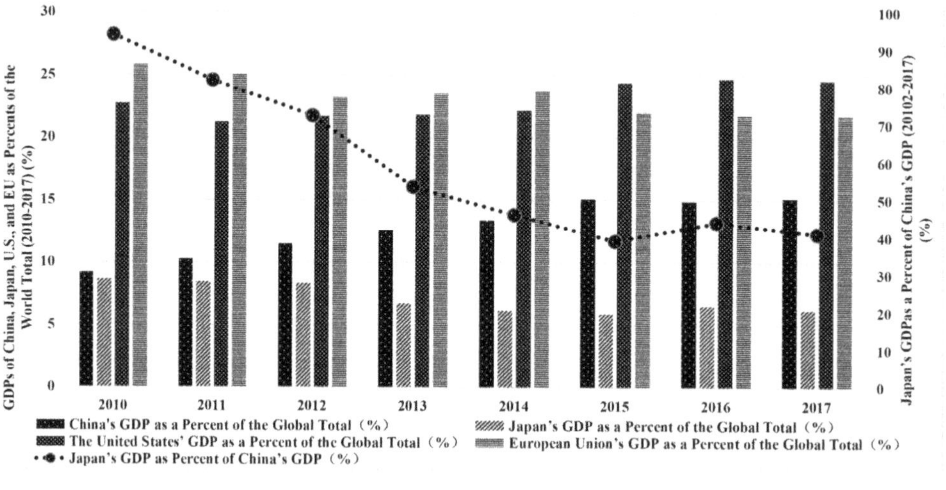

Figure 3.3: The Relative Positions of China, Japan, the United States, and the EU in the Global Economic System (2010-2017)

Source: Compiled and calculated by the author based on data provided by the International Monetary Fund

At the same time as the EU's position in the global economic system continued to decline, its significance within the broader architecture of international politics and strategic security also diminished, whereas the importance of China and the Asia-Pacific region in global politics—and particularly in the U.S. external strategic map—steadily increased. After 2011, the United States began to implement its "pivot to East Asia" and "rebalancing to the Asia-Pacific" strategies, explicitly shifting the center of its external strategic focus toward the Asia-Pacific region. In an analytical report released on May 26, 2016, Jan Joel Andersson of the European Union Institute for Security Studies noted that, at that time, the U.S. Pacific Command maintained approximately 360,000 troops and more than 200 naval vessels—including five aircraft carrier strike groups—within its area of responsibility, while the most advanced fighter aircraft of the U.S. Air Force were likewise deployed in the Asia-Pacific. By contrast, the U.S. European Command, which oversaw both Europe and Africa, had only 60,500 personnel in total, roughly half of whom were ground forces, with relatively limited naval and air assets. He further observed that, according to the U.S. Department of Defense budget, approximately 60 percent of expenditures on the U.S. Navy and overseas air forces in 2017 were allocated to the Asia-Pacific region, while the proportion devoted to Europe remained comparatively low, a distributional structure that was unlikely to change in the short term.[①]

The gradual marginalization of the EU in the international space, coupled with its declining position in U.S. global strategy, generated mounting pressure on EU decision-makers. Following the U.S. announcement of "pivot to Asia" in the autumn of 2011, segments of the EU's policymaking community and strategic research circles quickly developed a heightened sense of crisis, which in turn propelled efforts to formulate a new policy framework toward the Asia-Pacific region. The European Parliament convened special sessions in July 2012 and February 2013 to deliberate on the formulation of a new EU external strategy. At the February 2013 session, Swedish Foreign Minister Carl Bildt remarked that "the rise of Asia is changing the world," while Polish Foreign Minister Radosław Sikorski argued that shifts in the global economic landscape had placed the EU at a disadvantage, warning that "by 2050 no EU member state will rank among the world's top ten economies," and emphasizing the need for European countries to act collectively in redefining the Union's common strategic objectives.[②] On May 28, 2013, four leading foreign policy think tanks from key EU member states—the Istituto Affari Internazionali (IAI) of Italy, the Polish Institute of International Affairs (PISM), the Swedish Institute of International Affairs (UI), and Spain's Elcano Royal Institute (RIE)—jointly produced,

① Jan Joel Andersson, "US Forces: between Europe and Asia", Issue Alert, May 26, 2016, European Union Institute for Security Studies.

② European Parliament, Press Release, "External Policy: EU Must Raise Its Game or Become Irrelevant", Meeting of the Committee on Foreign Affairs, February 22, 2013.

following extensive consultations with 24 prominent European think tanks, a situational assessment report entitled *Towards a European Global Strategy: Securing European Influence in a Changing World*. This report, serving as the written articulation of an initiative launched by the foreign ministers of these four countries, catalogued major shifts in the EU's external environment—particularly in its neighborhood—argued that the existing policy framework had become inadequate, and called for a reassessment of external factors shaping internal policies, the revision of neighborhood policies, and more proactive engagement in global governance.① In July 2013, the foreign ministers of Italy, Poland, Spain, and Sweden, drawing on the above report, jointly launched an initiative calling on the EU to formulate a new external strategy.②

On this basis, the EU released in June 2016 *A Global Strategy for the European Union's Foreign and Security Policy*, which systematically articulated a new policy framework toward the Asia-Pacific region, explicitly proposing to "deepen economic diplomacy with Asia" and to "significantly enhance the EU's role in Asian security affairs".③ Concurrently with the conceptualization and formulation of this new Asia-Pacific policy framework, the EU intensified its efforts to advance free trade negotiations with countries across the region, concluding so-called "new-generation" free trade agreements with South Korea, Singapore, and Vietnam between 2011 and 2015, while also actively promoting negotiations on a bilateral investment agreement with China.

However, the EU's *Return to Asia* strategy yielded only limited results. On the one hand, the Union proved unable to exert substantive influence over a series of strategic confrontations that have emerged in the Asia-Pacific since 2012, including the North Korean nuclear crisis and maritime disputes in the East and South China Seas. A policy brief issued by the Stockholm International Peace Research Institute in February 2015 acknowledged

---

① "Towards a European Global Strategy: Securing European Influence in a Changing World", in Antonio Missiroli (Ed.), *An EU Global Strategy: Background, Process, References*, European Union Institute for Security Studies, October 2015, pp. 115-123.

② Emma Bonino, Radosław Sikorski, José Manuel García-Margallo y Marfil and Carl Bildt, "In Search of a Global Strategy", *POLITICO*, July 3, 2013.

③ European Union External Action Service, A Global Strategy for the European Union's Foreign and Security Policy, June 2016, https://eeas.europa.eu/archives/docs/top_stories/pdf/eugs_review_web.pdf, accessed March 5, 2018.

candidly that "in East Asian security affairs, the EU is widely perceived as a marginal actor".[①] Similarly, in November 2017, Fraser Cameron, Director of the Brussels-based EU-Asia Center, conceded that the EU's security policy engagement in Asia had achieved "rather limited" success.[②] On the other hand, the EU has exercised relatively limited discursive power and influence over regional economic integration processes in the Asia-Pacific, such as the development of the ASEAN Free Trade Area and the negotiations over the Regional Comprehensive Economic Partnership. In other words, the contrasting trajectories of China and the EU in the global economic system, as well as the disparities in their respective roles and influence within the structures of international politics and global strategic security, constitute structural characteristics that are likely to persist over the long term, with a profound influence over the EU's situational assessments and strategic cognition.

The simultaneous decline of the EU's position in the global economic and strategic-security order, and the rise in China's global importance, have compelled the EU to reassess its role and position in the international system, to recalibrate the distribution of interests between China and the EU in the ongoing reconfiguration of global power structures, and to redefine its interests and policy objectives in the context of EU-China relations. At the same time, shifts in the EU's internal political landscape, together with growing dissatisfaction and political demands among grassroots populations regarding European integration and globalization, have prompted EU leaders to re-evaluate the potential socio-political consequences of trade liberalization and regional integration, and to consider revising external economic policies by adopting protectionist, mercantilist, and economic nationalist measures aimed at "defending" against competitive pressures from external economies, thereby safeguarding domestic output and employment while alleviating internal discontent. Moreover, the first Trump administration's evident departure from the international multilateral trading system has compelled the EU to reassess the practical viability of WTO-centered multilateralism and global governance rules, while simultaneously strengthening selective unilateralist and protectionist measures and further refining its system of defensive economic policies. Consequently, the confluence of these three dimensions of structural

① Mathieu Duchatel and Fleur Huijskens, "The European Union's Principled Neutrality on the East China Sea", SIPRI Policy Brief, February 2015.

② Fraser Cameron, "It's Asia, Stupid: Time for the European Union to Deepen Relations with Asia", EU-Asia Center, November 9, 2017.

change has driven a fundamental shift in the EU's situational assessment and strategic cognition in its approach toward China.

II. The EU's Situational Assessment and Strategic Cognition in Advancing Defensive Economic Decision-Making toward China

During the second term of the Obama administration, populist forces in the United States began to rise, eventually facilitating the ascent of the Trump administration, which took a forceful posture in externally advancing economic nationalism and launched trade investigations against major economies closely connected to the United States through trade and investment by invoking three key provisions of U.S. trade law—Sections 301, 232, and 201—, thus contributing to a gradual intensification of China-U.S. economic tensions. For the EU, on the one hand, its modes of situational assessment and conceptual frameworks of strategic cognition were deeply influenced by the United States; on the other hand, since 2015, under the cumulative impact of multiple internal and external crises, the EU began to pay increasing attention to the negative consequences of globalization and regional integration, while EU-China trade and investment slowed down, and bilateral economic relations became increasingly strained due to issues such as "steel overcapacity", China's "market economy status," and the intensification of EU anti-dumping measures against China. These two sets of factors jointly shaped the EU's assessment and strategic perception of its economic relationship with China, leading to a growing prevalence of negative evaluations. Such assessments, perceptions, and evaluations, in turn, constituted an important driving force behind the EU's acceleration of defensive economic policymaking toward China during 2016-2017.

2.1 The EU's Assessment of Gains and Losses in EU-China Relations in the Process of Economic Globalization, 2016-2018

Under the influence of the United States, EU decision-makers increasingly came to perceive that the Union had incurred substantial losses from globalization, whereas China had "unfairly" extracted disproportionate benefits—particularly by leveraging the international multilateral trading system to its advantage to make sizable gains at the expense of the EU. Within both EU policymaking circles and the strategic research community, a growing consensus emerged that Chinese firms had taken full advantage of the cross-border mobility of goods and capital enabled by globalization, while relying on strong state intervention and support to engage in dumping practices and even so-called "social dumping" against the EU, thereby placing the EU in a structurally disadvantaged and increasingly marginalized position in the global distribution of benefits shaped by globalization. Although the EU decision-making elite continued, at least rhetorically, to affirm globalization, since early 2016 it had in practice engaged in a critical reassessment of the imbalanced internal and external distribution of benefits generated by globalization, while actively exploring new policy frameworks to rectify its unfavorable position. In both Europe and the United States, segments of the policymaking and strategic communities advocated the continuous strengthening of barriers against foreign products and investment, with the aim of preventing the "hollowing-out" of traditional manufacturing industries and safeguarding employment and welfare among grassroots populations. These perspectives contributed to the growing influence of populist and protectionist currents on both sides of the Atlantic.

In the United States, a prominent representative of populist, conservative, and protectionist thought among the think tank and academic communities was Peter Navarro, who served as Director of the National Trade Council under the first Trump administration and had previously been a professor of economics at the University of California, Irvine. Navarro argued that, in the fifteen years following its accession to the World Trade Organization in 2001, China had risen by exploiting the global trading system, while the United States had been effectively "devastated" by the flood of Chinese imports. He articulated these views in his book *Death by China: Confronting the Dragon-A Global Call to Action,*[①] which he also adapted into a documentary film, sharply criticizing the state of China-U.S. trade relations and exerting broad influence in the United States, representing a significant current of opinion in the American strategic research community and wider society. In such a powerful discursive environment, U.S. politicians and top-level decision-makers, regardless of whether they fully endorsed anti-globalization positions, were

① Peter Navarro and Greg Autry, *Death by China: Confronting the Dragon-A Global Call to Action*, Pearson Education, Inc., 2011.

compelled to respond to these demands and to express some degree of negative evaluation of economic relations with China, finding it difficult to resist prevailing public opinion pressures.

Under the strong influence of the United States, European strategic research circles and policymaking elites likewise began to adopt increasingly negative assessments of the distribution of gains and losses between China and the EU during the course of globalization. Since early 2016, Cecilia Malmström, European Commissioner for Trade, has increasingly emphasized the importance of "fair trade" in major public speeches when addressing EU-China economic relations.[①] The policy document *Elements for a New EU Strategy on China*, issued by the European Commission on June 22, 2016, focused almost entirely on managing economic relations with China and conveyed an overall tone of skepticism and concern.[②] Correspondingly, since early 2016, the European Commission has initiated anti-dumping and anti-subsidy investigations against Chinese products—particularly steel—at an increasing frequency, while decision-making activity surrounding the formulation of trade protection measures combining anti-dumping, anti-subsidy, and safeguard instruments has intensified. In early 2017, the acquisition of the German robotics firm KUKA by China's Midea Group triggered widespread controversy across Europe, prompting a profound reassessment among European policymakers and strategic analysts and serving as a critical turning point in the overall shift of the EU and its major member states toward a more cautious and negative stance in managing economic relations with China.[③] In February 2017, the ministers of economy of Germany, France, and Italy jointly addressed a letter to Trade Commissioner Malmström, calling for the establishment of an EU-level investment screening mechanism to constrain—or even resist—large-scale Chinese investment in Europe.[④] On March 20, the European Parliament, under the initiative of

---

① Commissioner for Trade Cecilia Malmstrom, "The EU and China: Trade and Investment in the Global Economy", Speech on the China Association Event, London, February 25, 2016.

② European Commission, "Joint Communication to the European Parliament and the Council, Elements for a New EU Strategy on China", JOIN (2016) 30 final, Brussels, June 22, 2016.

③ Based on interviews conducted by the author with European think tank scholars, including Claudia Schmucker, Hanns Günther Hilpert of the German Institute for International and Security Affairs, and Sven Biscop of the Egmont Royal Institute for International Relations, October 15-25, 2017.

④ Brigitte Zypries, Michel Sapin, and Carlo Calenda, Letter to Cecilia Malmström, February 2017, http://www.bmwi.de/Redaktion/DE/Downloads/S-T/schreiben-de-fr-it-an-malmstroem.pdf?__blob=publicationFile&v=5.

certain political groups, introduced a proposal calling for strengthened screening of foreign investment.① During the first half of 2017, EU decision-makers encouraged major Brussels-based think tanks to conduct systematic analyses of Chinese trade and investment in Europe. On this basis, the European Commission, on September 13, 2017, formally introduced a series of preliminary proposals for establishing an investment screening framework, and, for the first time, explicitly advanced the notion of "harnessing globalization," which signaled a significant shift in its underlying policy orientation.② On December 20, 2017, the EU formally implemented new regulations that substantially strengthened its anti-dumping and anti-subsidy regime, with the clear intention of imposing stricter constraints on Chinese exports to the European market③. These developments collectively show a significant shift in the EU's overall approach to managing economic relations with China.

2.2 EU Analyses of China's "Belt and Road Initiative" and the "16+1" Cooperation Mechanism, 2013-2017

In the EU's decision-making system, three categories of actors have kept track of and commented on the Belt and Road Initiative (BRI). First, there are the EU's institutional decision-making bodies and leading policymakers. More specifically, among the so-called institutional "troika" at the apex of the EU's decision-making structure, both the European Commission and the European Council have made explicit statements regarding the initiative. During Chinese President Xi Jinping's visit to the EU in 2014 and in the 2015 China-EU Summit, these institutions participated in official consultations with the Chinese

---

accessed March 4, 2018.

① European Parliament, Proposal for a Union Act Submitted under Rule 46 (2) of the Rules of Procedure on the Screening of Foreign Investment in Strategic Sectors, B[8-0000/2017], March 20, 2017.

② European Commission, Proposal for a Regulation of the European Parliament and of the Council establishing a Framework for Screening of Foreign Direct Investments into the European Union, COM (2017) 487 final, 2017/0224 (COD), Brussels, September 13, 2017; A Balanced and Progressive Trade Policy to Harness Globalization, COM (2017) 492 final, Brussels, September 13, 2017.

③ Regulation (EU) 2017/2321 of the European Parliament and of the Council of December 12th 2017 amending Regulation (EU) 2016/1036 on Protection against Dumped Imports from Countries not Members of the European Union and Regulation (EU) 2016/1037 on Protection against Subsidized Imports from Countries not Members of the European Union, *Official Journal of the European Union*, December 19, 2017, L338/1-L338/7.

side as representatives of the Union. Consequently, the then President of the European Council Herman Van Rompuy and his successor Donald Tusk, as well as the former President of the European Commission José Manuel Barroso and his successor Jean-Claude Juncker, all gave positive assessments of the BRI in the two China-EU joint statements issued in 2014 and 2015. In addition, the EU's High Representative for Foreign Affairs and Security Policy, Federica Mogherini, also explicitly commented on the BRI in May 2015.

Second, there exists the European strategic research community, composed primarily of leading think tanks engaged in foreign-policy analysis and advisory work both at the EU level and in EU member states. These institutions closely monitored and assessed the development of the BRI, and made various policy recommendations for how the EU should respond to the initiative.

Third, European interest groups, particularly representatives from the business community specializing in foreign trade and investment, also showed a certain degree of interest in the BRI, with the British business sector demonstrating especially pronounced attention. Among these three categories of actors, however, European think tanks produced the earliest, most systematic, and most detailed assessments, and their analyses have had a discernible influence on EU policymakers.

The EU decision-making system's perception of the BRI evolved through three distinct phases from 2013 to 2017. The first phase extended from September 2013 to the end of March 2014, that is, from the initial proposal of the *Silk Road Economic Belt* to the period immediately preceding President Xi Jinping's visit to the EU. During this phase, the overall attitude among elites in the EU's decision-making system was rather lukewarm. Senior EU policymakers did not issue any response to the proposal of the Silk Road Economic Belt, while at the EU level only the European Institute for Asian Studies (EIAS) expressed attention and commented on it in early March 2014. At the level of EU member states, however, two think tanks from Poland and Romania responded positively to the proposal.

The second phase lasted from April 2014 to the end of February 2015, beginning after President Xi Jinping's visit to the EU and ending shortly before the Chinese government issued the policy blueprint entitled *Vision and Actions on Jointly Building the Silk Road Economic Belt and the 21st Century Maritime Silk Road*. During this stage, EU policymakers began to make more explicit responses. In the China-EU Joint Statement issued on March 31, 2014, the EU expressed interest in the concept of the *New Silk Road Economic Belt*. Subsequently, on October 16, 2014, then President of the European Council Herman Van Rompuy reiterated this interest during a speech delivered at the Asia-Europe Business Forum. Meanwhile, at the EU level, both the European Institute for Asian Studies and the European Union Institute for Security Studies (EUISS) produced systematic introductions to the initiative and offered fairly detailed projections regarding its potential trajectory. At the level of EU member states, leading strategic research institutions such as the German Institute for International and Security Affairs and the Stockholm International Peace Research Institute also offered their analyses of the BRI, suggesting that the EU could utilize the platform created by the initiative to pursue cooperation with China in areas such as security governance.

The third phase began in March 2015 and extended to early 2017, following the official release on March 28, 2015 of the Chinese government's planning document for the BRI. During this period, the level of attention devoted to the initiative by EU policymakers increased rapidly, and responses became more frequent. On May 5, 2015, in her meeting with Chinese State Councilor Yang Jiechi during the China-EU Strategic Dialogue, High Representative Federica Mogherini proposed for the first time the idea of linking the BRI with the EU's Investment Plan for Europe. Subsequently, in the Joint Statement issued at the China-EU Summit on 29 June 2015, the EU side proposed connecting China's BRI investment framework with the EU's Trans-European Transport Network (TEN-T) planning scheme, thereby establishing a common platform for infrastructure investment cooperation. Simultaneously, European think tanks noticeably stepped up their attention and commentary regarding the initiative. At the EU level, the European Union Institute for Security Studies, the European Council on Foreign Relations, and the European Centre for International Political Economy all showed a strong interest and incorporated analysis of the BRI into their broader studies of China's foreign policy strategy. At the level of EU member states at the time, major British institutions such as the Royal Institute of International Affairs and the International Institute for Strategic Studies also maintained sustained analytical attention.

Table 3.4: Three Stages in the Responses of the European Union Decision-Making System to the Belt and Road Initiative

Stage / Actor	Stage I (September 2013-March 2014)	Stage II (April 2014-End of February 2015)	Stage III (March 2015-early 2017)
EU Decision-Making Leadership	No official comment was made	On March 31, 2014, the EU made its first positive response in the EU-China Joint Statement; on October 16, 2014, Herman Van Rompuy, President of the European Council, gave another positive response.	On May 5, 2015, Federica Mogherini, the High Representative of the Union for Foreign Affairs and Security Policy, issued a response; on June 29, 2015, the EU again responded in the Joint Statement of the EU-China Summit.
EU-Level Think Tanks	EIAS: 1 commentary	EIAS: 1 commentary; EUISS: 1 commentary; ECFR: 1 commentary	EIAS: 5 commentaries; ECIPE: 2 commentaries; ECFR: 5 commentaries; EUISS: 2 commentaries
Member-State-Level Think Tanks	PISM: 1 commentary; Aspen Institute Romania: 1 commentary	SWP: 1 commentary; PISM: 1 commentary; SIPRI: 1 commentary	SWP: 1 commentary; IISS: 3 commentaries; RIIA: 3 commentaries
European Interest Groups	Foreign Trade Association (FTA): 1 commentary	—	Confederation of British Industry (CBI): 1 commentary; European Union Chamber of Commerce in China: 1 commentary

Note: EIAS refers to the European Institute for Asian Studies; EUISS to the European Union Institute for Security Studies; ECFR to the European Council on Foreign Relations; ECIPE to the European Centre for International Political Economy; PISM to the Polish Institute of International Affairs; SWP to the German Institute for International and Security Affairs; SIPRI to the Stockholm International Peace Research Institute; RIIA to the Royal Institute of International Affairs (UK); and IISS to the International Institute for Strategic Studies (UK).

Source: Compiled by the author

Analyses of the BRI by EU policymakers and the European strategic research community have largely unfolded along five analytical dimensions.

The first dimension concerns the BRI's place in China's domestic economic development strategy. EU policymakers and strategic analysts have argued that the initiative is closely linked to China's economic structuring and domestic spatial rebalancing. In their view, the implementation of the BRI aims to address issues such as excess capital and overcapacity in China's manufacturing and infrastructure sectors, reduce the developmental disparities between coastal and inland regions, promote economic growth in China's western interior and frontier regions, and strengthen national energy security. For instance, François Godement, an expert from the European Council on Foreign Relations (ECFR), argued in a research report issued on June 10, 2015 that one of the primary motivations behind the BRI was the need for China to absorb its infrastructure construction overcapacity.① Meanwhile, a study published by the European Union Institute for Security Studies (EUISS) in May 2014 emphasized that the concept of the Silk Road Economic Belt also had the objective of ensuring the stability and security of China's energy supply.② Another report issued by the same institute in January 2015 further noted that the widening economic gap between China's western frontier regions—such as Xinjiang—and the prosperous southeastern coastal regions—such as Shanghai and Guangdong—had prompted Beijing to use the BRI framework to connect Xinjiang more closely with Europe, so as to facilitate deeper economic integration between China's western inland provinces and the global economy.③

The second dimension involves the role of the initiative within China's broader geostrategic security framework. Some analysts in the EU policymaking and strategic research communities have argued that, from a geopolitical perspective, the BRI constitutes a strategic initiative designed to stabilize China's western frontier regions and respond to tensions in the South China Sea. In this interpretation, the initiative represents a form of China's "westward and southward neighborhood diplomacy" and may also be viewed as part of the broader policy architecture surrounding the Shanghai Cooperation Organization. As such, the BRI carries not only economic significance but also important strategic and security implications. Two analytical reports on the BRI issued by the European Union Institute for Security Studies in 2014 and 2015 respectively both suggested that one of the objectives of the initiative was to stabilize China's western frontier regions by promoting economic development as a means of containing the influence of terrorist organizations.④ Similarly, China specialist Tim Summers from the Royal Institute of International Affairs argued on October 28, 2013 that China had launched a new "charm offensive" toward its

---

① Francois Godement, "One Belt One Road": China's Great Leap Forward Outward, China Analysis, June 2015, European Council on Foreign Relations.

② Camille Brugier, "China's Way: The New Silk Road", Brief Issue, the European Union Institute for Security Studies, May, 2014.

③ Raffaello Pantucci, "Central Asia: The View from China", Issue Alert, the European Union Institute for Security Studies, January 2015.

④ Camille Brugier, China's Way: The New Silk Road, Brief Issue, the European Union Institute for Security Studies, May, 2014; Raffaello Pantucci, Central Asia: The View from China, Issue Alert, the European Union Institute for Security Studies, January 2015.

neighboring countries, particularly by elevating its relations with Central Asian states to the level of "strategic partnerships," strengthening the institutional framework of the Shanghai Cooperation Organization, and incorporating the newly proposed Silk Road Economic Belt as part of this broader diplomatic strategy.①

The third dimension concerns the initiative's impact on regional economic cooperation frameworks along two major strategic corridors: 1). the westward route stretching from Central Asia through the Black Sea region to Central Europe; and 2). the southwestern route extending from the Asia-Pacific through Southeast Asia toward the Indian Ocean. Researchers at European and American think tanks have argued that, given the existing institutional landscape of regional economic cooperation, the westward Silk Road Economic Belt is likely to be easier to implement than the southward Maritime Silk Road. Scholars such as Justyna Szczudlik-Tatar from the Polish Institute of International Affairs and Tim Summers from the Chatham House have noted that the vast region extending westward from Central Asia through the Caucasus and the Black Sea to Central and Eastern Europe, although influenced by Russia's Eurasian integration initiatives, lacks a mature or powerful multilateral economic cooperation framework. Consequently, China's proposal of the Silk Road Economic Belt may encounter relatively fewer institutional constraints in this region, allowing Beijing's influence to expand more rapidly. By contrast, along China's southwestern strategic direction from Southeast Asia through the South China Sea and across the Indian Ocean to East Africa, China faces more substantial obstacles due to factors such as the United States' "pivot to Asia" strategy, the promotion of the Trans-Pacific Partnership framework, persistent sovereignty disputes in the South China Sea, and the rise of extremist organizations in parts of West Asia and East Africa.②

The fourth dimension relates to the geopolitical security implications of the BRI for the strategic balance along these two corridors. Analysts at EU institutions and European

---

① Tim Summers, China's New Charm Offensive, Expert Comment of Royal Institute of International Affairs, October 28, 2013.

② Justyna Szczudlik-Tatar, China's New Silk Road Diplomacy, PISM Policy Paper, No. 34 (82), December 2013; Silk Road as a Tool to Facilitate Europe-China and Intra-Europe Ties, November 13, 2014, Friends of Europe, http://www.friendsofeurope.org/global-europe/silk-road-tool-facilitate-europe-china-intra-europe-ties, accessed on August 8th, 2015; Tim Summers, China's New Charm Offensive, Expert Comment of Royal Institute of International Affairs, http://www.chathamhouse.org/media/comment/view/195157, accessed August 7 2015.

think tanks have argued that the initiative represents China's attempt to respond to shifting power balances in both Central Asia and the Asia-Pacific region. In Central Asia, the initiative could potentially reshape the existing geopolitical configuration characterized by competition among China, Russia, the United States, and the EU. In the Asia-Pacific region, meanwhile, the initiative might evolve into a strategic counterweight to the United States' rebalancing strategy. A policy report published by the European Institute for Asian Studies in March 2014 argued that China's advancement of the Silk Road Economic Belt in Central Asia might generate tensions among major powers, reminiscent of the strategic rivalry between Britain and Russia in the late nineteenth century, potentially giving rise to what has been described as a "New Great Game".[①] Tim Summers likewise suggested that the intensification of maritime sovereignty disputes in the South China Sea and the East China Sea, combined with Russian President Vladimir Putin's increasing willingness to employ coercive measures to draw former Soviet states into Russia's geopolitical orbit, might constrain the realization of China's strategic ambitions.[②]

Meanwhile, Oliver Brauner of the Stockholm International Peace Research Institute argued that the EU's European Neighbourhood Policy was experiencing an unprecedented crisis, as the tensions in eastern Ukraine, the short-lived rise of the so-called "Islamic State" along the eastern Mediterranean, and the continuing instability in North Africa since the Arab Spring had all severely strained the EU's strategic capacity. Under these circumstances, the EU could consider utilizing the cooperative platform created by the BRI to deepen security cooperation with China.[③] Similar arguments were also advanced in analytical reports published by the European Union Institute for Security Studies in 2014 and 2015.[④]

The fifth dimension concerns the potential impact of the BRI on the overall trajectory of China-EU relations and on interregional cooperation across Eurasia. Analysts at European

---

① Yu Xichao, China's Rise in Central Asia: Implications for EU Interests, EIAS Policy Paper, March, 2014.

② Tim Summers, China's New Charm Offensive, Expert Comment of RIIA, http://www.chathamhouse.org/media/comment/view/195157, accessed August 7, 2015.

③ Oliver Brauner, Deepening China-EU Security Cooperation along the "Silk Road Economic Belt", http://www.friendsofeurope.org/global-europe/deepening-china-eu-security-cooperation-along-silk-road-economic-belt/, accessed on August 7, 2015.

④ Camille Brugier, "China's Way: The New Silk Road", Brief Issue, the European Union Institute for Security Studies, May, 2014; Raffaello Pantucci, "Central Asia: The View from China", Issue Alert, the European Union Institute for Security Studies, January 2015.

and American think tanks have argued that the initiative provides new opportunities for China-EU cooperation. In particular, the BRI could be linked institutionally with frameworks such as the European Fund for Strategic Investments and the EU-China 2020 Strategic Agenda for Cooperation. It could also project its influence through interregional platforms such as the Asia-Europe Meeting, and contribute to strengthening Eurasian connectivity through projects such as railway corridors linking China's coastal regions with Germany, Spain, and Poland. These arguments were advanced in a series of reports issued between May and July 2015 by the European Council on Foreign Relations, as well as in studies published by the German Institute for International and Security Affairs and the European Union Institute for Security Studies.[①]

From early 2016 to the end of 2018, the EU faced a series of overlapping crises including the Brexit, repeated terrorist attacks, the refugee influx into Europe, persistent instability within the eurozone, and the rise of anti-globalization populist politics, all of which compelled EU policymakers to reassess and adjust their perspectives on globalization. At the same time, European trade and investment with China slowed down, while European companies operating in China increasingly perceived a deterioration in the Chinese business environment and declining profit margins. Consequently, European think tanks began to produce a growing number of negative evaluations regarding the present condition and future prospects of China-EU economic relations.

In response to these developments, the EU gradually moved closer to Japan with the aim of strengthening and expanding EU-Japan economic cooperation, while simultaneously beginning to distance itself from China and recalibrate its overall China strategy. The rhetoric employed by EU leaders during the China-EU Summit and Business Summit in June 2017, the State of the Union address delivered by the European Commission leadership in September of the same year, the policy documents on the establishment of an investment screening mechanism, the major revision of anti-dumping regulations approved on

---

① Francois Godement, "One Belt One Road": China's Great Leap Forward Outward, China Analysis, June 2015, European Council on Foreign Relations; Agatha Kratz, "Paying the China Price: the Costs of Chinese Investment", July 20, 2015, European Council on Foreign Relations; Hanns Gunther Hilpert and Gudrun Wacker, "Geoeconomics Meets Geopolitics: China's New Economic and Foreign Policy Initiatives, SWP-Aktuell 52/2015; Raffaello Pantucci, "Central Asia: the View from China", Issue Alert, the European Union Institute for Security Studies, January 2015.

December 4, and the report issued on December 20 concerning alleged "distortions" in the Chinese economy all suggested that the EU's overall assessment of China had begun to take on an increasingly negative tone.

Influenced by these developments, both EU policymakers and the European strategic research community produced a greater number of critical evaluations of the BRI, and they also adopted a strongly skeptical attitude toward the associated "16+1" cooperation framework between China and Central and Eastern European countries. In March 2018, the Brussels office of the German Marshall Fund of the United States (GMF) released a report entitled *Europe's Response to the Belt and Road Initiative*, which argued that the BRI posed three major threats to European interests. First, the initiative could undermine internal cohesion within the EU, particularly because the "16+1" framework might drive a wedge between Central and Eastern Europe on the one hand and Western Europe and the EU institutions on the other. Second, China's economic assistance to countries participating in BRI projects was portrayed as financially unsustainable, potentially generating domestic instability in those states and consequently threatening the stability of maritime trade and energy supply routes linking Europe to the Asia-Pacific region. Third, BRI projects were said to put competitive pressure on Europe's exports and investments in the Indian Ocean and Pacific regions. According to the report, such concerns were gradually growing rather than diminishing.

Under the influence of these analyses produced by European think tanks, the EU adopted a cautious and increasingly suspicious posture toward the BRI, reflecting a complex dual attitude: on the one hand, European policymakers hoped that the initiative would bring substantial investment capital to the EU through the BRI framework, while on the other hand they remained reluctant to witness a continuous expansion of China's political and economic influence across Europe. To a considerable extent, this report captured the prevailing mindset within the EU's policymaking circles.

Given the strongly negative attitudes held by European think tanks and EU policymakers alike, BRI-related projects in Europe had only managed to make slow progress, with the numbers of infrastructure projects fully completed and mergers and acquisitions finalized remaining limited at the end of 2018. Even in Central European countries such as Hungary, Poland, and the Czech Republic, the advancement of BRI projects has not proceeded particularly rapidly, partly due to subtle obstruction from the

EU and partly because of the relatively low degree of structural complementarity between China's economy and the economies of these Central European states. For example, Hungarian scholar Tamas Matura of Corvinus University of Budapest observed on November 30, 2017 that the volume of investment brought by China to Central Europe through the BRI framework and the "16+1" mechanism had remained quite limited.①

In practice, China's investment and project cooperation in Europe within the BRI framework were concentrated primarily in three sub-regional clusters: the four states of the Visegrád Group in Central Europe, Greece in Southern Europe, and several countries in the Western Balkans such as Serbia and Montenegro. Among these regions, China's project cooperation with countries in the Western Balkans, particularly Serbia and Montenegro, was the most successful in comparative terms. At the level of national leadership, moreover, the governments of Hungary, Poland, Serbia, and Greece were most positive about both the BRI framework and the "16+1" cooperation mechanism, at least at the end of 2018.

2.3 EU Perceptions of China's Basic Economic System and the Question of China's "Market Economy Status," 2013-2018

Between 2013 and 2018, the EU's perception of the fundamental characteristics and developmental trajectory of China's economic system underwent a gradual yet profound shift, as EU institutions increasingly adopted a critical and skeptical stance toward China's basic economic institutions and expressed growing pessimism regarding the direction of China's economic and social development. More specifically, both the EU policymaking establishment and the European strategic research community came to believe that China's economic reform process had made little substantive progress and that the country's overall trajectory of economic and social development was moving further away from the normative framework of a market economy. This assessment led them to adopt an increasingly pessimistic view on the long-term prospect of the Chinese economy.

A particularly notable development in 2017, distinguishing that year from earlier periods, was the extent to which researchers at European and American think tanks began to focus more intensively on China's state sector and state-owned enterprises (SOEs). On the

① POLITICO, "China Hits Roadblocks in Central Europe: Tough Competition Laws and Investment from the Bloc Slow Beijing's Infrastructure Push", November 26, 2017.

one hand, they expressed stronger disapproval of the distinctive practices through which the Chinese state intervenes in economic decision-making and market operations; on the other hand, they demonstrated an unprecedented degree of vigilance toward both Chinese SOEs and private firms that receive various forms of state subsidy or government support, and consequently began to advocate much greater resistance to investment activities undertaken by these two categories of Chinese enterprises in Europe.

This shift in policy thinking was reflected in several concrete regulatory developments. On September 13, 2017, the European Commission released a framework document on the establishment of an EU-level investment screening mechanism, while on December 20 of the same year the EU formally put revised anti-dumping regulations into implementation. Both policy instruments contained detailed and stringent provisions designed to restrict the activities of precisely these categories of Chinese enterprises.[①] On the same date, the European Commission also issued an unprecedented analytical report, examining what it described as "distortions" in the Chinese economy.[②] This report—prepared under the auspices of the European Commission and jointly drafted by Bruegel and several other European think tanks—extended to more than 450 pages and presented a comprehensive analysis of the structural characteristics of China's socialist market economic system. In this extensive document, the authors offered a detailed synthesis of the institutional features of China's economic system and provided an elaborate examination of the mechanisms governing the allocation of key factors of production in China's domestic economy, including land, labor, capital, raw materials, and energy. The report ultimately concluded that China would be unable to escape several core structural characteristics inherited from the planned economy system and that the state sector and SOEs would continue to play a dominant role in China's economic structure in the near future.

---

① European Commission, Proposal for a Regulation Establishing a Framework for Screening of Foreign Direct Investments into the European Union, COM (2017) 487 final, 2017/0224 (COD), SWD (2017) 297 final, Brussels, September 13, 2017; Regulation (EU) 2017/2321 amending Regulation (EU) 2016/1036 on Protection against Dumped Imports from Countries not Members of the European Union and Regulation (EU) 2016/1037 on Protection against Subsidized Imports from Countries not Members of the European Union, L 338, *Official Journal of the European Union*, December 19, 2017.

② European Commission, SWD (2017) 483 final/2, Commission Staff Working Document on Significant Distortions in the Economy of the People's Republic of China for the Purposes of Trade Defense Investigations, Brussels, December 20, 2017.

Taken together, the publication of this report signaled that both the European think tank community and EU policymakers had developed a relatively deep and systematic understanding of the institutional characteristics of China's economic system, while simultaneously adopting a broadly negative evaluation of China's basic economic institutions and expressing an increasingly explicit lack of normative acceptance of the structural features of China's political economy. Since March 2017, the President of the European Commission, Jean-Claude Juncker, together with the EU Commissioner for Trade, Cecilia Malmstrom, repeatedly stated in public that China could not be regarded as a market economy. Their position, which had by then become quite explicit, indicated that the EU would not be prepared to grant China official recognition as a market economy, although this stance was not directly communicated in such unequivocal terms to China's senior leadership.[①]

III. The Basic Architecture and Substantive Content of the EU's Defensive Economic Policy toward China

The brief "decision window" that emerged between February and May 2012 quickly disappeared. Owing to internal disagreements and opposition during that period, the EU was unable to establish a comprehensive and systematic defensive economic policy toward China, nor did it succeed in constructing a coherent and tightly organized protectionist policy framework specifically directed at China. However, the prevailing social attitude and political fabrics in Europe have undergone profound shifts since 2016. Under the repeated impact of multiple internal and external crises, the EU is compelled to engage in a painful reassessment of its earlier strategic assumptions and make significant adjustment to its existing policy architecture.

In this broader context, following the emergence of two additional "Decision Windows": the first between February and June 2016 and the second between January and May 2017, EU institutions gradually sped up their policy discussions and decision-

---

① EU Trade Commissioner Cecilia Malmstrom, "A Progressive Trade Policy in a Protectionist Age", Speech in EESC Plenary Session, Brussels, March 29, 2017; "Europe's Progressive Trade Policy", Speech on the European Business Summit, Brussels, May 22, 2017; "Trade in a Protectionist World", Speech in the Lunch hosted by the Friedrich Naumann Foundation, Hamburg, May 23, 2017.

making activities concerning defensive economic measures toward China. As a result, the EU progressively established a systematic and increasingly stringent policy framework encompassing multiple policy domains, including trade, investment, industrial policy, technology transfer, and intellectual property protection. By this stage, the overall architecture of the EU's defensive economic policy toward China had become relatively comprehensive, and several of its component policy areas were clearly defined. Based on an examination of more than three hundred policy documents issued by the European Commission, the European Council, the Council of the European Union, and the European Parliament between 2012 and the end of 2018, this policy system can be summarized as comprising six major aspects or in other words, domains, as illustrated in Table 3.5. Taken together, this evolving policy framework has several notable characteristics that are likely to profoundly influence the long-term trajectory of China-EU relations, particularly in the domain of economic relations.

First, the overall orientation of this policy framework indicates that the EU's assessment of the essential characteristics of the Chinese economy, as well as its broader interpretation of China-EU economic relations, has undergone a significant shift from the prevailing perspectives of 2012-2013. On the one hand, the EU has come to recognize more clearly the scale and significance of China's rise in the global economic system. On the other hand, EU policymakers and analysts have developed a more explicit and systematic assessment of the structural features of China's basic economic institutions and of what they perceive to be the fundamental contradictions embedded into China-EU economic relations. In particular, many EU policy documents argue that China's economic system inherently produces "market distortions" and "industrial overcapacity," and that these structural characteristics make it difficult to avoid underlying tensions or structural conflict in China-EU economic relations.①

Such an assessment carries two significant implications. On the one hand, it has the potential to negatively influence the EU's conceptualization of the broader EU-China Comprehensive Strategic Partnership. On the other hand, it suggests that the EU may adopt a more assertive and uncompromising stance when addressing disputes over China-EU economic relations in the future. In fact, since 2013 the EU's official characterization

① European Commission, Commission Staff Working Document on Significant Distortions in the Economy of the People's Republic of China for the Purposes of Trade Defense Investigations, SWD (2017), 483 Final/2, Brussels, December 20, 2017.

and expectations regarding the China-EU strategic partnership have gradually become less clearly defined. During the China-EU Summit held in November 2013, EU leaders still expressed an explicitly positive assessment of the strategic partnership and articulated relatively high expectations for its future development. At that time, the President of the European Council, Herman Van Rompuy, stated that the EU hoped "to elevate the EU-China strategic partnership to a new level".① Yet the new generation of EU leadership that assumed office after 2013 did not provide a similarly clear conceptual definition of the strategic partnership framework.

The China-EU Summit held in 2015 focused primarily on technical issues of bilateral cooperation, while the ensuing summits convened in 2016 and 2017—amid widening disagreement between the two sides—did not produce joint communiqués. Although the joint statement issued following the 2018 China-EU Summit once again mentioned the concept of the strategic partnership, it did not provide a substantive elaboration of its meaning. Instead, much like the 2015 summit, it focused predominantly on technical areas of cooperation and dialogue. It is therefore evident that by the end of 2018 the EU leadership no longer harbored the same level of enthusiasm or expectation regarding the China-EU strategic partnership that was apparent in 2013.

Table 3.5: The Structure and Content of the EU's Defensive Economic Policy toward China

Provision / Domain	1. General Principles	2. Detailed Points
I.Fundamental Positioning	**I-1:** (1) China has become one of the world's most important economic powers and is therefore of major significance to the EU; (2) however, China's institutional system of "state capitalism" is believed to make contradictions and tensions in bilateral economic relations inevitable; (3) the EU should emphasize the principle of reciprocity and strive to establish a "level playing field" for European enterprises.	**I-2:** (1) China is considered not to have fully fulfilled its commitments upon accession to the World Trade Organization, and the EU therefore refuses to recognize China's Market Economy Status; (2) the economic system dominated by China's state sector is regarded as inevitably producing "market distortions," "overcapacity," and "unfair" investment practices, which are seen as harming the EU and must therefore be taken seriously.

① European Commission, Press Release, The 16th EU-China Summit in Beijing, November 21, 2013, IP/13/1099.

Provision / Domain	1. General Principles	2. Detailed Points
II.Overall Policy Framework	**II-1:** (1) Strengthen coordination among EU decision-making institutions and among member states, and address economic relations with China from the perspective of a "whole-of-the-EU strategy." (European Commission, Joint Communication to the European Parliament and the Council: Elements for a New EU Strategy on China, JOIN (2016) 30 final, Brussels, June 22, 2016); (2) emphasize the principles of "openness" and "fairness," and incorporate EU-China economic relations into the EU's broader strategic vision of "taming globalization."	**II-2:** (1) Promote further opening of the Chinese market to EU businesses; (2) treat the EU-China 2020 Strategic Agenda for Cooperation as a key guiding document for bilateral relations, while maintaining a skeptical attitude toward the Belt and Road Initiative and the "16+1 Cooperation" framework; (3) regard the advancement of negotiations on a EU-China Comprehensive Investment Agreement as a major priority, while refraining from initiating negotiations on a EU-China Free Trade Area for the time being; (4) closely monitor and guard against the potential challenges posed by China's industrial and technological policies, especially the "Made in China 2025" strategy, to Europe's high-end economic sectors.
III.Trade Policy	**III-1:** (1) The EU should regard the Asia-Pacific as a major direction for advancing its trade strategy, while maneuvering flexibly among China, Japan, and other Asia-Pacific economies; (2) substantially update and strengthen the EU's system of Trade Defence Instruments (TDI) in order to safeguard fair trade; (3) advocate changes to the existing WTO rules framework in order to place stronger constraints on China.	**III-2:** (1) While increasing the transparency and predictability of anti-dumping and anti-subsidy investigations, strengthen the authority and efficiency of the European Commission in conducting such investigations; (2) under certain circumstances suspend the "lesser duty rule," which is intended to reduce market disruption, in order to enhance the effectiveness of anti-dumping and countervailing measures; (3) discontinue the "analogue country" methodology for "non-market economies" such as China and instead adopt a case-by-case investigation of "market distortions."
IV.Investment Policy	**IV-1:** (1) Chinese investment in Europe has grown rapidly; acquisitions of strategic assets and high-technology enterprises are viewed as potentially altering the existing structure of the European economy and gradually posing a challenge to Europe, thereby requiring close monitoring and precaution; (2) establish a rigorous investment screening mechanism between the European Commission and EU member states, based on mutual notification and information sharing.	**IV-2:** (1) Establish concrete institutional arrangements and mechanisms for a Europe-wide cooperative investment screening system; (2) identify specific sectors such as energy, infrastructure, critical raw materials, and high-technology research and development, in which foreign investment should be subject to review; (3) clarify the operational procedures governing mutual notification between the European Commission and EU member states.

Domain \ Provision	1. General Principles	2. Detailed Points
V.Industrial Policy	**V-1:** (1) The EU must adopt a comprehensive strategic approach to respond to strong competition from countries such as China in global value chains and high-technology industries; (2) the EU should support research and development in industries associated with "smart manufacturing," while restricting foreign acquisitions of strategic assets; (3) develop specific industries through government procurement and public investment, while monitoring foreign participation in public procurement markets; (4) conduct ex ante assessments of major infrastructure projects in order to prevent improper foreign participation.	**V-2:** (1) Identify 27 "critical raw materials" and promote diversification of supply channels; (2) advance the digitalization of manufacturing sectors while restricting outward technology transfers, thereby strengthening Europe's position within global value chains; (3) prioritize support for a series of emerging industries capable of widely applying digital technologies and artificial intelligence, increasing investment and strengthening their information security; (4) promote indigenous research and development; (5) support these measures through policies that promote fair trade and investment.
VI.Intellectual Property Policy	**VI-1:** Approximately 80 percent of counterfeit and pirated products entering the EU originate from China, making China the most serious concern in the field of intellectual property protection and thus requiring the EU's highest level of attention.	**VI-2:** (1) Argue that China's regulations governing technology import and export, as well as technology transfer requirements in joint ventures, harm EU interests, and therefore initiate litigation against China within the WTO framework; (2) promote the EU-China Intellectual Property Dialogue and customs cooperation mechanisms in order to combat infringements of intellectual property rights.

Source: Compiled by the author

Second, the three principles repeatedly emphasized in this policy framework—openness, fairness, and reciprocity—constitute recurrent discursive themes in EU policy documents and reflect the EU's longstanding perception of and strategic interests in China-EU economic relations. From the EU's perspective, these relations have long suffered from a lack of symmetry: the European market is more open to Chinese goods and capital than the Chinese market to European products and investment.① For this reason, the EU has increasingly treated reciprocity as a fundamental guiding principle in the management of its economic relations with China. Numerous policy documents emphasize that economic interactions between the two sides should be conducted on the basis of parity and mutual openness, frequently invoking the concept of establishing "a level playing field" in which conditions of market access, competition, and regulatory treatment are perceived as equitable. In particular, EU policymakers have repeatedly stressed that China should further

① Anna Saarela, A New Era in EU-China Relations: More Wide-Ranging Strategic Cooperation? A Study Report for the European Parliament, July 19, 2018.

open its domestic market to European products and capital.

At present, the EU has come to interpret what it identifies as structural problems in China-EU economic relations as part of the broader challenges generated by globalization per se, and has accordingly incorporated these issues into the EU's wider strategic agenda aimed at "managing" or "constraining" globalization. This shift in perspective has strengthened the strategic dimension of the EU's approach to managing relations with China and has simultaneously rendered China-EU relations more complex and politically sensitive.

In summary, the EU's defensive economic policy toward China has developed into a complex and highly systematic policy architecture that is already profoundly influencing both the dynamics and the future trajectory of China-EU relations. As an important component of European civil society, European think tanks have played a subtle yet consequential role in the EU's deliberation and formulation of its defensive economic policy toward China. In particular, they have exerted a significant, if often understated, influence over the construction of the ideas and discursive frameworks of EU decision-makers, especially in such stages of the policymaking process as problem identification, agenda-setting, and the provision and selection of policy options.

For this reason, the following three chapters of this book will focus on three prominent European think tanks as case studies, examining in detail the mechanisms through which these institutions have influenced the development and implementation of the EU's defensive economic policy toward China.

Chapter 4: EU-Level Think Tanks' Influence over the EU's Defensive Economic Policy toward China: A Case Study of the Brussels European and Global Economic Laboratory (Bruegel)

According to the latest statistics presented in the *Global Go To Think Tank Index Report* released by the University of Pennsylvania at the end of January 2018, there were a total of 1,942 think tanks in Europe (excluding Russia) in 2017, accounting for 24.8% of the global total, globally second only after the United States.[①] Unlike the United States, however, the European think tank system has already evolved into a 'two-tier, four-actor' interactive structure. Given the profound Europe-wide influence exerted by the supranational-level EU, a number of European think tanks have consequently focused their research on issues pertaining to the EU and the pan-European region such as the EU's external policies and security strategies, its modes of engagement in world and regional affairs as a global actor, and the broader process of European integration, rather than concentrating solely on the affairs of any single European state. As such, these think tanks constitute what may be termed EU-level think tanks, and, due to their high degree of specialization and division of labor in research, they occupy a relatively distinctive and structurally significant position in the EU's decision-making system.

Existing literature often refers to EU-level think tanks as Brussels think tanks. However, in reality, not all EU-level think tanks are located in Brussels. For example, the Jacques Delors Institute (Notre Europe) is headquartered in Paris, while the European Council on Foreign Relations (ECFR) is based in London and has offices in Berlin, Paris, Rome, Madrid, and Sofia, but not in Brussels. Philippa Sherrington has pointed out that most

① James G. McGann, 2017 Global Go To Think Tank Index Report, Think Tanks and Civil Societies Program, University of Pennsylvania, January 31, 2018.

think tanks focusing primarily on EU affairs only emerged after the mid-1980s, whereas think tanks established in the European Commission itself were not created until after 1989. During the two decades since the 1980s, it was precisely alongside the expansion of EU competency and the increasing impact of EU decision-making on member states that think tank activities at the pan-European level gradually developed.① According to the statistical analysis conducted by Stephen Boucher in 2004, from the establishment of the European Coal and Steel Community in 1951 to the late 1970s, only five EU-level think tanks emerged in nearly three decades, while only ten additional institutions were established during the 1980s. By contrast, during the 1990s, against the backdrop of accelerated European integration and accompanied by the establishment of the Single Market and the Eurozone, 24 EU-level think tanks emerged, a number which is 1.6 times the total established over the preceding forty years. After 2000, however, the pace of development slowed, with only six new institutions established between 2000 and 2004.② More recent scholars, such as Dieter Plehwe and Ramona Coman, have argued that, since the beginning of the twenty-first century, two major crises of European integration have given rise to a substantial expansion in the number of EU-level think tanks. The first of these crises occurred in 2005, when France and the Netherlands rejected the Treaty establishing a Constitution for Europe through referendums, signaling widespread public skepticism at the grassroots level regarding the legitimacy of the then rapidly advancing process of European political integration. The second crisis emerged during the sovereign debt crisis in the euro area between 2009 and 2010, during which the demand among EU decision-making bodies for information, data, and consulting services rose sharply. In the aftermath of these two crises, the number of EU-level think tanks expanded significantly, and their position in the EU decision-making system was correspondingly strengthened.③ It is therefore evident that

① Philippa Sherrington, "Sharing European Union Policy: The Significance of Think Tank Activity, a Paper presented to the European Community Studies Association Sixth Biennial Conference", University of Pittsburgh, Pennsylvania, June 2-5, 1999.

② Stephen Boucher, *Europe and Its Think Tanks: A Promise to be Fulfilled*, Notre Europe, Paris, Studies and Research, No. 35, October, 2004, pp. 9-11. Simon Nichelson, in his unpublished master's thesis completed in 2009, likewise articulated this perspective.

③ Dieter Plewhe, Moritz Neujeffski, and Werner Kramer, "Saving the Dangerous Idea: Austerity Think Tank Networks in the European Union", *Policy and Society*, Vol. 37, No. 2, June 2018, pp. 188-205; Ramona Coman, "Why and How do Think Tanks Expand Their Networks in Times of Crisis? The Case of Bruegel and the Center the development of EU-level think tanks has been closely synchronized, both in speed and rhythm, with the broader process of European integration.

Stephen Boucher further observes that, among think tanks headquartered in EU member states, 149 institutions regard research on European regional issues as an important field, yet only 36 can be classified as genuinely EU-level think tanks.① The Bureau of European Policy Advisers (BEPA),② an internal advisory body of the European Commission, identified six of the most prominent Brussels think tanks in 2012: the Centre for European Policy Studies (CEPS), the European Policy Centre (EPC), the Lisbon Council, Bruegel, Friends of Europe, and the Egmont Institute.③ Since the 2016-2018 period, a number of scholars have shifted their focus to three prominent EU-level think tanks—Bruegel, Centre for European Policy Studies, and European Council on Foreign Relation—examining the relationship between their policy advice records and the EU's external economic policymaking.④ However, a comprehensive review of the existing literature suggests that, after the research report by Stephen Boucher was published in 2004, no subsequent study has provided a precise and systematic estimate of the overall number of EU-level think tanks. Currently, EU-level think tanks are generally characterized by their relatively small number, limited size, and limited access to resources. Consequently, they do not feature high in the University of Pennsylvania's annual global think tank rankings. Nevertheless, as these

---

for European Policy Studies," *Journal of European Public Policy*, Vol. 26, No. 2, 2019, pp. 268-301.

① Stephen Boucher, *Europe and Its Think Tanks: A Promise to be Fulfilled*, Notre Europe, Paris, Studies and Research, No. 35, October, 2004, P. 2.

② Following the inauguration of a new European Commission in September 2014, the Bureau of European Policy Advisers was restructured and renamed the European Political Strategy Centre (EPSC), with its status elevated to that of a Directorate-General-level body. Subsequently, after the formation of a new Commission under Ursula von der Leyen at the end of 2019, the institution was once again reorganized and rebranded as the Inspire, Debate, Engage and Accelerate Action (I.D.E.A.) unit.

③ Antonio Missiroli and Isabelle Ioannides (Eds.), "European Think Tanks and the EU", September 2012, Bureau of European Policy Advisers, EU Commission, P. 14.

④ Rosetta Collura, "Bruegel, EU Think Tank in the EU Multilevel Governance", LUISS School of Government, Working Paper Series, SOG-WP35/2016, Italy, October 2016; Ramona Coman, "Why and How do Think Tanks Expand Their Networks in Times of Crisis? The Case of Bruegel and the Center for European Policy Studies," *Journal of European Public Policy*, Vol. 26, No. 2, 2019, pp. 268-301; Jasa Veselinovic, "The Making of the EU's Geoeconomic 'Bazooka': The Anti-Coercion Instrument and the Role of Think Tanks in European Union Foreign Policy", *Journal of Common Market Studies*, Vol. 46, No. 1, 2024, pp. 79-97.

think tanks specialize in EU policy issues and are, in most cases, geographically proximate to the core institutions of EU decision-making, their influence on EU policymaking should by no means be underestimated.

I. Existing Literature on the Study of EU-Level Think Tanks

As the only supranational political entity in the world, the EU is not a naturally evolved nation-state, but rather a political construct shaped by European elites on the basis of abstract ideas and normative principles. European countries have not yet developed a highly unified sense of European identity, and the Europe-wide public sphere continues to exhibit a fragmented structure. As a consequence, the EU's decision-making system is built upon a framework of multi-level governance, rendering it considerably more complex than the policymaking systems of typical nation-states. This institutional complexity, in turn, makes theoretically grounded analyses of EU-level think tanks more difficult to develop than studies focusing on think tanks operating in EU member states. Although EU-level think tanks have attracted attention in the academic community, there remains a relative lack of dedicated and systematic studies.

A review of existing literature suggests that the evolution of research on EU-level think tanks can be broadly divided into several distinct phases. The first phase precedes the outbreak of the euro area sovereign debt crisis in 2009-2010. During this period, the body of literature was extremely limited in scope, and only rarely engaged with the question of how think tanks influence EU decision-making processes. The conference paper submitted by Philippa Sherrington in 1999 may be regarded as the earliest work focusing on EU-level think tanks; however, it primarily concentrates on classifying types of think tanks and provides only limited and somewhat cursory discussion of the mechanisms through which think tanks influence EU decision-making.① The research report *Europe and Its Think Tanks: A Promise to be Fulfilled*, published in 2004 by the Jacques Delors Institute under the direction of Stephen Boucher, offers a detailed and systematic study statistical overview

① Philippa Sherrington, "*Sharing European Union Policy: The Significance of Think Tank Activity*", Paper presented to the European Community Studies Association Sixth Biennial Conference, University of Pittsburgh, Pennsylvania, June 2-5, 1999.

of think-tanks at the EU level.[①] In the same year, a chapter included in the edited volume *Think Tank Traditions: Policy Research and the Politics of Ideas*, published in the United Kingdom, offers a general overview of EU-level think tanks, discussing their typologies, theoretical frameworks, and modes of influence, providing a fairly comprehensive picture.[②]

The second phase spans the period from 2010 to 2016. After 2010, as the euro area sovereign debt crisis intensified and became protracted, the demand among the EU and the political leaderships of its major member states for information and data about European economic and social conditions increased dramatically. At the same time, this crisis not only generated severe shocks to the global economy but also triggered profound structural transformations in the international strategic landscape. Through its far-reaching "ripple effect," it indirectly contributed to the outbreak of instability in the Middle East and North Africa at the end of 2010 and to the eruption of the Ukraine crisis in 2014, accelerating the fragmentation of Europe's surrounding geopolitical environment. As a consequence, European political elites developed an increasingly urgent demand for knowledge and information related to foreign policy and strategic affairs. Against this backdrop, the role of think tanks in economic and foreign policy decision-making in both the EU and its major member states began to become more pronounced. Scholarly research on European think tanks also expanded in response to these developments. During this period, seven academic articles and research reports specifically addressing EU-level think tanks were produced.[③] In addition, major disciplinary handbooks published during this period, which were primarily characterized by their function as compendia of scholarly knowledge, made reference to European think tanks multiple times. However, such treatments were largely cursory in

---

① Stephen Boucher, *Europe and Its Think Tanks: A Promise to be Fulfilled*, Notre Europe, Paris, Studies and Research, No. 35, October, 2004, pp. 9-11. Simon Nichelson, in his unpublished master's thesis completed in 2009, likewise articulated this perspective.

② Heidi Ullrich, "European Union Think Tanks: Generating Ideas, Analysis and Debate", in Diane Stone and Andrew Denham (Eds.), *Think Tank Traditions: Policy Research and the Politics of Ideas*, New York: Manchester University Press, 2004.

③ Representative literature on think tanks at the EU-level during this period includes: Marybel Perez, "Does EU Policymaking Allow for Skillful Networkers But Limited Knowledge Managers? The Think Tanks' Tale", *International Journal of Politics, Culture, and Society*, Vol. 27, No. 3, 2014, pp. 323-342; Johan Eriksson, Think Tanks and European Foreign Policy: Transnational Politics of Expertise, Paper presented at the Pan-European EISA Conference in Warsaw, September 18-21, 2013.

nature and seldom engaged in substantive analysis of the mechanisms or extent of think tank influence on EU decision-making.① During this phase, a research report published in September 2012 by the Bureau of European Policy Advisers—an internal think tank of the European Commission—entitled *European Think Tanks and the EU*, offered a comparatively more refined definition of EU-level think tanks.② However, similar to the report published in 2004 by Stephen Boucher, these studies primarily focused on descriptive aspects of EU-level think tanks themselves, such as their number, typology, and organizational characteristics. Although they briefly addressed the European Commission's support for and management of think tanks, they did not systematically analyze the influence of think tanks on EU decision-making. In addition, a small number of academic articles provided more detailed discussions of the operational mechanisms, channels of influence, and target actors through which "Brussels-based think tanks" exert influence over the EU. Again, their scope and depth of analytical work remained limited.③

The third phase extends from 2016 to the present. The year 2016 represented a critical watershed in European integration. In 2016, a series of systemic and disruptive crises—including the refugee influx, terrorist attacks, the United Kingdom's decision to withdraw from the EU, and the election of Donald Trump—unfolded in rapid succession, sending profound shocks to both economic globalization and the process of European integration. As a consequence, the EU's existing governance structures and decision-making mechanisms faced an unprecedented legitimacy issue, while the EU's so-called "democratic deficit" problem became increasingly acute. Against this backdrop, think tanks gain growing recognition and importance among European political elites for their ability to provide strategic analysis and policy advice. As European think tanks acquire an elevation status in

① Andrew F. Cooper et al. (Eds.), *The Oxford Handbook of Modern Diplomacy*, Oxford, UK: Oxford University Press, 2013. 22 instances that refer to think tanks in it. David Coen et al. (Eds.), *The Oxford Handbook of Business and Government*, Oxford, UK and New York: Oxford University Press, 2010. 14 instances that refer to think tanks in it.

② Antonio Missiroli and Isabelle Ioannides eds., European Think Tanks and the EU, September 2012, Bureau of European Policy Advisers, EU Commission.

③ Simon Nichelson, EU Think Tanks in Brussels: Policy-Making Roles, Functions and Influence, Thesis for the Degree of Master of European Politics and Policies, Katholieke Universiteit Leuven, 2009; Lorenzo Allio, the Role of Brussels-based Think Tanks in the EU Decision-Making Process, Thesis for the Degree of Master of European Studies, College of Europe, May, 2002.

the EU decision-making system, scholarly research on EU-level think tanks has also made great strides. More than ten academic articles and five monographs have emerged during this period,[①] many of which focus explicitly on analyzing the role and influence of these think tanks in EU decision-making. Moreover, these studies increasingly place think tanks alongside both interest and advocacy groups as key actors in the EU's systems of multilevel governance and interest representation, arguing that think tanks constitute one of the core components of these broader institutional and political frameworks.

Existing literature generally classifies EU-level think tanks into four main types: The first category refers to think tanks embedded into EU decision-making institutions. Sherrington argues that the establishment of the Forward Studies Unit by Jacques Delors, then-President of the European Commission in 1989, marked the beginning of a trend whereby the EU's highest decision-making bodies, particularly the European Commission, gradually created internal research units to assist policymakers in addressing urgent and specific policy challenges.[②] However, Lorenzo Allio assumes that, although such in-house think tanks lack institutional independence, they nevertheless contribute to fostering a Europe-wide atmosphere of policy debate.[③]

The second category is Brussels-based think tanks. These think tanks are committed to advancing European integration by promoting policy debates and engaging with complex policy issues, thus contributing to the formation of a pan-European epistemic community

---

① The representative works included in these papers and monographs are: Marybel Perez, "The Governance Turn in EU Foreign Policy: Are EU Think Tanks out of the Picture?" in Stephen Brooks, Donald Abelson, and Xin Hua (Eds.), *Think Tanks, Foreign Policy and Geo-Politics: Pathways to Influence*, London and New York: Routledge, 2016, pp. 63-82; Tatyana Bajenova, "Rescaling Expertise in EU Policy-making: European Think Tanks and Their Reliance on Symbolic, Political and Network Capital," *Globalization, Societies and Education*, Vol. 17, No. 1, 2018, pp. 61-77; Dieter Plewhe, Moritz Neujeffski, and Werner Kramer, "Saving the Dangerous Idea: Austerity Think Tank Networks in the European Union", *Policy and Society*, Vol. 37, No. 2, June 2018, pp. 188-205; Jasa Veselinovic, "The Making of the EU's Geoeconomic 'Bazooka': The Anti-Coercion Instrument and the Role of Think Tanks in European Union Foreign Policy", *Journal of Common Market Studies*, Vol. 46, No. 1, 2024, pp. 79-97.

② Philippa Sherrington, "Sharing European Union Policy: The Significance of Think Tank Activity", Paper presented to the European Community Studies Association Sixth Biennial Conference, University of Pittsburgh, Pennsylvania, June 2-5, 1999.

③ Lorenzo Allio, "The Role of Brussels-based Think Tanks in the EU Decision-Making Process", Thesis for the Degree of Master of European Studies, College of Europe, May 2002, pp. 24-25.

centered in Brussels that supports the integration process. Sherrington and others contend that these think tanks, in practice, perform functions analogous to those of political lobbyists, actively and strategically influencing agenda-setting within the EU in a manner comparable to that of interest groups and advocacy groups, and shaping political ideas and decision-making paradigms among political elites,① while Simon Nichelson point out that they exhibit pronounced characteristics of institutions operating at the supranational level.②

The third category consists of leading think tanks headquartered in EU member states but specializing in research on EU policy issues. These include, in particular, institutions in countries such as Germany, the United Kingdom, and Italy that conduct in-depth research on foreign and economic policy. Such think tanks typically have offices both in Brussels—the EU's institutional center—and in major cities in core member states, and generally sustain institutionalized channels of interaction and exchange with "Brussels-based think tanks." As a result, they may be conceptualized as "transnational think tanks."③ However, Allio labels this type as "EU-oriented think tanks".④

The fourth category comprises social organizations endowed with functions of information gathering and analysis, including political party foundations, interest groups, and advocacy groups. According to Sherrington, this category of think tanks encompasses, in particular, certain German political party foundations as well as interest groups. He argues that many traditional interest groups have progressively established dedicated research units and employed teams of experts to support their activities, thereby gradually acquiring functions analogous to those of think tanks. Against the backdrop of intense debate and

---

① Philippa Sherrington, "Sharing European Union Policy: The Significance of Think Tank Activity", Paper presented to the European Community Studies Association Sixth Biennial Conference, University of Pittsburgh, Pennsylvania, June 2-5, 1999, P. 10.

② Simon Nichelson, *EU Think Tanks in Brussels: Policy-Making Roles, Functions and Influence*, Thesis for the Degree of Master of European Politics and Policies, Katholieke Universiteit Leuven, 2009, pp. 26-27.

③ Philippa Sherrington, "Sharing European Union Policy: The Significance of Think Tank Activity", Paper presented to the European Community Studies Association Sixth Biennial Conference, University of Pittsburgh, Pennsylvania, June 2-5, 1999, pp. 10-12; Tatyana Bajenova, "Rescaling Expertise in EU Policy-making: European Think Tanks and Their Reliance on Symbolic, Political and Network Capital," *Globalization, Societies and Education*, Vol. 17, No. 1, 2018, pp. 61-77.

④ Lorenzo Allio, the Role of Brussels-based Think Tanks in the EU Decision-Making Process, Thesis for the Degree of Master of European Studies, College of Europe, May 2002, pp. 25-26.

controversy generated by the process of European integration, the conventional boundaries between interest groups and think tanks at the EU level have become increasingly blurred. Indeed, some interest groups played a leading role in shaping policy debates during the early 1990s, particularly in the process of advancing the establishment of the European single market, in a manner functionally indistinguishable from that of think tanks.① Among more recent scholars, Jesper Dahl Kelstrup and Dieter Plehwe likewise conceptualize political party foundations in countries such as Germany and the Netherlands as a distinct type of think tanks. By examining their activities across transnational party alliances at the European level, party groups in the European Parliament, and parliamentary party structures in EU member states, they analyze the mechanisms through which such actors exert influence over EU decision-making.②

A review of existing literature reveals a notable convergence around several key arguments. First, scholars generally agree that the European Commission constitutes the primary institutional recipient of policy advice from Brussels-based think tanks, maintaining the closest and most longstanding relationships with these organizations among all EU decision-making bodies. Although interactions between the European Parliament and Brussels-based think tanks have increased significantly since 2016, they remain less extensive and less institutionalized than those between such think tanks and the European Commission.③ Second, it is widely argued that, following the outbreak of the euro area sovereign debt crisis in 2009-2010, the EU's "democratic deficit" problem has become increasingly acute, while the legitimacy of its regulations and policies has been subjected to unprecedented levels of scrutiny and contestation. In response, EU decision-making bodies have come to place greater emphasis on the data, policy-relevant information, strategic

---

① Philippa Sherrington, "Sharing European Union Policy: The Significance of Think Tank Activity", Paper presented to the European Community Studies Association Sixth Biennial Conference, University of Pittsburgh, Pennsylvania, June 2-5, 1999, pp. 6-8;

② Ibid, p. 13.

③ Marybel Perez, "Does EU Policymaking Allow for Skillful Networkers But Limited Knowledge Managers? The Think Tanks' Tale", *International Journal of Politics, Culture, and Society*, Vol. 27, No. 3, 2014, pp. 323-342; Tatyana Bajenova, "Rescaling Expertise in EU Policy-making: European Think Tanks and Their Reliance on Symbolic, Political and Network Capital," *Globalization, Societies and Education*, Vol. 17, No. 1, 2018, pp. 61-77; "European Think Tanks as a Channel of EU Public Diplomacy Towards Transnational Publics," *Politics and Governance*, Vol. 11, Issue 3, 2023, pp. 206-208.

analysis, and policy advice records provided by think tanks, becoming increasingly reliant on these institutions as a means of mitigating the democratic deficit. Consequently, Brussels-based think tanks has expanded significantly in numbers, their position in the EU decision-making system has been markedly strengthened, and they have entered a new phase of rapid development.① Third, a growing body of scholarship contends that, since 2016, Brussels-based think tanks—viewed as an integral component of Europe's "knowledge production system"—occupy a central position in the EU's "power-knowledge nexus," and therefore exert a considerable influence over EU decision-making.② Fourth, existing studies generally reveal that, as the sovereign debt crisis persists, Brussels-based think tanks have, since 2011, increasingly prioritized the construction of networks of communication and collaboration among themselves. These inter-think tank networks have gradually expanded across Europe through mechanisms such as joint conferences and collaborative research projects. At the same time, more think tanks from EU member states that are not headquartered in Brussels set up offices in the city in an effort to integrate into these networks of interaction and cooperation.③ Fifth, many scholars note that EU-level think tanks, which were traditionally focused on policy research and information exchange, have become progressively more active in political lobbying, resembling business-oriented lobbying groups to an increasing extent. In this sense, they have effectively evolved into a distinctive type of interest group

① Ramona Coman, "Why and How do Think Tanks Expand Their Networks in Times of Crisis? The Case of Bruegel and the Center for European Policy Studies," *Journal of European Public Policy*, Vol. 26, No. 2, 2019, pp. 268-301; Dieter Plewhe, Moritz Neujeffski, and Werner Kramer, "Saving the Dangerous Idea: Austerity Think Tank Networks in the European Union", *Policy and Society*, Vol. 37, No. 2, June 2018, pp. 192-194.

② Jasa Veselinovic, "The Making of the EU's Geoeconomic 'Bazooka': The Anti-Coercion Instrument and the Role of Think Tanks in European Union Foreign Policy", *Journal of Common Market Studies*, Vol. 46, No. 1, 2024, pp. 79-97; "European Foreign Policy Think Tanks and 'Strategic Autonomy': Making Sense of the EU's Role in the World of Geonomics," in Milan Babic et al. (Eds.), *The Political Economy of Geoeconomics: Europe in a Changing World*, Cham, Switzerland: 2022, pp. 81-87.

③ Tatyana Bajenova, "Rescaling Expertise in EU Policy-making: European Think Tanks and Their Reliance on Symbolic, Political and Network Capital," *Globalization, Societies and Education*, Vol. 17, No. 1 2018, pp. 61-77; "European Think Tanks as a Channel of EU Public Diplomacy Towards Transnational Publics," *Politics and Governance*, Vol. 11, Issue 3, 2023, pp. 206- 207; Dieter Plewhe, Moritz Neujeffski, and Werner Kramer, "Saving the Dangerous Idea: Austerity Think Tank Networks in the European Union", *Policy and Society*, Vol. 37, No. 2, June 2018, pp. 191-192.

and become highly active actors in the EU's system of interest representation.①

While existing literature provides detailed and largely consistent typologies of EU-level think tanks, there is a marked divergence in how scholars assess their position and role in the EU decision-making system. Sherrington argues that EU-level think tanks maintain dense and multifaceted connections with core EU decision-makers as well as with European business communities, and are therefore, to some extent, organizations that are influenced—if not shaped-by political elites embedded into the EU's decision—making architecture.② By contrast, Heidi Ullrich contends that, due to their relatively small number and the limited degree of competition among them, EU-level think tanks have not developed to their full potential, and consequently exert only indirect and constrained influence over EU decision-making.③ Similarly, Nichelson maintains that EU-level think tanks occupy a "marginal position" in EU policymaking.④ Stephen Boucher adopts a more moderate stance, characterizing the influence of these think tanks as one that "adds limited value" to EU affairs—"useful, but limited" in its overall effect. He further argues that the advisory services provided by such think tanks are, at times, overly general and insufficiently attuned to the concrete needs of EU policymakers, thus constraining their capacity to exert tangible influence over decision-making outcomes.⑤ The most positive assessment is offered by the Bureau of European Policy Advisers, which characterizes EU-level think tanks as important actors in the pan-European public sphere. According to this view, as the scope of

① Ramona Coman, "Why and How do Think Tanks Expand Their Networks in Times of Crisis? The Case of Bruegel and the Center for European Policy Studies," *Journal of European Public Policy*, Vol. 26, No. 2, 2019, pp. 286-301; Heloise Robino, EU Think Tanks' Lobbing Strategies: Think Tanks' Strategic Choices to Influence Public Policy, Master Thesis for MSc Public Administration, Leiden University, the Hague, June 11, 2018, pp. 10-14.

② Philippa Sherrington, "Sharing European Union Policy: The Significance of Think Tank Activity", a Paper presented to the European Community Studies Association Sixth Biennial Conference, University of Pittsburgh, Pennsylvania, June 2-5, 1999, P. 15.

③ Heidi Ullrich, "European Union Think Tanks: Generating Ideas, Analysis and Debate", in Diane Stone and Andrew Denham eds., *Think Tank Traditions: Policy Research and the Politics of Ideas*, New York: Manchester University Press, 2004, P. 56, pp. 67-69.

④ Simon Nichelson, "EU Think Tanks in Brussels: Policy-Making Roles, Functions and Influence", a Thesis for the Degree of Master of European Politics and Policies, Katholieke Universiteit Leuven, 2009, pp. 22-23.

⑤ Stephen Boucher, "Europe and Its Think Tanks: a Promise to be Fulfilled," Notre Europe, Paris, Studies and Research, No. 35, October, 2004, pp. 87-88.

EU governance expands and the complexity of its decision-making processes increases, the position of these think tanks is becoming progressively more prominent, and their influence is likely to grow, enabling them to play a formative role in shaping policy outcomes.① Taken together, these sharply divergent assessments not only underscore the extent to which evaluating the influence of think tanks on policymaking remains a highly contested and methodologically challenging issue—one that resists precise quantification and is therefore subject to differing interpretations—but also indicate that both the EU's political decision-making system and EU-level think tanks themselves are undergoing continuous and dynamic transformations.

The above-mentioned literature, when illustrating successful examples of "Brussels-based think tanks," consistently refers to the Brussels European and Global Economic Laboratory (Bruegel) as one of the most representative cases. As early as 1999, Sherrington observed that this think tank maintains close and multifaceted connections with EU administrative officials, members of the European Parliament, political actors in EU member states, corporate executives, the academic community, and the media.② Heidi Ullrich holds a similar view, characterizing the institute as "a key voice in the EU decision-making process."③ In other words, this think tank constitutes a paradigmatic example of what Thomas Medvetz conceptualizes as the "central space of the field of power," situated at the intersection of the political, economic, academic, and media spheres. Stephen Boucher places Bruegel alongside the Centre for European Policy Studies (CEPS) as the two "most well-known, most respected, and most influential" Brussels-based think tanks, further arguing that these two institutions command the greatest share of resources within this community.④ Similarly, Lorenzo Allio identifies Bruegel and CEPS as the two dominant

① Antonio Missiroli and Isabelle Ioannides eds., European Think Tanks and the EU, September 2012, Bureau of European Policy Advisers, EU Commission, P. 13.

② Philippa Sherrington, "Sharing European Union Policy: The Significance of Think Tank Activity", a Paper presented to the European Community Studies Association Six Biennial Conference, University of Pittsburgh, Pennsylvania, June 2-5, 1999, P. 9.

③ Heidi Ullrich, "European Union Think Tanks: Generating Ideas, Analysis and Debate", in Diane Stone and Andrew Denham eds., *Think Tank Traditions: Policy Research and the Politics of Ideas*, New York: Manchester University Press, 2004, P. 57.

④ Stephen Boucher, "Europe and Its Think Tanks: a Promise to be Fulfilled, Notre Europe", Paris, Studies and Research, No. 35, October 2004, pp. 44-45.

Brussels-based think tanks, while noting that Bruegel demonstrates particular strength in cultivating interpersonal networks with EU policymakers and the European financial sector.① Nichelson, for his part, includes Bruegel—together with the Centre for European Policy Studies, the European Policy Centre, and the European Centre for International Political Economy—among the think tanks capable of exerting substantial influence over EU economic policymaking.② Furthermore, in the 2012 report issued by the Bureau of European Policy Advisers, Bruegel is ranked third among six prominent Brussels-based think tanks. More recent studies since 2016 have also devoted exclusive attention to Bruegel, with at least two articles offering in-depth analyses of its role in shaping the agenda, ideas, and policy narratives of EU decision-makers.③ In light of Bruegel's prominent position in the community of Brussels-based think tanks, this chapter takes the institute as a primary case study in order to examine its influence over EU decision-making.

II. The Rhythm and Effectiveness of Bruegel's Influence over the EU's Defensive Economic Policymaking toward China: A Comparison between Policy Advice Records and EU Official Policy Documents

Current literature on think tanks generally does not deny that think tanks can exert subtle and indirect influence over policymaking. However, there is also a wide acknowledgement that, in highly complex and rapidly evolving decision-making processes, it is extremely difficult to clearly identify and verify the extent of such influence, let alone to conduct precise quantitative analysis of its magnitude. Nevertheless, if policymakers are indeed influenced by think tanks, it can be inferred that the situational assessments and policy advice articulated in the records of think tanks policy recommendations will exhibit

---

① Lorenzo Allio, "the Role of Brussels-based Think Tanks in the EU Decision-Making Process", a Thesis for the Degree of Master of European Studies, College of Europe, May, 2002, P. 55.

② Simon Nichelson, "EU Think Tanks in Brussels: Policy-Making Roles, Functions and Influence", a Thesis for the Degree of Master of European Politics and Policies, Katholieke Universiteit Leuven, 2009, P. 33.

③ Rosetta Collura, Bruegel: EU Think Tank in the EU Multilevel Governance, LUISS School of Government, Working Paper Series, SOG-WP35/2016, Italy, October 2016; Ramona Coman, "Why and How do Think Tanks Expand Their Networks in Times of Crisis? The Case of Bruegel and the Center for European Policy Studies," *Journal of European Public Policy*, Vol. 26, No. 2, 2019, pp. 286 301.

similarities or correspondences with the ideas, opinions, conceptual systems, and discursive structures employed by policymakers in their deliberation and formulation of specific policy frameworks. Accordingly, by comparing think tanks' policy advice records with official decision-making documents—examining the linkages between their concepts, discourses, and viewpoints—and further analyzing the specific forms and timing with which particular points and ideas of policy components are articulated in think tank outputs, in comparison with how and when the same components appear in official policy documents, it is possible to identify both the substantive effects and the temporal dynamics of think tank influence over policymaking. Admittedly, given that multiple think tanks in the broader think tank system engage in frequent interactions with policymakers, it is difficult to establish definitively that a specific policy component adopted by policymakers is attributable to the influence of any single think tank. However, insofar as a particular think tank ranks among the leading and most prominent institutions and occupies a significant position within the policymaking epistemic community, it is reasonable to infer that it, as an important part of the think tank system, exerts a meaningful influence over policymakers' deliberation and formulation of that policy component.

Bruegel is widely recognized in the European think tank and academic community as one of the three most influential Brussels think tanks and as maintaining the closest connections with EU decision-making bodies.[①] Consequently, comparing its policy advice records with EU official policy documents carries clear empirical significance. On this basis, drawing upon the six categories and twelve specific components of the EU's Defensive Economic Policy toward China listed in Table 3.5, the author conducts a systematic analysis of 176 policy advice records produced by Bruegel between June 2006 and September 2018,[②] as well as more than 300 EU official policy documents issued from the opening of

① Between 2013 and 2019, the author conducted extensive fieldwork and interviews across Europe, engaging in broad-based interactions with both the think tank community and the academic community. Insights gathered from these exchanges indicate a broad consensus among practitioners and scholars alike that, in addition to Bruegel, the two other Brussels-based think tanks most widely recognized for their influence are the Centre for European Policy Studies (CEPS) and the European Policy Centre (EPC).

② The 176 advisory outputs produced by Bruegel that address the key elements of the EU's defensive economic policy toward China cannot be listed exhaustively here; however, the publications that most comprehensively or most distinctly reflect the Institute's stances and perspectives include the following: Andre Sapir, "Some Ideas for Reforming the Community Anti-Dumping Instrument", Bruegel Policy Contribution, Issue 3, July 2006; Noclas the first policy window in February 2012 to September 2018.[①] By recording and comparing the timing and forms in which both Bruegel and EU decision-making bodies address the specific policy components listed in Table 3.5, the author constructs Table 4.1.

Veron, "Should Emerging Multinationals be Kept Out?", Bruegel Blog Post, October 7, 2006; Nicolas Veron, "A Multipolar Business World", *La Tribune*, February 19, 2007; Lars-Hendrik Roller, "Safe and Sound: An EU Approach to Sovereign Investment", Bruegel Policy Brief, Issue 08, November, 2008; Jean Pisani-Ferry, "China and the World Economy: A European Perspective", Bruegel Policy Contribution, Issue 2010/03, March 2010; Jean Pisani-Ferry, "International Asymmetries Redux", April 5, 2010; Reinhilde Veugelers, "A G2 for Science?", Bruegel Policy Brief, Issue 2011/03, April 2011; Philippe Aghion, Julian Boulanger, and Elie Cohen, "Rethinking Industrial Policy", Bruegel Policy Brief, Issue 2011/04, June 2011; "China Invests in Europe: Patterns, Impacts, and Policy Issues", Bruegel Conference Records, June 7, 2012; Reinhilde Veugelers, "The World Innovation Landscape: Asia Rising?", Bruegel Policy Contribution, Issue 2013/02, February 2013, (Ed.), *Manufacturing Europe's Future*, Bruegel Blueprint Series Vol. XXI, October 2013; Mario Mariniello, "Is Chinese Competition Policy a Cause for Concern?", Bruegel Policy Contribution, Issue 2013/14, October 2013; Jim O'Neill and Alessio Terzi, "Changing Trade Patterns, Unchanging European and Global Governance", Bruegel Working Paper, 2014/02, February 2014; Andre Sapir and Guntram B. Wolff, "The Great Transformation: Memo to the Incoming EU Presidents", Issue 2014/04, July 2014; Alicia Garcia Herrero, "MERICS Report on China's FDI in Europe: Some Comments and Ideas", Bruegel Conference Records, June 29, 2015; Guntram B. Wolff and Thomas Walsh, "The Dragon Sneezes, Europe Catches a Cold", Bruegel Blog Post, August 26, 2015; Alicia Garcia Herrero, "China Continues to Focus on Growth, not Reform", Bruegel Blog Post, March 4, 2016; Alicia Garcia Herrero and Jianwei Xu, "China's Belt and Road Initiative: Can Europe Expect Trade Gains?", Bruegel Working Paper, Issue 5/2016; Alicia Garcia Herrero, "China's State-owned Enterprises Reform Still Lacking Bite", Bruegel Opinion, October 4, 2016; Maria Demertzis, "Europe in a New World Order", Bruegel Policy Brief, Issue 2, February 2017; Alicia Garcia Herrero and Jianwei Xu, "How to Handle State-owned Enterprises in EU-China Investment Talks", Bruegel Policy Contribution, Issue 18, June 2017; Reinhilde Veugelers, "The Challenge of China's Rise as a Science and Technology Powerhouse", Bruegel Policy Contribution, Issue 19, July 2017; Alicia Garcia Herrero, K. G. Kwok, Liu Xiangdong, Tim Summers and Zhang Yansheng, "EU-China Economic Relations to 2025: Building a Common Future", September 2017.

① The policy documents referred to in this study denote the official documents of the European Commission, the European Council, the Council of the European Union, and the European Parliament. These official documents represent the outcomes of discussions and deliberations conducted by the respective institutions on a given issue, thereby articulating their official stances and positions. Consequently, the proposals and rules recorded in these official documents, along with the intentions, conceptions, and policy designs extrapolated from them, possess a considerable degree of decisional rigidity. The specific forms of official documents issued by the EU's decision-making institutions include: Communications and Proposals from the European Commission; Conclusions, Decisions, and Outcomes from the European Council and the Council of the European Union; Resolutions from the European Parliament; as well as Regulations and Directives published in the *Official Journal of the European Union*.

Table 4.1: Comparative Timelines of Bruegel's Policy Recommendations and EU Official Policy Documents on the EU's Defensive Economic Policy toward China (February 2006-September 2018)

Key Policy Points / Entity Proposing or Formulating Key Policy Points			Bruegel's Reference to and Commentary on Relevant Policy Elements (Format / Time)	Explicit Reference to Relevant Policy Elements in Official Decision-Making Documents of EU Authorities (Format/Time)		
				The European Commission	**The European Parliament**	**The European Council and The Council of the EU**
I. Fundamental Positioning	I-1 General Principles	Format	Media commentaries; research briefs; policy reports; conference speeches	Policy communications	Opinions; resolutions	Council decisions
		Time	Feb 2007; Mar & Oct 2010; Nov 2013; Mar 2014; Jun 2015; Feb, Jun & Sep 2017	Jun 2016; Sep 2017	Apr, May & Jun 2016	Jul 2016
	I-2 Detailed Points	Format	Media commentaries; research reports	Policy communications; analytical reports	Analytical reports	Council decisions
		Time	Apr 2010; Apr & Nov 2013; Mar 2016; Jun & Sep 2017	Jun-Jul 2016; May, Sep & Dec 2017	Nov 2017	Jun & Jul 2016
II. Overall Framework	II-1 General Principles	Format	Policy advisory reports; policy briefs	Policy communications; evaluation reports	Research reports	Council decisions
		Time	Sep 2014; Sep 2017	Jun 2016; May 2017	Apr 2017	Jul 2016
	II-2 Detailed Points	Format	Policy advisory reports; joint research reports	Policy communications; research reports	Analytical reports	—
		Time	Apr 2011; Jun & Oct 2015; Feb 2017	Jun 2016; May, Sep & Dec 2017	Nov 2017	—

Key Policy Points	**Entity Proposing or Formulating Key Policy Points**	**Bruegel's Reference to and Commentary on Relevant Policy Elements (Format / Time)**	**Explicit Reference to Relevant Policy Elements in Official Decision-Making Documents of EU Authorities (Format/Time)**			
			The European Commission		**The European Parliament**	**The European Council and The Council of the EU**
III. Trade Policy	III-1 General Principles	Format	Policy advisory reports; joint research reports	Evaluation reports; policy communications	Evaluation reports; legislative drafts	Legislative acts; Council decisions
		Time	Jul 2006; Oct 2013; Feb & Sep 2014; Feb & Mar 2017; Apr 2018	Apr 2013; Oct-Nov 2016	Oct 2013; Jun 2017	Jun, Oct & Nov 2016
	II-2 Detailed Points	Format	Policy advisory reports; policy briefs; media commentaries.	Evaluation reports; working documents; legislative drafts; proposals; press releases	Voting records; resolutions	Meeting conclusions; legislation; press releases
		Time	Jul 2006; Jun 2013; Sep 2015; Feb 2017	Apr 2013; Jun, Oct & Nov 2016; Sep & Dec 2017; Jan, Apr, Jun & Jul 2018	Jun 2016; Jun 2017; May 2018	Oct 2016; Nov-Dec 2017; Apr 2018
IV. Investment Policy	IV-1 General Principles	Format	Media commentaries; policy briefs; conference speeches	Working reports; policy communications	Legislative drafts; debate records	Press releases
		Time	Jul 2006; Nov-Dec 2008; Jun 2012; Dec 2014; May & Oct 2015; Apr (twice) & Sep (twice) 2017	May & Sep 2017	Mar 2017; May-Jun 2018	Jun 2018
	IV-2 Detailed Points	Format	Media commentaries; joint research reports	Working reports; technical issue lists; policy communications	Draft legislative revisions	—
		Time	Dec 2014; May 2015; Apr & Sep 2017	Sep 2017 (multiple)	Jun 2018	—

Key Policy Points \ Entity Proposing or Formulating Key Policy Points			Bruegel's Reference to and Commentary on Relevant Policy Elements (Format / Time)	Explicit Reference to Relevant Policy Elements in Official Decision-Making Documents of EU Authorities (Format/Time)			
				The European Commission		The European Parliament	The European Council and The Council of the EU
V. Industrial Policy	V-1 General Principles	Format	Policy advisory reports; policy briefs	Explanatory notes; policy communications		Resolutions	Council decisions
		Time	Jun 2011; Feb 2013; Jul 2014	Mar 2016; Sep 2017		Jul 2017	May 2017
	V-2 Detailed Points	Format	Research reports	Policy communications; working reports; technical issue lists		Resolutions	—
		Time	Jun 2011	Sep 2017 (twice); Oct-Nov 2017		Jul 2017	—
VI. Intellectual Property Policy	VI-1 General Principles	Format	Research reports	Working reports; press releases		—	—
		Time	Mar 2014	Feb-Mar 2018		—	—
	VI-2 Detailed Points	Format	Joint research reports	Policy communications; working reports; press releases		—	Press releases
		Time	Apr 2017	Nov 2017; Feb-Mar & Jun 2018		—	Jun 2018

Source: Compiled by the author

Table 4.1 demonstrates that, prior to the emergence of the two policy windows in February 2012 and February 2016 concerning the EU's defensive economic policymaking toward China, Bruegel had already conducted sustained observation and research on the relevant issues. It had produced a range of outputs, including media commentaries, research reports, and working papers, while also organizing and documenting a series of related seminars and conferences. Among the twelve specific policy components of the EU's defensive economic policy toward China listed in Table 3.5, a number of components appeared both in Bruegel's policy advice records and in EU official policy documents. A comparison between the formats and dates of Bruegel's records and those of EU documents on these components reveals a clear temporal sequence, thematic linkage, discursive consistency, and convergence of viewpoints between the two. Given that Bruegel is widely recognized as one of the three major Brussels think tanks and constitutes an important member of the EU-level epistemic community in policymaking, it can therefore be reasonably inferred that Bruegel has exerted a discernible influence over the EU's decision-making process regarding its defensive economic policy toward China.

From a temporal perspective, prior to the opening of the first policy window in February 2012, Bruegel's research had already extended to multiple domains of the EU's defensive economic policy toward China, albeit with relatively low frequency. Following the gradual completion of the decision-making process triggered by this first policy window by the end of 2012, and up until the full opening of the second policy window between February and June 2016, Bruegel's research activities became more frequent. After the emergence of the third policy window in January 2017, Bruegel's research progressed in parallel with the EU's decision-making process. Overall, in four major domains of the EU's policy toward China—fundamental positioning, overall framework, trade policy, and investment policy—the rhythm of Bruegel's research activities exhibits a high degree of correspondence with the progression of EU decision-making. Furthermore, a closer examination of the frequency and temporal distribution with which Bruegel's policy advice records address the policy components listed in Table 3.5 also reveals several notable characteristics.

First, there are clear differences in the degree of attention and depth of research that Bruegel devotes to different policy domains within the EU's defensive economic policy toward China. Among the six policy domains identified in Table 3.5, Bruegel's policy advice records most frequently and extensively address the four domains of fundamental positioning, overall framework, trade policy, and investment policy. Following the issuance of programmatic official policy documents by the EU in these domains in the second half of 2016 and throughout 2017, Bruegel continued to conduct extensive follow-up research, producing a series of reports, working papers, and academic studies. This indicates that Bruegel attaches the highest level of importance to these four domains and conducts the most in-depth and systematic research on these areas. By contrast, Bruegel devotes rather limited attention to the domains of industrial policy and intellectual property policy. Its policy advice records only make infrequent reference to policy components in these two domains, often merely in passing, while intellectual property policy is only briefly mentioned in two research reports. This suggests that, as a think tank specializing in economic policy, Bruegel concentrates its analytical focus on the traditional core areas of economic policy with direct strategic significance—namely, the broader political and diplomatic implications of economic policy, as well as trade and investment—while largely excluding more technical and data-intensive domains such as industrial policy and intellectual property, which are also more closely connected to practical policy implementation.

Second, by comparing the distribution of policy components addressed by Bruegel between the "General Principles" and "Detailed Points" in Table 3.5 in each policy domain, it can be observed that, with the exception of "Overall Framework", Bruegel more frequently deals with policy components at the level of "General Principles" than at the level of "Detailed Points". This discrepancy is particularly pronounced in the domain of investment policy, which indicates that Bruegel's research orientation is primarily long-term, macro-level, strategic, and systemic in nature, rather than focused on the design of specific, technical policy instruments. Indeed, in the field of think tank research, there has long been a debate on think tank's choice of prioritization between a strategic orientation and a problem-solving (or operational) orientation. One group of scholars argues that think tanks should play a high-level strategic role by assessing shifts in the balance of power, analyzing long-term macro trends, providing forecasts regarding overall developments, and constructing strategic policy frameworks. In contrast, another group contends that think tanks should prioritize providing decision-makers with concrete policy solutions to urgent and complex problems, particularly in times of rapid change or crisis. The former emphasizes long-term strategic analysis, whereas the latter focuses on technical and problem-specific policy advice. The evidence presented in Table 3.5 suggests that Bruegel places greater emphasis on strategic research and corresponding advisory functions, which reflects its overall institutional orientation and operational philosophy.

Third, a comparison across the four policy domains in which Bruegel makes most reference to the EU's key policy elements reveals a differentiated pattern of attention. The institute devoted a longer period of sustained attention to and a higher degree of analytical focus on two areas in particular: fundamental positioning, and investment policy, especially the latter. References to key EU policy elements were also most frequent in these two domains. By contrast, its attention to the overall policy architecture and to trade policy was more limited. The comparatively dense attention devoted to basic positioning suggests that Bruegel was highly sensitive to changes in the broader environment and attached considerable importance to assessing the overall configuration and longer-term strategic trends. More broadly, this indicates that the institute possessed strong capabilities in collecting and analyzing macro-level political information and economic data. Meanwhile, the fact that its policy recommendations were more heavily concentrated in the field of investment policy than in that of trade policy suggests that it devoted more research resources to issues of capital and finance than to the more traditional domain of goods circulation. This pattern not only reflects Bruegel's comparative research strengths in particular areas, but also indicates that, from the perspective of the EU decision-making process, its research agenda displayed a notable degree of forward-looking capacity and was able, to some extent, to anticipate and even shape the EU policy agenda. Indeed, as early as 2008, when the study of sovereign wealth funds was only beginning to emerge in international economics, experts at Bruegel had already argued that, in order to safeguard European economic security, an EU-level investment screening mechanism should be established and that closer attention should be paid to investment activities undertaken by Chinese state-owned enterprises (SOEs). By contrast, it was not until September 2017 that the European Commission formally introduced a proposal to establish a coordinated investment screening framework at the EU level, led by the Union and implemented in cooperation with its member states. In other words, Bruegel advanced this pioneering policy idea fully a decade before the European Commission placed the issue of investment screening onto the formal decision-making agenda.①

III. Bruegel's Short-Term Influence over the EU's Defensive Economic Policy toward China: An Examination of the Meetings Convened by Bruegel

As discussed in Chapter 2, think tank conferences constitute a crucial platform through which think tanks—conceptualized as occupying the central space of the field of power—engage in processes of information exchange and resource interaction with the four constituent spheres of the broader field of power, namely the political, economic, academic, and media spheres. In settings where policymakers are present, such interactions enable think tanks to exert a certain degree of direct influence over the decision-making process. Table 2.1 provides a systematic typology and characterization of the various forms of think

① Lars-Hendrik Roller and Nicolas Veron, "A European Framework for Foreign Investment", Bruegel Blog Post, December 5, 2008.

tank conferences. Building upon this analytical framework, the author conducts a statistical analysis of 49 conferences organized by Bruegel between December 2011 and June 2018 that are directly related to China-EU economic relations and the EU's economic policy toward China, the results of which are presented in Table 4.2. An analysis of Table 4.2 reveals the structural characteristics of the interaction mechanisms through which Bruegel engages, by means of think tank forum as a platform, with the EU's decision-making bodies, as well as with other components of the EU "field of power," and, on this basis, allows for an assessment of the pathways and mechanisms through which the institute exerts influence over EU decision-making in this policy domain.

Table 4.2: Statistics on Meetings Convened by Bruegel Directly Related to EU-China Relations and the EU's Economic Policy toward China (December 2011-June 2018)

Structural Characteristics / **Meeting Types**			**I. High-Level Forums**	**II. Lectures**	**III. Policy Report Launch Events**	**IV. Large-Scale Symposiums**	**V. Closed-Door Workshops**	**Total**
1. Meetings with clear records of EU decision-making body officials (including former officials) participating as guests	Including officials from the European Commission's Directorates-General (DGs)	Number of meetings attended	4	1	2	4	10	17
		Participation rate (percentage of attendees compared to the total number of such meetings)	44.4%	12.5%	28.6%	44.4%	55.6%	34.7%
	Including officials from EU financial decision-making and management bodies	Number of meetings attended	7	—	—	—	—	7
		Participation rate	77.8%	—	—	—	—	14.3%
	Total participation of officials from EU decision-making bodies (after removal of duplicates)	**Number of meetings attended**	**7**	**1**	**3**	**4**	**11**	**25**
		Participation rate	**77.8%**	**12.5%**	**42.6%**	**44.4%**	**61.1%**	**51%**

Structural Characteristics \ Meeting Types			I. High-Level Forums	II. Lectures	III. Policy Report Launch Events	IV. Large-Scale Symposiums	V. Closed-Door Workshops	Total
2. Meetings with clear records of EU member state decision-making body officials (including former officials) participating as guests	Including officials from EU member states' economic decision-making departments	Number of meetings attended	7	—	1	3	2	12
		Participation rate	77.8%	—	14.3%	33.3%	11.1%	24.5%
	Including officials from EU member states' foreign affairs systems	Number of meetings attended	1	—	1	1	—	2
		Participation Rate	11.1%	—	14.3%	11.1%	—	4.1%
	Total participation of officials from EU member state decision-making bodies (after removal of duplicates)	**Number of meetings attended**	**7**	**—**	**1**	**4**	**2**	**13**
		Participation rate	**77.8%**	**—**	**14.3%**	**44.4%**	**11.1%**	**26.5%**
3. Meetings with clear records of international economic organization decision-makers (including former officials) participating as guests		Number of meetings attended	8	3	7	6	5	24
		Participation rate	**88.9%**	**37.5%**	**77.8%**	**66.7%**	**27.8%**	**49%**
4. Meetings with clear records of officials from Chinese decision-making departments and embassies/consulates (including former officials) participating as guests		Number of meetings attended	3	1	—	1	5	9
		Participation rate	**33.3%**	**12.5%**	—	**11.1%**	**27.8%**	**18.4%**
5. Meetings with clear records of representatives from the European financial sector (including banks, investment companies, asset management firms, stock exchanges, rating agencies, etc.) and their interest groups participating as guests		Number of meetings attended	7	1	2	3	4	16
		Participation rate	**77.8%**	**12.5%**	**22.2%**	**33.3%**	**22.2%**	**32.7%**

Structural Characteristics \ Meeting Types		I. High-Level Forums	II. Lectures	III. Policy Report Launch Events	IV. Large-Scale Symposiums	V. Closed-Door Workshops	Total
6. Meetings with clear records of representatives from the European business and industry sectors outside of finance and their interest groups participating as guests	Number of meetings attended	3	—	2	4	2	9
	Participation rate	**33.3%**	—	**22.2%**	**44.4%**	**11.1%**	**18.4%**
7. Meetings with clear records of representatives from European professional service firms (including law firms, accounting firms, business consultancies, lobbying and public relations firms) participating as guests	Number of meetings Attended	3	1	3	6	3	12
	Participation rate	**33.3%**	**12.5%**	**33.3%**	**66.7%**	**16.7%**	**24.5%**
8. Meetings with clear records of representatives from the European media participating as guests	Number of meetings attended	—	—	—	1	2	3
	Participation rate	—	—	—	**11.1%**	**11.1%**	**6.1%**
9. Meetings with clear records of scholars from European universities and think tanks participating as guests	Number of meetings attended	9	4	5	7	9	31
	Participation rate	**100%**	**50%**	**55.6%**	**77.8%**	**50%**	**63.3%**
10. Total number of each meeting type as a percentage of all meetings (including two closed-door meetings with unspecified details, the total number of meetings is 49)	Total number of this meeting type	9	8	9	9	18	49
	Percentage of total meetings	**18.4%**	**16.3%**	**14.3%**	**14.3%**	**36.7%**	**100%**

Notes:

1) For the first five columns of data in the table (from "I. High-Level Forum" to "V. Closed-Door Thematic Workshop"), the "Participation rate" metrics indicates the ratio of the number of attendances of a specific type of participants for each meeting type to the total number of that meeting type. In the final column ("Total Attendance After Duplicate Removal and Its Percentage of Total Meetings"), the "Participation rate" metrics indicates the ratio of the total number of attendances of a specific type of participants across all meetings to the total of 49 meetings counted in this table.

2) The identification of a participant's background is based on the institution of their current or former full-time employment.

3) "Participation as a guest" refers to instances where attendees were invited to deliver a keynote speech during the

opening or closing ceremonies, present a thematic address during discussion sessions, or serve as a moderator or discussant during the seminar portions of the meetings.

4) Due to the fact that the same participant might attend different types of meetings, and some meetings possess attributes of more than one type (such as being simultaneously a lecture and a policy report launch). There are overlaps in the statistics in the table. Furthermore, because of the limited space here, the first and second categories cannot list all types of institutional backgrounds of decision-making body attendees. Therefore, the numbers in the table cannot be directly summed vertically or horizontally.

5) Specialized EU technical decision-making and management bodies refer to institutions responsible for specific economic and financial affairs, such as the European Central Bank (ECB), the European Investment Bank (EIB), the European Investment Fund, and the European Union Agency for Cybersecurity (ENISA), among others.

Source: Compiled by the author based on records of 49 meetings held by the Institute between December 2011 and June 2018

Table 4.2 provides an overall picture of the operational structure of Bruegel's think tank conference system in the field of the EU's defensive economic policy toward China. It shows that, among the four constituent spheres of the field of power—namely the political, economic, academic, and media spheres—Bruegel maintains the closest connections with the academic community through the platform of think tank conferences, followed by the political sphere, then the economic sphere, and finally the media. Particularly noteworthy is that, by organizing such conferences, the institute has also maintained a certain degree of contact with Chinese decision-makers, in fact a function akin to Track Two communication between China and the EU. Through a more detailed analysis, several key characteristics are revealed. First, in the political sphere of the field of power, Bruegel maintains significantly closer ties with EU-level decision-makers and international economic organizations than with decision-makers in EU member states. Officials from EU decision-making bodies and international economic organizations participate as speakers or guests in the five types of conferences at a markedly higher frequency than officials from member states. On the one hand, this reflects the institute's identity as a Brussels think tank, in the sense that it is able to leverage its geographical proximity to exert influence directly over EU-level policymakers. On the other hand, it also indicates that the institute places a high degree of emphasis on, and conducts in-depth research into, the international multilateral trading system and the architecture of global economic governance. This is evidenced by its ability to attract officials from institutions such as the International Monetary Fund, the World Bank, and the Organisation for Economic Co-operation and Development to participate in its conferences. More broadly, this suggests that Bruegel possesses a certain degree of influence over agenda-setting and the conception of policy ideas not only at the EU level but also in the wider global economic governance system.

Second, in the EU decision-making system, Bruegel maintained relatively close ties with the European Commission's Directorates-General (DGs), whereas its connections with specialized EU bodies responsible for monetary and financial affairs—such as the European Central Bank (ECB) and the European Investment Bank (EIB)—were noticeably more limited. At the level of EU member states, the institute was more closely connected to economic decision-making departments than to diplomatic institutions, with which its ties remained comparatively weak. Officials from the Commission's DGs participated in all five types of meetings organized by the institute, and did so especially frequently in small-scale seminars, which were more specialized and more tightly focused on specific issues. By contrast, officials from EU financial authorities such as the ECB participated only in high-level forums. This suggests that the principal targets of the think tank's influence were officials in the Commission's DGs, especially DG Trade and DG ECFIN, who exercised macro-level responsibility for steering and advancing the EU's defensive economic decision-making toward China. At the same time, officials from the economic decision-making departments of EU member states participated in twelve meetings across four categories, whereas officials from diplomatic institutions participated in only two. The disparity is striking. It indicates that the institute exerted only limited influence over member states in the diplomatic and strategic domains, a pattern that in turn reflects its professional character as a think tank specializing in economic policy.

Third, in the domain of EU policymaking on economic relations with China, Bruegel maintains closer interactions with the European financial sector than not only with industrial and commercial actors in the real economy and professional service providers such as law and accounting firms, but also with decision-makers in EU member states. This indicates that the European financial sector demonstrates a high level of attention to and participation in China-EU economic relations and EU economic policymaking toward China, which makes it a significant interest group and influential factor that cannot be overlooked. Among the 49 conferences included in Table 4.2, representatives from the financial sector participated in 16, only one fewer than the number of participations by officials from the European Commission, and they also took part in four highly specialized closed-door workshops, demonstrating a notably high level of engagement. This finding also suggests that, in the domain of the EU's economic policy toward China, the financial sector constitutes one of the key channels through which Bruegel is able to exert indirect influence over decision-making. Similarly, the institute maintains relatively close ties with professional organizations such as law firms and accounting firms, indicating that such actors also play a certain intermediary or brokerage role in the processes of information exchange and resource circulation across the four spheres of the field of power.

Finally, an examination of the frequency with which different components of the field of power participate in various types of think tank conferences also reveals important structural characteristics of the institute's conference platform system. In terms of the total number of events, the three types of conferences—namely high-level forums, lectures, and policy reports launches—are strikingly similar in number, whereas the number of closed-door thematic workshops is approximately twice as large. This clearly indicates that closed-door thematic workshops constitute the most important operational format of think tank conferences in the field of the EU's economic policy toward China. Such workshops are characterized by a limited number of participants, a high level of technical specialization, and a relative homogeneity in participants' professional backgrounds and policy concerns. As a result, participants tend to share similar analytical perspectives and approaches to the issues under discussion, thereby enabling more focused, intensive, and effective communication and mutual influence. The institute treated such meetings as its principal platform for engagement in EU economic decision-making toward China. Given that officials from the Commission's DGs participated in more than half of these meetings, this format was the primary and most critical channel through which the institute exerted influence over EU decision-makers in this field.

IV. Bruegel's Long-Term Indirect Influence over the EU's Defensive Economic Policy toward China: An Analysis of Its Participation in Inter-Think Tank Research Collaboration Platforms

Institutionalized inter-think tank research collaboration platforms refer to structured arrangements through which multiple think tanks, by way of mutual agreement, establish mechanisms of coordination and cooperation by jointly undertaking research projects, co-authoring and publishing reports or academic papers, co-organizing seminars, and engaging in regular exchanges of information and data. Through such arrangements, each platform generates synergies in research capacity, thereby collectively enhancing the empirical accuracy, theoretical depth, and evidentiary richness of studies in a given academic discipline or policy domain. In functional terms, inter-think tank research collaboration platforms bear a strong resemblance to what Pierre Bourdieu conceptualizes as the field of cultural production, in that they are capable of generating spillover effects across the four constituent spheres of the field of power—namely the political, economic, academic, and media domains—, thereby producing a certain degree of influence. Accordingly, much like think tank conferences, such platforms can also serve as operational hubs linking these four spheres in the broader field of power. However, unlike think tank conferences, research collaboration platforms of think tanks typically operate without frequent participation from decision-makers; as a result, their influence tends to be indirect in nature. Nevertheless, insofar as such platforms are sustained over time, the influence they generate can persist and accumulate in the long term.

On this basis, the author compiles and systematizes relevant information on three inter-think tank research collaboration platforms in which Bruegel participates that are directly related to EU economic decision-making toward China and China-EU economic relations during the 2016-2018 period, the results of which are presented in Table 4.3. An analysis of Table 4.3 makes it possible to identify the operational modes and mechanisms through which the institute exerts long-term indirect influence over the EU's defensive economic policymaking toward China. The specific characteristics of the three research collaboration platforms in this policy domain in which the Bruegel participates are presented in Table 4.3. Among these three platforms, the platform that most intensively focuses on China-EU economic relations and the EU's economic policy toward China is the Asia-Europe Economic Forum (AEEF) mechanism. This mechanism is composed of economic policy research think tanks from Germany, France, China, and South Korea, alongside Bruegel at the EU level and the research department of the Asian Development Bank. It takes as its principal mode of interaction one to two high-level forums per year, during which key issues of mutual concern to decision-makers in the Asia-Pacific region and the EU—particularly those relating to bilateral economic relations—are intensively discussed. From 2011 to the end of 2018, every high-level forum organized under this platform included discussions on China-EU economic relations and the EU's economic policy toward China. Among these, the 10th forum, held in May 2014 under the theme of "Asia and Europe in a Changing Global Context," and the 12th forum, held in October 2015 under the theme of "Global Public Goods Governance: Asian and European Perspectives," featured particularly extensive deliberations on China-EU economic relations and the EU's trade policy toward China. A number of the assessments and viewpoints articulated during these forums were subsequently reflected in the EU's official policy documents following the opening of the second policy window in February 2016. Besides, the 13th forum, held in September 2016 under the theme of "Navigating the New Wave: Economic Perspectives from Europe and Asia," provided an evaluation of China-EU economic relations under the broader framework of global economic governance and put forward a number of forward-looking policy recommendations regarding the EU's economic policy toward China. Some of these forward-looking recommendations were subsequently incorporated into the EU's defensive trade and investment policies toward China adopted between September 2017 and the end of 2018.

Table 4.3: Think Tank Collaboration Platforms Involving Bruegel in EU Economic Decision-Making on China (2016-2018)

Name / Characteristics	Asia-Europe Economic Forum (AEEF) Mechanism	Bruegel Annual Conference Mechanism	Brussels Think Tank Dialogue (BTTD)
Institution(s) responsible for leading and operating the platform	With responsibilities for leading and operating the platform rotate among its member institutions	Organized and operated by Bruegel	With responsibilities for organizing and operating the platform in rotation among its member institutions
Membership composition of the platform	Composed of seven think tanks and foundations: Bruegel, the Bertelsmann Stiftung (Germany), the Centre d'Études Prospectives et d'Informations Internationales (CEPII, France), the Asian Development Bank Institute (ADBI), the Chongyang Institute for Financial Studies at Renmin University of China, and the East Asian Studies Center at Korea University	Composed of important members of Bruegel's membership assembly, particularly companies, interest groups, and the EU's decision-making departments and its member states that pay high annual fees to Bruegel	Composed of three think tanks and foundations: Bruegel, the Bertelsmann Stiftung (Germany), and the Centre for European Policy Studies (CEPS)

Characteristics \ Name	Asia-Europe Economic Forum (AEEF) Mechanism	Bruegel Annual Conference Mechanism	Brussels Think Tank Dialogue (BTTD)
Regular exchange mechanism of the platform	High-level forums held once or twice annually	A high-level forum held annually in September or October, lasting one day, often accompanied by a closed-door annual dinner that facilitates direct exchange between EU leadership and various sectors of society	An annual high-level forum held at the end of January; however, this mechanism has not been convened since 2016.
Research areas of the platform and their relevance to the EU's economic policy toward China	The platform focuses on interregional and bilateral economic relations between Europe and East Asia, as well as comparative studies of economic dynamics and policies between the two regions. Given that China is the largest economy in East Asia, EU-China economic relations and the EU's economic policy toward China constitute integral components of its research focus,	The platform focuses on the annual hot-button issues that are of greatest concern to the EU's decision-making hierarchy and are most widely discussed within European civil society, among which the analysis of hot topics in EU-China economic relations is included.	The platform focuses on studying changes in the EU's economic and political systems, discussing the annual State of the Union address, and selecting the most critical decision-making issues prioritized by the EU's leadership for in-depth research and exchange.
Connection between the platform and the EU's decision-making bodies	Officials from the European Commission's Directorates-General for Trade (DG TRADE) and Economic and Financial Affairs (DG ECFIN), as well as from the European Central Bank (ECB) and the European Bank for Reconstruction and Development (EBRD), occasionally participate in its annual high-level forums.	Tusk, then-President of the European Council, the European Commissioners responsible for Trade, Economic and Financial Affairs, and Members of the European Parliament (MEPs) sometimes attend its annual conference.	The leaderships of the European Council, the Council of the European Union, and the European Commission may participate in its annual forum. For instance, Herman Van Rompuy, then-President of the European Council, and José Manuel Barroso, then-President of the European Commission, attended the annual forum in 2013.
The Platform's influence over the EU's economic policy-making toward China	The perspective on "Asia-Europe cooperation to strengthen the international multilateral trading system," proposed at the 2014 forum, was reflected in the European Commission's 2016 communication *Elements for a New EU Strategy on China*. The new trends in trade and investment policy discussed at the 2016 forum were evident in the EU's official policy documents on defensive trade and investment measures toward China, issued between September and November 2017.	The 2015 annual conference explored "New Dynamics in Relations between Emerging Markets and the EU," offering perspectives on how the EU could cooperate with emerging market countries like China to advance global governance, while also evaluating the structural characteristics of the Chinese economy. These points were reflected in the 2016 communication *Elements for a New EU Strategy on China* and the EU's trade and investment policy documents concerning China released in September 2017.	The fourth session of the 2013 annual forum and the third session of the 2014 annual forum focused on deliberating the direction of the EU's new foreign policy, presenting strategic visions for future EU-China economic relations. Several of these points were incorporated into the 2016 communication *Elements for a New EU Strategy on China*.

Source: Compiled by the author

On the other hand, as indicated in Table 4.3, the collaboration platform that maintains the closest connections with the EU decision-making bodies is the Bruegel Annual Meetings mechanism. The core component of this mechanism is the annual conference convened in Brussels by Bruegel, which brings together a diverse set of participants, including representatives of member organizations that provide financial contributions to the institute, representatives of pan-European interest groups based in Brussels, and members of the EU. Notably, former Presidents of the European Council, including Herman Van Rompuy and Donald Tusk, as well as former Presidents of the European Commission, such as José Manuel Durão Barroso and Jean-Claude Juncker, have all participated in these annual meetings. In addition to the conference itself, a complementary event—namely the Annual Dinner—is typically before or after the main sessions. This event is frequently attended by senior EU leaders, officials from the various Directorates-General of the European Commission, and leading figures from EU monetary and financial authorities, including the European Central Bank. Through face-to-face and intensive interactions with representatives from European interest groups, the business and financial sectors, professional organizations, the media, universities, and think tanks, the Annual Dinner functions as one of the most direct channels and venues through which think tanks and broader societal actors can articulate interests and exert influence over EU decision-makers. At the same time, the institute also makes use of the annual meetings and the Annual Dinner as platforms for disseminating its annual reports, in which it synthesizes the major developments and underlying drivers of change in the international environment over the preceding year, while also providing forward-looking assessments of future trends.

In fact, some of the research collaboration platforms in which Bruegel participates implicitly incorporate two linkage channels to different components of the field of power. On the one hand, these platforms are connected to the political decision-making layer through large-scale research projects funded by the European Commission. On the other hand, they are linked to the broader public and other components of the field of power through major events—such as regular high-level forums—at which the institute occasionally disseminates the research outputs generated through these collaboration platforms. Although the three research platforms listed in Table 4.3 are not directly associated with specific research projects, they nonetheless perform the function of facilitating the exchange of information and resources in the "central space" of the field of power.

V. Bruegel's Long-Term Direct Influence over the EU's Defensive Economic Policy toward China: An Analysis of the "Revolving Door" Mechanism

The 'revolving door' mechanism refers to relatively stable, long-term channels of interpersonal communication established by researchers and administrators in think tanks on the basis of their prior professional experience, or their concurrent appointments at other institutions, through which enduring networks of personal relationships and institutional linkages are accumulated and maintained. This mechanism is most prominently manifested in the U.S. think tank system. According to several European think tank experts interviewed by the author, however, the revolving door mechanism is less pronounced among EU-level think tanks in Brussels. This is primarily because a considerable number of officials in the EU decision-making system tend, both prior to and following their departure from office, to take up positions in the parliaments or governments of their respective member states. Nevertheless, a systematic analysis of the personnel composition and professional trajectories of Brussels-based think tanks still reveals the existence of certain patterns of institutional and interpersonal linkage, from which it is possible to identify the networks connecting specific think tanks with various components of the EU's field of power through interpersonal interaction.

The organizational structure of Bruegel comprises several distinct layers. 1) it includes a Board of Directors composed of elite figures drawn from various sectors of society. The Board is responsible for reviewing and determining all strategic matters, including the institute's budget, the list of research projects, and its overall development direction, although it does not directly manage financial or research operations. In other words, the Board constitutes the highest decision-making body exercising substantive authority in the institute. Members of the Board typically hold full-time positions at other institutions and serve on Bruegel's Board in a part-time capacity, without receiving remuneration from the institute. They generally possess extensive professional experience and maintain close connections with all components of the EU and member-state field of power. Then-Chair of the Board in 2018, Jean-Claude Trichet, is a French national who has held senior positions in France's Ministry of Finance, Ministry of Economy, and central bank, and has also worked at the International Monetary Fund and the World Bank. 2) Bruegel includes a Scientific Council composed of scholars with distinguished research achievements. This body is responsible for evaluating and guiding the institute's research activities, as well as providing recommendations to the Board on professional and academic matters, and it effectively oversees the day-to-day operation of the institute's research work. Then-Chair of the Scientific Council in 2018 was Guntram B. Wolff, who had previously taught at the University of Pittsburgh and the Université libre de Bruxelles.

Bruegel is a relatively small think tank and does not maintain dedicated area studies teams. As of September 30, 2018, its research team consisted of 50 experts, while its management team comprised 19 members, although the curriculum vitae of three members of its management were not publicly disclosed. Based on a systematic review and statistical analysis of the professional backgrounds of 50 research staff and 16 members of the management team who were in post as of 30 September 2018, the author has compiled the results presented in Table 4.4.

Table 4.4: Bruegel's "Revolving Door": A Statistical Overview (as of September 30, 2018)

Category and Member Type	Department	Research Expert Team		Think Tank Senior Management Team	
		Number	% of Expert Team	Number	% of Senior Management Team
1. EU decision-making and administrative authorities	EU Commission (DGs)	12	24%	1	6.25%
	Specialized EU bodies responsible for monetary and financial affairs (e.g., ECB, EBRD)	9	18%	1	6.25%
	Other EU institutions and bodies (e.g., European Parliament, Council of the EU)	—	—	3	18.8%
	Total with professional experience in EU decision-making and administrative authorities	*21*	*42%*	*5*	*31.3%*
2. Official decision-making bodies of European countries	Economic advisory teams of heads of government, or ministries of finance, or ministries of economy in European countries	6	12%	4	25%
	Central banks of European countries	10	20%	3	18.8%
	Other economic decision-making and management bodies of European countries	2	4%	—	—
	Foreign affairs and external relations systems of European countries	2	4%	—	—

Category and Member Type \ Department		Research Expert Team		Think Tank Senior Management Team	
		Number	% of Expert Team	Number	% of Senior Management Team
2. Official decision-making bodies of European countries	Other departments in European countries (e.g., foreign/intelligence services, parliaments, local governments)	2	4%	2	12.5%
	Total with Professional experience in official decision-making bodies of European countries	***22***	***44%***	***9***	***56.2%***
3. Official decision-making bodies of countries outside Europe		***2***	***4%***		
4. International economic organizations		***11***	***22%***	***3***	***18.8%***
5. Financial sector (e.g., banking, securities, insurance, trust) and its interest groups	European financial sector	7	14%	4	25%
	Financial sector outside Europe	3	6%	—	—
	Total with professional experience in the financial sector	***10***	***20%***	***4***	***25%***
6. General business and industry (real economy sectors) and their interest groups	European general business and industry	4	8%	3	18.8%
	General business and industry outside Europe	1	2%	—	—
	Total with professional experience in general business and industry	***5***	***10%***	***3***	***18.8%***
7. Professional service firms (e.g., law firms, accounting firms, business consultancies, political lobbying and public relations firms)	European professional service firms	3	6%	1	6.3%
	Professional service firms outside Europe	4	8%		
	Total with experience in professional service firms	*7*	***14%***	***1***	***6.3%***
8. European Media		***3***	***6%***	—	—
9. Think tank sector	Other European think tanks	18	36%	9	56.3%
	Non-European think tanks	5	10%	—	—
	Total with experience in other think tanks	***23***	***46%***	***9***	***56.3%***
10. Universities	European universities	21	42%	10	62.5%
	Non-European Universities	10	20%	1	6.3%
	Total with professional experience in universities	***31***	***62%***	***11***	***68.8%***

Note:

"Professional experience" refers to current or past stable and institutionalized employment history. Specifically, this includes full-time employment in a certain capacity or part-time service as a member of a formal, permanent body in an institution (e.g., serving as an independent director on a company's board, or holding a formal academic position at a university). If an individual included in the statistics had experience in several sub-categories of a single major category listed in the table above, to avoid duplicate counting, they were counted under the sub-category where they held the longest tenure. In case of equal tenure length, they were counted under the sub-category where they held the most recent position. Therefore, there is no duplicate counting for each major category in the table. However, because many experts and managers have rich professional experiences across several major categories in the table, duplicate counting between the major categories is unavoidable; thus, the totals across the major categories cannot be aggregated vertically. As of 30 September 2018, the institute had 50 research experts with identifiable professional backgrounds and 16 senior managers.

Source: Compiled by the author

Table 4.4 reveals several key characteristics of the 'revolving door' mechanism within Bruegel:

First, the degree of connection between the institute's researchers and experts and the EU-level decision-making bodies is broadly comparable to that between these researchers and decision-makers at the level of EU member states; however, the institute's senior management maintains significantly closer ties with member states than with EU decision-making bodies. A substantial proportion of the senior management consists of members of the Board of Directors, and these individuals generally possess far more extensive professional experience in member-state institutions than at the EU level. This characteristic is not entirely consistent with the relational structure of the institute's conference platform as revealed in Table 4.2. To some extent, this suggests that, when the institute exerts influence over EU decision-making through the interpersonal communication channels established by the 'revolving door' mechanism, the "national route (also called the member-state pathway)" and the "Brussels route (also known as the "Brussels pathway") as discussed in Chapter 2, are of equal importance. In other words, at the level of informal interpersonal interaction and personnel linkages, a considerable proportion of the institute's influence over EU policymaking is mediated through the economic decision-making departments of EU member states.

Second, in the EU-level decision-making system, the personnel linkages between members of the institute and EU monetary and financial authorities-such as the European Central Bank-were nearly as close as those between the institute and the European Commission's DGs. At the level of EU member states, moreover, the institute maintained closer ties with national central banks than with general economic policymaking bodies such as ministries of finance or economy. This pattern suggests that the institute possesses a comparative advantage in research on macro-level and strategic issues related to monetary and financial policy at the EU level, relative to other policy domains. In this field, its accumulated strengths in professional networks and research capacity enable it to access key information and data more readily and to conduct more detailed and in-depth analysis. As a result, the institute demonstrates a relative research advantage in monetary and financial issues related to China-EU economic relations and the EU's economic policy toward China. By contrast, it shows no comparable advantage in more technical trade-related issues, and accordingly does not allocate significant resources to this area. This helps to explain the pattern observed in Table 4.1, where reference to key elements of the EU's defensive economic policy toward China appears more frequently in the domain of investment than in that of trade. Put differently, because EU investment policy is closely linked to financial issues such as capital flows and foreign exchange movements-areas in which the institute has particular expertise-it devotes greater resources and attention to this domain.

Indeed, the institute has paid sustained attention to three issues in particular: the stability of China's monetary system, the internationalization of the renminbi, and China's participation in global financial governance. Between 2011 and September 2018, research outputs in this area were produced on an almost quarterly basis.

VI. Summary of Chapter 4

The influence of think tanks over policymaking constitutes one of the most challenging yet most widely debated focal points in think tank studies, and has long been characterized by a diversity of perspectives. Simon James argues that think tanks primarily exert what he terms "atmospheric influence," that is, by defining policy problems, constructing discursive frameworks, and shaping policy ideas, they influence the broader environment within which decisions are made, thereby altering the paradigms through which policymakers interpret and analyze issues.[①]

By contrast, Diane Stone and others contend that think tanks operate through mechanisms such as epistemic communities, advocacy coalitions, or discourse coalitions, through which they contribute to the social construction of policy ideas and, in doing so,

① Simon James, "Influencing Government Policy-making", in Diane Stone (Ed.), *Banking on Knowledge: The Genesis of the Global Development Network*, London: Routledge, 2000, pp. 162-180.

exert latent and indirect influence over agenda-setting processes.① Donald E. Abelson observes that "almost everyone acknowledges that measuring think tank influence is difficult, yet few can resist attempting to do so." He attributes this persistent effort to three factors: the demands of empirical research, the competitive pressures among think tanks and the needs of policymakers, media actors, and the broader public who rely on think tanks for information and policy advice.② He further emphasizes that informal and non-public interpersonal exchanges between think tank actors and policymakers constitute one of the most significant channels of influence, metaphorically describing such activities as operating under an "invisibility cloak."③ Nevertheless, these scholars broadly agree that the influence of think tanks over policymaking remains inherently difficult to measure. The relatively limited body of literature focusing on EU-level think tanks generally concurs that such institutions exert a discernible influence over EU policymaking. For instance, Stephen Boucher suggests that EU-level think tanks have a "potentially significant influence" over EU decision-making and constitute an important component of the European political system's "soft power."④ A report published in September 2012 by the Bureau of European Policy Advisers likewise characterizes EU-level think tanks as "shapers of ideas" in EU policy debates and notes their increasing importance.⑤ At the same time, however, these studies also acknowledge that the influence of EU-level think tanks remains uncertain and difficult to quantify. Accordingly, any analysis of the mechanisms through which EU-level think tanks influence EU decision-making requires the development of a robust analytical framework.

This chapter focuses on Bruegel as a representative case of the EU-level think tanks, and adopts the analytical framework developed in the preceding sections—one that

① Diane Stone, *Public Policy Analysis and Think Tanks*, in Frank Fischer (Ed.), *Public Policy Analysis: Theories, Politics, and Methods*, London: CRC Press, 2007, P. 156.

② Donald E. Abelson, Stephen Brooks and Xin Hua (Eds.), *Think Tanks, Foreign Policy and Geopolitics: Pathways to Influence*, London: Routledge, 2016, P. 3.

③ Donald E. Abelson, *A Capital Idea: Think Tanks and US Foreign Policy*, McGill-Queen's University Press, 2006, P. 178.

④ Stephen Boucher, *Europe and Its Think Tanks: a Promise to be Fulfilled*, Notre Europe, Paris, Studies and Research, No. 35, October, 2004, pp. 11-13.

⑤ Antonio Missiroli and Isabelle Ioannides (Eds.), European Think Tanks and the EU, September 2012, Bureau of European Policy Advisers, EU Commission, P. 1.

integrates the multiple streams model of agenda-setting with the perspective of the central space of the field of power—to examine and explain the mechanisms through which the institute exerts influence over the EU's defensive economic policy toward China. This study argues that the influence of Bruegel over EU decision-making in this policy domain can be analyzed from four principal dimensions.

First, by comparing the institute's policy advice records with EU official policy documents, and by examining both the substantive alignment of policy components and their temporal sequencing, it is possible to identify the overall patterns of its influence. In particular, prior to the opening of the three "policy windows" discussed in Chapter 1, Bruegel had already addressed key elements across multiple domains of the EU's defensive economic policy toward China. Notably, during the period between the opening of the first policy window in February 2012 and the full opening of the second policy window in June 2016, the frequency with which the institute engaged with subsequent key EU policy issues reached its peak. In the domain of investment policy, moreover, the institute demonstrated a high degree of forward-looking capacity, having proposed policy recommendations closely aligned with the EU's eventual policy framework as early as a decade before the formal adoption of relevant EU official policy documents.

Second, by examining the conferences organized by the institute, especially by analyzing how it utilizes think tank conferences as a distinctive platform for information exchange in the field of power, it is possible to identify the structural patterns of interaction it establishes with different components of this field, particularly with EU institutions and member states, and go on to infer the pathways through which it exerts short-term influence over EU decision-making.

Third, by identifying and analyzing the inter-think tank research collaboration platforms in which the institute participates, especially those focusing on China-EU economic relations and EU economic policymaking toward China, it is possible to uncover the channels through which the institute exerts long-term indirect influence. Finally, through an examination of the institute's personnel structure and professional trajectories, it is possible to reconstruct the contours of its 'revolving door' mechanism

Within the broader landscape of EU policymaking, issues related to regional economic integration occupy a particularly prominent position, often taking precedence over external relations. As a result, in comparison with think tanks in the United States and in EU member states, EU-level think tanks are generally smaller in size and allocate a greater proportion of their resources to the study of European integration. However, their research capacity in the fields of EU external relations and area studies remains relatively underdeveloped.

Data compiled by the author, based on information available on the official websites of the respective think tanks as of late September 2018, show that among the world's leading think tanks, the Brookings Institution had more than 300 experts in its research team, including 55 specialists in its Asia-Pacific program; the Royal Institute of International Affairs (RIIA) had 262 members in its research teams, including 23 in its Asia-Pacific program; and the German Institute for International and Security Affairs (SWP) had over 110 research experts, of whom 15 specialized in Asia-Pacific studies. By contrast, the three most prominent EU-level think tanks—The Centre for European Policy Studies, European Policy Centre, and Bruegel—each employ fewer than 50 researchers and do not maintain dedicated teams for area and country studies. Nevertheless, since the entry into force of the Treaty of Lisbon at the end of 2009 and the establishment of the European External Action Service at the end of 2010, the importance of external relations in EU policymaking has been steadily increasing. Consequently, EU-level think tanks are likely, in the future, to strengthen their research on EU foreign policy and area studies, and to expand their influence over EU external policymaking. For this reason, a systematic analysis of the mechanisms through which EU-level think tanks influence EU external decision-making is of considerable theoretical and practical significance.

Chapter 5: German Think Tanks' Influence over the EU's Defensive Economic Policy toward China: A Case Study of the German Institute for International and Security Affairs (SWP)

Given Germany's dominant position in the EU, German think tanks inevitably play a pivotal, irreplaceable role in the European think tank scene and the EU's core policymaking process. According to the historical data compiled in the annual *Global Go To Think Tanks Report*, arguably the world's most authoritative, widely cited annual audit and rankings report of global think tanks that is overseen and edited by James G. McGann of the University of Pennsylvania, the total number of think tanks in Germany rose from 187 in 2007 to 214 in 2017, representing an average annual addition of approximately three institutions.① In 2017, Germany, then with 214 think tanks, came fifth globally in terms of think tank tally, second only to the United Kingdom among European nations, accounting for 11 percent of the total number of think tanks operating across the European continent. Among the Top 30 Think Tanks in Western Europe, the share of German institutions increased from three in 2008 to seven in 2018. These figures clearly show that, alongside Germany's expanding steering and hegemonic role in the EU and the deepening and proliferation of successive, overlapping crises confronting the European bloc, German think tanks have achieved sustained growth in terms of numerical size and research capacity.

From early 2015 to the end of 2018, the EU entered a period of profound, unprecedented turbulence both internally and externally, marked by a cascading sequence of mutually reinforcing crises. These included a protracted sovereign debt crisis, a spate of

① James G. McGann, The Global Go-To Think Tanks: The Leading Public Policy Research Organizations in the World, 2007, 2008; 2017 Global Go To Think Tank Index Report, Think Tanks and Civil Societies Program, University of Pennsylvania, January 31, 2018.

devastating terrorist attacks across the bloc, the United Kingdom's withdrawal from the EU or Brexit, and the large-scale refugee influx across its external borders, all of which threw the EU's policymaking and operational procedures into a higher level of heightened complexity and chronic unpredictability. Against this volatile, crisis-ridden backdrop, Germany's central position in the EU's policymaking process became more prominent, with German think tanks' influence over EU legislative, strategic and policy formulations continuing to expand in lockstep.

In *The 2016 Global Go To Think Tanks Index* published by the University of Pennsylvania, the German Institute for International and Security Affairs (whose German name is Stiftung Wissenschaft und Politik, abbreviated as SWP) ranked in the top 15 in three high-profile, globally recognized categories: *Top Think Tanks Worldwide (Non-US)*, *Top Think Tanks in Western Europe*, and *Top Think Tanks in Foreign Policy and International Affairs*. Notably, in the latter category, SWP secured the 3rd place among all European think tanks and came on top of all German institutions, firmly establishing it as the most influential, academically rigorous, and paradigmatic think tank in Germany in terms of structural sway over national and European foreign and security policymaking. In the course of EU policymaking between 2013 and 2016, during which period the bloc's decision-making elites deliberated and formulated the landmark European Union Global Strategy (EUGS) for Foreign and Security Policy, SWP held a prominent, agenda-shaping position in the initial, agenda-setting phases of the entire policy formulation cycle. Taking SWP as its core case study and focusing attention on the EU's defensive economic policy toward China, this book systematically examines the causal mechanisms through which SWP exerts its structural and discursive influence over the formulation and evolution of the EU's China-related defensive economic policy framework, with the overarching academic objective of providing a clearer, more empirically grounded, and theoretically precise analytical context for scholarly research on the policy influence of think tanks across EU member states.①

① A joint report entitled "Towards a European Global Strategy: Securing European Influence in a Changing World", released on May 28, 2013 by four think tanks-the Istituto Affari Internazionali (IAI) of Italy, the Swedish Institute of International Affairs (UI), the Polish Institute of International Affairs (PISM), and the Elcano Royal Institute for International and Strategic Studies (RIE) of Spain-effectively initiated the EU's decision-making process for the formulation of a new Global Strategy. Although the report was formally co-authored by these four institutions, its drafting process involved a much broader deliberative exercise: a total of 25 think tanks from across Europe participated in discussions organized under the auspices of the European Union Institute for

This chapter takes SWP as its object of study, focusing on the EU's defensive economic policy toward China. It sets out to look at the mechanisms through which SWP influences the formulation of the EU's defensive economic policy toward China, with a view to providing a clearer theoretical picture of member state think tanks' influence over EU policymaking in relation to specific issues.

I. Existing Literature on the Study of German Think Tanks

Existing literature contains relatively few dedicated studies on European think tanks' policy influence over EU decision-making. Still, there are even fewer academic works and monographs focused specifically on the study of German think tanks. Owing to the fact that, before 2020, among all the EU member states, the United Kingdom hosted the largest number of the earliest think tanks, whose tangible and well-documented influence over national government decision-making has long stood out in European scholarly research, so a substantial proportion of the existing literature on European think tanks focuses overwhelmingly on UK-based institutions.① Only a very small number of studies have examined the role of EU-level think tanks in influencing the EU policymaking process.②

However, specific analyses of German think tanks remain limited to a handful of scattered works. Some papers compare German think tanks with their counterparts in other countries, or provide general overviews of the overall German think tank landscape, rather than offering dedicated and in-depth elaboration on the influence of German think tanks over policymaking. ③ Crucially, there is no identified academic literature specifically dedicated to

Security Studies (EUISS), with SWP being an active contributor.

① Representative studies on the role of British think tanks in the UK decision-making system include: Hugh Pemberton, *Policy Learning and British Governance in the 1960s*, Hampshire: Palgrave Macmillan, 2004; Peter A. Hall, "Policy Paradigms, Social Learning, and the State: The Case of Economic Policy Making in Britain", *Comparative Politics*, Vol. 25, No. 3, 1993, pp. 275-296; Bill Coxall, *Pressure Groups in British Politics*, Harlow: Pearson Education Limited, 2001.

② Representative studies on the influence of EU-level think tanks over EU decision-making include: Stephen Boucher, Europe and Its Think Tanks: a Promise to be Fulfilled, Notre Europe, Paris, Studies and Research, No. 35, October 2004; Antonio Missiroli and Isabelle Ioannides eds., European Think Tanks and the EU, September 2012, Bureau of European Policy Advisers, EU Commission.

③ Existing literature on German think tanks remains limited, with the following works representing the main examining the influence of German think tanks over the EU decision-making process.

Literature available to date has synthesized the current state of development of German think tanks into the following key aspects.

First, a number of scholarly works have come up with typological classifications of German think tanks. Martin Thunert categorizes German think tanks into four core types: academic research-oriented think tanks, contract research think tanks, policy advice-oriented think tanks, and party-affiliated think tanks. Among these, the academic research-oriented category is further subdivided into four sub-types: think tanks founded by the federal government, the so-called "Blue List" think tanks which receive equal funding from the federal government and the governments of Germany's federal states, university-affiliated research centers, and privately funded academic research institutions.[①] He further points out that a number of Germany's national academic consortia of an academic-research association nature, including the Leibniz Association, Max Planck Society, and Helmholtz Association,

---

contributions identified to date: Martin Thunert, "Think Tanks in Germany", *Society*, May/June 2004, Vol. 41, No. 4, pp. 66-69; "Think Tanks in Germany", in Diane Stone and Andrew Denham (Eds.), *Think Tank Traditions: Policy Research and the Politics of Ideas*, Manchester and New York: Manchester University Press, 2004, pp. 72-80; "Expert Policy Advice in Germany", in Stephen Brooks et al. (Eds.), *Policy Expertise in Contemporary Democracies*, Surrey: Ashgate Publishing Limited, 2012, pp. 113-131; "Non-University Research Institutes: between Basic Research, Knowledge Transfer to the Public and Policy Analysis", in Sonja Blum and Klaus Schubert (Eds.), *Policy Analysis in Germany*, Bristol: Policy Press, 2013, pp. 247-263; James G. McGann and Erik C. Johnson, *Comparative Think Tanks, Politics and Public Policy*, Cheltenham of UK: Edward Elgar, 2005; Rick Vogel and Jetta Frost, "Innovating in the German Public Sector: How a Think Tank Frames the Debate on NPM", *Innovation Journal*, 2009, Vol. 14, Issue 2, pp. 1-21; Hartwig Pautz, "Think Tanks in the United Kingdom and Germany: Actors in the Modernization of Social Democracy", *British Journal of Politics and International Relations*, 2010, Vol. 12, pp. 274-294; Sven Jochem, "Think Tanks: Bridging Beltway and Ivory Tower", in Sonja Blum and Klaus Schubert (Eds.), *Policy Analysis in Germany*, Bristol: Policy Press, 2013, pp. 231-244; Ihor Petrenko, "The Features of German Think Tanks Development and Their Interactions with the Authorities," *Ukrainian Policymaker*, Vol. 5, pp. 61-67. In addition, the Shanghai Office of the Friedrich Ebert Foundation published a briefing paper in September 2011 that provided a brief comparative assessment of think tanks in China, the United States, the United Kingdom, and Germany. See: Friedrich Ebert Stiftung, *Think Tanks in Policy Making: Do They Matter?* Briefing Paper Special Issue, September 2011, Shanghai Office.

① Martin Thunert, "Think Tanks in Germany", in Diane Stone and Andrew Denham (Eds.), *Think Tank Traditions: Policy Research and the Politics of Ideas*, Manchester and New York: Manchester University Press, 2004, pp. 72-80; Sven Jochem, "Think Tanks: Bridging Beltway and Ivory Tower", in Sonja Blum and Klaus Schubert (Eds.), *Policy Analysis in Germany*, Bristol: Policy Press, 2013, pp. 231-241.

also exhibit the core functional characteristics of think tanks (Thunert, 2004, 2013).① Sven Jochem has put forward a similar classification framework, noting that German think tanks represent a special category of research entities that operate in the intermediate space between the "corridors of power" and the "ivory tower" of academia (Jochem, 2013).②

Second, some researchers have observed that since the beginning of the new century, German think tanks have gradually learned from the operational models of American think tanks, devoting increasing attention to strengthening their public relations and policy advice activities, and expanding their engagement with media outlets. Through these efforts, they seek to shape media narratives and public policy debates, build their own discursive power, and establish tangible influence over social and public opinion. Some German think tanks have even evolved in the direction of the so-called "do-tanks" (Jochem, 2013).③

Third, several scholarly works have assessed the policy influence of German think tanks. For instance, Thunert argues that the groups most susceptible to the influence of German think tanks are universities and research institutions, followed by members of parliament and parliamentary groups, with the bureaucratic apparatus of various cabinet ministries—the day-to-day decision-makers in the state—ranking third. He further argues that party-affiliated think tanks and policy advice-oriented think tanks wield significant influence during the initial phases of the highest-level decision-making process, especially the stages of problem definition and agenda-setting; contract research think tanks, by contrast, exert their strongest influence during the policy implementation phase, while academic research-oriented think tanks maintain a moderate degree of influence across all stages of the decision-making cycle (Thunert, 2004).④ Hartwig Pautz, however, argues that compared with their UK counterparts, German think tanks have a markedly lower level of participation in domestic party politics, policy advice, and lobbying activities, and exert a far

① Martin Thunert, "Non-University Research Institutes: between Basic Research, Knowledge Transfer to the Public and Policy Analysis", in Sonja Blum and Klaus Schubert (Eds.), *Policy Analysis in Germany*, Bristol: Policy Press, 2013, pp. 247-263.

② Sven Jochem, "Think Tanks: Bridging Beltway and Ivory Tower", in Sonja Blum and Klaus Schubert (Eds.), *Policy Analysis in Germany*, Bristol: Policy Press, 2013, P. 240.

③ Ibid.

④ Martin Thunert, "Think Tanks in Germany", *Society*, May/June 2004, P. 68; "Think Tanks in Germany", in Diane Stone and Andrew Denham (Eds.), *Think Tank Traditions: Policy Research and the Politics of Ideas*, Manchester and New York: Manchester University Press, 2004, P. 85.

weaker influence over the ideological shifts of Germany's political parties (Pautz, 2010).① Overall, existing literature lacks in-depth analysis of the magnitude and effectiveness of German think tanks' influence over policymaking, and there is no thorough elaboration on the operational mechanisms through which German think tanks exert their influence over policy outcomes. Existing accounts of the differential influences of distinct types of German think tanks are largely grounded in specific researchers' own intuitive judgments, lacking robust supporting evidence derived from statistical data analysis or critical textual interpretation.

Fourth, some researchers have analyzed and assessed, to varying degrees, the position of German think tanks in Germany's political decision-making structure. Thunert, for one, points out that German politics has a long tradition of corporatism, as a result of which interest groups and parliamentary groups are often able to exert a more direct and forceful influence over the media, the general public, and top decision-makers, particularly with regard to agenda-setting. Relative to the highly organized and developed interest groups in Germany—most notably business and industrial interest groups—think tanks are in a comparatively disadvantaged position, with far weaker capacity to influence policymaking, let alone agenda-setting (Thunert, 2004).② (Rudolf Speth, by contrast, argues that German think tanks constitute a core component of the interest representation system and knowledge production structure in contemporary German politics. He contends that in Germany's political system, think tanks can leverage their specialized expertise in political thought and scientific knowledge to function as a key channel of political communication, serving as a vital mechanism through which different sections of political elites conduct interest mediation and articulate their interest demands, both among themselves and to the broader public (Speth, 2011).③

① Hartwig Pautz, "Think Tanks in the United Kingdom and Germany: Actors in the Modernization of Social Democracy", *British Journal of Politics and International Relations*, 2010, Vol. 12, P. 279.

② Martin Thunert, "Think Tanks in Germany", in Diane Stone and Andrew Denham (Eds.), *Think Tank Traditions: Policy Research and the Politics of Ideas*, Manchester and New York: Manchester University Press, 2004, P. 83.

③ Rudolf Speth, "Think Tanks as New Channels of Influence within the Political System of Germany", in Friedrich Ebert Stiftung, *Think Tanks in Policy Making: Do They Matter?* Briefing Paper Special Issue, September 2011, Shanghai Office, P. 55.

Fifth, researchers have generally noted that German think tanks have developed fast since the end of the Cold War, with even greater acceleration from the turn of the new century onward. They further argue that this rapid expansion is not only correlated with the growing demand for policy advisory service from Germany's decision-making authorities, but also inextricably linked to the EU's increasingly complex decision-making structure and process. For example, Sven Jochem characterizes Germany's think tank system as a "growth industry" since the 1990s, and links this expansion directly to the deepening of the European integration process.[①] Martin Thunert similarly notes that the number of German think tanks has continued to grow steadily,[②] pointing out that German think tanks are securing an increasing volume of funding from the EU.[③] Rudolf Speth, meanwhile, argues that more than half of Germany's current think tanks were established after 1975, and that they represent a core structural component of Germany's political and social modernization process since the late 20th century (Speth, 2011).[④]

Overall, existing literature on the policy influence of think tanks focuses primarily on American think tanks, with a secondary body of work examining the influence of UK think tanks over British domestic policymaking, and British economic policymaking in particular. Notably, in the mid-1990s, alongside the rise of conservative forces in the United Kingdom and the United States and the accompanying paradigm shift in their economic policymaking models, a cohort of scholars conducted intensive research on the pivotal role played by UK think tanks in the British government's shift in economic policy preference from Keynesianism to neoliberalism. These works remain the most seminal and widely cited scholarly contributions to date on the mechanisms through which non-state actors including think tanks exert influence over policymaking. By contrast, scholarly works on German

---

① Sven Jochem, "Think Tanks: Bridging Beltway and Ivory Tower", in Sonja Blum and Klaus Schubert (Eds.), *Policy Analysis in Germany*, Bristol: Policy Press, 2013, P. 232.

② Martin Thunert, "Non-University Research Institutes: between Basic Research, Knowledge Transfer to the Public and Policy Analysis", in Sonja Blum and Klaus Schubert (Eds.), *Policy Analysis in Germany*, Bristol: Policy Press, 2013, pp. 247.

③ Martin Thunert, "Think Tanks in Germany" in Friedrich Ebert Stiftung, *Think Tanks in Policy Making: Do They Matter?* Briefing Paper Special Issue, September 2011, Shanghai Office, P. 48.

④ Rudolf Speth, "Think Tanks as New Channels of Influence within the Political System of Germany", in Friedrich Ebert Stiftung, "Think Tanks in Policy Making: Do They Matter?" Briefing Paper Special Issue, September 2011, Shanghai Office, P. 55.

think tanks, based on the literature identified to date, remain largely at the stage of general descriptive overviews of the sector, and still lack in-depth, systematic, and detailed analytical and theoretical elaboration.

II. Efficacy and Rhythm of SWP' Influence over the EU's Defensive Economic Policymaking toward China: A Comparison Between Policy Advice Records and EU Official Policy Documents

As Germany's preeminent foreign policy think tank, SWP maintained a consistently active presence in the relevant policy debates in the EU's policymaking architecture around the opening of the three decision-making windows in the EU's defensive economic policymaking process toward China, as discussed in Chapter 1. While the Institute's archival records contain barely any documented trace of hosting or organizing relevant conferences, its formal policy advice records in this policy domain—particularly its research reports, academic articles, and working papers, which are distinguished by their in-depth research, rigorous data accuracy, and acute sensitivity to evolving geopolitical and economic developments—have been comprehensively and systematically preserved.

A rigorous comparative analysis between the Institute's research outputs and policy advice records on the EU's defensive economic policy toward China, and the EU's official policy documents—especially those issued by EU decision-making authorities following the opening of the three aforementioned decision-making windows (February to June 2012, February to June 2016, and January to July 2017)—can therefore reveal the overall rhythm and efficacy of the Institute's influence over EU policymaking within this policy framework.① This analysis will focus specifically on comparing the framing and timing

---

① From 2006-2018, a total of 63 policy advisory outputs produced by SWP address key elements of the EU's defensive economic policy toward China. Due to limited space, it is not possible to list them individually here. The most representative publications-those that most clearly articulate the institute's core positions-include: Christine Wong, "Can China Change Development Paradigm for the 21st Century?", SWP Working Paper FG 7, 2005/03, April 2005; Kay Moller, "A Rising China and the World's Response", Paper for the 11th Arrabida Meeting, May 26-28, 2005; Bates Gill and Gudrun Wacker (Eds.), *China's Rise: Diverging U.S.-EU Perceptions and Approaches*, SWP, Berlin, August 2005; Jens van Scherpenberg, "Coping with China as an Economic Power: European versus American Approaches", SWP Working Paper FG 4, 205/04, September 2005; Hanns of articulation of the twelve core elements of the EU's defensive economic policy toward China listed in Table 3.5 in both sets of documents, and evaluating the degree of uptake of the Institute's arguments and recommendations in the EU's official policy outputs.

Indeed, SWP has a long history of focusing on and examining issues related to defensive economic policy toward China. As early as 2005, it published more than a dozen research reports and working papers, in which it accurately forecasted China's economic rise and the resulting disruptive impact it would have on China-EU economic relations. In 2006 and 2008 alone, the Institute, on four separate occasions, published nearly ten working papers and research reports. In these publications, it argued that inherent and unavoidable frictions and contradictions existed between the Chinese and EU economies stemming from fundamental differences in their domestic economic systems, and recommended to the decision-making authorities of both Germany and the EU that they consider adopting more stringent defensive measures in the management of their economic relations with China. This happened several years prior to the opening of the first decision-making window for the EU's defensive economic policymaking toward China in February 2012.

In October 2006, the European Commission released a policy planning document, in which it argued that new shifts in the global economy were likely to expose the EU's foreign trade to fresh pressures, and that more robust trade defense instruments were therefore required to protect the bloc's domestic industries and employment. It further resolved to launch a public consultation on this issue.① This marked the first time the EU considered

---

Guenther Hilpert, "China's Economic Rise and Asian-Pacific Security: Economic Perspectives", Discussion Paper for a Conference jointly organized by SWP and Germany's Federal Ministry of Defense, Berlin, December 15, 2005; Gudrun Wacker ed., "China's Rise: The Return of Geopolitics?" SWP Research Paper, RP 1, February 2006; David Shambaugh and Gudrun Wacker (Eds.), "American and European Relations with China: Advancing Common Agendas", SWP Research Paper, RP 3, June 2008; Hanns Gunther Hilpert, "The EU's Strategic Economic Dialogue with China: a New Chance for European Trade Policy", SWP Comments 16, June 2008; Volker Perthes and Barbara Lippert (Eds.), "Expect the Unexpected: Ten Situations to Keep an Eye On", SWP Research Paper, RP 1, January 2012; Gudrun Wacker, "China-Europe Relations and the European Perspectives on the 'New Type of Major Power Relations'", Discussion Paper, July 28-31, 2013; Hanns Gunther Hilpert, "China's Trade Policy: Dominance without the Will to Lead", SWP Research Paper, RP 1, January 2014; Hanns Gunther Hilpert and Gudrun Wacker, "Geo-economics meets Geopolitics: China's New Economic and Foreign Policy Initiatives", SWP Comments, June 2015; Nadine Godehardt, "No End of History: A Chinese Alternative Concept of International Order?" SWP Research Paper, RP 2, January 2016;

① European Commission, DG Trade, Global Europe: Europe's Trade Defense Instruments in a Changing updating its defensive economic policy framework since the start of the 21st century. Notably, the research reports published by SWP between early 2006 and March 2006 put forward highly similar assessments and recommendations, six months prior to the European Commission's policy document in October 2006. This clearly demonstrates the forward-looking nature of the Institute's research on China and China-EU relations.

Table 5.1: Comparative Timelines of SWP's Policy Recommendations and EU Official Policy Documents on the Twelve Key Points of EU Defensive Economic Policy toward China (February 2006–July 2018)

Key Policy Points / Entity Proposing or Formulating the Key Policy Points			SWP's Reference to and Commentary on the Relevant Policy Element (Format/Time)	Explicit Reference to the Relevant Policy Element in Official Decision-Making Documents of EU Authorities (Format/Time)		
				The EU Commission	**The European Parliament**	**The European Council and the Council of the EU**
I. Fundamental Positioning	I-1. General Principles	Format	Conference proceedings, research papers, joint research reports	Policy communication	Opinions, resolutions	Council decisions
		Time	Feb & Oct 2006; Jun 2008 (twice); May 2013; Jan 2014; Jan 2016; Jan 2017; Apr 2018	Jun 2016; Sep 2017	Apr, May & Jun 2016	Jul 2016
	I-2. Detailed Points	Format	Conference/project papers, media commentaries, thematic research	Policy communications, analytical reports	Analytical reports	Council decisions
		Time	Oct 2006; Jun 2008; Jan, Mar & May 2013; Jan 2014; Apr 2018	Jun & Jul 2016; May, Sep & Dec 2017	Nov 2017	Jul 2016; Jun 2017
II. Overall Framework	II-1. General Principles	Format	Conference papers, thematic research	Policy communications, evaluation reports	Research reports	Council decisions
		Time	Oct 2006; Jun 2008 (×2); Jan 2014; Jun 2015; Jan 2016; Apr 2018	Jun 2016; May 2017	Apr 2017	Jul 2016
	II-2. Detailed Points	Format	Thematic research papers	Policy communications, research reports	Analytical reports	—
		Time	Jan 2014; Jun 2015; Jan 2017	Jun 2016; May, Sep & Dec 2017	Nov 2017	—

Global Economy. A Green Paper for Public Consultation, October 2006.

Entity Proposing or Formulating the Key Policy Points / Key Policy Points			SWP's Reference to and Commentary on the Relevant Policy Element (Format/Time)	Explicit Reference to the Relevant Policy Element in Official Decision-Making Documents of EU Authorities (Format/Time)		
				The EU Commission	**The European Parliament**	**The European Council and the Council of the EU**
III. Trade Policy	III-1. General Principles	Format	Conference papers, research reports, thematic studies	Evaluation reports, policy communications	Evaluation reports, draft legislative texts	Legislative documents, Council decisions
		Time	Feb 2006; Jun 2008; Aug 2012; Jan 2014; Jan 2017	Apr 2013; Oct & Nov 2016	Oct 2013; Jun 2017	Jun, Oct & Nov 2016
	III-2. Detailed Points	Format	—	Evaluation reports, working group documents, legislative drafts, proposal communications, press releases	Scrutiny records, resolutions, voting records	Council conclusions, legislative documents, press releases
		Time	Conference proceedings, research papers, joint research reports	Apr 2013; Jun, Oct & Nov 2016; Sep & Dec 2017; Jan, Apr, Jun & Jul 2018	Jun 2016; Jun 2017; May 2018	Oct 2016; Nov & Dec 2017; Apr 2018
IV. Investment Policy	IV-1. General Principles	Format	Feb & Oct 2006; Jun 2008 (×2); May 2013; Jan 2014; Jan 2016; Jan 2017; Apr 2018	Working group reports, policy communications	Draft legislative texts, debate records	Press releases
		Time	Conference/project papers, media commentaries, thematic research	May 2017; Sep 2017	Mar 2017; May & Jun 2018	Jun 2018
	IV-2. Detailed Points	Format	Oct 2006; Jun 2008; Jan, Mar & May 2013; Jan 2014; Apr 2018	Working group reports, technical question lists, policy communications	Draft amendments to legislative texts	—
		Time	Conference papers, thematic research	Sep 2017 (×6)	Jun 2018	—
V. Industrial Policy	V-1. General Principles	Format	Oct 2006; Jun 2008 (×2); Jan 2014; Jun 2015; Jan 2016; Apr 2018	Fact sheets, proposal communications	Resolutions	Council decisions
		Time	Thematic research papers	Mar 2016; Sep 2017 (×2)	Jul 2017	May 2017

Key Policy Points (rows) / Entity Proposing or Formulating the Key Policy Points (columns)			SWP's Reference to and Commentary on the Relevant Policy Element (Format/Time)	Explicit Reference to the Relevant Policy Element in Official Decision-Making Documents of EU Authorities (Format/Time)		
				The EU Commission	The European Parliament	The European Council and the Council of the EU
V. Industrial Policy	V-2. Detailed Points	Format	Jan 2014; Jun 2015; Jan 2017	Policy communications, working group reports, technical question lists	Resolutions	—
		Time	Conference papers, research reports, thematic studies	Sep 2017 (×2); Oct & Nov 2017	Jul 2017	—
VI. Intellectual Property Policy	VI-1. General Principles	Format	Feb 2006; Jun 2008; Aug 2012; Jan 2014; Jan 2017	Working group reports, press releases	—	—
		Time	None	Feb & Mar 2018	—	—
	VI-2. Detailed Points	Format	Conference proceedings, research papers, joint research reports	Policy communications, working group reports, press releases	—	Press releases
		Time	Feb & Oct 2006; Jun 2008 (×2); May 2013; Jan 2014; Jan 2016; Jan 2017; Apr 2018	Nov 2017; Feb, Mar & Jun 2018	—	Jun 2018

Source: Compiled by the author

As shown in Table 5.1, SWP exhibits several prominent characteristics in its intention and rhythm of engagement in policy debates and influence exertion throughout the EU's decision-making process on defensive economic policy toward China.

First, as evidenced by its policy advice records, the Institute has shown varying degrees of attention and research focus on the six domains of the EU's defensive economic policy toward China as listed in Table 3.5, resulting in a marked divergence in the distribution of the frequency and rhythm of its reference to individual policy elements across these domains. Overall, among the six domains of the EU's defensive economic policy toward China, the Institute's experts have referenced the policy elements in the two domains of fundamental positioning and overall framework with notably high frequency. Reference to elements in the two domains of trade policy and investment policy is significantly less frequent, while mentions of elements in the domains of industrial policy and intellectual property protection policy are extremely scarce, and even when addressed, are only touched upon in passing.

Second, there is also a considerable and significant disparity in the Institute's attention and research focus between the general principles and detailed points in each domain of the EU's policy framework. In other words, the frequency with which the Institute's policy advice records reference policy elements in each domain is highly unevenly distributed between the general principles and detailed provisions of that domain. As can be seen from Table 5.1, nearly all of the policy elements addressed by the Institute are concentrated in the general principles of each domain, while the elements in the detailed provisions of each domain are rarely mentioned. Specifically, the policy elements of the trade and industrial policy parts are not referenced by the Institute at all.

Third, the frequency of the Institute's attention to and commentary on the policy elements of this framework also varies across different phases of the EU's decision-making process for this policy architecture. Across the distinct periods delineated by the three "decision-making windows" discussed in Chapter 1 of this book, the Institute devoted most of its attention and commentary to the EU's policy frameworks, and referenced its policy elements with the highest frequency, during the period between the conclusion of the policymaking activities triggered by the first decision-making window and the opening of the second—that is, the period from the end of 2012 to before February 2016.

The disparities in the Institute's degree of attention and research focus across the different domains of the EU's defensive economic policy framework toward China reflect its specific institutional positioning and core research strengths. As a traditional foreign policy think tank rather than an economic policy think tank, its long research tradition prioritizes the assessment and grasp of long-term, strategic macro-level trends, and the formulation of overarching policy recommendations capable of shaping the broader landscape, rather than focusing on highly technical and specialized specific policy and detailed operational issues. Formulating policy recommendations for the two domains of fundamental positioning and overall framework of the EU's defensive economic policy toward China requires the establishment of a rigorous assessment of the long-term trajectory and fundamental structural characteristics of China-EU economic relations. Conducting such assessment aligns precisely with the research tradition the Institute has cultivated over many years, which explains its intensive and detailed research focus on these two domains.

In contrast to these two domains, research and policy advice on trade and investment policy demand the consideration of far more technical details, resulting in a reduced level of attention and research from the Institute, and a correspondingly lower frequency of reference to policy elements in these two domains in its policy advice records. Industrial policy and intellectual property policy, meanwhile, are far less strategic and far more technical in nature, requiring more granular technical data and information. For this reason, the Institute has devoted even less attention and research to these two domains, with correspondingly minimal reflection and elaboration on their core policy elements.

In sum, Table 5.1 demonstrates a clear chronological sequence between the articulation of specific elements of the EU's defensive economic policy framework toward China in the Institute's policy advice records and in the EU's relevant decision-making documents. Given the Institute's prominent position in the entire EU decision-making system as Germany's preeminent foreign policy think tank, it can be reasonably concluded that SWP has indeed exerted a tangible influence over the EU's decision-making process surrounding this policy architecture.

III. SWP's Long-Term Indirect Influence over the EU's Defensive Economic Policy toward China: An Analysis of Research Projects and Inter-Think Tank Collaboration Platforms

Figure 2.2 demonstrates that research projects and inter-think tank research collaboration platforms represent a critical mechanism through which think tanks exert long-term, indirect influence over decision-making authorities. As specialized policy research institutions, think tanks require a steady stream of funding from research projects to sustain their operation and development, and must also continuously disseminate the outputs of these research projects to enhance their academic reputation and public profile. An analysis of the funding sources and research team composition of a think tank's research projects enables the identification of the segments of the field of power most closely aligned with the institution, and in turn, the delineation of the think tank's precise position in this field of power. Correspondingly, an analysis of the substantive content of the research outputs produced by the think tank within the framework of these projects, and the identification of conceptual, argumentative, and discursive linkages between these outputs and the policy architecture formulated by decision-makers, allows for a robust assessment of the think tank's policy influence.

Meanwhile, the European think tank community places strong emphasis on the importance of establishing research collaboration platforms (also referred to as collaborative networks) between think tanks of different types and geographic locations. The establishment of institutionalized collaboration platforms through mutual agreement enables individual think tanks to broaden their research horizons, enhance their sensitivity to evolving developments, secure access to research resources, information, and data that would be difficult to obtain through their own efforts alone, and thereby elevate the depth and precision of their research. An analysis of the research projects and inter-think tank collaboration platforms in which SWP participates can therefore further clarify the institution's position and influence in the EU's decision-making system.

3.1 Relevant Research Projects Operated by SWP

Table 5.2 lists all research projects hosted or participated in by the Institute that relate to the EU's economic policy toward China. While the Institute's archival records contain fragmented information on the operational processes of these projects, the research outputs of the projects are fully and comprehensively documented. From the information available on these research projects and their outputs, a number of characteristics of the Institute's research and operational model can be identified:

First, the consistent analytical perspective, research orientation, and intellectual preferences underpinning the Institute's work are evident from the titles and substantive content of its research projects. The research content of the five projects listed in Table 5.2 all relates to the EU's economic policy toward China, yet lack a concentrated or explicit linear connection to one another. The research content of these five projects is distinctly marked by a strong theoretical and strategic orientation, requiring comprehensive assessments of long-term trends. Given China's considerable size and the strategic significance of China-EU relations, these research projects inevitably entailed an assessment of the trajectory of China-

EU relations in the course of their analysis, and in turn, policy recommendations for the EU's management of its economic relations with China. As such, the research on the EU's economic policy toward China undertaken in these five projects is inevitably framed from a macro, holistic perspective, centered on strategic analysis and reasoning. This characteristic corroborates the pattern identified in Table 5.1: namely, that the Institute prioritizes strategic research on long-term, macro-level issues, while undertaking far less technical research that requires large volumes of granular data and specialized technical expertise.

Second, in its engagement with EU decision-making authorities in the field of economic policy toward China through the operation of research projects, the Institute relies primarily on the national route, while also making some use of the Brussels route. Of the five projects listed in Table 5.2, three were hosted by the Institute with funding from the German Federal Foreign Office, while the other two received funding from the European Commission but only involved the Institute as a participant rather than a lead institution. This indicates that in terms of funding acquisition and project implementation, the Institute maintains closer ties with German decision-making authorities and a relatively more distant relationship with EU-level decision-makers.

Table 5.2: Research Projects Hosted or Participated in by SWP Related to EU Economic Policy toward China (September 2015-September 2018)

Project Name, Duration & Characteristics	Research Funding Source	Project's Lead Institution (s)	Research Team Composition	Research Outputs and Linkage to the EU's Economic Policy Toward China
Diplomacy in the 21st Century Duration: January 2016-July 2018	German Federal Foreign Office; Zeit Foundation (Germany)	Led by Volker Stanzel, former German Ambassador to China	Composed of more than 20 experts from think tanks and universities across Europe	The project's research reports① included an assessment of China's position in the global economy and global governance system, which was reflected in the EU's September 2016 document *New Elements of the EU Strategy on China*, and the EU's policy documents on China trade and investment policy issued between September and December 2017.

① Alexandra Friede, Report of the Workshop on "Diplomacy in the 21st Century", September 8, 2016, Project Paper for Project "Diplomacy in the 21st Century", 2016/No.1, SWP, Berlin; Rudine Emrich and David Schulze, "Diplomacy in the 21st Century: What Needs to Change?", Presentation of the Main Findings of SWP's "Diplomacy in the 21st Century" Project, SWP Working Paper, December 2017.

Project Name, Duration & Characteristics	Research Funding Source	Project's Lead Institution (s)	Research Team Composition	Research Outputs and Linkage to the EU's Economic Policy Toward China
The Future of the International Order Duration: September 2015-June 2016	Fritz Thyssen Foundation; German Federal Foreign Office; Friedrich Ebert Stiftung (FES)	Co-led by SWP, the East Asia Institute (South Korea), the East-West Center in Honolulu, and Jawaharlal Nehru University (India)	Composed of 35 experts in total, including officials from the German Federal Foreign Office, and experts from think tanks and universities in Europe, the United States, and Asia	A policy recommendation report issued by the project in December 2015, which defined China's role in the international multilateral economic order, China's domestic economic situation and its foreign policy intentions, was reflected in the EU's 2016 *New Elements of the EU Strategy on China* document and the EU's September 2017 policy document on China trade policy.
New Power, New Responsibility: Elements of a Changing German Foreign Policy Duration: Autumn 2012-End of 2013	German Federal Foreign Office	Co-led by SWP and the German Marshall Fund of the United States (GMF)	Composed of 31 experts from the German Bundestag, German Chancellery, Federal Foreign Office, German business and industrial community, and think tanks and universities across Europe	The project's final report① defined the relationship between China and the existing international order, as well as its impact on the strategic interests of Germany and Europe, which was reflected in the EU's *2016 New Elements of the EU Strategy on China* document.
EU Global Strategy Duration: July 2012-June 2013	Foreign Ministries of Italy, Poland, Spain and Sweden; European External Action Service (EEAS); European Commission	Led by the Istituto Affari Internazionali (IAI, Italy), Polish Institute of International Affairs (PISM), Real Instituto Elcano (RIE, Spain), and Swedish Institute of International Affairs (UI)	Composed of in-house experts from the European Commission and the EEAS, as well as experts from 28 of Europe's most prominent foreign policy think tanks; exact number of participants unknown	The project's research report released on May 28, 2013 put forward an assessment of China's position in the international order and global governance, as well as recommendations on the EU's overall strategy toward China and its economic policy intentions, which were reflected in the EU's September 2016 *New Elements of the EU Strategy on China* document.
Think Global, Act European Duration: May 2008-May 2013	European Commission; governments of EU member states including France, Luxembourg and Denmark	Led by the Institut Jacques Delors, an EU-level think tank headquartered in Paris	Composed of more than 40 experts from 16 leading think tanks across Europe	The project's final report released in May 2013 put forward recommendations on the overarching principles for the EU's management of its economic relations with China, which were reflected in the EU's September 2016 *New Elements of the EU Strategy on China* document.

Source: Compiled by the author

① SWP and GMF, "New Power, New Responsibility: Elements of a German Foreign and Security Policy for a Changing World", December 2013.

As a German foreign policy think tank headquartered in Berlin, the Institute is geographically detached from the EU's decision-making center in Brussels. Unlike Bruegel, it cannot be directly integrated into the EU decision-making process or operate in lockstep with EU policymakers. However, it naturally leverages its geographical proximity to establish close links with Germany's top decision-making bodies when implementing research projects. Table 5.3 presents the composition of the research team for one of the Institute's projects, "New Power, New Responsibility: Elements of German Foreign and Security Policy in a Changing World," and in doing so illustrates the close linkages between the Institute and German policymaking circles. Funded by the German Federal Foreign Office, the Institute provides research output and policy advice to German decision-makers and, through this channel, is able to shape German positions. Given Germany's presence in the European Council and the Council of the European Union and, in particular, the European Council, such influence can subsequently be transmitted to the EU level in an indirect manner. Accordingly, when seeking to shape EU decision-making on China through research projects, the Institute appears to rely primarily on the "national route".

Table 5.3: Composition of the Research Team of the SWP-Led Project "Elements of German Foreign and Security Policy in a Changing World" (Autumn 2012-End of 2013)

Background of Project Participants \ Project Name		Research Project on *New Power, New Responsibility: Elements of German Foreign and Security Policy in a Changing World*
1. EU decision-making institutions (current officials)		None
2. German decision-making institutions (current officials)	Bundestag (German Parliament)	7 participants
	Federal Chancellery	1 participant
	Federal Foreign Office	6 participants
	Armed Forces and Ministry of Defense	2 participants
	Other central government departments	3 participants
3. German business and financial sector and interest groups		2 participants, respectively from Daimler AG and the Federation of German Industries (BDI)
4. German media		2 participants, respectively from Frankfurter Allgemeine Zeitung and Die Zeit
4. Experts from other German think tanks & universities		14 participants
5. Other European think tanks & universities		2 participants
6. Think tanks & universities outside Europe		5 participants

Source: Compiled by the author

3.2 Inter-Think Tank Collaboration Platforms in Which SWP Participates

Table 5.4 sets out a series of inter-think tank collaboration platforms in which SWP holds formal membership and participates in substantive activities, the core areas of focus and deliberative research remits of which bear direct and material relevance to the EU policy toward China. The policy recommendations formulated and advanced through these platforms—whether embedded into their formally published research outputs or articulated in the outcomes of the thematic conferences and expert dialogues they convene—all exert a tangible, if varying, degree of influence over the EU's economic policymaking process with regard to China.

In parallel with the research projects detailed in Table 5.2, these inter-think tank collaboration platforms not only reflect the deeply entrenched research preferences, strategic orientations, and core analytical perspectives that the Institute has consolidated and refined over decades of operation, but also serve to further illuminate the Institute's structural position in the broader EU decision-making ecosystem, alongside the specific pathways and operational modalities through which it translates its research insights into policy influence.

Inter-think tank collaboration platforms originate from the coordination mechanisms established by multiple think tanks for the joint implementation of research projects or the co-hosting of large-scale conferences. When these coordination mechanisms are sustained over the long term and evolve into formal, stable cooperative structures, they solidify into full-fledged inter-think tank collaboration platforms. As such, these platforms typically incorporate a set of interconnected, granular operational architectures, including recurring conferences, dedicated publication series, and collaborative research projects, or center their core operational model around one of these structural elements. All the four inter-think tank collaboration platforms listed in Table 5.4 embed an operational mechanism for the regular convening of large-scale conferences, alongside a steady stream of periodic publications that put forward targeted policy recommendations. Of these, the first, second and fourth platforms host collaborative research projects that receive funding from the European Commission, and officials from the European Commission also regularly participate in their recurring conferences. The third platform, by contrast, does not operate formal collaborative research projects, and instead takes the convening of an annual high-level forum as its core operational form, with senior officials from both the European External Action Service

(EEAS) and the European Commission in regular attendance at its annual forum. All the four inter-think tank collaboration platforms listed in Table 5.4 are therefore capable of exerting some degree of influence over EU decision-making authorities.

The areas of focus and deliberation across all the four of these inter-think tank collaboration platforms fall firmly within the scope of macro-level strategic research, encompassing holistic judgments on long-term trends and overarching assessments of the macro strategic landscape, with no engagement with granular, technical or highly specialized policy issues. Of these, the first two collaboration platforms do not directly address or center their deliberations on issues related to the EU's policy toward China. However, in the course of assessing the long-term trajectory of the macro strategic environment, they do reference issues related to the EU's policy toward China, and on occasion put forward detailed, targeted recommendations in this regard. The third collaboration platform, by contrast, the Berlin Conference on Asian Security (BCAS) Collaborative Framework, is directly linked to the EU's policy toward China, and has therefore conducted extensive in-depth deliberations on the EU's economic policy toward China and China-EU economic relations. The fourth collaboration platform takes the implementation of research projects as its core operational form; notably, the third phase of its flagship project in 2013 focused specifically on EU trade strategy, and included intensive, in-depth research on the EU's economic policy toward China and China-EU economic relations.

In sum, all the four inter-think tank collaboration platforms listed in Table 5.4 embody the consistent analytical perspective and research preferences that SWP has long maintained, while also reflecting the Institute's structural position in the EU's decision-making system. A systematic synthesis of the relevant information on these four platforms can reveal the specific pathways and modalities through which the Institute exerts influence over EU decision-making by virtue of its participation in these research collaboration platforms.

Table 5.4: Inter-Think-Tank Collaborative Platforms Involving SWP with Potential Influence over the EU's Economic Policy toward China

Characteristics \ Name	European Policy Institutes Network (EPIN)	OSCE Think Tank Network	Berlin Conference on Asian Security (BCAS)	*Think Global – Act European* Platform
Lead and Coordinating Institutions	Led and operated by four EU-level think tanks, including the Centre for European Policy Studies (CEPS)	Led and operated by 7 think tanks including the Institut Français des Relations Internationales (IFRI), Finland's Tampere Peace Research Institute (TAPRI), and the Carnegie Endowment for International Peace	Led by (SWP, with funding from the Konrad Adenauer Foundation and the German Federal Foreign Office	Notre Europe – Jacques Delors Institute
Membership Composition	41 think tanks and university research institutes across Europe, including 15 core members	84 think tanks and academic institutions from 41 countries in Europe and beyond	20+ foreign policy think tanks from Europe, China, Japan, South Korea, South Asia, and the United States	16 think tanks from the EU level and 7 European countries
Regular Exchange Mechanisms	3-4 major conferences annually in Brussels and elsewhere; joint research reports	One annual plenary meeting; biennial elections to appoint a coordinator; additional ad hoc workshops and research projects organized by leading institutions	Annual major conference in Berlin	One joint research report every 6-12 months; platform ceased operation after the end of 2013
Research Focus and Relevance to EU Policy toward China	Developments in European domestic politics and their implications for EU external policy, including the overall strategic orientation of EU-China relations	European strategic security and EU external strategy, including assessments and policy orientations regarding EU-China and EU-East Asia relations	Security dynamics in East and Southeast Asia, particularly China's bilateral and multilateral relations with neighboring countries, including assessments of overall trends in EU-China economic relations	Addresses key and urgent policy issues faced by EU decision-makers; during 2012-2013, focused on EU external relations, including discussions of EU policy toward China
Linkages with EU Decision-Making Institutions	Has received multiple research grants from the European Commission since 2002; Commission officials have participated in its annual meetings	Some projects funded by the European Commission; EU Commission officials and members of the European Parliament participate in its workshops.	Annual conferences attended by officials from the European External Action Service (EEAS) and the European Commission	Funded by the European Commission's Directorate-General for Education and Culture and by rotating EU Council presidencies; its reports are sometimes prefaced by European Commission officials

Characteristics \ Name	European Policy Institutes Network (EPIN)	OSCE Think Tank Network	Berlin Conference on Asian Security (BCAS)	*Think Global – Act European* Platform
Influence on EU Economic Policy toward China	Recommendations on EU decision-making approaches toward China (published in its 2015 newsletter) were reflected in EU policy processes between June 2016 and September 2017.	Assessments of the global strategic environment (2014-2015 reports) were reflected in the EU's 2016 policy document *Elements for a New EU Strategy on China*.	Recommendations on the future of China-EU economic relations, deliberated in the third session *Economic Interdependence and New Trade Agreements* of the platform's 2014 annual conference, were reflected in the EU's 2016 *New Elements of the EU Strategy on China* and the 2017 State of the Union Address.	Recommendations put forward in the platform's April 2013 report around the two themes of EU Trade Strategy and How to Advance EU Economic Interests with China were reflected in the EU's June 2016 *New Elements of the EU Strategy on China* document.

Note: All information and data are current as of the end of September 2018.

Source: Compiled by the author

VI. SWP's Long-Term Direct Influence over the EU's Defensive Economic Policy toward China: An Examination of the "Revolving Door" System

The "revolving door" has long been a major focus of scholarship on think tanks. Members of think tanks inevitably retain institutional and professional ties to organizations in which they previously served or with which they are concurrently affiliated, thereby creating channels of relatively direct and durable influence. The extent to which revolving-door dynamics develop, however, is closely related to the structural characteristics of power alternation and interest representation in the political system in which a think tank operates. In the United States, the rapid turnover associated with party politics and presidential elections has produced the most highly developed form of the revolving door. Within the "two-level, four-actor" structure through which European think tanks operate, member-state think tanks likewise display a certain degree of revolving-door dynamics.

Examination of SWP's governance structure and human resource composition provides a window into its revolving door patterns. As of the end of September 2018, SWP's governance architecture comprised the following layers: (1) a Board of Trustees

(Kuratorium), which holds supreme decision-making authority over strategic direction and overall operations. At the time, the Chair of the Board of Trustees, Hans-Peter Keitel, also served as Vice President of the Federation of German Industries (Bundesverband der Deutschen Industrie, BDI), one of Germany's most important business associations. In 2018, one Vice Chair, Peter Altmaier, was Chief of Staff at the German Chancellery, while another, Angelika Niebler, was a Member of the European Parliament. Board members are drawn from academia, the think-tank community, the military, government, and the Bundestag; (2) an Executive Board (Vorstand) of three members, elected by the Board of Trustees, which serves as the institute's legal representative; (3) a Research Advisory Council composed primarily of German university and think-tank experts; (4) an Administrative Committee comprising the Director and three Deputy Directors; and (5) the research staff.

An analysis of the prior and concurrent affiliations of the Institute's research and management teams as of the end of September 2018 suggests that the most substantial revolving-door exchanges took place between the Institute, on the one hand, and other think tanks and universities, on the other. Nearly half of its research and management personnel had previously held positions at, or concurrently held appointments with, other think tanks and universities. Another notable feature is that, with the exception of two institutions, the universities with which team members had prior or concurrent affiliations were all located in Europe or the United States. The government departments in the German political system where members of the Institute have the highest concentration of prior or concurrent employment and part-time appointments are, in descending order: the German Federal Ministry of Defence and the German military, the Federal Foreign Office, economic decision-making authorities, the Bundestag, and the German Chancellery. Among these, the departments with the highest concentration of prior or concurrent appointments among research team members are the Ministry of Defence, the military, and the Federal Foreign Office, while members of the senior executive team are most likely to have held prior or concurrent positions in the Bundestag.

In addition, the Institute also maintained direct links with the European Commission and the European Parliament, with six members having previously worked at the European Commission. The Institute also had certain connections with civil society organizations, including advocacy groups. Another notable feature, as shown in Table 5.5, is that in the

Institute's Asia-Pacific research team, members with prior work experience in the media and think tanks outnumbered those with experience in any other sector.

Table 5.5: Analysis of the Revolving-Door Structure of SWP Personnel (as of the End of September 2018)

Professional Experience \ **Department**		**Asia-Pacific Research Team**		**Expert Teams of Other Fields**		**Think Tank Senior Management Team**	
		Headcount	**% of Team**	**Headcount**	**% of Team**	**Headcount**	**% of Team**
1. EU Decision-Making and Administrative Authorities	EU Commission (DGs)	—	—	2	1.9%	—	—
	Council of the EU & European Parliament	—	—	2	1.9%	—	—
	Other EU institutions and bodies (ECB, EESC, etc.)	1	6.7%	1	6.7%	1	3.7%
	Total with professional experience in EU decision-making and administrative authorities	***1***	***6.7%***	***5***	***4.9%***	—	—
2. German Official Decision-Making Bodies	German official economic decision-making bodies (Economic Policy Advisory Team of the German Chancellery, Federal Ministry of Finance, Federal Ministry for Economic Affairs, Deutsche Bundesbank, etc.)	—	—	4	3.9%	3	11.1%
	Federal Foreign Office	1	6.7%	6	5.8%	1	3.7%
	Federal Ministry of Defence & Armed Forces	—	—	8	7.8%	2	7.4%
	Federal Chancellery	—	—	2	1.9%	2	7.4%
	Bundestag	—	—	3	2.9%	4	14.8%
	Other German government bodies (other cabinet ministries, state legislatures and governments)	—	—	2	1.9%	3	11.1%
	Total with professional experience in German official decision-making authorities	***1***	***6.7%***	***25***	***24.3%***	***15***	***55.6%***
3. International Organizations		1	6.7%	5	4.9%	1	3.7%

Professional Experience	Department	Asia-Pacific Research Team		Expert Teams of Other Fields		Think Tank Senior Management Team	
		Headcount	% of Team	Headcount	% of Team	Headcount	% of Team
4. Financial Sector (banking, securities, insurance, asset management & associations)	European financial sector	1	6.7%	1	1%	—	—
	Financial sector outside Europe	—	—	—	—	—	—
	Total with professional experience in the financial sector	***1***	***6.7%***	***1***	***1%***	—	—
5. General Business & Industry (real economy sectors & associations)	European business & industry	—	—	7	6.8%	3	11.1%
	Business & industry outside Europe	—	—	—	—	—	—
	Total with professional experience in business & industry	—	—	***7***	***6.8%***	***3***	***11.1%***
6. European Media		—	—	5	4.9%		
7. Think Tanks	European think tanks	6	—	47	45.6%	3	11.1%
	Non-European Think tanks	—	—	7	6.8%	—	—
	Total with work experience with other think tanks	***6***	***40%***	***54***	***52.4%***	***3***	***11.1%***
8. Universities	European universities	6	40%	44	42.7%	4	14.8%
	Non-European Universities	—	—	7	6.8%	—	—
	Total with professional experience in universities	***6***	***40%***	***51***	***49.5%***	***4***	***14.8%***

Notes:

"Professional experience" refers to an individual's record of having engaged in a given occupation in a stable and institutionalized capacity, either at present or in the past. More specifically, it includes both full-time positions and formal part-time roles within established organizational structures, such as serving as an independent director on a corporate board or holding a formal academic appointment at a university.

In cases where an individual has held positions in multiple subcategories of the same major category listed in the table, only one affiliation is counted in order to avoid double counting. Specifically, the subcategory in which the individual has held the longest tenure is selected. If the durations are equal, the subcategory corresponding to the most recent position is recorded. As a result, no double counting occurs within each major category. However, given that many experts and senior administrators possess diverse professional backgrounds and may have held positions across multiple major categories, double counting across different categories cannot be avoided. Consequently, the figures across major categories should not be aggregated vertically.

At the end of September 2028, the total number of members in SWP's Asia-Pacific research team was 15, the number of members in other research fields was 103, and the number of members in the senior management team was 27.

Source: Compiled by the author

However, across different political systems and decision-making architectures, the strength of ties between a think tank's central space and the four aforementioned domains of the field of power varies significantly. The preceding analysis of SWP's revolving door system demonstrates that, as Germany's preeminent think tank occupying this central space, the Institute maintains the closest links to the academic domain of the field of power, followed by the political domain, then the financial and economic domain, and finally the media domain. In relative terms, American foreign policy think tanks of comparable standing to the Institute maintain far closer ties to the political domain.

V. Summary of Chapter 5

Building on Pierre Bourdieu's theory of the field of power, American think tank scholar Thomas Medvetz conceptualizes think tanks as a central space in the field of power, situated at the intersection of four core domains: politics, media, finance and economics, and academia. Indeed, the exchange of information and resources between think tanks and these four domains constitutes a critical link in the political decision-making process. The prevailing two-tier, four-quadrant system of European think tanks means that SWP occupies a central space in the EU's field of power, at the nexus of the EU's decision-making architecture and member states' national power systems. Through the dual channels of the national route and the Brussels route, it forges connections with the political, academic, media, and financial-economic domains of the EU's field of power, and in turn exerts influence over EU decision-making. Overall, the mechanisms of interaction between EU member state think tanks and the EU's decision-making system are considerably more complex and multi-layered than the relationship between American think tanks and the U.S. decision-making architecture.

As an intricate and multifaceted system, the EU's field of power is in a constant state of flux and evolution. From the perspective of the multiple streams model of decision-making, think tanks including SWP form a core component of the policy stream in the EU system. The EU's unwieldy, sprawling organizational structure and cumbersome, slow-moving operational procedures have long kept the three streams of the EU's field of power—the policy stream, the politics stream, and the problem stream—largely separate from one another, with only rare moments of convergence. It was only against the backdrop of dramatic, cascading shifts in the external and internal environment that decision-making windows in the field of power opened up: the prolonged economic downturn triggered by the sovereign debt crisis in early 2012; the successive shocks of overlapping internal and external crises from the second half of 2015 to early 2016, including the refugee influx, terrorist attacks across the bloc, and the Brexit process; and the profound volatility in early 2017, driven by the surge of populist forces into mainstream political arenas and the widespread public and political uproar triggered by Chinese corporate acquisitions in Europe. These seismic shifts enabled the policy stream, into which SWP and other think tanks are embedded, to converge with the other two streams, driving the EU's incremental advancement of the decision-making process for its defensive economic policy toward China. It is therefore of paradigmatic and representative significance to combine the analytical lens of the central space in the field of power with the multiple streams decision-making model, to examine and dissect the mechanisms through which SWP exerts its influence over the EU's defensive economic policymaking toward China.

In practice, there are substantial differences between think tanks in the Anglo-American system, those in continental European states such as Germany, and Brussels-based think tanks operating at the EU level, with each group exhibiting distinct characteristics in their operational models, organizational structures, human resource composition, and mechanisms for influencing decision-making. Think tanks in the Anglo-American system operate in an environment of fierce competition and rapid change, demonstrating high degrees of flexibility; they maintain exceptionally close ties to the political and media domains of the field of power, and prioritize the policy utility of their research. By contrast, think tanks in continental European states such as Germany maintain the closest links to the academic domain of the field of power, exhibit far greater institutional stability, and place greater emphasis on the academic rigor of their research. In turn, Brussels-based think tanks operating at the EU level are often smaller in size with more limited resources, and more focused on building collaborative networks and institutional frameworks than either of the other two groups.

These differences and characteristics have been shaped by the long-term structural imprint of the political and decision-making systems into which each group of think tanks is embedded, and also reflect divergences in the functional positioning that each set of institutions has defined for itself. Comparative research on think tanks across different systems therefore warrants further granular, in-depth scholarly exploration in future research.

Chapter 6: British Think Tanks' Influence over the EU's Defensive Economic Policy toward China: A Case Study of the Royal Institute of International Affairs (RIIA)

Of all the European countries, the United Kingdom has the largest number of think tanks, the earliest emergence of such institutions, and the most profound think tank influence over government decision-making. As early as 1955-1961, while U.S. think tanks such as the RAND Corporation and the Brookings Institution were starting to enter America's foreign and security decision-making system, the first cohort of British think tanks to develop after World War II—such as Political and Economic Planning (PEP)—had already been incorporated into cabinet advisory mechanisms. They shaped Britain's economic and social policymaking system and helped form the earliest "epistemic community" in the country[①] In the post-Cold War era, the political leadership's demand for policy advice increased, and British think tanks entered a new phase of development. According to the annual global think tank rankings published since 2007 by James McGann of the University of Pennsylvania, between 2007 and 2017 approximately 16 think tanks were added in Britain per year;[②] by 2017, the country had 444 think tanks, ranking third globally and first

---

① On the position and role of Britain's earliest think tanks in the British political system after the Second World War, reference is made to a report published in 1960: Political and Economic Planning (PEP), *Advisory Committees in British Government, a PEP report*, London: George Allen and Unwin Ltd., 1960. This report documents the rapid expansion of the decision-making advisory committee system across British Cabinet departments from the early 1950s onward. It also describes the operational framework, membership composition, and mechanisms and processes through which advisory committees participated in public policy-making within the British Cabinet, including accounts of the earliest cohort of think tanks to emerge in Britain after the Second World War. This constitutes the earliest known specialized research record on British think tanks in existing literature.

② James G. McGann, *The Global Go-To Think Tanks: The Leading Public Policy Research Organizations in the World 2007, 2008; 2017 Global Go To Think Tank Index Report*, Think Tanks and Civil Societies Program, in Europe. Moreover, the United Kingdom had the largest share of think tanks on the "Top Think Tanks Worldwide (Non-U.S.)" top-30 list. ①This indicates that British think tanks are important actors with considerable influence over decision-making in the United Kingdom and, indirectly, in the EU.

Among the many British think tanks that study international affairs and provide foreign policy advice, the Royal Institute of International Affairs—better known as the Chatham House—is widely regarded as the most prominent and representative.② Since 2007, it has consistently ranked among the top three in the University of Pennsylvania's annual Global Go To Think Tank Index across the following categories: "Top Think Tanks Worldwide (Non-U.S.)," "Top Think Tanks in Western Europe," and "Top Foreign Policy and International Affairs Think Tanks." As one of Britian's top think tanks, it remains among the top ten in the "Top Think Tanks on Foreign Economic Policy" category. In recent years, its influence has continued to rise. Therefore, examining its influence over EU decision-making holds exemplary significance and can shed light on the distinctive position and function of British think tanks in the EU decision-making system.

I. Existing Literature on British Think Tanks' Influence over Decision-Making

Given the central role of UK think tanks in Britain's political decision-making system, scholarly inquiry into their influence has evolved in tandem with research on governmental decision-making structures and processes. Many new concepts originally proposed to interpret changes in decision-making mechanisms were first used to explain how think tanks and similar actors influence British government decisions and the resulting policy outcomes. Overall, existing literature offers multiple theoretical perspectives that help elucidate the influence of British think tanks.

First, from the perspective of policy idea construction, British think tanks are embedded

University of Pennsylvania, January 31, 2018.

① James G. McGann, *2017 Global Go To Think Tank Index Report*, Think Tanks and Civil Societies Program, University of Pennsylvania, January 31, 2018.

② The full English name of this think tank is the "Royal Institute of International Affairs". In academic literature, think tank publications, and official policy documents, it is usually abbreviated as the Chatham House or RIIA.

within institutional structures such as "epistemic communities," "discourse coalitions," "advocacy coalitions," or "policy networks." This body of scholarship contends that these structures enable think tanks to participate catalyzing "paradigm shifts" in government decision-making. British scholarship pays particular attention to the cognitive construction of policy, as well as to the interaction between expert knowledge and political decision-making. Peter M. Haas offered an early and exact definition of "epistemic community," analyzing how such communities influence government external decision-making and international relations, and incorporating think tank-like research institutions and academic associations into this category (Haas, 1992)①. Building on this, Maarten A. Hajer proposed the concept of "discourse coalition," and other scholars have used "advocacy coalition" to examine, from different angles, the mechanisms by which social forces—including think tanks—shift the UK government's environmental policy ideas (Hajer, 1993; Smith, 1999)②. Hugh Pemberton and Peter M. Hall argued that think tanks, through their specialized expertise, become key components of "policy networks" or "advocacy coalitions." Alongside interest groups, advocacy associations, political parties, and decision-making elites, they contributed to a three-stage paradigm shift in UK policy—from welfareism and Keynesianism in the 1960s to neoliberalism and monetarism in the 1980s (Pemberton, 2004; Hall, 1993)③.

Second, from the perspective of political power distribution, British think tanks are treated as a special type of pressure group, advocacy group, or lobbying organization. Such literature explains the role of think tanks in UK lobbying politics and in the ideological renewal of social groups. Bill Coxall noted that because traditional bureaucracies, university research institutions, and party-affiliated research departments were often ill-equipped to respond to emergency issues, the Conservative Party from the 1970s and the Labor Party

---

① Peter M. Hass, "*Epistemic Communities and International Policy Coordination*", *International Organization*, Winter 1992, Vol. 46, No. 1, pp. 1-35.

② Maarten A. Hajer, "*Discourse Coalitions and the Institutionalization of Practice: The Case of Acid Rain in Britain*", in Frank Fischer and John Forester (Eds.), *The Argumentative Turn in Policy Analysis and Planning*, Durham and London: Duke University Press, 1993, pp. 43-78; Adrian Smith, "*Policy Networks and Coalitions: Explaining Policy Change and Stability in UK Industrial Pollution Policy?*", *Environment and Planning C Government and Policy*, Vol. 18, No. 1, February 2000, pp. 95-114.

③ Hugh Pemberton, *Policy Learning and British Governance in the 1960s*, Hampshire: Palgrave Macmillan, 2004, P. 283; Peter A. Hall, "Policy Paradigms, Social Learning, and the State: The Case of Economic Policy Making in Britain", *Comparative Politics*, Vol. 25, No. 3, April 1993, pp. 275-296.

from the 1990s increasingly relied on think tanks as sources of new policy thinking—thereby turning think tanks into a special type of pressure group (Coxall, 2001).① Hartwig Pautz, viewing think tanks as "suppliers of ideology," compared interactions between think tanks and the UK Labor Party versus Germany's SPD, and concluded that UK think tanks exert a greater influence in the ideological renewal of political parties (Pautz, 2010). ②Other scholars examined how think tanks cooperate with interest groups to influence public decisions in specific areas, detailing their importance in lobbying politics (Harkins, 2010; Hawkins & McCambridge, 2014).③

Third, British think tanks are positioned as "idea brokers." The "idea brokers" and "marketplace of ideas" perspective was originally proposed by U.S. scholars to explain④ American think tanks. When later applied to the UK context, it underwent further development, to the point where its meaning approaches the "central space of the field of power" perspective. Simon James, for example, looked at the relationships between the Institute of Economic Affairs and the Centre for Policy Studies and Thatcher's cabinet in the 1980s. He described how the think tanks helped translate neoliberal economic insight into the Conservative Party's governing ideas, arguing that UK think tanks functioned as "idea brokers" between academia and politics (James, 1993).⑤

However, most existing studies focus on the influence of British think tanks on UK government decisions, while relatively few explicitly examine their influence over EU decision-making. Among the limited literature, one study by Wells (2012) examines

① Bill Coxall, *Pressure Groups in British Politics*, Harlow: Pearson Education Limited, 2001, pp. 75-79.

② Hartwig Pautz, *Think Tanks in the United Kingdom and Germany: Actors in the Modernization of Social Democracy*, *British Journal of Politics and International Relations*, 2010, Vol. 12, pp. 274-294.

③ Miller D. Harkins, *Corporate Strategy, Corporate Capture: Food and Alcohol Industry Lobbing and Public Health*, *Critical Social Policy*, 2010, 30 (4), pp. 564-589; Benjamin Hawkins and Jim McCambridge, *Industry Actors, Think Tanks, and Alcohol Policy in the United Kingdom*, *American Journal of Public Health*, August 2014, Vol. 104, No. 8, pp. 1364-1369; John Turnpenny et al, *Mapping Actors involved in Climate Change Policy Networks in the UK*, January 2005, Tyndall Center for Climate Change Research, Working Paper no. 66.

④ James Allen Smith was the first to systematically elaborate the concept of the "idea broker" and use it to explain the developmental history and structural characteristics of the influence mechanism of American think tanks on U.S. government decision-making. For details, see James Allen Smith, *The Idea Brokers: Think Tanks and the Rise of the New Policy Elite*, New York: Macmillan Inc., 1991.

⑤ Simon James, "The Idea Brokers: The Impact of Think Tanks on British Government", *Public Administration*, Vol. 71, No. 3, Winter 1993, pp. 491-506.

how British think tanks affect UK regional policy under the EU's multi-level governance framework, but its focus remains on their influence over UK central government decision-making, concluding that British think tanks mainly influence central government and national party politics, while paying relatively little attention to—and exerting limited influence over—subnational local politics and the EU level.[①] Dedicated studies on how the United Kingdom influences EU external decision-making remain scarce. Thus, analyzing the mechanisms of UK influence over EU decision-making carries both theoretical significance and practical relevance.

II. The "National Route" of British Think Tanks' Influence over EU Decision-Making

Britain joined the European Communities relatively late, but it was never part of the euro area. In practice, it occupied a relatively peripheral position within the EU system. Domestically, Eurosceptic and isolationist forces had long been strong, and certain interest groups and social constituencies harbored deep distrust of the EU. The widely watched Brexit referendum process that unfolded from early 2016 is a clear illustration. As later analysis of the RIIA's "revolving door" mechanism reveals, a substantial share of its experts and senior managers have held positions in the British cabinet or Parliament, whereas few—if any—have served in EU decision-making institutions. Compared with the "Brussels route" and the "national route" available to think tanks from EU member states, UK think tanks have generally relied more heavily on the latter. The "Brussels route" has been summarized earlier. To understand the "national route" of British think tanks in depth—i.e., how British think tanks exert indirect and latent influence over EU decision-making—one must examine the political structure of UK foreign policy making and the position of think tanks within it, along with the mechanisms they employ. Unlike the U.S. political system which is built on a codified constitution and systematic institutional design, the British political system developed historically as one of the earliest representative democracies. It therefore exhibits a degree of fragmentation and a more complex and less linear internal structure. This makes theoretical generalization of UK decision mechanisms difficult. To clarify the structure of

① Peter Wells, Prescriptions for Regional Economic Dilemmas: Understanding the Role of Think Tanks in the Governance of Regional Policy, *Public Administration*, Vol. 90, No. 1, 2002, pp. 211-229 the UK executive decision-making system, Garsten Greve and Mathew Flinders proposed the "Russian doll model" (RDM), dividing the UK system into seven nested layers with the "core executive" at the center and semi-official public bodies at the periphery. Information, resources, interests, and decision-making authority flow inward, while policy implementation flows outward; the deeper the layer, the lower the autonomy and the higher the transparency (Greve, 1999; Flinders, 2004, 2008). ①Because the UK system often features overlapping functions and intersecting lines of authority—including cross-departmental decision-making and implementation involving both horizontal and vertical interactions—RDM cannot fully account for all phenomena. Flinders later proposed a "spider-web model," which retains a nine-layer nested structure but foregrounds the complex circulation, overlap, and intersection among various layers. He further noted that the layers may vary in scale, with no clear hierarchy in terms of autonomy and transparency② (Flinders, 2009). While the spider-web model highlights dynamic interactions, it nevertheless falls short of clearly identifying the routes and mechanisms through which overlap occurs in relation to specific issues.

Any national decision-making system must rely on mechanisms that collect, filter, process, and transmit the interests, preferences, information, and resources of various social groups from the grassroots upward. Hence, the structures between governing elites and grassroots society—political parties, interest groups, civil society, etc.—are indispensable. The above models focus mainly on the administrative apparatus that holds formal decision-making authority and thus do not explain relationships between executive decision-making departments and political actors, nor do they provide a macro-level overview of UK political structure. In this chapter, the "pyramid" structure (Figure 6.1) is proposed to depict the overall UK foreign policymaking system.

As Figure 6.1 suggests, UK foreign policymaking is a highly composite multi-level architecture. Parliamentary committees relevant to foreign policy and the cabinet led by

① Mathew Flinders, *"Distributed Public Governance in Britain"*, *Public Administration*, 2004, Vol.82, pp. 883-909; *"the Politics of Public-Private Partnerships"*, *British Journal of Politics and International Relations*, 2005 (7), pp. 543-567; *Delegated Governance and the British State: Walking without Order*, Oxford: Oxford University Press, 2008. Garsten Greve and Mathew Flinders, *"Quangos: What's in a Name?"*, *Governance*, 1999 (12), pp. 129-147.

② Mathew Flinders, *Chapter 17: Delegation*, in Mathew Flinders, Andrew Gamble, Colin Hay and Michael Kenny (Eds.), *the Oxford Handbook of British Politics*, Oxford: Oxford University Press, 2009, P. 318.

the prime minister occupy the most central position. Within this architecture, the UK think-tank system occupies a distinctive place: it sits between political parties, interest groups, academia, the media, business and finance, grassroots civil society, and decision-making elites. Through its channels of connection to these actors, it transmits interests, preferences, and policy positions upward to the core decision-making level, watches and interprets core decision-making activities, and thereby exerts influence over UK foreign policymaking.

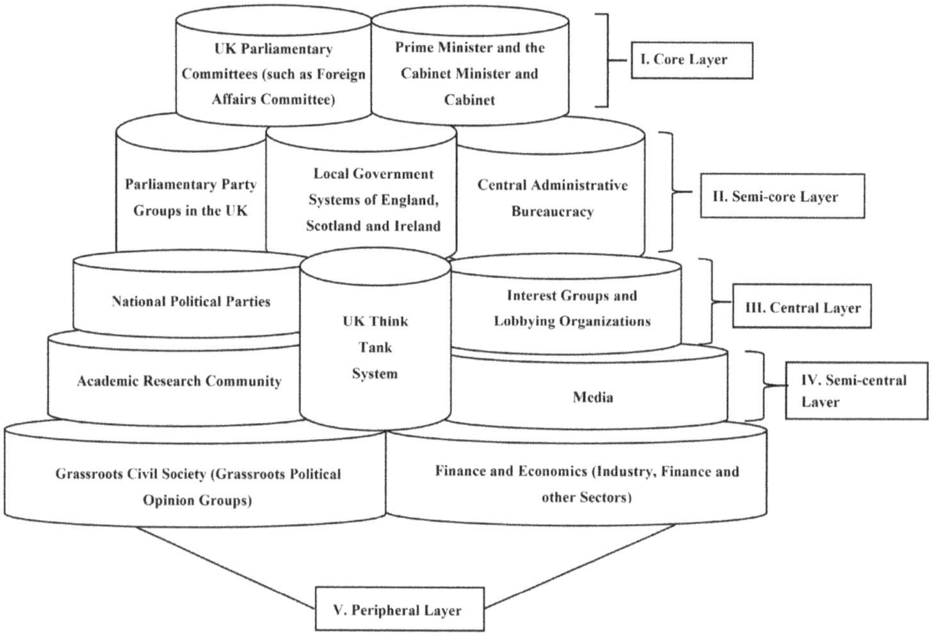

Figure 6.1: Pyramid Structure of the UK Foreign Policymaking System

Source: Compiled by the author

As shown in Figure 2.2, a coordinate system based on the duration and salience of think-tank influence can classify influence methods into four types comprising thirteen distinct modes. These modes are not universally applicable across all layers and departments; some work only in specific settings. Based on existing literature and practice, these four types/thirteen modes can be mapped onto the five layers and eleven actors in the UK foreign-policy "pyramid" structure. By analyzing the potential influence on each actor, and connecting this to how core UK decision-making departments—operating through the UK's status as an EU member state at the time—participated in and influenced EU decision-making, one can construct a comprehensive route map of how UK think tanks influence the EU via the "national route" (see Figure 6.2).

Figure 6.2 shows that within the "national route," different UK think-tank influence methods operate via different routes and affect different parts of the decision-making system. Indirect influence methods can affect all parts, whereas direct influence methods tend to concentrate on the most central decision-making hub. Overall, UK think tanks influence five layers of UK foreign-policy decision-making via four types of methods, forming a composite system of frequent interactions. By leveraging the top UK decision-making level, they can extend their influence to EU decision-making institutions.

Compared with the "Brussels route," the "national route" contains more layers and involves more procedures and links, making it more complex. Its endpoint also differs. Specifically, it operates across three levels: (1) Think-tank level—interest groups and civil society transmit interests and preferences to think tanks via commissioned or funded research, participation in seminars, holding of positions, etc.; (2) UK top decision-making level—think tanks transmit these demands and preferences via policy debates and advisory services to key decision-makers within the UK political system—parliamentary foreign-affairs committee members, heads of cabinet departments such as the Foreign Office, and even the prime minister; (3) EU decision-making level—before 2020, when Britain was still a member of the EU, UK top decision-makers could transmit these domestic interests and preferences to the EU Council through the European Council summits, Council of Ministers meetings, and other Council-level meetings. This occurs through bargaining, negotiation, and coordination among member states, and is ultimately reflected in Council decisions, declarations, and other documents. Meanwhile, the UK cabinet and central bureaucracy can exert some indirect influence over the European Commission through routine administrative interactions.

Thus, the "national route" ultimately focuses on the European Council and the Council of the European Union as the main institution that can clearly receive think-tank influence along this route. The most critical intermediate link is the high-ranking bureaucrats and executive leadership of the central governments of the EU's member states, which determines whether the think tank's influence can be transmitted smoothly to the EU level. In short, the process by which UK think tanks convey their demands, preferences, and information to EU decision-making institutions—especially the Council—via the pathways in Figure 6.2 constitutes the overall picture of the "national route" for UK think tanks.

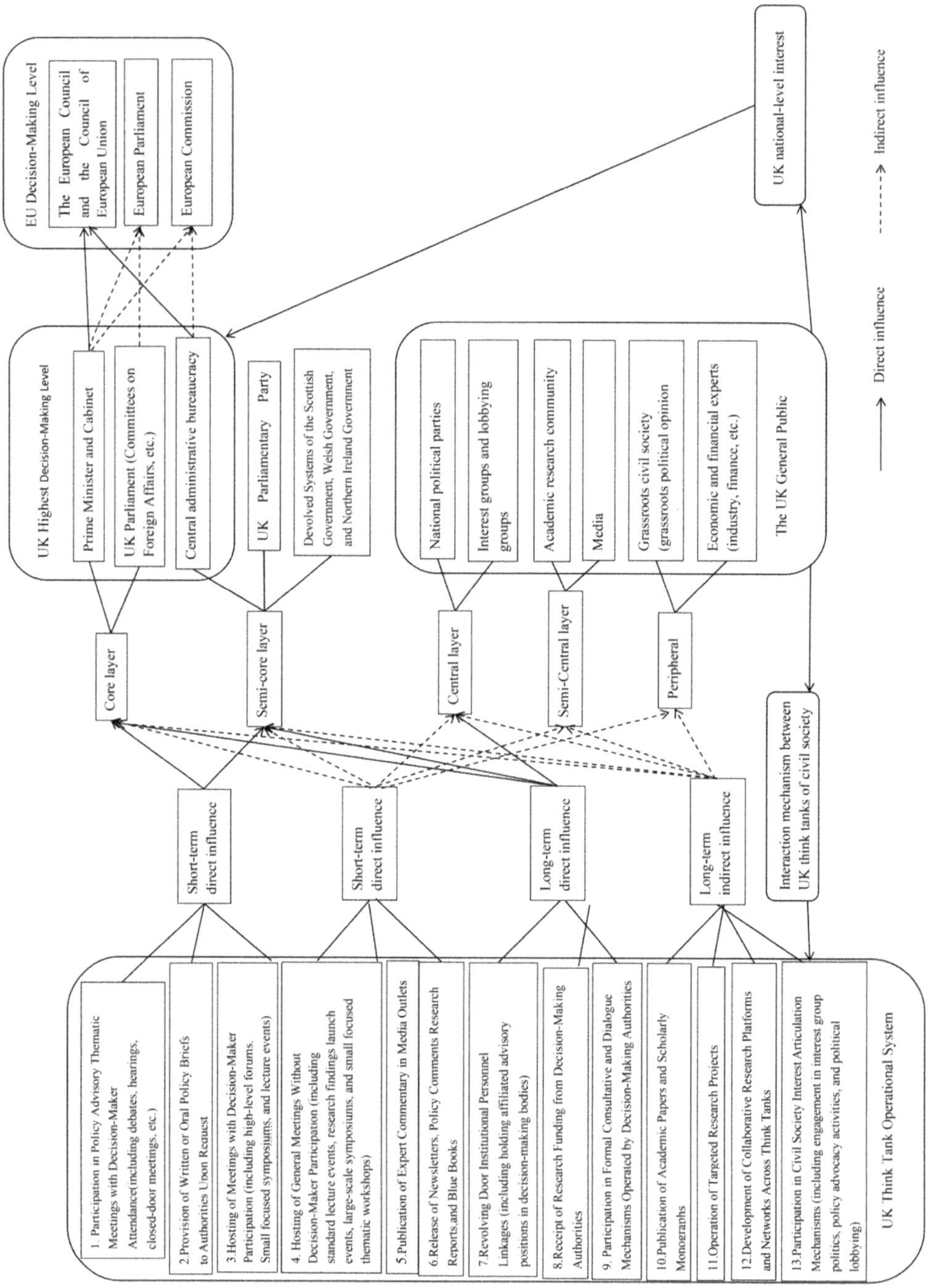

Figure 6.2: The Pathways of the "National Route" for British Think Tanks to Influence EU Decision-Making

Source: Compiled by the author

Of course, relying on the "national route" does not mean abandoning the "Brussels route." The EU relies on institutionalized communication with "organized civil society" to ensure representation and facilitate governance; accordingly, EU multi-level governance provides channels (e.g., Commission public consultations and social dialogue mechanisms; EESC participation) for member-state think tanks and interest groups to express demands directly. EU-level lobbying and think-tank networks are also highly developed, so UK think tanks do not exclude the Brussels route. For the RIIA specifically, it has in practice used both routes.

III. British Think Tanks and the European Think Tank System in the Context of Brexit

On June 23, 2016, Britain held a referendum in which Leave won a narrow majority. The result sent shockwaves beyond the UK borders to reach the EU. Prime Minister David Cameron announced his resignation the following day, on June 24, stating that Brexit negotiations would be handled by his successor's cabinet. After taking office as prime minister on July 13, 2016, Theresa May invoked Article 50 of the Treaty on European Union on March 31, 2017, triggering formal withdrawal negotiations. Talks commenced on June 19, 2017 and proceeded through subsequent phases. However, the negotiation process was fraught with twists and turns, punctuated by prolonged stalemates. The EU and the United Kingdom engaged in repeated back-and-forth over bilateral trade relations and Britain's stance on EU legislation. After years of meticulous price negotiations, Britain formally left the EU in early 2020. Following a one-year Brexit transition period, the "transition phase" was concluded by the end of 2020, completing full UK separation from the EU. With it, Britain diverged its economy from the European Single Market to establish an independent economic system.

Although UK withdrawal from the EU to establish its own independent system has become an irreversible trend, ambiguities remain in how both sides define their bilateral relationship. While the overall trajectory of Brexit proved difficult to reverse and the future UK-EU relationship remained unclear, Europe had already formed a well-developed, networked think-tank ecosystem characterized by extensive exchange and coordination. UK think tanks maintained relatively close cooperation and communication with their

European counterparts. As global rankings suggest, Britain has led Europe in both the number and quality of think tanks. UK think tanks have accumulated profound expertise on Europe, including rich materials and data, and often demonstrate strong theoretical depth and sensitivity to changing circumstances. For EU decision-makers and European strategic research communities, UK think tanks—especially top foreign-policy think tanks—remain important voices in debates concerning EU decision-making. In other words, UK think tanks still occupy a position within the broader European think tank system and can continue to influence EU decision-making. This is reflected in three aspects:

(1) Since the early 2000s, several major EU-focused "Brussels-level think tanks" have located their headquarters in the United Kingdom, most notably RAND Europe and the European Council on Foreign Relations (ECFR). Both occupy prominent positions in EU policy debates, comment frequently in the media, and publish substantial high-quality research—advantages that confer upon them significant discursive power.

(2) Since the 2008 global financial crisis, UK think tanks have been important participants in successive major EU policy adjustments, playing significant roles in problem identification, agenda-setting, and option selection. Their research strengths are widely recognized by EU decision-makers and European strategic research communities. Notably, in the run-up to the *EU's Global Strategy for Foreign and Security Policy* issued on June 28, 2016, multiple UK think tanks collaborated with continental counterparts in research and debate, delivering reports and articulating distinct viewpoints, and in doing so, building close ties with EU decision-makers and major member-state think tanks.

(3) Top UK foreign-policy think tanks engage in pan-European collaboration networks and are members of Europe-wide epistemic and policy communities, thus continuing to influence EU idea formation, issue identification, and policy debate. For instance, the RIIA participates in platforms such as the European Security and Defence Forum (ESDF), Vision Europe platform, and European Think-tank Network on China (ETNC). These collaborative platforms maintain institutionalized tight connections with high-ranking officials of the EU political leadership and decision-making. Within the organizational frameworks that propel the daily operations of these platforms, there are highest-ranking EU policymakers and officials. And many important symposiums and forums sponsored by these platforms are participated in by high-level officials from the core decision-making bodies of the European

Commission and the European Central Bank, and by members of the European Parliament.

For instance, William Shapcott, a member of the steering committee of the first aforementioned platform, had headed the EU Intelligence and Situation Centre (EU INTCEN), the EU's core intelligence agency, prior to 2018. In September 2018, he took office as Head of the Directorate-General for Administration at the General Secretariat of the Council of the European Union in September 2018. Meanwhile, those annual conferences sponsored or organized by the second and third aforementioned platforms consistently draw attendance from officials of relevant Directorates-General of the European Commission that are responsible for economic and social policies, as well as members of the European Parliament. Therefore, it is evident that through the institutional frameworks and operational mechanisms forged by these think tank collaboration networks, British think tanks retain the capacity to voice their views and exert influence over EU affairs.

IV. RIIA's Influence over the EU's Defensive Economic Policy toward China: Comparing Policy Advice Records with EU Official Policy Documents

The EU's defensive economic policy toward China evolved—through a gradual process—into a large and systematic framework. During this process, changes in internal and external circumstances created three "policy windows" that put pressure on EU decision-makers and led to intensive decision-making activities. After the first window period (February-May 2012), the EU only supplemented and revised its existing framework in response to internal disputes, without undertaking deep structural adjustment. However, after the policy windows of February-July 2016 and January-May 2017, the EU made major structural adjustments and constructed a systematic, defensive economic policy framework toward China. These years coincided with the rise of populism in the United Kingdom and the acceleration of Brexit. Studying the role of a distinctive member state like Britain in shaping EU policy is both academically valuable and practically significant: it can illuminate the actual effects, mechanisms, pathways, and structural characteristics of how think tanks from a centrifugal member state influence EU external decision-making.

Accordingly, this chapter continues to focus on the EU's defensive economic policy toward China, combining a "central space of the field of power" perspective with the

Multiple Streams Framework to examine the RIIA's influence over the EU's major structural adjustments of these policy frameworks, so as to provide an integrated theoretical and empirical picture.

The EU's first policy window period (February-June 2012) saw an intensive review of the Union's defensive trade policy toward China, resulting mainly in revisions and consolidation. Only after the policy windows in 2016 and 2017 did the EU establish a new comprehensive framework. Compared with the EU's policymaking time and pace, the RIIA undertook relevant assessments and developed policy ideas much earlier, maintaining sustained attention to China, EU-China economic relations, and defensive economic policy issues. As the global financial crisis and the European sovereign debt crisis broke out in succession from 2008 to 2009, the RIIA published a dozen outputs discussing new changes in the world economy and how China's rise might affect EU-China economic relations, offering insightful views. For example, a report in June 2009 explicitly stated that within the existing multilateral trade system, China's rise would create a "crowding-out effect" on European industry.[①] Multiple reports in the 2009-2010 period discussed growing Chinese investment in Europe;[②] a report in November 2009 titled "China and the EU: Time for a Change" argued that EU-China economic relations would undergo deep transformation and called for a new policy framework.[③] These judgments preceded the EU's 2012 review by three to four years, demonstrating the RIIA's foresight and sensitivity to shifting international trends.

On this basis, the author has reviewed 109 formal RIIA publications (reports, working papers, commentaries, etc.) between early 2005 and the end of September 2018[④] and

---

① Francoise Nicolas, "Chinese Direct Investment in Europe: Facts and Fallacies", Chatham House Briefing Paper, IE BP 2009/01, June 2009.

② Kerry Brown, "The UK and China: Dealing with a New-Old Friend", Asia Program Briefing Note: ASP 2009/01, Chatham House, June 2009; Nora Burghart and Vanessa Rossi, "China's Overseas Direct Investment in the UK", Program Paper IE PP 2009/06, December 2009; Francois Nicolas, "Chinese Direct Investments in France: No French Exception, No Chinese Challenge", IE Program Paper IE PP 2010/02, Chatham House, January 2010.

③ Kerry Brown and Stanley Crossick, "The EU and China: Time for a Change?" Asia Program Paper" ASP PP 2009/03, November 2009.

④ The 109 publications of the Royal Institute of International Affairs cannot be listed one by one here. Among its most important and sharply argued research outputs are the following: Francoise Nicolas, "Chinese Direct Investment in Europe: Facts and Fallacies", Chatham House Briefing Paper, IE BP 2009/01, June 2009;

identified the forms and timing in which they addressed the twelve key elements listed for the EU's policy framework, then compared them with EU decision documents to produce Table 6.1.

Table 6.1: Comparison of Timings and Formats of the RIIA's Policy Advice and the EU's Policy Documents on Twelve Key Points of EU's Defensive Economic Policy toward China (December 2005-September 2018)

Entity Proposing or Formulating Key Policy Points / Key Policy Points			RIIA's Reference or Commentary on Key Policy Points (Format / Time)	Explicit Reference to Relevant Policy Elements in Official Decision-Making Documents of EU Authorities (Format/Time)		
				European Commission	European Parliament	The European Council and the Council of the EU
I. Fundamental Positioning	I-1. General Principles	Format	Project team reports, policy briefs, research papers, conference speeches	Policy and Program briefings	Opinions, resolutions	Council decisions
		Time	Jan 2008, Jun 2009 (twice), Jul 2009 (twice), May 2010 and Oct 2010 (twice), Jan, May, and Jul 2011 (twice), Mar 2012, Jul 2013, Sep 2017	Jun 2016, Sep 2017	Apr, May, and Jun 2016	Jul 2016

Vanessa Rossi, "Towards a Post-Crisis Global Economy: Not out of the Woods yet, Europe Now the Key Risk?" Program Paper: IEP PP 09/01, Chatham House, July 2009; Nora Burghart and Vanessa Rossi, "China's Overseas Direct Investment in the UK", Program Paper IE PP 2009/06, December 2009; Francois Nicolas, "Chinese Direct Investments in France: No French Exception, No Chinese Challenge", IE Program Paper IE PP 2010/02, Chatham House, January 2010; Carlo Pietrobelli, "The Marco Polo Effect: Chinese FDI in Italy", IE Program Paper: IE PP 2010/04, February 2010; Lawrence Saez, "Chinese Outward Direct Investments in Spain", International Economics Program Paper 2010/06, March 2010; Kerry Brown and Loh Su Hsing, "Trying to Read the New 'Assertive' China Right", Asia Program Paper: ASP PP 2011/02, January 2011; David Miliband, Speech Transcript, "Europe between America and China", May 12, 2011; Steven McGuire, "The Changing Landscape of the Aircraft Industry", Chatham House Briefing Paper, IE WIT BP 2011/02, July 2011; Sylvia Hui, "Engaging an Emerging Super Power: Understanding China as a Foreign Policy Actor", Asia Program Paper: ASP 2011/05, July 2011; Donald Hepburn, "Mapping the World's Changing Industrial Landscape", Chatham House Briefing Paper, IE WIT BP 2011/01, July 2011; Robert Ash, Robin Porter and Tim Summers, "China, the EU and China's 12th Five-Year Program", ECRAN Research Paper, March 2012; Jeremy Clegg and Hinrich Voss, "Chinese Overseas Direct Investment in the European Union", ECRAN Research Paper, September 2012; Bates Gill and Andrew Small, "Untapped Trilateralism: Common Economic and Security Interests of the European Union, the United States and China", ECRAN Research Paper, November 2012; Donald Hepburn et al., "The World Industrial Transformation: A Chatham House Report", July 2013; Stephen Pickford et al., "Towards a More Effective G20 in 2016: Chinese and UK Perspectives", Chatham House Research Paper, March 2016.

Key Policy Points \ Entity Proposing or Formulating Key Policy Points			RIIA's Reference or Commentary on Key Policy Points (Format / Time)	Explicit Reference to Relevant Policy Elements in Official Decision-Making Documents of EU Authorities (Format/Time)		
				European Commission	European Parliament	The European Council and the Council of the EU
I. Fundamental Positioning	I-2. Detailed Points	Format	Policy briefs, research reports, project team reports, research papers	Policy and Program Briefings, Analytical Reports	Analytical reports	Council decisions
		Time	Jun and Jul 2009 (twice), Nov 2009, Fe 2010, Jan 2011, Mar and Sep 2012, March 2013	Jun and Jul 2016, May, Sep, and Dec 2017	Nov 2017	Jul 2016, Jun 2017
II.Overall Framework	II-1. General Principles	Format	Policy analysis report, projecst team reports, research papers	Policy and program briefings, evaluation reports	Research papers	Council decisions
		Time	Jun and Nov 2009, Mar and Sep 2012, May and Sep 2017	Jun 2016, May 2017	Apr 2017	Jul 2016
II.Overall Framework	II-2. Detailed Points	Format	Research papers, project team reports	Policy document releases, research reports	Analytical reports	—
		Time	Jul 2011 (twice), Mar and Sep 2012, Jul 2013, Sep 2017	Jun 2016, May 2017, Sep 2017, and Dec 2017	Nov 2017	—
III.Trade Policy	III-1. General Principles	Format	Research papers, project team reports, and conference presentations	Evaluation reports, policy proposal notifications	Evaluation reports, draft legislative documents	Legislative documents, council decisions
		Time	May 2010, Jan 2011, Jul 2011, Oct 2011, Mar 2012	Apr 2013, Oct and Nov 2016	Oct 2013, Jun 2017	Jun, Oct, and Nov 2016
	III-2. Detailed Points	Format	Research papers	Assessment reports, working group documents, legislative drafts, proposal notifications, press releases	Review records, resolutions, and voting records	Meeting conclusions, legislative documents, press releases
		Time	Jun 2016	Apr 2013, Jun 2016, Oct and Nov 2016, Sep and Dec 2017, Jan, Apr, Jun and Jul 2018	Jun 2016, Jun 2017, May 2018	Oct 2016, Nov and Dec 2017, Apr 2018

Key Policy Points \ Entity Proposing or Formulating Key Policy Points			RIIA's Reference or Commentary on Key Policy Points (Format / Time)	Explicit Reference to Relevant Policy Elements in Official Decision-Making Documents of EU Authorities (Format/Time)		
				European Commission	European Parliament	The European Council and the Council of the EU
IV. Investment Policy	IV-1. General Principles	Format	Policy analysis reports, conference speeches, research papers, project team reports	Working Group reports, policy program briefings	Draft legislative legislations, debate records	News announcements
		Time	Jun and Dec 2009, Jan and Feb 2010, May and Oct 2011, Mar and Sep 2012, May and Sep 2017	May 2017, Sep 2017	Mar 2017, May and Jun 2018	Jun 2018
	IV-2. Detailed Points	Format	Research papers, project team reports	Working group reports, technical lists, policy options briefings	Revised drafts of legislative documents	—
		Time	Mar and Sep 2012	Sep 2017 (six time)	Jun 2018	—
V. Industrial Policy	V-1. General Principles	Format	Research reports, survey reports	Situation statements, proposal notifications	Resolutions	Council decision
		Time	Jan 2008, Jul 2011 (three times), Jul 2013	Mar 2016, Sep 2017 (twice)	Jul 2017	May 2017
	V-2. Detailed Points	Format	Situation briefings, research reports, research papers	Policy briefings, working group reports, technical issue lists	Resolution	—
		Time	Jul 2011 (three times), Mar 2012, Jul 2013	Sep 2017 (twice), Oct and Nov 2017	Jul 2017	—
VI. Intellectual Property Policy	VI-1. General Principles	Format	Project team reports, research papers	Working group reports, press releases	—	—
		Time	Marc 2012, July 2013	Feb and Mar 2018	—	—
	VI-2. detailed Points	Format	Project Team Report	Policy briefings, working group reports, press releases	—	News announcements
		Time	March 2012	Nov 2017, Feb, Mar, and Jun 2018	—	Jun 2018

Source: The author compiled the data based on 109 officially published articles and relevant EU decision-making documents from 2005 to 2018 obtained from the RIIA.

Table 6.1 reveals several key features of the RIIA's research on China-EU economic relations and its reflections on the EU's defensive economic policy toward China.

First, in terms of research rhythm, the Institute was most active in its analysis in the run-up to the "decision-making window" between February and June 2012, during which time it most frequently discussed and elaborated on the key elements of the EU policy framework outlined in Table 3.5. By contrast, discussions of the EU's defensive economic policy toward China were relatively sparse around the "decision-making window" from February to June 2016. This can largely be attributed to the profound disruptions caused by the Brexit referendum to the internal and external environments of both the EU and Britain, which diverted the Institute's research focus and resources heavily toward Brexit-related issues, leaving little capacity for sustained, intensive research on China-EU economic ties and the EU's economic policy toward China.

Second, regarding the distribution of mentions across different dimensions of the EU's policy framework, the Institute's policy contributions most frequently referenced the fundamental positioning and overall framework of the EU's defensive economic policy toward China, suggesting that these two areas received the greatest attention and most in-depth analysis. Table 6.1 further indicates that the Institute also devoted considerable attention to policy dimensions related to investment and industrial policy. It showed relatively limited interest, however, in trade policy—traditionally the core area of China-EU economic relations. This pattern, to some extent, reflects the Institute's distinctive research priorities, analytical perspective, and thematic focus.

The Institute's frequent engagement with the fundamental positioning and overall framework of the EU's policy underscores its identity as a traditional foreign-policy think tank, which tends to prioritize strategic issues. Its long-standing research strength lies in assessing long-term, systemic shifts in the global landscape and analyzing macro-level strategic questions. Meanwhile, the Institute closely focuses on policy issues in investment and industrial policy. As early as the second half of 2009 and early 2010, it published a series of country-specific reports on Chinese investment in the Europe, providing detailed assessments of Chinese firms' investment activities in major EU member states including the United Kingdom, France, Italy, and Spain, and identifying the potential implications of Chinese investment for EU industrial dynamics.①

① Nora Burghart and Vanessa Rossi, "China's Overseas Direct Investment in the UK", Program Paper IE PP

Political elites in continental European countries such as Germany, along with EU policymakers, only began to closely monitor Chinese investment in Europe and conduct substantive policy debates in late 2016 and early 2017. This demonstrates the Institute's strong foresight and sensitivity to emerging global trends, enabling it to identify developments beyond the immediate horizon of international affairs. Its research is therefore highly forward-looking, allowing it to accurately capture evolving trends in China-EU economic relations and significant new issues in the EU's economic policy toward China.

In conclusion, a comparison between the Institute's policy research and EU official documents reveals a clear temporal sequence, a conceptual and discursive coherence, and a substantive relevance between the Institute's analysis of the EU's defensive economic policy toward China and the positions articulated by EU decision-makers. On this basis, it can reasonably be concluded that the RIIA exerted a discernible influence over EU policy deliberations concerning this framework.

V. RIIA's Short-Term Influence: An Examination of Its Conferences

As discussed above, think tanks act as a "central space" linking politics, business/finance, academia, and the media. Conferences involving outside participants provide platforms for think tanks to engage in information exchange and resource circulation, and are an important way for them to generate and deploy discourse power. Conferences can shape public debate, attract attention, influence agendas, and create pressure or momentum for decision-makers. Therefore, the types and number of conferences reflect a think tank's prominence and position in a decision-making system. The RIIA keeps detailed conference records. By analyzing the characteristics of RIIA-organized conferences, one can reveal the pathways and mechanisms of RIIA influence. Since 2006, the RIIA held 107 conferences focusing on EU-China economic relations and EU economic policy toward China. The author's statistics are presented in Table 6.2, which illustrates the RIIA's communication and

2009/06, December 2009; Francois Nicolas, "Chinese Direct Investments in France: No French Exception, No Chinese Challenge", IE Program Paper IE PP 2010/02, Chatham House, January 2010; Carlo Pietrobelli, "The Marco Polo Effect: Chinese FDI in Italy", IE Program Paper: IE PP 2010/04, February 2010; Lawrence Saez, "Chinese Outward Direct Investments in Spain", International Economics Program Paper 2010/06, March 2010.

exchange structure with parts of the EU "field of power" in this policy domain, and helps identify channels and mechanisms of influence.

Table 6.2: Statistics on Meetings Convened by RIIA on Issues Directly Related to EU-China Relations and the EU's Economic Policy toward China (November 2006-June 2018)

Structural Characteristics \ Meeting Type			I. High-Level Forums	II. Lectures	III. Policy Report Launch Events	IV. Large-Scale Symposiums	V. Small-scale Thematic Workshops	Total
1. Meetings with explicit records of attendance by officials from EU decision-making bodies (including former members) as guests	Including officials from various DGs of the European Commission	Number of meetings attended	6	—	—	3	2	11
		Participation rate (percentage of attendees compared to the total number of such meetings)	42.9%	—	—	37.5%	6.9%	10.3%
	Including officials from other decision-making and administrative departments outside the European Commission.	Number of meetings attended	3	2	—	—	1	6
	Including officials from other decision-making and administrative departments outside the European Commission.	Participation rate	21.4%	3.8%	—	—	3.4%	5.6%
	Total attendance of officials from EU decision-making bodies (after duplicate removal)	**Number of meetings attended**	**7**	**2**	**—**	**3**	**3**	**14**
		Participation rate	**50%**	**3.8%**	**—**	**37.5%**	**10.3%**	**13.1%**

Structural Characteristics		Meeting Type	I. High-Level Forums	II. Lectures	III. Policy Report Launch Events	IV. Large-Scale Symposiums	V. Small-scale Thematic Workshops	Total
2. Meetings with explicit records of attendance by UK decision-making body officials (including former members) as guests	Including officials from the UK's economic decision-making departments (including the Ministry of Finance, the Department for Trade and Industry, etc.)	Number of meetings attended	5	—	—	2	2	10
		Participation rate	35.7%	—	—	25%	6.9%	9.3%
	Including officials from the UK Foreign Service (including departments such as the Foreign Office, Brexit Office, and Immigration and Security Department).	Number of meetings attended	4	3	—	—	2	9
		Participation rate	28.6%	5.9%	—	—	6.9%	8.4%
	Total attendance of UK decision-making officials at the meeting (after duplicate removal)	**Number of meetings attended**	**11**	**3**	**—**	**2**	**5**	**21**
		Participation rate	**78.6%**	**5.7%**	**—**	**25%**	**17.2%**	**19.6%**
3. Meetings with clear records of international economic organization decision-makers (including former) participating as guests		Number of meetings attended	5	1	1	2	3	11
		Participation rate	35.7%	1.9%	5.3%	25%	10.3%	10.3%
4. Meetings with clear records of officials from Chinese decision-making departments and embassies/consulates (including former) participating as guests		Number of meetings attended	8	5	1	1	2	17
		Participation rate	57.1%	9.4%	5.3%	12.5%	6.9%	15.9%
5. Meetings with clear records of representatives from the European financial sector (including banks, investment companies, asset management firms, stock exchanges, rating agencies, etc.) and their interest groups participating as guests		Number of meetings attended	7	4	3	1	4	17
		Participation rate	50%	7.5%	15.8%	12.5%	13.8%	15.9%

Structural Characteristics \ Meeting Type		I. High-Level Forums	II. Lectures	III. Policy Report Launch Events	IV. Large-Scale Symposiums	V. Small-scale Thematic Workshops	Total
6. Meetings with Clear records of representatives from the European business and industry sectors outside of finance and their interest groups participating as guests	Number of meetings attended	12	1	3	4	5	21
	Participation rate	85.7%	1.9%	15.8%	50%	17.2%	19.6%
7. Meetings with clear records of representatives from European professional service firms (including law firms, accounting firms, business consultancies, lobbying and public relations firms) participating as guests	Number of meetings attended	10	3	2	4	7	22
	Participation rate	71.4%	5.7%	10.5%	50%	24.1%	20.6%
8. Meetings with clear records of representatives from European media professionals as guests	Number of meetings attended	5	7	4	1	7	21
	Participation rate	35.7%	13.2%	21.1%	12.5%	24.1%	19.6%
9.Meetings with clear records of scholars from European universities and think tanks participating as guests	Number of meetings attended	12	18	9	5	14	47
	Participation rate	85.7%	34%	47.4%	62.5%	48.2%	43.9%
10. Percentage of meetings of the same type in total (total meetings of all types: 107)	**Total number of such meetings**	**14**	**53**	**19**	**8**	**29**	**107**
	Percentage of all meeting types	**13.1**	**47.7%**	**17.8%**	**7.5%**	**27.1%**	**100%**

Notes:

1) "Participation rate" in the first five columns of the table (from "I. High-Level Forums" to "V. Small-Scale Thematic Seminars") indicates the proportion of attendees in a specific category attending each type of meeting relative to the total number of meetings in that category. The participation rate in the last column ("Total Meetings After Deducting Double Counts") reflects the proportion of attendees in a given category attending all meetings compared to the total 49 meetings recorded in this table.

2) The identification of participants' backgrounds is based on their current or former full-time employment status.

3) "Guest attendee" refers to participants invited to deliver keynote speeches at opening or closing ceremonies, make thematic presentations during discussion sessions, or serve as moderators or commentators in the conference's discussion sessions.

4) Due to the fact that the same participant might attend different types of meetings, and some meetings possess attributes of more than one type (such as being simultaneously a lecture and a policy report launch). There are overlaps in the statistics in the table. Furthermore, because of the limited space here, the first and second categories cannot list all types of institutional backgrounds of decision-making body attendees. Therefore, the numbers in the table cannot be directly summed vertically or horizontally.

Source: The author independently compiled and plotted the data based on records from the 107 meetings conducted by the RIIA between 2006 and 2018.

Table 6.2 reveals several key characteristics of the external relations structure of the RIIA in the domain of the EU's economic policy toward China.

First, regarding its linkage with political decision-makers in the "field of power", the RIIA's ties with EU decision-makers are generally weaker than those with UK decision-makers, yet the gap is relatively marginal. In practice, officials from the various Directorates-General (DGs) of the European Commission attended different types of meetings with higher frequency than their counterparts in Britain's economic decision-making departments and foreign affairs system. This demonstrates that, as a traditional British foreign-policy think tank, the RIIA—despite its geographical distance from the EU's decision-making hub in Brussels, and the imperfect alignment between its research/operational rhythm and that of the EU policymaking process—still maintains substantially close connections with EU decision-makers, particularly the DGs of the European Commission, in the fields of China-EU economic relations and the EU's economic policy toward China. In other words, the Institute's influence over EU decision-makers is undeniable and cannot be overlooked.

Second, within the realm of the EU's economic policy toward China, the RIIA fosters very close ties with the media. The level of media professionals' participation in its meetings is not only on par with that of UK decision-makers and representatives from the British real economy and industrial and commercial sectors, but also higher than the participation rate of EU decision-making officials. Compared with EU-level think tanks such as Bruegel and prominent German think tanks like SWP, close engagement with the media stands out as a defining feature of the RIIA as a British foreign-policy think tank. British media outlets exhibit a high degree of sensitivity to evolving situations and maintains a strong focus on international affairs, endowing them with unique advantages in collecting and synthesizing the information and data essential for international affairs research. For this reason, many of the Institute's events—especially small-scale seminars and lectures—are chaired by senior media professionals with extensive experience in international affairs. Meanwhile, leveraging media channels, the Institute can disseminate its research findings more efficiently and articulate its perspectives on specific issues within policy debates, thereby effectively establishing its discourse influence in specific EU policymaking areas and proposals.

Third, Table 6.2 further indicates that the RIIA maintains, through its meeting platforms, fairly close connections with various professional institutions, such as law and accounting firms, business consulting firms, political public relations agencies, and other similar organizations. Among its linkages with different components of the "field of power", the strength of its ties with professional institutions ranks second only to those with think tanks and universities. This not only surpasses its connections with the financial sector and the general industrial and commercial community, but also exceeds its links to UK and EU decision-makers. This represents another distinctive trait of the RIIA as a British foreign-policy think tank, setting it apart from the EU-level think tanks and those in continental European countries such as Germany and France. Naturally, this pattern is closely tied to the characteristics of the economic and political systems of the Anglo-American system. In contrast to continental Europe, electoral and lobbying politics in the Anglo-American system are marked by greater competitiveness. Consequently, professional institutions like law firms, business consulting firms, and political public relations agencies in the Anglo-American system hold comparative advantages over general industrial, commercial, and financial institutions and their interest groups in terms of professional information processing and adaption to situational changes. They also demonstrate heightened sensitivity to evolving circumstances and possess more sophisticated professional methodologies for assessing situations in electoral and lobbying politics. Thus, the RIIA's close ties with professional institutions are fully warranted and well-justified.

VI. RIIA's Long-Term Indirect Influence: Research Projects and Cooperation Platforms

Operating research projects is a core daily function of think tanks and the foundation for then to providing advisory service. Project topic selection and funding reflect information and resource exchange between think tanks and decision-makers or other domains of the field of power. In general, unless directly commissioned by decision-making institutions, routine research projects do not yield immediate, explicit impacts on specific decisions; even when decision-making institutions fund them, the motivation often comes from the need for supporting public interests and accumulating basic information for long-term strategic planning rather than urgent demand for specific policy design advice. Thus, such projects tend to exert long-term and indirect influence.

As policy issues become increasingly more complex and decision-making environments change rapidly, think-tank projects often span multiple disciplines and require continuous tracking of developments, while any single think tank is resource-constrained. Collaboration platforms help think tanks enhance project efficiency and quality. In Europe, such platforms have formed multi-level, multi-field communication mechanisms around joint projects, co-publications, and joint large conferences, creating a "project-publication-conference" integrated system. Mature platforms can also function as a type of advocacy group and build discourse power. Therefore, examining the RIIA's research projects and collaboration platforms can shed light on mechanisms of its long-term indirect influence.

Table 6.3 presents the research projects currently underway at the Institute that are directly related to China-EU economic relations, from which several key features can be identified. First, the RIIA's research projects on China-EU economic relations establish a platform for communication and interaction between EU decision-makers and the European business community, reflecting the think tank's role as a "central space in the field of power" that facilitates the exchange of information and resources between political decision-makers and the business and financial circles. The first project listed in Table 6.3 is funded by major corporations from Britain and continental Europe, and its research team includes officials from the European Commission. Its findings on China-EU economic relations and the EU's economic policy toward China can thus be disseminated to both the business community and EU decision-makers simultaneously. This also enables the Institute to exert its policy influence over both groups through the platform created by these research projects. Second, the Institute's research projects on China-EU economic relations aim to assess long-term trends in China-EU ties and analyze the macro and systemic implications of China's rise for China-EU relations and even the world order. Research is therefore approached from the perspective of the overall structure of the world economy and international politics. Its outputs consist of strategic, macro-level analyses rather than technical discussions of specific issues or the formulation of detailed policies. Consequently, the influence of the Institute's research projects on the EU's defensive economic policy framework toward China generally focuses on the general principles across all areas of the framework, particularly the general principles concerning its basic orientation and overall structure.

Table 6.3: Research Projects Operated by RIIA Directly Related to EU-China Relations (Early 2014–September 2018)

Project Title / Project Characteristics	**"China and Europe in 2025"**	**"China and the Future of the International Legal Order"**
Project Start and End Dates	February 2016 to July 2017	Since early 2014
Sources of Research Funding	Huawei Technologies Co., Ltd., Airbus Corporation, and GlaxoSmithKline plc	Huawei Technologies Co., Ltd., Airbus Corporation, and GlaxoSmithKline plc
Organizers	Co-hosted by RIIA, the Bruegel Institute, the Chinese University of Hong Kong, and the China International Economic Exchange Center	Unclear
Research Team Composition	A "Senior Advisory Team" composed of over 30 experts from the European Commission and the academic community of Central Europe provided guidance for the research project, while full-time researchers from the aforementioned four think tanks completed the study.	All researchers of the Asia-Pacific Regional Research Team and International Law Research Team at RIIA
The Relationship between Research Results and EU Economic Policy toward China	The project's three policy briefings and one research report, released successively from February to September 2017, assessed the tensions in China-EU bilateral economic relations and proposed measures to address EU-China trade and investment ties. These insights were incorporated into the EU's trade and investment policy document on China from September to December 2017.	The project's commentary on China's strategic considerations regarding the dispute settlement mechanisms of the international multilateral trading system and bilateral investment treaties, published in a report in March 2017, was reflected in the EU's trade and investment policy document with China from September to December 2017.

Source: Compiled by the author

Table 6.4 presents information on two interthink tank collaboration platforms in which the RIIA participates, both of which are directly related to China-EU economic relations and the EU's economic policymaking toward China. Both platforms center their operations on regularly co-hosted large-scale conferences, while also producing a range of publications, forming a composite structure of a "major conference-publication" dual model. Unlike the two research projects listed in Table 6.3, these two collaboration platforms focus on the latest trends in evolving circumstances and the most pressing issues facing European societies, so their thematic focus and research areas are not fixed. Given the growing importance of China-EU relations and the gradual strengthening of the EU's defensive economic policy framework toward China, the large conferences organized by these two platforms since 2014 have sometimes featured focused discussions on issues concerning China-EU economic relations and the EU's economic decision-making toward China. At the same time, the two platforms maintain institutionalized and close ties with EU decision-makers. Officials from top EU decision-making and regulatory bodies—including the DGs of the European Commission, the European Central Bank, and the European External Action Service—attend the annual largescale conferences hosted by the platforms. Furthermore, the policy recommendations and visions put forward in the platforms' conference declarations, annual reports, and other documents and publications have been reflected in EU decision-making documents since 2016. This demonstrates the clear influence of these two platforms over EU decision-makers. In addition, both platforms are jointly operated by prominent and leading think tanks from across Europe, with the RIIA as a key member. The Institute has taken part in all major conferences and publication launches organized by the two platforms since 2016. This indicates that Brexit has not significantly weakened the Institute's standing within the European strategic research community. It remains part of the "epistemic community" of the EU decision-making system and continues to actively participate in EU policy debates.

Table 6.4: Think Tank Collaboration Platforms Involving RIIA in EU Economic Decision-Making on China (early 2016–September 2018)

Platform Name / Platform Features	Vision Europe Think Tank Collaboration Platform	European Think Tank China Research Network (ETNC)
Platform responsible for institutional leadership and operation	Each member unit takes turns assuming leadership and operational responsibilities. In 2017, the unit responsible for leadership was the Italian 'Compagnia Di San Paolo' Foundation.	Operated by three think tanks: the French Institute of International Relations (IFRI), Spain's Royal Elcano Institute, and Germany's Mercator China Institute (MERICS)
Membership composition of the platform	The consortium comprises eight think tanks and foundations: RIIA, Germany's Bertelsmann Foundation, the EU-level Bruegel Institute, Lisbon's Calouste Gulbenkian Foundation, Warsaw's Centre for Social and Economic Research, Italy's Compagnia di San Paolo Foundation, Paris' Jacques Delors Institute, and the Finnish Innovation Fund.	Composed of 16 think tanks from the European Union level, Belgium, the Czech Republic, Denmark, Finland, Greece, Hungary, Italy, Latvia, the Netherlands, Norway, Poland, Portugal, Romania, Slovakia, Sweden, and the United Kingdom.

Platform Name / Platform Features	Vision Europe Think Tank Collaboration Platform	European Think Tank China Research Network (ETNC)
Periodic communication mechanism of the platform architecture	The periodic communication mechanism of the platform architecture	Meetings are held semi-annually, with an annual research report released in December each year.
Research field of this architectural study is related to the EU's economic policy toward China	The framework focuses on the most pressing and high-profile issues at the EU level and within European society. Its 2017 focus was on "Globalization Winners and Losers," examining the divisions caused by globalization within Europe and their impact on EU foreign policy. It also provided policy recommendations on how the EU should manage its economic relations with China.	The framework focuses on the latest developments in China-EU relations, addressing the most discussed policy issues regarding China among European society and the most challenging topics for EU decision-makers. Its 2016 annual report centered on "The New Silk Road between Europe and China," while the 2017 annual report analyzed "Country-specific patterns of China's investments in Europe."
The platform architecture's connection with EU decision-making levels	Officials from the European Commission's General Directorates and the European Central Bank, as well as members of the European Parliament, sometimes attend its annual summit.	Officials from the European External Action Service and the various operational directorates of the European Commission, as well as Members of the European Parliament, may occasionally attend its meetings.
Impact of the platform architecture on the EU's economic decision-making toward China	The views on the overall direction of EU-China economic relations and the policy intentions to be adopted, as outlined in the 2017 Annual Summit Declaration, were further reflected in the EU State of the Union Address delivered on September 13,2017, as well as in the European Commission's policy document on managing globalization.	The perspectives articulated in its annual reports for 2016 and 2017 were reflected in the Alliance Situation Report dated September 13,2017, the European Commission's policy documents on trade defense and investment review covering September to December 2017, and the joint statement issued at the China-EU Summit in July 2018.

Source: Compiled by the author

VII. RIIA's Long-Term Direct Influence: Funding Sources and the "Revolving Door" Mechanism

Receiving financial support from decision-making authorities and forging personnel ties through the "revolving door" mechanism represent the primary channels through which think tanks establish stable, long-term direct links with decision-makers. They also constitute an important means for think tanks to exert sustained and direct influence over policymaking. Think tanks generally uphold the operational independence of their research programs. Funding from decision-making authorities does not directly dictate or control the management of think tank projects, and is often disconnected to any specific research program. However, long-term, institutionalized financial support from decision-makers implicitly fosters enduring direct connections between think tanks and the circles of policymakers and political leadership. This, in turn, enables think tanks to exert direct influence over decision-makers in the processes of issue identification, agenda-setting, and policy option selection, by virtue of their expertise in analyzing complex policy issues and their capacity to assess rapidly evolving developments. Meanwhile, the "revolving door" mechanism creates extensive and intimate direct links between think-tank experts, senior executives, and decision-making circles, thereby revealing the structural characteristics of think tanks' direct influence over policy outcomes.

7.1 Analysis of Funding Sources at RIIA

Categorizing the sources of financial support received by the RIIA yields the data presented in Table 6.4. Several noteworthy features can be identified from the table. First, the business and financial sectors constitute a critical funding source for the Institute. The business and financial community holds a prominent position in its funding structure, whether for Asia-Pacific regional research, specific research projects, or the Institute's daily operations. Among the institutions supporting the Institute's general operations are six major European financial institutions, 22 financial institutions from North America, Japan, and other regions, and 34 large corporations in the real economy. Sponsors of the Institute's Asia-Pacific research include 11 major financial institutions and large real-economy enterprises. This pattern demonstrates that the Institute maintains close connections with the financial and economic domain within the "field of power". Given that large European business and financial corporations and their interest groups conduct highly active political lobbying at the EU level, and that EU decision-making bodies responsible for shaping the EU's defensive economic policy toward China—such as the European Commission's Directorate-General for Trade—are frequently affected by lobbying efforts from these firms and interest groups, it can be concluded that close ties with the business and financial community serve as an important channel for the Institute to exert influence over EU decision-makers. Second, from the perspective of funding sources, the Institute maintains strong connections with EU decision-makers, UK decision-makers, and the governmental authorities of EU member states. In other words, in terms of transmitting policy influence, both the "Brussels route" and the "national route" are equally significant to the Institute. The RIIA's network of connections with the political decision-making system of the "field of power" is highly diverse and extends far beyond EU and UK institutions. It also maintains extensive links with the foreign affairs ministries of EU member states and government agencies of countries such as Japan and Canada. An analysis of its funding sources confirms that the Institute forms an integral part of the "central space" within the EU's "field of power."

Table 6.5: Overview of Funding Sources for Research at the RIIA (2014-2017)

Method of Research Grant Funding / Category of funding institutions		Institutions providing financial support for research on the Asia-Pacific region	Institutions receiving funding support for specific research projects	Institutions providing non-targeted funding to the research of this think tank
1. EU decision-making level		The European Commission	Directorate-General for Research, the European Commission	European Parliament and European Bank for Reconstruction and Development
2. British policymakers		Department for International Development, the UK Government	Office of the UK Cabinet, Department of Public Health, the UK Government	The Bank of England, UK Government Department for International Development, the Commonwealth Secretariat, the British Army, Labor Party of the UK, London Municipal Government
3. Government decision-makers in other countries	**Government agencies in other European countries**	—	• Ministries of Foreign Affairs of Switzerland, Netherlands, Norway, and Sweden • International development Agencies of Switzerland and Sweden	• Foreign ministries of Germany, Austria, Finland, and Ireland • Norwegian Ministry of Defense • German Central Bank
3. Government decision-makers in other countries	**Government agencies in countries outside Europe**	Japanese Ministry of Foreign Affairs	○ Ministry of Finance of Japan ○ United States Agency for International Development	○ Canada's Ministry of Defense and Ministry of Foreign Affairs, Trade and Development
4. International organization		The World Bank, NATO Intelligence Aggregation Center	The World Bank, NATO, the United Nations Foundation for Support of Arms Control Cooperation, Food and Agriculture Organization of the United Nations, United Nations Refugee Agency	Food and Agriculture Organization of the United Nations, the International Monetary Fund

Category of funding institutions / Method of Research Grant Funding		Institutions providing financial support for research on the Asia-Pacific region	Institutions receiving funding support for specific research projects	Institutions providing non-targeted funding to the research of this think tank
5. The financial sector (including industries such as banking, insurance, and securities) and its interest groups	**The European Financial Sector and Its Interest Groups**	Credit Suisse Group, Banca San Paolo Unita	Credit Suisse	Barclays Bank, Blackstone (UK), the Warsaw Stock Exchange, Commonwealth Investment Group Actis, and two Italian financial industry associations, "European Financial Markets Association"
5. The financial sector (including industries such as banking, insurance, and securities) and its interest groups	**The financial sector and relevant interest groups outside Europe**	American International Group (AIG)	Merrill Lynch-American Bank, Quantum Global Fund, Citibank	Morgan Stanley Group, JPMorgan Chase Group, Japan's Daiwa Capital Markets Europe Ltd., Japan Development Bank, Angola Investment Bank, American International Group, and 16 other financial institutions
6. General business community (various sectors of the real economy) and their interest groups	**The European general business community**	Eni Chemicals S.p.A., Airbus AG, GlaxoSmithKline plc	The European Federation of Pharmaceutical Industries (EFPIA), German Technical Cooperation Agency (GIZ)	A total of 12 European manufacturing companies were involved, spanning industries such as energy, automotive, aircraft manufacturing, logistics, and publishing, along with 7 professional institutions including business consulting firms, law firms, and accounting firms.
	The general business community outside Europe	Yamato Seiko Group, Olayan Group, Chevron Energy Company, ExxonMobil, and Huawei Technologies	ExxonMobil Corporation of the United States	A total of 22 large manufacturing companies headquartered outside Europe were involved, spanning industries such as petrochemicals, mining, automotive, aircraft manufacturing, defense, logistics, and publishing. Additionally, there were 6 consulting firms, law firms, and accounting firms.
7. Non-governmental organizations and other institutions	**UK non-governmental organizations and other institutions**	Aga Khan Foundation, UK	British Red Cross, the British Foundation, and three other institutions	Four UK foundations
	Other European non-governmental organizations and other institutions	—	One non-governmental organization from Norway, and two foundations from Germany	Three institutions: the British Academy, the German Foundation

Category of funding institutions \ Method of Research Grant Funding		Institutions providing financial support for research on the Asia-Pacific region	Institutions receiving funding support for specific research projects	Institutions providing non-targeted funding to the research of this think tank
7. Non-governmental organizations and other institutions	Non-governmental organizations and other institutions outside Europe	• Three foundations in Japan • Korea International Exchange Foundation • The Lutheran World Relief Organization	There are four foundations in the United States and two foundations in Japan.	Two foundations in Japan
8. Think tanks and other research institutions		South Korea National Institute of Security Strategy	One think tank each from Sweden, Switzerland, and Norway	Two UK think tanks and one Italian think tank

Source: This table was compiled by the author based on information provided in the annual reports of the RIIA from 2014 to 2018.

The organizational structure of the RIIA consists of seven tiers: 1) Honorary leadership: the Institute's Patron, who is the British monarch; 2) The President(s) responsible for the Institute's day-to-day administration. As of September 2018, the Institute had three Presidents: Elizabeth Lydia Manningham-Buller, a senior intelligence expert who long headed Britain's core intelligence agency MI5; John Major, a veteran Conservative leader and former British Prime Minister; and Patricia Scotland, a Labor lawyer and former Attorney General for England and Wales, and Queen's Counsel; 3) The Council, elected by the Institute's members, which is primarily responsible for deliberating and setting the Institute's strategic direction for future development and overseeing its daily operations; 4) The Board of Directors, which provides professional guidance for the Institute's academic research, outreach and publications, external relations, and other operational activities; 5) The Panel of Senior Advisers; 6) Research specialist teams in specific fields; 7) The administrative team. Among these, the first five tiers—the Patron, Presidents, Council, Board of Directors, and Panel of Senior Advisers—constitute the Institute's leadership, namely its senior executive team. In addition, the Institute has bodies including a Finance Committee.

The author has classified and compiled the career backgrounds of each member of the Institute's research team and senior executive team focusing on China and Asia-Pacific issues as of September 2018, as detailed in Table 6.9. According to the statistics, the Institute's research team on China and Asia-Pacific issues comprises 23 experts, and its team of senior executives and administrative staff as a whole has 65 members—1.5 times the number of researchers in SWP's Asia team and 1.7 times the size of SWP's executive and administrative team, respectively. The types of institutions where each member previously served or currently holds concurrent positions, along with their respective proportions, are shown in the table below. Since some members worked in multiple sectors and institutions before joining the Institute, the same individual may be counted under several different institutional categories. As a result, the percentages in the two "Percentage of Total" columns cannot be summed vertically.

Table 6.6: Analysis of the Revolving-Door Structure of RIIA Personnel (as of the End of September 2018)

Type of Work Experience	Department and Member Type	Asia-Pacific Research Expert Team		Think Tank Senior Management Team	
		Number of People	**Proportion of the Total Expert Team**	**Number of People**	**Percentage of Total Executive Team Members**
1. EU decision-making and administrative departments	GDs of the European Commission	—	—	1	3.6%
	Other EU institutions and departments (European Parliament, Council of the European Union, European Central Bank, etc.)	—	—	1	3.6%
	Total number of individuals with experience in EU decision-making and administrative departments	—	—	*2*	*7.1%*
2. British official decision-making body	The Foreign Affairs System of the United Kingdom	5	21.7%	2	7.1%
	UK Ministry of Defense, military forces, and national intelligence systems	—	—	1	3.6%
	The British Prime Minister's Decision-Making Advisory Team and Cabinet Office	1	4.3%	1	3.6%
	The official economic decision-making bodies in the UK (including the Ministry of Finance, Department of Trade and Industry, and the Bank of England)	—	—	2	7.1%
	Other UK government departments (other cabinet departments, Parliament, local councils and governments, etc.)	1	4.3%	2	7.1%
	Total number of individuals with experience in official decision-making departments in the UK	*7*	*30.4%*	*8*	*28.6%*

Type of Work Experience \ Department and Member Type		Asia-Pacific Research Expert Team		Think Tank Senior Management Team	
		Number of People	Proportion of the Total Expert Team	Number of People	Percentage of Total Executive Team Members
3. International organization		***2***	***8.7%***	***2***	***7.1%***
4. The financial sector (including banking, securities, insurance, trust industries) and its interest groups	The European financial sector	1	4.3%	5	17.6%
	The financial sector outside Europe	1	4.3%	1	3.7%
	Total number of individuals with professional experience in the financial sector	***2***	***8.7%***	***6***	***21.4%***
5. General business community (various sectors of the real economy) and their interest groups	The European general business community	1	4.3%	6	21.4%
	The general business community outside Europe			1	3.6%
	Total number of individuals with professional experience in general business sectors	***1***	***4.3%***	***7***	***25%***
6. Professional institutions (law and accounting firms, business consulting companies, political public relations and lobbying firms)	European professional institutions	1	4.3%	9	32.1%
	Professional institutions outside Europe	1	4.3%	1	3.6%
	Total number of individuals with professional experience at specialized institutions	***2***	***8.7%***	***10***	***35.7%***
7. The media industry		***5***	***21.7%***	***4***	***14.3%***
8. The think tank community	Other European think tanks	6	26.1%	5	17.9%
	Think tanks outside Europe	2	8.7%	2	7.1%
	Total experience at other think tanks	***8***	***34.8%***	***7***	***25%***
9. Universities	European University	9	39.1%	4	14.2%
	Universities outside Europe	5	21.7%	1	3.6%
	Total number of individuals with academic appointments at universities	***14***	***60.9%***	***5***	***17.9%***

Note:

"Professional experience" refers to a stable and institutionalized history of engaging in specific work activities, either currently or previously. Specifically, it encompasses full-time employment in a particular role or part-time position as member of formal permanent institutions within organizations, such as serving as an independent director on corporate boards or holding formal academic positions at universities. For individuals listed in the table who have held positions across multiple subcategories within major categories, the longest-serving institution within that subcategory is counted so as to avoid duplicate entries. If multiple institutions have the same tenure duration, the institution with the most recent employment record is selected. This ensures no overlap in data aggregation within each major category. However, given that many experts and executives have extensive professional experience across multiple institutions, overlapping entries between categories are unavoidable, making vertical consolidation between categories impossible. At the end of September 2018 , the RIIA in Britain had 23 members in its Asia Studies expert team, 239 members in other field expert teams, and 28 members in executive leadership teams.

Source: The author.

Data in Table 6.6 reveals several notable characteristics of the "revolving door" mechanism at the RIIA, which distinguish it from the Bruegel think tank and SWP as discussed earlier: First, the Institute's Asia-Pacific research team maintains close ties with the media. As Table 6.6 shows, the share of experts on the Asia-Pacific team with prior media experience ranks second only to those with backgrounds from universities, think tanks, and official UK policymaking bodies, further reflecting the Institute's strong links with the media.

Second, in the statistical breakdown of senior executive backgrounds at the RIIA, the proportion of individuals from the financial sector, general business and finance circles, and professional institutions is remarkably high. Specifically, the share of senior executives from professional bodies such as law and accounting firms, business consulting companies, and political public relations firms is notably higher than that from think tanks and universities. By contrast, only two experts on the Asia-Pacific team come from professional institutions and the financial sector respectively, and just one from general industry and commerce. This indicates that the think tank maintains close connections and exerts significant mutual influence with the business, industrial and financial communities, as well as professional intermediaries operating across different segments of the "field of power" in its overall operation and strategic development. Yet, in order to preserve research professionalism in the Asia-Pacific field, the RIIA retains traditional ties with think tanks, universities, and UK policymaking authorities. In contrast, SWP has very few experts and senior staff with backgrounds in industry, commerce and finance.

Third, the Institute's personnel connections with UK policymaking bodies are significantly closer than those with EU decision-making institutions. Both its Asia-Pacific research team and senior management maintain relatively strong links with the UK policy establishment. The Asia-Pacific research team draws the largest number of experts from the UK diplomatic and foreign affairs system, while the share of senior executives from the

UK diplomatic and foreign affairs system equals that from economic policymaking bodies. However, none of the RIIA's Asia-Pacific research experts have served in EU decision-making bodies, and only two of its senior executives have such experience, representing a very low proportion. This suggests that, compared with SWP, the RIIA keeps a greater distance from and stronger independence toward EU institutions.

In summary, data in Table 6.5 indicates that, from the perspective of the "central space of the field of power", the RIIA maintains close revolving-door personnel ties with all four sectors of the field of power. Relatively speaking, however, its Asia-Pacific research team has the closest links with universities and think tanks, followed by the UK policy establishment, then the media, and finally industry, commerce and finance. Its senior executive team maintains the closest connections with professional institutions, followed by the UK political and policymaking establishment, with roughly equivalent ties to the financial sector, general industry and commerce, and think tanks, but the weakest links to EU decision-making bodies and international organizations. The divergence between the two teams reflects differing focuses and external influences between the think tank's professional researchers and its management. As a whole, however, the Institute's external personnel connections showcase its pivotal role as a "central space of the field of power" bridging the four sectors.

VIII. Summary of Chapter 6

Simon James argues that, compared with its U.S. counterpart, the UK think-tank system is much smaller in scale and exerts far weaker influence over government decision-making. He attributes this gap to three differences between the British and American political systems and political cultures. First, the U.S. political decision-making system tends to "outsource" highly professional and technical decision-making processes to social organizations. Second, U.S. politics features stronger partisan competition, with a prominent spoils system after elections and rapid turnover in the composition of the decision-making circles, resulting in a more diverse "policy community". By contrast, Britain maintains a stable, politically neutral Civil Service that performs substantial internal decision-making functions. Third, the U.S. decision-making system is far more open than Britain's. Fourth, the culture of charitable donations from private enterprises is considerably more developed in the United States than in Britain, with a much larger scale of giving.① Scholarly literature on British think tanks generally regards the early 1980s, following the arrival of the Thatcher government, as a critical period of rapid growth for the UK think-tank system.②

Nevertheless, the UK think-tank system remains far more developed than those of the EU and continental European countries. According to the 2017 Global Go To Think Tank Index Report released by the University of Pennsylvania, Britain was home to 444 think tanks, compared with 225 in Germany and 197 in France. The total number of British think tanks was roughly 50 percent higher than that of Germany and 2.25 times that of France. Leading British foreign-policy think tanks are also larger in scale than their German counterparts. At the end of September 2018, the RIIA had a research team of 262 experts, including a 23-member research division on Asia-Pacific studies, whereas SWP had only 15 experts specialized in Asia-Pacific studies out of a 118-member workforce of researchers. Across Europe until nowadays, British think tanks remain the largest in both number and scale.

Comparing the RIIA with Bruegel and SWP as respectively discussed in Chapters 4 and 5 reveals several distinctive features in the operational and influence mechanisms of this think tank:

First, from the perspective of the "central space of the field of power", the RIIA maintains much closer direct ties with British business and financial circles, professional institutions, and the media than do Bruegel and SWP. A comparison of Tables 4.4, 5.5 and 6.5 shows that, while the expert team of the RIIA has weaker revolvingdoor links with the financial sector and general business circles than Bruegel, the number and proportion of its senior executives drawn from major British corporations and financial institutions are remarkably high. At the same time, the Institute's connections with professional bodies such as law and accounting firms, business consultancies, and political public relations agencies

① Simon James, "The Idea Brokers: The Impact of Think Tanks on British Government", Public Administration, Vol. 71, Winter 1993, pp. 491506.

② John Turnpenny et al., Mapping Actors involved in Climate Change Policy Networks in the UK, January 2005, Tyndall Centre for Climate Change Research, Working Paper No. 66; Hugh Pemberton, Policy Learning and British Governance in the 1960s, Hampshire: Palgrave Macmillan, 2004, p. 283; Peter A. Hall, "Policy Paradigms, Social Learning, and the State: the Case of Economic Policy Making in Britain", Comparative Politics, April 1993, Vol. 25, pp. 275296.

are far closer than those of Bruegel and SWP. These professional institutions, which serve business and financial interests and operate between the corporatefinancial world and political decision-making, can be regarded as extensions of the business and financial circles in public life. This shows that, among the four domains of the "field of power"—politics, finance, academia and media—the RIIA is most closely connected to the financial and economic spheres, even though its core research focus is neither financial issues nor exclusively external economic policy, but foreign policy in a general sense. This feature reflects the considerable influence of the British business and financial circles over national political decision-making, a trait shared to some extent with the American political system. In this sense, the RIIA's influence over any policy area in Britain and the EU, including their respective China policies, largely reflects the interests of the British financial and economic circles, especially the financial sector.

Second, the "two-level, four-sided" system in which contemporary European think tanks operate is highly complex and dynamic. The European "field of power" thus effectively operates at both the EU level and the national level of member states. While the RIIA maintains close relations with the financial and media spheres within Britain's national field of power, its connections across different domains at the EU level and in other member states follow a different logic. Table 6.5, which maps personnel links formed through the "revolving-door" mechanism , shows almost no substantial connection between the RIIA and EU-level decision-making bodies, reflecting the relative detachment of British foreign-policy think tanks from the EU's core decision-making circles. This aligns with the strong presence of Eurosceptic social attitudes and political forces in Britain. However, Tables 6.2, 6.3 and 6.4 indicate that the RIIA remains actively engaged in the field of power at the EU level and in other member states through high-level forums, thematic seminars, research projects, research funding, and participation in collaborative think-tank platforms. In particular, Tables 6.2 and 6.4 show that the Institute has established direct links with EU decision-making bodies through high-level forums, thematic seminars, and research funding, enabling it to exert direct influence over the EU's core decision-making layers. The RIIA therefore remains an active member of the EU-level "policy community". These tables also reveal various connections between the RIIA and political and financial circles in EU member states, with Table 6.4 especially highlighting close ties with foreign-policy departments across the EU. Based on available information, it remains difficult to find out which of the four domains of the EU-level and member-state "fields of power" the RIIA engages more closely or more distantly, or to establish clear hierarchical relationships. Overall, however, this Institute functions as a "central space" within the EU-level field of power, maintaining close exchanges of information and resources across all domains.

Third, from the perspective of the multiple-streams decision-making model, Tables 6.1 and 6.2 and Figure 6.3 reveal that the RIIA forms an important part of the "policy stream" within the multiple flows shaping EU policy toward China. Its operational rhythm of influence largely aligns with the "problem stream"—namely, shifts in EU-China economic relations—and is clearly correlated with the pace and progress of EU decision-making. Out of the six domains of the EU's defensive economic policy toward China, the RIIA's assessments and advice on the fundamental positioning, overall framework, investment policy, and industrial policy demonstrate a strong forward-looking vision. Following the sharp deterioration of the situation and the opening of a "policy window" between March and May 2015, the Institute provided timely supplementary and extended advice to support the EU's substantial revision of its original framework. As early as 2008-2009, the RIIA's series of research reports, along with numerous sporadic commentaries and newsletters, had already offered predictive analyses of the inherent structural contradictions and tensions in EU-China economic relations, as well as the potential impact of China's economic rise on EU-China economic ties. From the perspective of evolving decision-making streams, the RIIA is thus able to anticipate macro and long-term strategic threats, foresee sharp fluctuations in the "problem stream", and identify emerging "policy windows".

Fourth, the RIIA distinguishes itself from other foreign-policy think tanks by its ability not only to provide strategic advice mapping long-term trends and assessing systemic change for EU decision-making, but also to conduct highly specialized technical research, particularly in the economic domain. Table 6.1 shows that its recommendations on the EU's defensive economic policy toward China include both strategic analyses of the long-term trajectory, institutional design, overall policy framework, and detailed, sector-specific analyses and policy proposals focused on the highly technical areas of investment and industry. The think tank therefore effectively integrates strategic research on systemic issues with specialized research on specific economic, diplomatic and security domains.

As Britain's most academically rigorous and representative foreign-policy think tank, the RIIA's operational mechanisms and distinctive features of influence over the EU's defensive economic decision-making toward China to a certain extent reveal and outline the broader mechanisms and structural characteristics of the UK think-tank system in providing policy advice to the EU.

Conclusion

Scholarly research on American think tanks now dominates academic attention. Scholars have mapped out a coherent theoretical landscape and produced nuanced, exhaustive scholarly explications of the institutional architecture and operational dynamics of U.S. think tanks. While Europe and the United States share broadly aligned political cultures and historical traditions, the two-tier, four-dimensional composite system of European think tanks stands in stark contrast to the think-tank ecosystem of the United States as a unitary nation-state. Further, the distinct systems formed by think tanks operating at the EU level, in the United Kingdom, and in the Federal Republic of Germany each exhibit unique structural and operational characteristics. Conversely, however, all European think tanks operate within the broader ecosystem of the EU's political decision-making system and thus share fundamental commonalities, enabling the derivation of generalizable models of European think-tank influence through granular case study and analysis of the core mechanisms and operational pathways through which they shape EU policy outcomes. A systematic comparative analysis of the commonalities and divergences between European and U.S. think tanks, as well as across distinct typologies of European think tanks themselves, lays bare the defining intrinsic features and evolutionary dynamics of European think-tank ecosystems.

I. Sources of the Gap Between European and U.S. Think-Tank Systems

While think tanks leverage their research and analysis of policy issues to deliver advisory services to decision-makers and thereby exert influence over policy outcomes, the policymaking process itself is not an absolutely rational, value-neutral scientific exercise, but rather a deeply political process of intense contestation between competing ideologies and interest groups, the trajectory and tempo of which are fundamentally shaped by the structure of the overarching macro-political institutional framework. Put differently, the think-tank ecosystem of every region and nation-state is both constrained and fundamentally structured by the architecture of the macro-political institutional environment within which it is embedded. Only through a systematic analysis of macro-political institutional structures, and a granular unpacking of the constraining effects these structures exert on think-tank development, can scholars effectively explicate the underlying causal mechanisms that shape the structural features and evolutionary trajectories of distinct think-tank systems.

Virtually all of the canonical literature in think tank studies acknowledges that the United States currently hosts the world's largest, most extensive, and most influential think-tank ecosystem, one marked by unrivaled scholarly rigor, policy advisory capacity, and tangible influence over policy outcomes. Across each of these dimensions, however, European think-tank systems exhibit a pronounced gap relative to their U.S. counterparts. The origins of this disparity can be directly traced to the structural features of the political decision-making systems of both the EU and its member states that diverge fundamentally from those of the United States. While the political institutions and political cultures of the EU and Western European nations are broadly aligned with those of the United States, two seemingly modest yet substantively consequential structural differences account for the systematically lower level of development across the entire European think-tank ecosystem—encompassing both EU-level institutions and those based in major member states including the United Kingdom and Germany—along every measurable dimension, including total number, operational scale, scholarly quality, and tangible policy influence.

First, the intensity of partisan competition and electoral politics in the United States vastly outstrips that of the EU and its member states, a structural dynamic that generates a far stronger demand among American political decision-makers for external policy expertise of the kind provided by think tanks than that exhibited by their counterparts in the EU and its member states. The United States operates a rigorous system of checks and balances between Congress and the Presidency, with each branch filled through entirely separate and independent elections; its legislative and presidential electoral contests further operate under a first-past-the-post (FPTP) system, under which the candidate who secures the highest number of votes in a given single-member electoral district wins the seat outright, while all other competing candidates in that district are defeated regardless of their overall vote share, which is a structural design that effectively institutionalizes a winner-takes-all electoral model. Compounding this dynamic, the United States' two major political parties—the Democratic Party and the Republican Party—are perennially evenly matched in national electoral competition, meaning that party members seeking election to Congress or the Presidency must navigate extraordinarily intense, often cutthroat electoral contests, and even after securing electoral victory and taking office, they must expend substantial time and resources carefully navigating the unrelenting checks, balances, and partisan competition from opposing political forces. As a direct result, the allocation of executive-branch cabinet positions by a newly elected American president bears the strong imprint of the spoils system. This creates a pattern in which the turnover of senior staff, policy aides, and auxiliary support personnel within the executive branch's power structure synchronizes directly with the rhythm of the national electoral cycle—yielding exceptionally rapid, frequent, and high-magnitude personnel changes, together with extreme institutional fluidity. Under these structural conditions, senior decision-makers at the highest levels of the American legislative and executive branches cannot rely on a permanent, stable, in-house team of full-time professional policy advisors for exclusive decision-making advice, and are therefore compelled to seek high-quality policy advisory services from non-governmental organizations outside the formal state apparatus—a demand that emerges as early as the initial stages of a candidate's political career, when they first assemble their core campaign team for electoral office. It is for this reason that Abelson has observed that the influence of American think tanks over presidential and cabinet-level policymaking frequently originates in the sustained advisory services and policy support they provide to a presidential candidate during their electoral campaigns, long before that candidate secures victory and accedes to the Oval Office.[①]

In stark contrast, the EU and its major member states possess a long-standing, deeply entrenched tradition of parliamentary governance, wherein, whether at the level of the United Kingdom, the Federal Republic of Germany, or the EU itself, the political party or coalition of parties that secures a majority of seats in parliamentary elections gains control

① Donald E. Abelson, *A Capital Idea: Think Tanks and US Foreign Policy*, Montreal: McGill-Queen's University Press, 2006, pp. 18-22.

over the executive branch and exercises executive authority through the formal government formation process. Furthermore, parliamentary elections in continental European countries are universally conducted under a proportional representation system, under which political parties are allocated legislative seats in the national parliament in direct proportion to the share of the popular votes they receive in national elections. Barring periods of extreme and acute social and political upheaval, major established political parties are able to consistently and stably occupy the dominant position within the parliamentary system, while smaller political parties, even if they remain on the ideological and political margins, are still able to retain a small but consistent number of parliamentary seats over the long term. For these reasons, electoral competition across all sectors of European society is significantly less intense and polarized than in the United States, with a correspondingly diminished role for spoils system-style patronage in the allocation of government positions, thus enabling the development of a highly professional, permanent civil service that operates independently of partisan political contestation and is vastly more stable and institutionally robust than its counterpart in the United States. This permanent, career civil service not only ensures the consistent, stable day-to-day functioning of the policymaking and administrative process, but also leverages its decades of accumulated institutional knowledge, on-the-ground policy experience, and specialized technical expertise to deliver high-quality, in-house policy advice services directly to senior decision-makers, including systematic and comprehensive information gathering, rigorous qualitative and quantitative data analysis, and targeted, actionable policy recommendations. As a direct and inevitable consequence, the demand among senior decision-makers in the EU, the United Kingdom, and Germany for external policy expertise from think tanks is substantially weaker and less urgent than that of their counterparts at the highest levels of the U.S. government.

Second, the United States possesses an extraordinarily well-developed system of corporate and private philanthropic giving, marked by exceptionally large donation volumes and high levels of sustained philanthropic activity; as a result, the U.S. think-tank ecosystem was built and has expanded primarily through the financial support of private foundations, granting it abundant, highly flexible funding streams. In sharp contrast, systems of private philanthropic giving at both the EU and member state level lag far behind those of the United States, with a large proportion of European think tanks established through the impetus of government or partisan actors, and with total available funding volumes that are dwarfed by those of their US counterparts. The modern U.S. system of private philanthropy gradually took shape following the U.S. tax code reforms of the early 20th century, and the substantial endowments provided by private philanthropic donations enabled the establishment of the earliest cohort of U.S. think tanks during the first two decades of the 20th century in what Abelson terms the "first generation of U.S. think tanks" and McGann identifies as the first developmental phase of the U.S. think-tank ecosystem.[①] This stark disparity has been noted with explicit envy in scholarly work on domestic think tanks by both British and German academics (James, 1993; Thunert, 2012).[②] While the United Kingdom's legal framework governing philanthropic giving is broadly similar to that of the United States, the total scale of charitable donations in Britain remains vastly smaller than in the United States. The rapid expansion of UK think tanks since the early 1980s has been driven in large part by partisan political support, while German think tanks maintain deeply intertwined, multifaceted relationships with the federal government and major parties represented in the Bundestag; for EU-level "Brussels-based think tanks," institutional and financial support from the EU is indispensable, with EU funding accounting for more than one-third of their total annual revenue.[③] Of course, the highly developed U.S. private philanthropic system also grants substantial capacity for political advocacy and the advancement of policy priorities to private corporations and business interest groups, which explains why U.S. think tanks, on the whole, engage in political lobbying activities to a far greater extent than their European counterparts, particularly German think tanks (Jochem, 2013).[④]

---

① Donald E. Abelson, *A Capital Idea: Think Tanks and US Foreign Policy*, Montreal: McGill-Queen's University Press, 2006, pp. 19-22; James G. McGann, *Think Tanks and Policy Advice in the United States: Academics, Advisors, and Advocates*, New York: Routledge, 2007, pp. 8-9.

② Simon James, "The Idea Brokers: The Impact of Think Tanks on British Government", *Public Administration*, Vol. 71, No. 3, Winter 1993, pp. 491-506; Martin Thunert, "Expert Policy Advice in Germany", in Stephen Brooks at al eds., *Policy Expertise in Contemporary Democracies*, Surrey: Ashgate Publishing Limited, 2012, P. 253.

③ During field interviews conducted by the author in Brussels in the second half of 2013, a number of researchers from the European Policy Centre (EPC) and the European Institute for Asian Studies (EIAS) raised this very point with the author.

④ Friedrich Ebert Stiftung, *Think Tanks in Policy Making: Do They Matter?* Briefing Paper Special Issue, September 2011, Shanghai Office; Sven Jochem, "Think Tanks: Bridging Beltway and Ivory Tower", in Sonja

II. The Precise Positioning of European Think Tanks in the EU's Political Decision-Making System

The policy influence of think tanks and its underlying mechanisms represent the most widely studied, yet most fiercely contested, domain within the broader field of think-tank studies, with nearly all scholars in the field acknowledging that the policy impact of think tanks is exceptionally difficult to verify empirically or measure with granular precision. As Abelson categorically states: "Scholars of think tanks must recognize that they will never complete their research if they seek to draw definitive conclusions about the precise magnitude of think-tank influence. The simple reality is that the impact of think tanks cannot be measured with precision, leaving scholars with no alternative but to conduct case-by-case assessments of individual think tanks and the policy issues they address" (Abelson, 2006).① Diane Stone similarly puts it bluntly: "One of the most intractable questions surrounding think tanks is whether they actually exert any meaningful policy influence at all," noting that "attempting to market policy analysis to decision-makers does not equate to delivering a direct, transformative impact on the thinking of legislative or executive bodies." She thus argues that the role think tanks play within the broader macro-policy system is analogous to that of cogs in a complex machine—one that cannot be neatly defined or quantified (Stone, 2007).② Numerous other scholars have advanced parallel arguments, which explains why the annual *Global Go To Think Tank Index Report*, produced under the direction of James McGann at the University of Pennsylvania, focuses on assessing and ranking think tanks based on their public profile, scholarly rigor, and quality of advisory service, rather than on the precise quantification of their policy impact. Published annually without interruption from 2007 to 2021, the report had released 9 consecutive editions by the time of this study, yet it has still failed to develop a systematic, universally accepted set of quantitative metrics for evaluating think tanks' policy influence, and the index itself has faced substantial

Blum and Klaus Schubert eds., *Policy Analysis in Germany*, Bristol: Policy Press, 2013, pp. 231-244.

① Donald E. Abelson, *A Capital Idea: Think Tanks and US Foreign Policy*, Montreal: McGill-Queen's University Press, 2006, P. 230.

② Diane Stone, "Public Policy Analysis and Think Tanks", in Frank Fischer, Gerald J. Miller and Mara S. Sidney (Eds.), *Handbook of Public Policy Analysis: Theory, Politics and Methods*, Boca Raton of Florida: CRC Press of Taylor & Francis Group, 2007, P. 145.

criticism and contestation from the global think-tank research community. To date, no authoritative ranking system or quantitative measurement framework for assessing the policy influence of think tanks has gained widespread, cross-sectoral acceptance among scholars, practitioners, and policymakers globally.

Even as the policy impact of think tanks remains stubbornly resistant to systematic measurement, the core rationale for the existence and sustained development of think tanks lies precisely in their ability to shape policy outcomes, rendering the study of think tanks' policy influence a central, extensively elaborated focus of nearly every scholarly article and monograph published in the field of think tank studies. In the context of this persistent inability to accurately quantify the magnitude of think tanks' policy influence, a highly valid and rigorous methodological approach to the study of such influence remains the systematic observation and explication of the mechanisms through which think tanks shape policy outcomes: this approach entails analyzing the specific nodes and branches of the policymaking structure that are amenable to think-tank influence, identifying the distinct phases of the policy process in which decision-makers actively receive and incorporate inputs from think tanks, cataloging the full range of modalities and pathways through which think tanks exert their influence, synthesizing these discrete data points into a comprehensive roadmap of how think-tank influence is transmitted within a given political and administrative institutional structure, and mapping the critical nodes and focal points through which that influence circulates and gains traction within the system. Crucially, however, the distribution of these pathways of influence is fundamentally constrained by the overarching structure of the EU's macro-political decision-making system and the precise positioning of think tanks within that system; for this reason, a holistic macro-level analysis of the institutional structure of the political system within which think tanks operate, and a clear mapping of the relative positions and interactive dynamics between all relevant actors in that system—including think tanks themselves—constitutes the necessary logical starting point for any rigorous analysis of the mechanisms behind think tanks' policy influence.

The inherent "two-tier, four-dimensional" structure of the European think-tank ecosystem is already inherently more complex than that of the United States, and this complexity is further amplified by the fact that the EU's policymaking system and its signature multi-level governance framework are vastly more elaborate and multi-faceted than the political decision-making and social governance systems of the United States as a modern nation-state. As a result, the mechanisms through which European think tanks exert influence over EU policy outcomes exhibit substantially greater diversity and dynamism than those of their U.S. counterparts, rendering the theoretical explication and empirical analysis of these European mechanisms significantly more challenging both methodologically and analytically.

Figures 2.4, 2.5, and 6.2 of this book provide a detailed explication of the precise positioning of European think tanks within the EU's political decision-making system, as well as the relative positions and interactive dynamics between the various actors operating within this system. As illustrated in Figure 2.4, European think tanks consistently function as intermediaries for the transmission of interest claims and policy preferences between grassroots European civil society and the EU's core decision-making institutions, operating within both the EU's policymaking framework and its broader European interest representation system. For this reason, scholarly literature on the EU's political decision-making system generally positions European think tanks as actors situated between pressure groups, interest groups, advocacy organizations, and mainstream civil society organizations, with a substantial body of literature conceptualizing them as a distinct, specialized category of interest groups or pressure groups (Coxall, 2001; Greenwood, 2011; Hix, 2012).a The operational pathways through which European think tanks influence EU foreign policy decision-making within the broader EU political system—specifically, via the "Brussels route" and the "member state route"—are described in detail in Figures 2.5 and 6.2. These illustrations reveal that while the overall pathways of influence utilized by European think tanks to shape EU policy are broadly similar to those employed by conventional interest groups and pressure groups, they nevertheless contain notable, nuanced differences: most notably, European think tanks engage with the EU-level political lobbying system to a significantly lesser degree than traditional interest groups, and the core modalities through which they exert their influence differ substantially from those of mainstream interest and pressure groups. European interest and pressure groups primarily seek to advance their goals

① Bill Coxall, *Pressure Groups in British Politics*, London: Pearson Education Limited, 2001, pp. 74-76; Justin Greenwood, *Interest Representation in the European Union*, Hampshire: Palgrave Macmillan, 2011, P. 10; Simon Hix and Bjorn Hoyland, *The Political System of the European Union*, New York: Palgrave Macmillan, 2011, P. 165

through direct meetings with officials of the EU's decision-making institutions, particularly the specialized DGs of the European Commissiona, using these direct engagements to articulate their policy demands and conduct political lobbying. While they occasionally host workshops and seminars or publish research outputs, their utilization of these modalities is quite infrequent. In stark contrast, European think tanks rely primarily on the 12 distinct mechanisms of policy influence outlined in Figure 2.2, with the four core modalities being utilized with the highest frequency: hosting workshops, conferences, and seminars; publishing research outputs and policy briefs; managing and executing collaborative research projects; and participating in formal and informal trans-European think tank collaboration networks. Notably, the archival records of the three think tanks examined in this study contain the most extensive documentation of their activities related to these four core mechanisms of influence.

III. Three Defining Features of the Mechanisms Through Which European Think Tanks Shape the EU's Defensive Economic Policy toward China

A systematic comparative analysis of the structural divergences between the political institutions of the United States and Europe enables a comprehensive understanding of the overall landscape and defining characteristics of the European think-tank ecosystem. Building on this foundation, this study applies the analytical framework outlined in the preceding chapters—which integrates the theoretical perspective of the "central space of the field of power" with the Multiple Streams Framework (MSF)—to analyze the mechanisms through which three leading European think tanks (Bruegel, SWP, and the RIIA) exerted influence over the EU's policymaking process for defensive economic policy toward China. This analysis reveals three core defining features of these influence mechanisms, which are

① According to the author's statistical analysis of publicly available officially documented records, Cecilia Malmström, the European Commissioner for Trade of the European Commission, held a total of 50 direct meetings with representatives from all sectors of society between early January and the end of November 2015; of these meetings, 15 were convened with representatives of various interest groups and pressure groups, while a mere 6 were held with representatives from think tanks and universities, a breakdown that clearly lays bare the heavy reliance of interest groups and pressure groups on direct meetings as a core mechanism to exert their policy influence.

outlined below.

First, from the perspective of the "central space of the field of power," European think tanks operate within a "two-tier field of power" constituted jointly by the EU and its member states, maintaining close linkages with the four core domains of this field of power. Critically, however, the three think tanks examined in this study all occupy distinct, unique positions within this "two-tier field of power," and differ substantially in the strategic priorities they place on information exchange and resource reciprocity with each of the four domains of the field.

In terms of their respective positioning within the "two-tier field of power," Bruegel—as a preeminent Brussels-based think tank specializing in EU affairs and European regional studies—maintains only minimal linkages with the national-level fields of power of EU member states. Instead, it sustains direct, robust connections with the political and financial-economic domains of the EU-level field of power, particularly with the European Commission (the EU's core executive body) and EU-level business and industry interest groups, while maintaining comparatively more distant relationships with the media and academic domains of the field. By contrast, both SWP and the RIIA maintain far closer, more institutionalized linkages with their respective national fields of power than with the EU-level field of power, with the RIIA maintaining a notably more distant relationship with the core EU decision-making institutions than SWP. As a quintessential continental European think tank, SWP's level of engagement with the four domains of the German national field of power ranks in the following order: the academic domain, the political domain, the financial-economic domain, and the media domain. Simultaneously, however, it maintains explicit, direct linkages with the EU-level field of power through the well-documented "revolving door" mechanism between national and EU-level political and advisory institutions. The RIIA, by contrast, is a quintessential UK-based foreign policy think tank that maintains exceptionally close, direct institutional linkages with the financial-economic domain of the British national field of power, particularly with the financial sector, the business and industrial community, and the specialized professional services firms closely tied to the financial and business sectors, including law and accounting firms, management consultancies, political lobbying firms, and public relations agencies. Its connections to the EU-level field of power, by contrast, are maintained almost exclusively through the receipt of research funding and participation in trans-European think tank collaboration networks, rendering these linkages significantly more tenuous and distant than those of SWP.

In terms of the strategic modalities each think tank prioritizes for engagement with the various domains of the field of power, all three institutions share a core reliance on timely, targeted, concise policy-oriented outputs designed to deliver actionable recommendations to decision-makers, including op-eds, policy updates, policy briefs, situational analysis reports, research findings, and meeting memoranda. Simultaneously, however, Bruegel and the RIIA both host a dense calendar of high-level convenings, including high-level policy forums, thematic workshops and seminars, and keynote lecture series, leveraging these events to exert influence over decision-makers and advance their policy recommendations. By contrast, the archival record contains minimal documentation of similar convening activities by SWP, a pattern that suggests the institute places far less strategic emphasis on this modality of influence. In addition, all the three think tanks participate in a range of cross-European inter-think tank research collaboration platforms operated jointly by multiple institutions across the continent. These platforms almost universally incorporate multi-layered, cross-sectoral collaboration and coordination mechanisms, including joint convenings, collaborative research project implementation, and co-publication of research outputs, forming a deeply integrated, multi-faceted collaborative ecosystem. This pattern demonstrates that intra-sectoral coordination and cooperation within the European think tank community has reached an exceptionally high level of institutionalization and sophistication.

Second, from the perspective of the Multiple Streams Framework, a systematic comparison of the policy recommendations issued by the three think tanks and the corresponding official EU policy documents reveals that all the three institutions were core, influential components of the policy stream during the advancement of the multiple decision-making streams shaping the EU's defensive economic policy toward China. The timing and tempo of their situational assessments and policy recommendations remained broadly synchronized with the problem stream—defined as the evolving dynamics of China-EU bilateral economic relations—and also exhibited a clear, statistically significant correlation with the timing and tempo of the political stream, defined as the decision-making activities of the EU's core institutional bodies.

The archival record of policy recommendations from all three think tanks demonstrates a consistent degree of forward-looking strategic foresight. For example, Bruegel's and the RIIA's analyses of the growth trajectory and potential implications of Chinese outbound investment into Europe, the RIIA's research on the impact of Chinese investment on the operational dynamics of European industrial sectors and its accompanying policy recommendations, and SWP's assessment of the inescapable structural contradictions in China-EU economic relations stemming from fundamental differences in the two sides' institutional systems, were all subsequently reflected in the EU's official situational assessments, strategic framing, and corresponding policy design. This pattern confirms that the research produced by all three think tanks exhibited clear strategic foresight, enabling them to generate relatively accurate assessments of systemically important long-term trends, as well as incisive, actionable policy proposals for macro-level strategic issues.

As outlined in the preceding chapters, a long-standing debate within the field of think tank studies centers on the core comparative advantages of think tank policy advice services, relative to the in-house staff advisory systems, executive support structures, and intelligence services embedded into formal political decision-making institutions: specifically, whether their core advantages lie in assisting decision-makers to forecast and respond to major unforeseen crises, or in providing sustained advisory services for high-priority issues in the routine policymaking process. The analysis of the three think tanks' policy influence mechanisms presented in the preceding chapters demonstrates that while think tanks cannot directly deliver precise crisis forecast to decision-makers, or mount an immediate, rapid response to unfolding crisis events, they can nevertheless leverage their long-accumulated institutional knowledge and expertise, through years of sustained, systematic monitoring and analysis of specialized policy domains, to detect early warning signs of major impending and disruptive shifts in the policy landscape, thereby providing decision-makers with a meaningful degree of advance warning. Put differently, think tanks are uniquely positioned to discern the faint, easily overlooked storm clouds on the horizon, and thereby anticipate the approaching storm beyond the line of sight, even as they struggle to deliver definitive forecasts of the storm's precise speed, scale, and intensity.

Third, all the three think tanks integrate, to varying degrees, strategic research focused on long-term, system-wide issues with technically rigorous, specialized research on discrete policy challenges, forming a comprehensive, integrated research architecture. Overall, all the three institutions prioritize strategic macro-level research, with a core focus on assessing the evolution of long-term structural trends and analyzing emerging issues and dynamics within the broader systemic landscape, while devoting comparatively fewer resources to granular research on narrow, specific, and highly technical policy issues. That said, there are notable divergences in their research priorities: Bruegel devotes significantly more attention and research capacity to discrete issues within the traditional field of international economics, particularly trade and investment; SWP prioritizes analysis of the interlinkages between the core architecture of the EU's defensive economic policy toward China and the broader strategic security landscape; and the RIIA focuses its research primarily on issues across three core domains: investment, industrial policy, and monetary affairs.

In fact, another long-standing, defining debate within the think tank studies field concerns the optimal focus of think tank research: whether institutions should prioritize macro-level, system-wide strategic research, or more granular, micro-level analysis of specific policy issues. The practice of all the three think tanks examined in this study demonstrates that they integrate strategic and issue-specific research, dynamically calibrating the balance between the two based on their proprietary data holdings, institutional expertise, and long-established research strengths. This finding makes clear that there is no universal, one-size-fits-all answer to this long-standing debate; instead, the optimal balance must be determined through context-specific analysis tailored to the unique characteristics of each individual think tank and each specific policy domain.

China-EU economic relations have consistently occupied a position of central importance within the EU's external strategic architecture. Bilateral economic ties constitute the core, most consequential component of the China-EU Strategic Partnership, and EU policymaking in this domain provides a uniquely clear lens through which to observe the defining structural and procedural features of the EU's broader decision-making system. The in-depth case study and analysis of the mechanisms through which European think tanks influence EU policymaking in this critical domain, presented in this monograph, enables a clear mapping of the precise positioning of European think tanks within the EU's overarching political power structure, and in turn facilitates a deeper, more nuanced understanding of the defining intrinsic features and evolutionary dynamics of both European think tanks and the EU's policymaking structure and process. That said, the existing scholarly literature on European think tanks remains incomplete and underdeveloped, with numerous critical questions regarding the specific cases and operational details of European think tank influence over EU policymaking remaining to be addressed through further rigorous, in-depth empirical analysis.

References

I. English Literature

1.1 English Monographs and Articles

Abelson, D. E. (2002) *Do Think Tanks Matter? Assessing the Impact of Public Policy Institute,* London: McGill-Queen's University Press.

Abelson, D. E. (1995) 'From Policy Research to Political Advocacy: The Changing Role of Think Tanks in American Politics', *Canadian Review of American Studies,* 25(1), pp. 93-126.

Abelson, D. E. (2024) 'Old World, New World: the Evolution and Influence of Foreign Affairs Think Tanks', *International Affairs,* 90(1), pp. 125-142.

Allio, L. (2002) 'The Role of Brussels-based Think Tanks in the EU Decision-Making Process', a Thesis for the Degree of Master of European Studies, College of Europe.

Baird, T. (2018) 'Interest Groups and Strategic Constructivism: Business Actors and Border Security Policies in the European Union', *Journal of Ethnic and Migration Studies*, 44(1), pp. 118-136.

Bajenova, T. (2018) 'Rescaling Expertise in EU Policy-Making: European Think Tanks and their Reliance on Symbolic, Political and Network Capital', *Globalisation, Societies and Education*, 16(1), pp. 1-17.

Baldwin, M. (2006) 'EU Trade Politics — Heaven or Hell?', *Journal of European Public Policy*, 13(6), pp. 926–942.

Balosin, M. A. (2009-2010) 'Think Tanks for the Promotion of a European Public Space', *L'Europe Unie,* 4(3-4), pp. 20-23.

Benz, A., Corcaci, A. and Wolfgang Doser, J. (2016) 'Unraveling Multilevel Administration: Pattern and Dynamics of Administrative Coordination in European Governance', *Journal of European Public Policy*, 23(7), pp. 999-1018.

Berardo, R. and Scholz, J. T. (2010) 'Self-Organizing Policy Networks: Risk, Partner Selection and Cooperation in Estuaries', *American Journal of Political Science*, 54(3), pp. 632-649.

Berardo, R. (2009) 'Processing Complexity in Networks: A Study of Informal Collaboration and Its Effect on Organizational Success', *Policy Studies Journal*, 37(3), pp. 521-539.

Berkhout, J., Carroll, B. J., Braun, C., Chalmers, A. W., Destrooper, T., Lowery, D. and Rasmussen, A. (2015) 'Interest Organizations Across Economic Sectors: Explaining Interest Group Density in the European Union', *Journal of European Public Policy*, 22(4), pp. 462-480.

Berman, S. (2001) 'Review: Ideas, Norms, and Culture in Political Analysis', *Comparative Politics*, 33(2), pp. 231-250.

Bertelli, A. M. and Wenger, J. B. (2008) 'Demanding Information: Think Tanks and the U.S. Congress', *British Journal of Political Science*, 39(2), pp. 225-242.

Besussi, E. (2006) 'Policy Networks: Conceptual Developments and Their European Applications', *UCL Working Papers Series*, Issue 102, pp. 1-17.

Beyers, J., Eising, R. and Maloney, W. A. (Eds., 2010), *Interest Group Politics in Europe: Lessons from EU Studies and Comparative Politics*, London: Routledge.

Birkland, T. A. (2011) *An Introduction to the Policy Process: Theories, Concepts, and Models of Public Policy Making*, 3rd Edition, New York: M. E. Sharpe.

Bogaards, M. (2002) 'Consociational Interpretations of the EU: A Critical Appraisal', *European Union Politics*, 3(3), pp. 357-381.

Boswell, C. (2008) 'The Political Functions of Expert Knowledge: Knowledge and Legitimation in European Union Immigration Policy', *Journal of European Public Policy*, 15(4), pp. 471-488.

Brooks, S., Stasiak, D. and Zyro, T. (Eds., 2012) *Policy Expertise in Contemporary Democracies*, Surrey: Ashgate Publishing Limited.

Broscheid, A. and Coen, D. (2007) 'Lobbying Activity and Fora Creation in the EU', *Journal of European Public Policy*, 14(3), pp. 346-365.

Bulmers, S. J. (1996) 'The European Council and the Council of the European Union: Shapers of a European Confederation', *Publius: The Journal of Federalism*, 26(4), pp. 17-42.

Bunea, A. and Thomson, R. (2014) 'Consultations with Interest Groups and the Empowerment of Executives: Evidence from the European Union', *Governance*, 28(4), pp. 517-531.

Bursens, P., Beyers, J. and Donas, T. (2014) 'Domestic European Union Coordination and Interest Group Mobilization in Three Member States: Looking Beyond the Formal Mechanisms', *Regional and Federal Studies*, 24(3), pp. 363-381.

Carter, R. G., Scott, J. M. and Rowling, C. M. (2004) 'Setting a Course: Congressional Foreign

Policy Entrepreneurs in Post-World War II U.S. Foreign Policy', *International Studies Perspective*, 5(3), pp. 278-299.

Cekik, A. (2017) 'Adapting to Europe? Business interests and civil society groups in accession countries', *West European Politics*, 40(5), pp. 1066-1087.

Chalmers, A. W. (2011) 'Interests, Influence and Information: Comparing the Influence of Interest Groups in the European Union', *Journal of European Integration*, 33(4), pp. 471-486.

Chalmers, A. W. (2013) 'Trading information for access: informational lobbying strategies and interest group access to the European Union', *Journal of European Public Policy*, 20(1), pp. 39-58.

Coen, D. (1997) 'The Evolution of the Large Firm as a Political Actor in the European Union', *Journal of European Public Policy*, 4(1), pp. 91-108.

Cohen, M. D., March, J. G. and Olsen, J. P. (1972) 'A Garbage Can Model of Organizational Choice', *Administrative Science Quarterly*, 17(1), pp. 1-25.

Collura, R. and Vercauteren, P. (2017) 'Theoretical Perspectives On Think Tanks in the European Governance', *Studia Universitatis Babes-Bolyai - Studia Europaea*, 62(1), pp. 27-53.

Collura, R. (2016) 'Bruegel, EU Think Tank in the EU Multi-level Governance', SOG Working Papers 36.

Coman, R. (2019) 'Why and How Do Think Tanks Expand their Networks in Times of Crisis? The Case of Bruegel and the Centre for European Policy Studies', *Journal of European Public Policy*, 26(2), pp. 286-301.

Constantelos, J. (2004) 'The Europeanization of interest group politics in Italy: Business Associations in Rome and the Regions', *Journal of European Public Policy*, 11(6), pp. 1020-1040.

Costa, O. and Magnette, P. (2003) 'The European Union as a Consociation? A Methodological Assessment', *West European Politics*, 26(3), pp. 1-18.

Coxall, B. (2001) *Pressure Groups in British Politics*. London: Pearson Education Limited, 2001.

Crawford, B. (2007) *Power and German Foreign Policy: Embedded Hegemony in Europe*. London: Palgrave Macmillan.

Critchlow, D. T. (1985) *The Brookings Institution, 1916-1952: Expertise and the Public Interest in a Democratic Society*, DeKalb: Northern Illinois University Press.

Crombois, J. F. (2019) 'Central and Eastern European Business Interest Associations and EU Policy

Making', *Journal of Public Affairs*, 19(1), pp. 1-8.

Cronin, T. E. and Greenberg, S. D. (1969) *The Presidential Advisory System*. New York: Harper and Row Publisher.

Cross, M. K. D. (2011) *Security Integration in Europe: How Knowledge-Based Networks Are Transforming the European Union*. Ann Arbor: The University of Michigan Press.

Czub, J. F. (2017) 'Business Groups and the Europe 2020 Strategy: Problem Analysis', *International Relations and Diplomacy*, 5(1), pp. 34-45.

Czub, J. F. (2016) 'Representation of Polish Business Groups in the Institutional System of the European Union', *International Relations and Diplomacy*, 4(3), pp. 177-188.

Damro, C. (2006) 'The New Trade Politics and EU Competition Policy: Shopping for Convergence and Co-Operation', *Journal of European Public Policy*, 13(6), pp. 867-886.

Daviter, F. (2011) *Policy Framing in the European Union*, Hampshire: Palgrave Macmillan.

De Bièvre, D. (2006) 'The EU Regulatory Trade Agenda and the Quest for WTO Enforcement', *Journal of European Public Policy*, 13(6), pp. 851-866.

De Bruycker, I. and Beyers, J. (2015) 'Balanced or Biased? Interest Groups and Legislative Lobbying in the European News Media', *Political Communication*, 32(3), pp. 453-474.

De Rynck, S. (2016) 'Banking on a Union: The Politics of Changing Eurozone Banking Supervision', *Journal of European Public Policy*, 23(1), pp. 119-135.

Denham, A. and Garnett, M. (1996) 'The Nature and Impact of Think Tanks in Contemporary Britain', *Contemporary British History*, 10(1), pp. 43-61.

Desai, R. (1994) 'Second Hand Dealers in Ideas: Think Tanks and Thatcherite Hegemony', *New Left Review*, 203(1), pp. 27-64.

Domhoff, G. W. (1990) *The Power Elite and the State: How Policy is Made in America*. New York: de Gruyter, A., Domhoff, G. W. and Dye, T. R. (Eds., 1987) *Power Elites and Organizations*. London: Sage Publications.

Dukenfield, M. E. (2006) *Business and the Euro: Business Groups and the Politics of EMU in Germany and the United Kingdom*, Basingstoke of Hampshire: Palgrave Macmillan.

Dye, T. R. (2000) *Top Down Policymaking*. New York: Chatham House Publishers.

Dür, A. and Mateo, G. (2014) 'The Europeanization of interest groups: Group type, resources and policy area', *European Union Politics*, 15(4), pp. 572-594.

Dür, A. and Mateo, G. (2012) 'Who lobbies the European Union? National interest groups in a multilevel polity', *Journal of European Public Policy*, 19(7), pp. 969-987.

Dür, A., Bernhagen, P. and Marshall, D. (2015) 'Interest Group Success in the European Union', *Comparative Political Studies*, 48(8), pp. 951-983.

Etzion, D. and Davis, G. F. (2008) 'Revolving Doors? A Network Analysis of Corporate Officers and U.S. Government Officials', *Journal of Management Inquiry*, 17(3), pp. 157-161.

Fabbrini, S. (2016) 'The Constitutional Conundrum of the European Union', *Journal of European Public Policy*, 23(1), pp. 84-100.

Fawcett, P. and Daugbjerg, C. (2012) 'Explaining Governance Outcomes: Epistemology, Network Governance and Policy Network Analysis', *Political Studies Review*, 10(2), pp. 195-207.

Fischer, F. (1990) *Technocracy and the Politics of Experience*. Newbury Park, CA: Sage Publications.

Fligstein, N. and McNichol, J. (1998) 'The Institutional Terrain of the European Union', in Sandholtz, W. and Stone Sweet, A. (Eds.), *European Integration and Supranational Governance*, Oxford: Oxford University Press, pp. 59-91.

Flinders, M. (2004) 'Distributed Public Governance in Britain', *Public Administration*, 82(4), pp. 883-909.

Flinders, M. (2005) 'The Politics of Public-Private Partnerships', *The British Journal of Politics and International Relations*, 7(2), pp. 215-239.

Flinders, M. (2008) *Delegated Governance and the British State: Walking without Order.* Oxford: Oxford University Press.

Flinders, M., Gamble, A., Hay, C. and Kenny, M. (Eds., 2009) *The Oxford Handbook of British Politics*. Oxford: Oxford University Press.

Gabel, M. J. (1998) 'The Endurance of Supranational Governance: A Consociational Interpretation of the European Union', *Comparative Politics*, 30(4), pp. 463-475.

Garrett, G. (1992) 'International Cooperation and Institutional Choice: The European Community's Internal Market', *International Organization*, 46(2), pp. 533-560.

Geddes, A. (2014) 'Relationships between Research and Policy on Migration in the European Union: A Practice-Based Analysis', Robert Schuman Centre for Advanced Studies Research Paper, Issue 2014/06.

Gornitzka, A. and Sverdrup, U. (2015), 'Societal Inclusion in Expert Venues: Participation of Interest Groups and Business in the European Commission Expert Groups', *Politics and*

Governance, 3(1), pp. 151-165.

Gray, V., Lowery, D., Fellowes, M., and Anderson, J. L. (2005) 'Legislative Agendas and Interest Advocacy: Understanding the Demand Side of Lobbying', *American Political Research*, 33(3), pp. 404-434.

Greenwood, J. and Halpin, D. (2007) 'The European Commission and the Public Governance of Interest Groups in the European Union: Seeking a Niche between Accreditation and Laissez Faire', *Perspectives on European Politics and Society*, 8(2), pp. 189-210.

Greenwood, J. (2011) *Interest Representation in the European Union*. Hampshire: Palgrave Macmillan.

Greve, C., Flinders, M., and Van Thiel, S. (1999) 'Quangos - What's in a Name? Defining Quangos from a Comparative Perspective', *Governance*, 12(2), pp. 129-146.

Gullberg, A. T. (2008) 'Lobbying Friends and Foes in Climate Policy: The Case of Business and Environmental Interest Groups in the European Union', *Energy Policy, 36(8)*, pp. 2964-2972.

Guttman, D. and Willner, B. (1976) *Shadow Government: How Government's Multi-Billion-Dollar Giveaway of Its Decision-Making Powers to Private Management Consultants, 'Experts', and Think Tanks., New York: Pantheon Books.*

Haas, P. M. (1992) 'Epistemic Communities and International Policy Coordination', I*nternational Organization*, 46(1), pp. 1-35.

Habermas, J. (1976) 'Verwissenshcaftlichte Politik und offentliche Meinung', in Habermas, J. (Ed.), *Technik und Wissenschaft als 'Ideologie'*. Frankfurt: Suhrkamp Verlag, pp. 120-145.

Hajer, M. A. (1993) 'Discourse Coalitions and the Institutionalization of Practice: The Case of Acid Rain in Britain', in Fischer, F. and Forester, J. (Eds.), *The Argumentative Turn in Policy Analysis and Planning*, Durham and London: Duke University Press, pp. 43-76.

Hall, P. A. (1993) 'Policy Paradigms, Social Learning, and the State: the Case of Economic Policy Making in Britain', *Comparative Politics*, 25(3), pp. 275-296.

Hall, R. L. and Deardorff, A. V. (2006) 'Lobbying as Legislative Subsidy', *American Political Science Review*, 100(1), pp. 69-84.

Hammack, D. C. and Anheier, H. K. (2013) *A Versatile American Institution: The Changing Ideals and Realities of Philanthropic Foundations*. Washington D.C.: the Brookings Institution Press.

Hanegraaff, M. and Pritoni, A. (2019) 'United in fear: Interest group coalition formation as a weapon of the weak?', *European Union Politics*, 20(2), pp. 198-218.

Haney, P. J. (2002) *Organizing for Foreign Policy Crises: Presidents, Advisers, and the Management of Decision Making*. Ann Arbor: The University of Michigan Press.

Hardacre, A. (Ed.) (2011) *How the EU Institution Work and How to Work with the EU Institutions*. London: John Harper Publishing.

Harkins, M. D. (2010) 'Corporate Strategy, Corporate Capture: Food and Alcohol Industry Lobbing and Public Health', *Critical Social Policy*, 30(4), pp. 564-589.

Hart, P. and Vromen, A. (2008) 'A New Era for Think Tanks in Public Policy? International Trends, Australian Realities', *The Australian Journal of Public Administration*, 67(2), pp. 135-148.

Hass, E. B. (1961) 'International Integration: The European and the Universal Process', *International Organization*, 15(3), pp. 366-392.

Hass, E. B. (1989) 'Do Regimes Matter? Epistemic Communities and Evolving Policies to Control Mediterranean Pollution', *International Organization*, 43(3), pp. 377-403.

Hawkins, B. and McCambridge, J. (2014) 'Industry Actors, Think Tanks, and Alcohol Policy in the United Kingdom', *American Journal of Public Health*, 104(8), pp. 1363-1369.

Hayden, F. G. (2002) Policymaking Network of the Iron-Triangle Sub-government for Licensing Hazardous Waste Facilities, *Journal of Economic Issues*, 36(2), pp. 477-484.

Heclo, H. (1978) 'Issue Networks and the Executive Establishment', in King, A. (Ed.). *The New American Political System*, Washington D.C.: The American Enterprise Institute, pp. 87-124.

Hill, C. and Smith, M. (2011) *International Relations and the European Union*, 2nd edition. Oxford: Oxford University Press.

Hird, J. A. (2005) *Power, Knowledge, and Politics: Policy Analysis in the States*. Washington, D.C.: Georgetown University Press, 2005.

Holmes, P. (2006) 'Trade and 'Domestic' Policies: The European Mix', *Journal of European Public Policy*, 13(6), pp. 815-831.

Holsti, K. J. (1988) *International Politics: A Framework for Analysis*. Englewood Cliffs of New Jersey: Prentice-Hall, 1988.

Hooghe, L. and Marks, G. (2001) 'Types of Multilevel Governance', *European Integration Online Papers*, Vol. 5, No. 11; http://eiop.or.at/eiop/texte/2001-011a.htm

Institute for European Studies (IES) of Vrije Universiteit Brussel (2008) *The European Commission and Interest Groups: Towards a Deliberative Interpretation of Stakeholder Involvement in EU*

Policy Making. Brussels: Brussels University Press.

Jacoby, R. N. and Townsley, E. (2011) *The Space of Opinion: Media Intellectuals and the Public Sphere*. New York: Oxford University Press.

Jochem, S. (2013) 'Think Tanks: Bridging Beltway and Ivory Tower', in S. Blum and K. Schubert (Eds.), *Policy Analysis in Germany*. Bristol: Policy Press, pp. 231-245.

Jones, E. (2006) 'Europe's Market Liberalization Is a Bad Model for a Global Trade Agenda', *Journal of European Public Policy*, 13(6), pp. 943-957.

Joos, K. (2011) *Lobbying in the New Europe: Successful Representation of Interests after the Treaty of Lisbon*. Weinheim of Germany: Wiley-VCH.

Kaya, C. (2019) 'Providing Information and Building Capacity: Interest Group Involvement in the Application of EU Law', *West European Politics*, 42(1), pp. 25-44.

Kaya, C. (2017) 'The impact of interest group diversity on legal implementation in the European Union', *Journal of European Public Policy*, 25(4), pp. 567-585.

Kelstrup, J. D. (2016) 'Quantitative Differences in Think Tank Dissemination Activities in Germany, Denmark and the UK', *Policy Sciences*, 50(1), pp. 125-137.

Keohane, R. and Hoffmann, S. (1991) 'Institutional Change in Europe in the 1980s', in Keohane, R. and Hoffmann, S. (Eds.), *The New European Community*. Boulder, Colorado: Westview Press, pp. 1-39.

Keohane, R. and Hoffmann, S. (1994) 'Institutional Change in Europe in the 1980s', in Nelsen, B. F. and Stubb, A. C-G. (Eds.), *The European Union*. Boulder, Colorado: Lynne Rienner Publisher, pp. 237-255.

Kingdon, J. W. (2007) *Agenda, Alternatives, and Public Policies*, New York: Longman.

Kluver, H. (2012) 'Lobbying as a Collective Enterprise: Winners and Losers of Policy Formulation in the European Union', *Journal of European Public Policy*, 20(1), pp. 59-76.

Klüver, H. and Mahoney, C. (2015) 'Measuring interest group framing strategies in public policy debates', *Journal of Public Policy*, 35(2), pp. 223-244.

Klüver, H. and Saurugger, S. (2013) 'Opening the black box: The professionalization of interest groups in the European Union', *Interest Groups and Advocacy*, 2(2), pp. 185-205.

Klüver, H., Braun, C. and Beyers, J. (2015) 'Legislative lobbying in context: towards a conceptual framework of interest group lobbying in the European Union', *Journal of European Public Policy*, 22(4), pp. 447-461.

Klüver, H., Mahoney, C. and Opper, M. (2015) 'Framing in context: how interest groups employ framing to lobby the European Commission', *Journal of European Public Policy*, 22(4), pp. 481-498.

Knodt, M., Quittkat, C. and Greenwood, J. (Eds., 2012), *Functional and Territorial Interest Representation in the EU*. London: Routledge.

Kohler-Koch, B. and Finke, B. (2007) 'The Institutional Shaping of EU-Society Relations: A Contribution to Democracy via Participation?', *Journal of Civil Society*, 3(3), pp. 205-221.

Kohler-Koch, B., Kotzian, P. and Quittkat, C., 'The multilevel interest representation of national business associations', *West European Politics*, 40(5), pp. 1046-1065.

Koppell, J. G. (2003) *The Politics of Quasi-Government: Hybrid Organizations and Dynamics of Bureaucratic Control*. Cambridge: Cambridge University Press.

Lasswell, H. D. (1956) *The Decision Process: Seven Categories of Functional Analysis*. College Park: University of Maryland Press.

Limani, A. Q. (2016) 'Impact of Interest Groups in United Kingdom, as State Member of European Union', *European Journal of Sustainable Development*, 5(1), pp. 97-107.

Lorenzo, A. G. (2003) 'The Role of Interest Groups in the European Union Decision-Making Process', *European Journal of Law and Economics*, 15(3), pp. 251-261.

Lowi, T. J. (1964) 'American Business and Public Policy: Case Studies and Political Theory', *World Politics*, 16(4), pp. 677-715.

Lowi, T. (1969) *The End of Liberalism*. New York: Norton Publisher.

Lukes, S. (2004) *Power: A Radical View*, 2nd edition, New York: Palgrave MacMillan.

Lüddecke, R. (2006) 'Think Tanks in Den USA Und Deutschland: Überzeugende Systematisierung', *Zeitschrift Für Parlamentsfragen*, 37(2), pp. 439-440.

Mahoney, C. (2009) *Brussels Versus the Beltway: Advocacy in the United States and the European Union*. Washington, D.C.: Georgetown University Press.

Majone, G. (1994) 'The Rise of the Regulatory State in Europe', *West European Politics*, 17(3), pp. 77-101.

Marks, G. and McAdam, D. (1996) 'Social Movements and the Changing Structure of Political Opportunity in the European Union', *West European Politics*, 19(2), pp. 249-278.

Massaro, M. (2019) 'Is Business Lobbying in the European Union Context-Dependent? Evidence from the Policy Field of Radio Spectrum', *Telecommunications Policy*, 43(10), pp. 1-8.

Matthijs, M. (201) 'The Three Faces of German Leadership', *Survival*, 58(2), pp. 135-154.

McFarland, A. (1987) 'Interest Groups and Theories of Power in America', *British Journal of Political Science*, 17(2), pp. 129-147.

McGann, J. G. (2001), *Global Think Tanks: Policy Networks and Governance*. London: Routledge.

McGann J. G. (2007) *Think Tanks and Policy Advice in the United States: Academics, Advisors, and Advocates*. New York: Routledge.

McGuire, S. (2006) 'No More Euro-Champions? The Interaction of EU Industrial and Trade Policies', *Journal of European Public Policy*, 13(6), pp. 887-905.

McNutt, K. and Marchildon, G. (2009) 'Think Tanks and the Web: Measuring Visibility and Influence', *Canadian Public Policy*, 35(2), pp. 219-236.

Medvetz, T. (2012) 'Scholar as Sitting Duck: The Cronon Affair and the Buffer Zone in American Public Debate', *Public Culture*, 24(1), pp. 47-53.

Medvetz, T. (2012) *Think Tanks in America*. Chicago: The University of Chicago Press.

Medvic, S. K. (2001) *Political Consultants in Congressional Elections*, Columbus: The Ohio State University Press.

Metcalfe, L. (1996) 'The European Commission as a Network Organization', *Publius: The Journal of Federalism*, 26(4), pp. 43-62.

Meunier, S., and Nicolaïdis, K. (2006) 'The European Union as a Conflicted Trade Power', *Journal of European Public Policy*, 13(6), pp. 906-925.

Mills, C. W. (1967) *The Power Elite*. New York: The Oxford University Press.

Miragliotta, N. (2018) 'Institutional dynamics and party think tank development: Britain and Germany compared', *Commonwealth and Comparative Politics*, 56(2), pp. 234-256.

Murray, C. (1993) 'The Coming White Underclass', *Wall Street Journal*, October 29, 1993.

Nichelson, S. (2009) *EU Think Tanks in Brussels: Policy-Making Roles, Functions and Influence*, A Thesis for the Degree of Master of European Politics and Policies, Katholieke Universiteit Leuven.

Nugent, N. (2010) *The Government and Politics of the European Union*, 7th edition. Houndmills of Hampshire: Palgrave Macmillan.

Parmar, I. (2004) 'Institutes of International Affairs: Their Roles in Foreign Policy Making, Opinion Mobilization, and Unofficial Diplomacy', in Stone, D. (Ed.), *Think Tank Traditions: Policy Research and the Politics of Ideas*. Manchester: Manchester University Press.

Pautz, H. (2008) 'Think-tanks in Germany: the Bertelsmann Foundation's Role in Labour Market Reform', *Zeitschrift Für Politikberatung*, 1(3-4), pp. 437-456.

Pautz, H. (2010a) 'The Role of Think Tanks in the Modernisation of the SPD', *German Politics*, 19(2), pp. 183-199.

Pautz, H. (2010b), 'Think Tanks in the United Kingdom and Germany: Actors in the Modernisation of Social Democracy', *The British Journal of Politics and International Relations*, 12(2), pp. 274-294.

Pautz, H. (2011) 'Revisiting the Think Tank Phenomenon', *Public Policy and Administration*, 26(4), pp. 419-435.

Pautz, H. (2012) 'The Think Tanks behind 'Cameronism', *British Journal of Politics and International Relations*, 15(3), pp. 362-377.

Pautz, H. (2016) 'Managing the Crisis? Think Tanks and the British Response to Global Financial Crisis and Great Recession', *Critical Policy Studies*, 11(2), pp. 191-210.

Pel., D. (1995) 'Knowledge Politics and Anti-Politics: Toward a Critical Appraisal of Bourdieu's Concept of Intellectual Autonomy', *Theory and Society*, 24(1), pp. 79-104.

Pemberton, H. (2004) *Policy Learning and British Governance in the 1960s*. Hampshire: Palgrave Macmillan.

Perez, M. (2014a) 'Does EU Policymaking Allow for Skilful Networkers But Limited Knowledge Managers? The Think Tanks' Tale', *International Journal of Politics, Culture, and Society*, 27(3), pp. 323-342.

Perez, M. (2014b) 'EU Think Tank Fora as Transaction Cost Reducers: A Study of Informal Interest Intermediation in the EU', *Journal of Contemporary European Research*, 10(2), pp. 146-165.

Peterson, J. (1995a) 'Decision Making in the European Union: towards a Framework for Analysis', *Journal of European Public Policy*, 2(1), pp. 69-93.

Peterson, J. (1995b) 'Playing the Transparency Game: Consultation and Policy Making in the European Commission', *Public Administration*, 73(3), pp. 473-492.

Peterson, J. (1996) 'Policy Networks and the European Union Governance'. Paper presented at the Conference of Europeanists, Chicago.

Peterson, J. (1999) 'The Santer Era: The European Commission in Normative, Historical, and Theoretical Perspective', *Journal of European Public Policy*, 6(1), pp. 46-55.

Plehwe, D. (2014) 'Think Tank Networks and the Knowledge-Interest Nexus: The Case of Climate

Change', *Critical Policy Studies*, 8(1), pp. 101-115.

Plehwe, D., Krämer, W., Neujeffski, M., Meland, A. and Guérot, U (2016) 'Time to Go beyond Interstate Federalism - or Something Different? The Response of New Pro-European Think Tanks to the EU Integration Crisis', Discussion Papers, Inequality and Social Policy SP I 2016-202, WZB Berlin Social Science Center.

Plehwe, D., Neujeffski, M. and Krämer, W. (2018) 'Saving the Dangerous Idea: Austerity Think Tank Networks in the European Union', *Policy and Society*, 37(2), pp. 188-205.

Political and Economic Planning (PEP) (1960) *Advisory Committees in British Government, A PEP Report*. London: George Allen and Unwin Ltd.

Polyakova, A., and Fligstein, N. (2016) 'Is European Integration Causing Europe to Become More Nationalist? Evidence from the 2007-9 Financial Crisis', *Journal of European Public Policy*, 23(1), pp. 60-83.

Rasmussen, M. K. (2014) 'The Battle for Influence: The Politics of Business Lobbying in the European Parliament', *JCMS: Journal of Common Market Studies*, 53(2), pp. 365-382.

Rhodes, R. A. W. (1994) 'The Hollowing Out of the State: The Changing Nature of Public Service in Britain', *The Political Quarterly*, 65(2), pp. 138-151.

Rhodes, R. A. W. (1997) *Understanding Governance: Policy Networks, Governance, Reflexivity and Accountability*. Buckingham: Open University Press.

Rich, A. (2004) *Think Tanks, Public Policy, and the Politics of Expertise*. Cambridge: Cambridge University Press.

Roth, W. and Metha, J. (2002) 'The Rashomon Effect: Combining Positivist and Interpretivist Approaches in the Analysis of Contested Events', *Sociological Methods and Research*, 31(2), pp. 131-173.

Ruser, A. (2018) 'What to Think About Think Tanks: Towards a Conceptual Framework of Strategic Think Tank Behaviour', *International Journal of Politics, Culture and Society*, 31(2), pp. 179-192.

Sabatier, P. A., and Weible, C. M. (2007) 'The Advocacy Coalition Framework: Innovations and Clarifications', in Sabatier, P. A. (Ed.) *Theories of the Policy Process*. London: Westview Press.

Sager, F. (2007) 'Habermas' Models of Decisionism, Technocracy and Pragmatism in Times of Governance: The Relationship of Public Administration, Politics and Science in the Alcohol

Prevention Policies of the Swiss Member States', *Public Administration*, 85(2), pp. 429-447.

Sandstrom, A. and Carlsson, L. (2008) 'The Performance of Policy Networks: The Relations between Network Structure and Network Performance', *Policy Studies Journal*, 36(4), pp. 497-524.

Savage, J. D. and Verdun, A. (2016) 'Strengthening the European Commission's Budgetary and Economic Surveillance Capacity since Greece and the Euro Area Crisis: A Study of Five Directorates-General', *Journal of European Public Policy*, 23(1), pp. 101-118.

Scharpf, F. W. (1988) 'The Joint Decision Trap: Lessons from German Federalism and European Integration', *Public Administration*, 66(3), pp. 239-278.

Schmidt, V. (2008) 'Discursive Institutionalism: The Explanatory Power of Ideas and Discourse', *Political Science*, 11(1), pp. 303-322.

Schmitter, P. C. (1969) 'Three Neo-functional Hypotheses about International Integration', *International Organization*, 23(1), pp. 161-166.

Schmitter, P. C. (1981) 'Interest Intermediation and Regime Governability in Contemporary Western Europe and North America', in Berger, S. (Ed.), *Organizing Interests in Western Europe*. Cambridge: Cambridge University Press.

Schulzinger, R. D. (1984) *The Wise Men of Foreign Affairs: The History of the Council on Foreign Relations*. New York: Columbia University Press.

Shaffer, G. (2006) 'What's New in EU Trade Dispute Settlement? Judicialization, Public-Private Networks and the WTO Legal Order', *Journal of European Public Policy*, 13(6), pp. 832-850.

Sharp, L. H. and Minter, W. (1977) *Imperial Brain Trust: The Council on Foreign Relations and United States Foreign Policy*. New York: Monthly Review Press.

Sherrington, P. (1999) *Shaping European Union Policy: The Significance of Think Tank Activity*. Belfast: Queens University Press.

Sherrington, P. (2000), 'Shaping the Policy Agenda: Think Tank Activity in the European Union', *Global Society*, 14(2), pp. 173-189.

Smith, A. (2000) 'Policy Networks and Advocacy Coalitions: Explaining Policy Change and Stability in UK Industrial Pollution Policy?', *Environment and Planning C Government and Policy*, 18(1), pp. 95-114.

Smith, J. A. (1989) 'Think Tanks and the Politics of Ideas', in Colander, D. C. and Coats, A. W. (Eds.), *The Spread of Economic Ideas*, New York: Cambridge University Press, pp. 175-194.

Smith, M. J. (1991) 'From Policy Community to Issue Networks: Salmonella in Eggs and the New Politics of Food', *Public Administration*, 69, pp. 235-255.

Stone, D. (1996) 'From the Margins of Politics: The Influence of Think Tanks in Britain', *West European Politics*, 19(4), pp. 675-692.

Stone, D. (2005) *Comparative Think Tanks, Politics and Public Policy*. Cheltenham of UK: Edward Elgar.

Stone, D. (2007a) 'Public Policy Analysis and Think Tanks', in Fischer, F., Miller, G. J., and Sidney, M. S. (Eds.), *Handbook of Public Policy Analysis: Theory, Politics and Methods*. Boca Raton of Florida: CRC Press of Taylor and Francis Group.

Stone, D. (2007b), 'Recycling Bins, Garbage Cans or Think Tanks? Three Myths Regarding Policy Analysis Institutes', *Public Administration*, 85(2), pp. 259-278.

Stone, D. and Denham, A. (2004) *Think Tank Traditions: Policy Research and the Politics of Ideas*. Manchester: Manchester University Press.

Stone, D. and Ullrich, H. (2003), 'Policy Research Institutes and Think Tanks in Western Europe: Development Trends and Perspectives', Local Government and Public Service Reform Initiative, Open Society Institute, pp. 1-49.

Streeck, W. and Elsässer, L. (2016) 'Monetary Disunion: The Domestic Politics of Euroland', *Journal of European Public Policy*, 23(1), pp. 1-24.

Thatcher, M. (1998) 'The Development of Policy Network Analyses: From Modest Origins to Overarching Frameworks', *Journal of Theoretical Politics*, 10(4), pp. 389-416.

Thunert, M. (2006) 'The Development and Significance of Think Tanks in Germany', *German Policy Studies*, 3(2), pp. 185-221.

Thunert, M. (2008) 'Think Tanks in Germany: Their Resources, Strategies and Potential', *Zeitschrift Für Politikberatung*, 1(1), pp. 32-52.

Thunert, M. (2004) 'Think Tanks in Germany', in Stone, D. and Denham, A. (Eds.), *Think Tank Traditions: Policy Research and the Politics of Ideas*. Manchester: Manchester University Press, pp. 71-88.

Tortola, P. D. (2017) 'Clarifying Multilevel Governance', *European Journal of Political Research*, 56(2), pp. 234-250.

Truman, D. B. (1951) *The Governmental Process: Political Interests and Public Opinion*. New York: Alfred A. Knopf.

Turnpenny, J., Haxeltine A., Lorenzoni I., O'Riordian T. and Jones M. (2005) 'Mapping Actors involved in Climate Change Policy Networks in the UK', Tyndall Center for Climate Change Research, Working Paper Issue 66.

Ullrich, H. (2004) 'European Union Think Tanks: Generating Ideas, Analysis and Debate', in Stone, D., and Denham, A. (Eds.), *Think Tank Traditions: Policy Research and the Politics of Ideas*. New York: Manchester University Press.

Verdun, A. (2008) 'Policy-Making and Integration in the European Union: Do Economic Interest Groups Matter?', *The British Journal of Politics and International Relations*, 10(1) pp. 129-137.

Vogel, R. and Frost, J. (2009) 'Innovating in the German Public Sector: How a Think Tank Frames the Debate on NPM', *Innovation Journal*, 14(2), 2009, pp. 1-21.

Wallace, H., Pollack, M. A. and Young, A. R. (Eds., 2010) *Policy-Making in the European Union*. 6th edition. Oxford: Oxford University Press.

Ward, V. and others (2009) 'Knowledge Brokering: The Missing Link in the Evidence to Action Chain?', *Evidence and Policy*, 5(3), pp. 267-279.

Warleigh, A., and Faribrass, J. (Eds. 2003). *Influence and Interests in the European Union: The New Politics of Persuasion and Advocacy*. London: Taylor and Francis Group.

Warleigh, A. (2007) 'Better the Devil You Know? Synthetic and Confederal Understandings of European Unification', *Western European Politics*, 21(3), pp. 1-18.

Warleigh, A. (2001) 'Europeanizing Civil Society: NGOs as Agents of Political Socialization', *Journal of Common Market Studies*, 39(4), pp. 619-639.

Weaver, R. K. (1989) 'The Changing World of Think Tanks', *Political Science and Politics*, 22(3), pp. 563-578.

Weber, M. *Economy and Society: An Outline of Interpretive Sociology*, Chapter 3 The Types of Legitimate Domination & Chapter 5, Political Communities, In Roth, G. and Wittich, C. (Eds.) Berkeley: University of California Press, October 2013.

Weidenbaum, M. (2009a) 'A Challenge to Washington Think Tanks', *Challenge*, 52(1), pp. 87-96.

Weidenbaum, M. (2009b) T*he Competition of Ideas: The World of Washington Think Tanks.* New Brunswick: Transaction Publishers.

Wells, P. (2002) 'Prescriptions for Regional Economic Dilemmas: Understanding the Role of Think Tanks in the Governance of Regional Policy', *Public Administration*, 90(1), pp. 211-229.

Wright, M. (Ed., 1987) *Comparative Government-Industry Relations: Western Europe, United States, and Japan*, Oxford: Clarendon Press.

Wu, S. and Keysar, B. (2007) 'The Effect of Culture on Perspective Taking', *Psychological Science*, 18 (7), pp. 600-606.

Young, A. R. and Peterson, J. (2006) 'The EU and the New Trade Politics', *Journal of European Public Policy*, 13 (6), pp. 795-814.

Zaun, N. (2016) 'Why EU Asylum Standards Exceed the Lowest Common Denominator: The Role of Regulatory Expertise in EU Decision-Making', *Journal of European Public Policy*, 23(1), pp. 136-54.

1.2 English Research Reports, Commentaries, Newsletters, Conference Proceedings, Archival Compilations, and Collections of Current Affairs Commentaries

Ahmadoun, S. (2014) 'Turkey's Policy Toward Syrian Refugees: Domestic Repercussions and the Need for International Support', SWP Comments, November 2014.

Angenendt, S. (2015) 'No Solidarity? Growing Refugee Inflows and the Need for EU Asylum Policy Reforms', Transatlantic Academy Comments, January 29, 2015.

Angenendt, S., Engler, M. and Schneider, J. (2013) 'European Refugee Policy: Pathways to Fairer Burden Sharing', SWP Comments, November 2013.

Angenendt, S. and Parkes, R. (2010) 'The Blue Card Impasse: Three Options for EU Policy on Highly Qualified Immigrant*s*', SWP Comments, June, 2010.

Asseburg, M. (Ed., 2012) 'Protest, Revolt and Regime Change in the Arab World: Actors, Challenges, Implications and Policy Options', SWP Research Paper, Berlin, February 2012.

Asseburg, M. (2014a) 'The EU in the Middle East and North Africa: Helpless Bystander rather than Effective Democracy Promoter or Stabilizing Force', SWP Comments, November 2014.

Asseburg, M. (2014b) 'The Networking of European Foreign Policy: from Cacophony to Choir', SWP Comments, November 2014.

Falkner, K., Moisi, D., Youngs, R. and Peet, J. (2014) 'The EU in the World: Foreign Policy after Economic Crisis', Meeting Transcript, March 5, 2014.

Bendiek, A. and Kempin, R. (2012) *Europe's Foreign and Security Policy Adrift: Strengthening the Role of the EU-3*, SWP Comments, December 2011.

Boucher, S. (2004) 'Europe and Its Think Tanks: a Promise to be Fulfilled', Notre Europe, Paris, Studies and Research, No. 35, October 2004.

Brozus, L. (Ed., 2016) *Unexpected, Unforeseen, Unplanned: Scenarios of International Foreign and Security Policy*, SWP Research Paper, January 2016.

Carrion, D. (2015) *'Syria Refugees in Jordan Confronting Difficult Truths'*, Research Paper, September 2015.

Chatham House (2014a) 'The Transatlantic Business Response to Foreign Policy Challenges: Russia, China and the Middle East', Meeting Note, June 12, 2014.

Chatham House (2014b) 'Syria's Conflict and the Impact on Its Neighbors: The Long View', Meeting Note, October 14, 2014.

Chatham House (2015a) 'Transatlantic Security Policy towards a Changing Middle East', Meeting Note, Paris, February 6, 2015.

Chatham House (2015b) "Crises across the Mediterranean: Confronting the Common Challenge.". London, UK. September 14, 2015.

Chatham House Middle East and North Africa Programme (2011a) *The Economics of the Arab Spring*, Summary of a Chatham House Conference held in partnership with FTI Consulting, September 12, 2011.

Chatham House Middle East and North Africa Programme (2011b) *A Changing Middle East and North Africa: Challenges and Opportunities*, November 26-27, 2011, Istanbul, Turkey, Chatham House International Roundtable Summary.

Hanson, P. (2011) 'On Europe's Fringes: Russia, Turkey and the European Union', Briefing Paper, July 2011, REP/EP BP 2011/01.

Hilpert, D. and Parkes, R. (2011) 'Split Citizenship: Immigrant Integration in an Age of Circular Migration', Fokus, 1/2011, Austria Institut fur Europa-und Sicherheitspolitik.

Kempin, R. and Lippert, B. (2013) *Membership, Neighborhood, Partnership: the EU's Foreign Policy Triptych needs Re-modelling*, SWP Working Paper, August 2013.

Kempin, R. and Scheler, R. (2015) 'The EU Must Focus on Root Causes of Migration', *Fair Observer*, April 30, 2015.

Kempin, R., von Ondarza, N. and Overhaus, M. (2012) *Tackling the Big Questions in the Little Steps: A Process towards a Comprehensive EU Strategy*, SWP Working Paper, October 2012.

Kinninmont, J., Stansfield, G. and Sirri, O. (2013a) 'Iraq on the International Stage: Foreign Policy and National Identity in Transition', Working Report, July 2013.

Kinninmont, J., Stansfield, G. and Sirri, O. (2013b) 'It's Time for Europe to Look After Its Own Backyard', *The World Today*, 69(5), October 2013.

Lacher, W. (2014) *Libya's Transition: towards Collapse*, SWP Comments, May 2014.

Lord William of Baglan (2015) 'No Diplomatic End in Sight in Syria', a Comment, March 13, 2015.

Lyall-Grant, M. and Dormandy, X. (2011) Is There an Arab Summer? The UN's Response to the Arab Spring, Meeting Transcript, June 27, 2011.

McGann, J. G. (2007-2016), 'Global Go To Think Tank Index Report', Think Tanks and Civil Societies Program, University of Pennsylvania, 2007, 2008, 2009, 2010, 2011, 2012, 2013, 2014, 2015, 2016.

Missiroli, A. (Ed., 2015), '*An EU Global Strategy: Background, Process, References*', European Union Institute for Security Studies, October 2015.

Missiroli, A. and Ioannides, I. (Eds., 2012) *European Think Tanks and the EU*, Bureau of European Policy Advisers, EU Commission, September 2012.

Niblett, R. (2012) 'Time to Build Bridges over the Mediterranean', February 15, 2012, *International Affairs*.

Niblett, R. (2013) 'Britain's EU Future: A Dangerous Period of Uncertainty', January 24, 2013.

Overhaus, M. (2011) Violence and Post-Conflict Transitions: Twin Challenges for the EU in the 'Arab Spring', SWP Comments, December 2011.

Oweis, K. Y. (2014a) 'Struggling to Build an Alternative to Assad: Structural Flaws and Lack of Protection Undermine Syria's Opposition Government', SWP Comments, June 2014.

Oweis, K. Y. (2014b) 'U.S.-Led Bombardment Challenges Islamic State's Hold on Eastern Syria', SWP Comments, October 2014.

Parkes, R. and Schneider, M. (2010a) 'Partnership: a New EU Approach to Fighting Irregular Immigration?' SWP Comments, November 2010.

Parkes, R. and Schneider, M. (2010b) 'When Home Affairs Becomes Foreign Policy: Lessons from EU Immigration Policy towards North Africa and Eastern Europe', SWP Comments, December 2010.

Perthes, V. (2010) *Turkey's Role in the Middle East; an Outsider's Perspective*, Commentaries of SWP, October 4, 2010.

Perthes, V. (2011) 'Europe and the Arab Spring', *Survival*, 53(6), pp. 73-84.

Perthes, V. and Barbara Lippert, B. (Eds., 2012) *Expect the Unexpected: Ten Situations to Keep an Eye on*, SWP Research Paper, January 2012.

Rogan, E. and Spencer, C. (2011) *The Arab Revolutions of 2011: the Struggle against Autocracy Resumed*, Meeting Transcript.

Sayigh, Y. and Azzam, M. (2012) One Year On: The Challenges of Democratic Transition in the Wake of the Arab Uprisings, Meeting Transcript, January 25, 2012.

Spencer, C. (2010) 'The Real Debate at the Heart of Europe's Middle East Policy', December 14, 2010.

Spencer, C., Bunt, G., Merlini, C. and Roy, O. (2012) *Arab States in Transition: The West's Mediterranean Challenge*, Meeting Transcript, November 8, 2012.

Spencer, C. and Kinzer, S. (2011a) 'Facing Disaster in the Middle East: Do We Only Have Bad Options?', Meeting Transcript, January 12, 2011.

Spencer, C. and Kinzer, S. (2011b) 'Future Prospects for EU Enlargement and Neighborhood Policy', Meeting Transcript, January 13, 2011.

Spencer, C., Philips, C. and Kinninmont, J. (2013) 'Western Policy towards Syria: Ten Recommendations', Working Paper, PP 2013/01, December 2013.

Steinberg, G. (2015) 'A German Strategy for Syria', SWP Comments, October 1, 2015.

Stiftung, F. E. (2011), *Think Tanks in Policy Making: Do They Matter?* Briefing Paper Special Issue, Shanghai Office, September 2011.

UK Foreign and Security Policy Working Group (2015) "Strengthening Britain's Voice in the World", a report of the UK Foreign and Security Policy Working Group, November 3, 2015.

Vandystadt, N. (2014) 'Syrian Refugees will not go back', in *Europolitics*, No. 4984, December 2, 2014.

Wimmen, H. (2014) *Divisive Rule: Sectarianism and Power Maintenance in the Arab Spring: Bahrain, Iraq, Lebanon and Syria*, SWP Research Paper, March 2014.

Wimmen, H. (2015) *Sleepwalking in Brussels*, SWP Comments, October 29, 2015.

1.3 Decision Documents of Core EU Decision-Making Bodies (Communications, Proposals, Decisions, Resolutions, Announcements, Evaluation Reports, etc.)

1) Presentations

Jean-Claude Juncker (2014) My Five Point Plan on Immigration, European People's Party, April 23,

2014.

Federica Mogherini and Strategic Planning Unit of European External Action Service (2015) 'The European Union in a Changing Global Environment: A More Connected, Contested and Complex World', Brussels, June 25, 2015.

2) Key Decision Documents of the European Commission

2021 Strategic Foresight Report on The EU's capacity and freedom to act, COM(2021) 750 final, Brussels, September 8, 2021.

A European Agenda on Migration, COM (2015) 240 final, Brussels, May 13, 2015.

Commission Delegated Regulation on amending the Annex to Regulation (EU) 2019/452 of the European Parliament and of the Council establishing a framework for the screening of foreign direct investments into the Union, (EU) 2020/1298, Brussels, September 18, 2020;

Commission Delegated Regulation on amending the Annex to Regulation (EU) 2019/452 of the European Parliament and of the Council establishing a framework for the screening of foreign direct investments into the Union, (EU) 2021/2126, Brussels, September 29, 2021;

Commission Delegated Regulation (EU) 2022/1 of 20 October 2021 on amending Regulation (EU) 2021/821 of the European Parliament and of the Council as regards the list of dual-use items, CELEX:32022R0001, Brussels, October 20, 2021;

Commission document COM (2008) 319 (Final), May 20, 2008;

Commission document COM (2011) 200 Final, March 8, 2011;

Commission document COM (2011) 303 Final, May 25, 2011;

Commission document JOIN (2012) 27 Final, October 3, 2012;

Commission document MEMO/11/638, September 27, 2011;

Commission document MEMO/13/81, February 8, 2013;

Commission Notice on Guidelines on ranking transparency pursuant to Regulation (EU) 2019/1150 of the European Parliament and of the Council, 2020/C 424/01, Brussels, December 8, 2020;

Commission Recommendation (EU) on Coordination of National Control Lists, 2025/683, April 8, 2025;

Commission Staff Working Document on Executive Summary of the Impact Assessment accompanying the amendment of Council Regulations (EC) No 1225/2009 and (EC) No 597/2009, COM(2013) 192 final; SWD(2013) 105 final; SWD(2013) 106 final, Brussels, April

10, 2013;

Commission Staff Working Document on Impact Assessment accompanying the Proposal for a Regulation on the modernisation of trade defence instruments, COM(2013) 192 final; SWD(2013) 106 final; SWD(2013) 105 final, Brussels, April 10, 2013;

Commission Staff Working Document Accompanying the document Proposal for a Regulation of the European Parliament and of the Council establishing a framework for screening of foreign direct investments into the European Union, SWD(2017) 297 final, Brussels, September 13, 2017;

Commission Staff Working Document on Foreign Direct Investment in the EU Following up on the Commission Communication 'Welcoming Foreign Direct Investment while Protecting Essential Interests' of 13 September 2017, SWD(2019) 108 final, Brussels, March 13, 2019;

Commission Staff Working Document on Single Market Performance Report 2019 accompanying the Annual Sustainable Growth Strategy 2020, COM(2019) 650 final; SWD(2019) 444 final, Brussels, December 17, 2019;

Commission Staff Working Document on Business Journey on the Single Market: Practical Obstacles and Barriers accompanying the Communication on Identifying and addressing barriers to the Single Market, COM(2020) 93 final; SWD(2020) 54 final, Brussels, March 10, 2020;

Commission Staff Working Document on EVALUATION of procedural and jurisdictional aspects of EU merger control, SEC(2021) 156 final; SWD(2021) 67 final; SWD(2021) 66 final, Brussels, March 26, 2021;

Commission Staff Working Document Impact Assessment Accompanying the Proposal for a Regulation of the European Parliament and of the Council on foreign subsidies distorting the internal market, SWD(2021) 99 final, Brussels, May 5, 2021;

Communication on An Integrated Industrial Policy for the Globalisation Era: Putting Competitiveness and Sustainability at Centre Stage, COM(2010) 614 final; SEC(2010) 1272; SEC(2010) 1276, Brussels, October 28, 2010;

Communication on Tackling The Challenges in Commodity Markets and on Raw Materials, COM(2011) 25 final, Brussels, February 2, 2011;

Communication on Industrial Policy: Reinforcing competitiveness, COM(2011) 642 final, Brussels, October 14, 2011;

Communication on A Stronger European Industry for Growth and Economic Recovery: Industrial Policy Communication Update, COM(2012) 582 final; SWD(2012) 297 final; SWD(2012) 298 final; SWD(2012) 299 final, Brussels, October 10, 2012;

Communication on Modernisation of Trade Defence Instruments: Adapting trade defence instruments to the current needs of the European economy, COM(2013) 191 final, Brussels, April 10, 2013.

Communication on For a European Industrial Renaissance, COM(2014) 14 final; SWD(2014) 14 final, Brussels, January 22, 2014;

Communication on An open and secure Europe: making it happen, COM(2014) 154 final, Brussels, March 11, 2014;

Communication on 5G for Europe: An Action Plan, COM(2016) 588 final; SWD(2016) 306 final, Brussels, September 14, 2016;

Communication on Europe's next leaders: the Start-up and Scale-up Initiative, COM(2016) 733 final; SWD(2016) 373 final, Strasbourg, November 22, 2016;

Communication on Investing in a smart, innovative and sustainable Industry: A renewed EU Industrial Policy Strategy, COM(2017) 479 final, Brussels, September 13, 2017;

Communication on the 2017 list of Critical Raw Materials for the EU, COM(2017) 490 final, Brussels, September 13, 2017;

Communication on Welcoming Foreign Direct Investment while Protecting Essential Interests, COM(2017) 494 final, Brussels, September 13, 2017;

Communication on A balanced IP enforcement system responding to today's societal challenges, COM(2017) 707 final; SWD(2017) 430 final, Brussels, November 29, 2017;

Communication on A renewed European Agenda for Research and Innovation - Europe's chance to shape its future: The European Commission's contribution to the Informal EU Leaders' meeting on innovation in Sofia on 16 May 2018, COM(2018) 306 final, Brussels, May 15, 2018;

Communication on Coordinated Plan on Artificial Intelligence, COM(2018) 795 final, Brussels, December 7, 2018;

Communication on Commission Work Programme 2020, COM(2020) 37 final, Brussels, January 29, 2020;

Communication on Secure 5G deployment in the EU - Implementing the EU toolbox, COM(2020)

50 final, Brussels, January 29, 2020;

Communication on A European strategy for data, COM(2020) 66 final, Brussels, February 19, 2020;

Communication on Long term action plan for better implementation and enforcement of single market rules, COM(2020) 94 final, Brussels, March 10, 2020;

Communication on A New Industrial Strategy for Europe, COM(2020) 102 final, Brussels, March 10, 2020.

Communication on An SME Strategy for a sustainable and digital Europe, COM(2020) 103 final, Brussels, March 10, 2020;

Communication on Guidance to the Member States concerning foreign direct investment and free movement of capital from third countries, and the protection of Europe's strategic assets, ahead of the application of Regulation (EU) 2019/452 (FDI Screening Regulation), C(2020) 1981 final, Brussels, March 25, 2020;

Communication on A new ERA for Research and Innovation, COM(2020) 628 final; SWD(2020) 214 final, Brussels, September 30, 2020;

Communication on An Open, Sustainable and Assertive Trade Policy (Trade Policy Review), COM(2021) 66 final, Brussels, February 18, 2021;

Communication on Trade Policy Review - An Open, Sustainable and Assertive Trade Policy, COM(2021) 66 final, Brussels, February 18, 2021;

Communication on the Global Approach to Research and Innovation: Europe's strategy for international cooperation in a changing world, COM(2021) 252 final, Brussels, May 18, 2021;

Communication on taking stock of and updating the reform recommendations for regulation in professional services of 2017, COM(2021) 385 final; SWD(2021) 185 final, Brussels, July 9, 2021;

Communication on 'Fit for 55': delivering the EU's 2030 Climate Target on the way to climate neutrality, COM(2021) 550 final, Brussels, July 14, 2021;

Communication on A competition policy fit for new challenges, COM(2021) 713 final, Brussels, November 18, 2021;

Communication on measures to counteract third-country economic coercion, COM(2021) 774 final, Brussels, December 8, 2021;

Communication on measures within the Commission's powers which the Commission can adopt when it determines, pursuant to the Regulation of the European Parliament and of the Council on the protection of the Union and its Member States from economic coercion by third countries, that the Union takes response measures to counteract a third-country measure of economic coercion, COM(2021) 774 final, Brussels, December 8, 2021;

Joint Communication, A Partnership for Democracy and Shared Prosperity with the Southern Mediterranean, COM (2011) 200 final, March 8, 2011;

Joint Communication, A New Response to a Changing Neighborhood: A Review of European Neighborhood Policy, Brussels, May 25, 2011;

Joint Communication, Delivering on a New Neighborhood Policy, JOIN (2012) 14 final, Brussels, May 15, 2012;

Joint Communication, European Neighborhood Policy: Working towards a Stronger Partnership, JOIN (2013) 4 final, March 20, 2013;

Joint Communication, Neighborhood at the Crossroads: Implementation of the European Neighborhood Policy in 2013, JOIN (2014), 12 final, Brussels, March 27, 2014;

Joint Consultation Paper: towards a New European Neighborhood Policy, Join (2015) 6 final, Brussels, March 4, 2015;

Joint Communication on The Global Gateway, JOIN(2021) 30 final, Brussels, December 1, 2021;

Next Operational Steps in EU-Turkey Cooperation in the Field of Migration, COM (2016), 166 finals, March 16, 2016;

Proposal for a Regulation on establishing a common procedure for international protection in the Union and repealing Directive 2013/32/EU, COM(2016) 467 final, Brussels, July 13, 2016;

Proposal for a Regulation on establishing a framework for screening of foreign direct investments into the European Union, COM(2017) 487 final, Brussels, September 13, 2017;

Proposal for a Regulation of the European Parliament and of the Council on establishing the space programme of the Union and the European Union Agency for the Space Programme and repealing Regulations (EU) No 912/2010, (EU) No 1285/2013, (EU) No 377/2014 and Decision 541/2014/EU, COM(2018) 447 final; SWD(2018) 327 final; SWD(2018) 328 final, 2018/0236 (COD), Brussels, June 6, 2018;

Proposal for a Regulation of the European Parliament and of the Council on European data governance (Data Governance Act), COM(2020) 767 final, 2020/0340 (COD), Brussels, November 25, 2020;

Proposal for a Regulation of the European Parliament and of the Council on Laying Down

Harmonised Rules on Artificial Intelligence (Artificial Intelligence Act) and Amending Certain Union Legislative Acts, COM(2021) 206 final; SEC(2021) 167 final; SWD(2021) 84 final; SWD(2021) 85 final, 2021/0106 (COD), Brussels, April 21, 2021;

Proposal for a Regulation of the European Parliament and of the Council on Foreign Subsidies Distorting the Internal market, COM(2021) 223 final; SWD(2021) 99 final; SWD(2021) 100 final; SEC(2021) 182 final, 2021/0114 (COD), Brussels, May 5, 2021;

Proposal for a Council Recommendation on a Pact for Research and Innovation in Europe, COM(2021) 407 final, 2021/0230 (NLE), Brussels, July 16, 2021;

Proposal for a Decision of the European Parliament and of the Council on establishing the 2030 Policy Programme 'Path to the Digital Decade', COM(2021) 574 final; SWD(2021) 247 final, 2021/0293 (COD), Brussels, September 15, 2021;

Proposal for a Decision of the European Parliament and of the Council on establishing the 2030 Policy Programme 'Path to the Digital Decade', COM(2021) 574 final, Brussels, September 16, 2021;

Proposal for a Regulation of the European Parliament and of the Council on the protection of the Union and its Member States from Economic Coercion by Third Countries, COM(2021) 775 final; SEC(2021) 418 final; SWD(2021) 371 final; SWD(2021) 372 final, 2021/0406 (COD), Brussels, December 8, 2021;

Quantum Europe Strategy: Quantum Europe in a Changing World, COM (2025) 363 final, July 2, 2025;

Report on the Implementation of the European Security Strategy: Providing Security in a Changing World, S407/08, December 11, 2008;

Report on the implementation of Regulation (EU) 2021/821 setting up a Union regime for the control of exports, brokering, technical assistance, transit and transfer of dual-use items, COM(2021) 716 final, Brussels, November 23, 2021;

Report on the implementation of Regulation (EU) 2021/821 setting up a Union regime for the control of exports, brokering, technical assistance, transit and transfer of dual-use items, COM(2022) 434 final, Brussels, September 1, 2022;

The EU Startup and Scaleup Strategy, Choose Europe to start and scale, COM (2025) 270 final, May 28, 2025;

The EU Startup and Scaleup Strategy, Choose Europe to start and scale, SWD (2025) 138 final, May

28, 2025;

The European Agenda on Security, COM (2015) 185 final, Strasbourg, April 28, 2015;

The Global Approach to Migration and Mobility, COM (2011) 743 Final, Brussels, November 18, 2011.

3) Key Decision Documents of the Council of the European Union

Council Conclusions on Developments in the Southern Neighborhood, 3069th Foreign Affairs Council Meeting, Brussels, February 21, 2011;

Council Conclusions on the European Neighborhood Policy, 3101st Foreign Affairs Council Meeting, June 20, 2011;

Council Conclusions on EU's Response to the Developments in Southern Neighborhood, 3130th Foreign Affairs Council Meeting, December 1, 2011;

Council Conclusions on Migration, EUCO 22/15, Brussels, June 26, 2015;

Council Conclusions on Migration, EUCO 26/15, October 16, 2015;

Council Conclusions on the Review of the European Neighborhood Policy, Press Release, 926/15, December 14, 2015;

Council Conclusions on European Council meeting (20 and 21 October 2016), EUCO 31/16, Brussels, October 21, 2016;Council Conclusions on European Council meeting (22 and 23 June 2017), EUCO 8/17, Brussels, June 23, 2017;

Council Conclusions on Jobs, Growth and Competitiveness, EUCO 1/18; CO EUR 1; CONCL 1, Brussels, March 23, 2018;

Council Conclusions on Accelerating knowledge circulation in the EU, 9507/18; RECH 241; COMPET 384, Brussels, May 29, 2018;

Council Conclusions on A future EU Industrial Policy Strategy, 14832/18; COMPET 824; IND 376; MI 904, Brussels, November 29, 2018;

Council Conclusions on Space as an enabler, 9248/19; ESPACE 50; RECH 260; COMPET 396; MI 433; IND 172; EU-GNSS 28; TRANS 331; TELECOM 220; ENER 266; EMPL 269; CSDP/PSDC 238; CFSP/PESC 376, Brussels, May 17, 2019;

Council Conclusions on an EU Industrial Policy Strategy: A Vision for 2030, 9263/19; 9706/19, Brussels, May 27, 2019;

Council Conclusions on 'Space as an Enabler', 9248/19; 9713/19, Brussels, May 28, 2019;

Council Conclusions on the future governance of the European Research Area (ERA) (Approval), 14126/21, Brussels, November 19, 2021;

Council Conclusions on European Council meeting (March 24 and 25, 2022), EUCO 1/22, Brussels, March 25th, 2022;Council of the EU document 6496/08 (Press 41), February 18, 2008;

Council of the EU document 7652/1/08 REV 1, May 20, 2008;

Council of the EU document 11887/08 (Press 213), July 15, 2008;

Council of the European Union, European Security Strategy: A Secure Europe in a Better World, Brussels, December 2003;

Foreign Affairs Council document of Background on Trade Issues, September 23, 2011;

Joint Staff Working Paper Document, Implementation of European Neighborhood Policy: Partnership for Democracy and Shared Prosperity with the Southern Mediterranean Partners Report, SWD (2015) 75 final, Brussels, March 25, 2015;

Position of the Council at first reading with a view to the adoption of a Regulation of the European Parliament and of the Council amending Regulation (EU) 2016/1036 on protection against dumped imports from countries not members of the European Union and Regulation (EU) 2016/1037 on protection against subsidised imports from countries not members of the European Union, 2013/0103 (COD), Brussels, April 3, 2018;

Press Release: European Council Conclusions on Migration, 72/16, February 18, 2016;

Proposal for a Regulation amending Regulation (EU) 2016/1036 on protection against dumped imports from countries not members of the European Union and Regulation (EU) 2016/1037 on protection against subsidised imports from countries not members of the European Union, 2016/0351 (COD), Brussels, November 9, 2016;

Providing Security in a Changing World: Report on the Implementation of the European Security Strategy, S407/08, Brussels, December 11, 2009;

Regulation on setting up a Community regime for the control of exports, transfer, brokering and transit of dual use items (Recast), (EC) No 428/2009, Brussels, May 5, 2009;

Statement of the EU Heads of State or Government, Brussels, March 7, 2016.

4) Key Decision Documents of the European Parliament

Amendments on the proposal for a regulation amending Council Regulations (EC) No 1225/2009 and (EC) No 597/2009 on protection against dumped and subsidised imports from non-EU countries, COM(2013)0192–C7-0097/2013–2013/0103(COD), Brussels, February 5, 2014;

Briefing - Distortive foreign subsidies regulation A level playing-field for the single market, PE 690.700, June 1, 2022;

EU-US EXPLAINER - Regulation of the digital sector, PE 696.179, July 1, 2021;

Parliament document B6-0295/2008, May 28, 2008;

Parliament document of Policy Briefing, May 30, 2008;

Parliament document B7-0199/2011, April 7, 2011;

Parliament document A7-0400/2011, December 14, 2011;

Parliament document SPEECH/12/23, January 24, 2012;

Report on the proposal for a regulation of the European Parliament and of the Council establishing a framework for screening of foreign direct investments into the European Union, A8-0198/2018, June 4, 2018.

5) Key Decision Documents of the European Parliament and the Council of the European Union

Directive (EU) 2013/33 of 26 June 2013 on standards for the reception of applicants for international protection (recast), CELEX:32013L0033, Brussels, June 29, 2013;

Directive on common procedures for granting and withdrawing international protection (recast), Directive 2013/32/EU, June 26, 2013;

Proposal for a Regulation on a Single Market For Digital Services (Digital Services Act) and amending Directive 2000/31/EC, COM(2020)825 final; 2020/0361(COD), Brussels, December 15, 2020;

Proposal for a Regulation on contestable and fair markets in the digital sector (Digital Markets Act), COM(2020)842 final; 2020/0374(COD), Brussels, December 15, 2020;

Proposal for a Regulation on the protection of the Union and its Member States from economic coercion by third countries, COM(2021)775 final; 2021/0406(COD), Brussels, December 8, 2021;

Regulation on applying a scheme of generalised tariff preferences and repealing Council Regulation (EC) No 732/2008, (EU) No 978/2012, Brussels, October 25, 2012;

Regulation on the protection of natural persons with regard to the processing of personal data and on the free movement of such data (General Data Protection Regulation), (EU) 2016/679, Brussels, April 27, 2016;

Regulation on protection against dumped imports from countries not members of the European Union (codification), Regulation (EU) 2016/1036, June 8, 2016;

Regulation on protection against subsidised imports from countries not members of the European Union (codification), Regulation (EU) 2016/1037, June 8, 2016;

Regulation on amending Regulation (EU) 2016/1036 on protection against dumped imports from countries not members of the European Union and Regulation (EU) 2016/1037 on protection against subsidised imports from countries not members of the European Union, 2016/0351(COD), October 3, 2017;

Regulation on amending Regulation (EU) 2016/1036 on protection against dumped imports from countries not members of the European Union and Regulation (EU) 2016/1037 on protection against subsidised imports from countries not members of the European Union, PE-CONS 50/17, Brussels, November 27, 2017;

Regulation on amending Regulation (EU) 2016/1036 on protection against dumped imports from countries not members of the European Union and Regulation (EU) 2016/1037 on protection against subsidised imports from countries not members of the European Union, Regulation (EU) 2017/2321, December 12, 2017;

Regulation on amending Regulation (EU) 2016/1036 on protection against dumped imports from countries not members of the European Union and Regulation (EU) 2016/1037 on protection against subsidised imports from countries not members of the European Union, Regulation (EU) 2018/825, May 30, 2018;

Regulation on establishing a framework for the screening of foreign direct investments into the Union, PE-CONS 72/18, Brussels, February 20, 2019;

Regulation on establishing a framework for the screening of foreign direct investments into the Union, Regulation (EU) 2019/452, March 19, 2019;

Regulation on ENISA and on information and communications technology cybersecurity certification (Cybersecurity Act) (Text with EEA relevance), (EU) 2019/881, Brussels, April 17, 2019;

Regulation on amending Regulation (EU) No 654/2014 concerning the exercise of the Union's rights for the application and enforcement of international trade rules, Regulation (EU) 2021/167, February 10, 2021;

Regulation on setting up a Union regime for the control of exports, brokering, technical assistance, transit and transfer of dual-use items (recast), (EU) 2021/821 (OJ L 206, 11.6.2021, p. 1),

Brussels, May 20, 2021;

Regulation on the access of third-country economic operators, goods and services to the Union's public procurement and concession markets and procedures supporting negotiations on access of Union economic operators, goods and services to the public procurement and concession markets of third countries (International Procurement Instrument-IPI), Regulation (EU) 2022/1031, Brussels, June 23, 2022;

Regulation on foreign subsidies distorting the internal market, (EU) 2022/2560, Brussels, December 14, 2022.

II. Literature in Chinese (Including Translated Works)

2.1 Books

Wang, Bo (2010) *A Study of the European Union's Middle East Policy* [欧盟中东政策研究]. Beijing: Current Affairs Press [Shishi Chubanshe].

Niu, Song (2011) *EU Governance of Democracy in the Middle East* [欧盟的中东民主治理研究]. Beijing: Current Affairs Press [Shishi Chubanshe].

Zhongguo Xiandai Guoji Guanxi Yanjiuyuan (Ed., 2004). *European Think Tanks and Their Research on China* [欧洲思想库及其对华研究]. Beijing: Current Affairs Press [Shishi Chubanshe].

Zhang, Chun (2007) *American Think Tanks and the One-China Policy* [美国思想库与一个中国政策]. Shanghai: Shanghai People's Publishing House [Shanghai Renmin Chubanshe].

Zhu, Xufeng (2009) *Chinese Think Tanks: Influence in the Policy Process* [中国思想库：政策过程中的影响力研究]. Beijing: Tsinghua University Press [Qinghua Daxue Chubanshe].

Wang, Lili (2010) *Revolving Door: A Study of American Think Tanks* [旋转门：美国思想库研究]. Beijing: National Academy of Governance Press [Guojia Xingzheng Xueyuan Chubanshe].

Chu, Ming (2013) *A Comparative Study of American and European Think Tanks* [美欧智库比较研究]. Beijing: China Social Sciences Press [Zhongguo Shehui Kexue Chubanshe].

Tang, Lei (Ed., 2015) *Knowledge Production in Contemporary Think Tanks* [当代智库的知识

生产]. Beijing: China Social Sciences Press [Zhongguo Shehui Kexue Chubanshe].

Li, Shangzhong (1994) *The Third Way: A Study of Marcuse and Habermas's Critical Social Theory* [第三条道路：马尔库塞和哈贝马斯的社会批判理论研究]. Beijing: Xueyuan Press [Xueyuan Chubanshe].

Zhang, Guofeng (2002) *A Utopian Vision of a Just World: Interpreting Habermas's Theory of Communicative Action* [关于一个公正世界的乌托邦构想：解读哈马贝斯交往行为理论]. Jinan: Shandong People's Press [Shandong Renmin Chubanshe].

Habermas, Jürgen. *The Horizon of Modernity: Interviews with Habermas* [现代性的地平线：哈贝马斯访谈录]. trans. Li Yaquns. Shanghai: Shanghai People's Publishing House [Shanghai Renmin Chubanshe], 1997.

2.2 Articles

Fang, Lexian (2012) 'Recent Trends in European Think Tanks' Perceptions of China: A Case Study of the European Council on Foreign Relations' [欧洲智库对华认知的近期倾向：以欧洲对外关系委员会为例]. *Shijie Jingji yu Zhengzhi Luntan [World Economics and Politics Forum]*, No. 1, pp. 95-104.

Pan, Zhongqi (2010) 'Recent Developments of European Think Tanks and Their Research on China' [欧洲智库的最新发展及其对华研究]. *Xiandai Guoji Guanxi [Contemporary International Relations]*, No. 10, pp. 8-14.

Wang, Yan (2009) 'The Role of European Think Tanks in EU Decision-Making toward China' [欧洲思想库在欧盟对华决策中的地位和作用]. *Ouzhou Yanjiu[European Studies]*, No. 2, pp. 92-104.

Shanghai Academy of Social Sciences Think Tank Research Center Project Group (2014) 'An Empirical Study on the Influence of Chinese Think Tanks and Policy Recommendations' [中国智库影响力的实证研究与政策建议]. *Shehui Kexue [Social Sciences]*, No. 4, pp. 4-21.

Yang, Ye and Zhang Jindi (2014) 'German Political Foundations in China: Operational Models and Characteristics of Public Diplomacy' [德国政治基金会在华的工作方式及其公共外交特征评析]. *Shehui Kexue [Social Sciences]*, No. 4, pp. 22-28.

Wu, Jiang (2015) 'German Think Tanks' Interpretation of the Belt and Road Initiative' [德国

智库解读‘一带一路’战略]. *Xuexi Shibao*, May 11, 2015.

2.3 Translated Works

Max Weber *Science and Politics* [学术与政治]. trans. Qian, Q. X. et al., Guilin: Guangxi Normal University Press [Guangxi Shifan Daxue Chubanshe], 2004.

Pierre Bourdieu. *Cultural Capital and Social Alchemy* [文化资本与社会炼金术]. trans. Bao, Y. M. Shanghai: Shanghai People's Publishing House [Shanghai Renmin Chubanshe], 1997.

Jürgen Habermas. *Technology and Science as 'Ideology'* [作为‘意识形态’的技术与科学]. trans. Li, L. and Guo, G. Y. Shanghai: Xuelin Press [Xuelin Chubanshe], 1999.

Jürgen Habermas et al. *Globalization and Politics* [全球化与政治]. trans. Wang, X. D. et al., Beijing: Central Compilation & Translation Press [Zhongyang Bianyi Chubanshe], 2000.

Jürgen Habermas, J. *The Structural Transformation of the Public Sphere* [公共领域的结构转型]. trans. Cao, W. D. et al., Shanghai: Xuelin Press [Xuelin Chubanshe], 1999.

Jürgen Habermas (2001) *Legitimation Crisis* [合法化危机]. trans. Liu, B. C. and Cao, W. D., Shanghai: Shanghai People's Publishing House [Shanghai Renmin Chubanshe], 2001.

Jürgen Habermas. *Communication and the Evolution of Society* [交往与社会进化]. trans. Zhang B. S., Chongqing: Chongqing Publishing House [Chongqing Chubanshe], 1989.

Appendix I: List of Field Interviews with Experts of European Think Tanks

Location	Institution	Position	Interviewee
Brussels	Madariaga – College of Europe Foundation	Executive Director	Pierre Defraigne
		Project Manager	Ariane de Bellefroid
Brussels	Carnegie Europe	Director	Jan Techau
Brussels	Friedrich Naumann Foundation	Head of Brussels Office	Hans H. Stein
Brussels	European Institute of Asian Studies (EIAS)	Chief Executive Officer	Axel Goethals
		Chairman	David Fouquet
Brussels	European Policy Centre (EPC)	Chief Executive Officer	Fabian Zuleeg
Brussels	Centre for European Policy Studies (CEPS)	Transatlantic Affairs Expert	Jacques Pelkmans
		Head of EU External Policy Research Team	Steven Blockmans
Dublin	Institute of International and European Affairs (IIEA)	Chairman	Brendan Halligan
		Vice Chairman	Jill Donoghue
		Head of East Asia Programme	Eoin McDonnell
Berlin	Free University of Berlin, NFG Research Centre	Head of Research Group	Dr. May-Britt U. Stumbaum
Berlin	Heinrich Böll Foundation	Head of Asia Programme	Clemens Kunze; Ella Daschkey
Berlin	German Institute for International and Security Affairs (SWP)	Head of Asia Division	Dr. Hanns Günter Hilpert
Berlin	Association of German Chambers of Industry and Commerce (DIHK)	Executive Director	Benjamin Leipold

Location	Institution	Position	Interviewee
Berlin	Friedrich Ebert Foundation	Head of International Cooperation, Asia-Pacific Department	Katja Müller
		Head of Brussels Office	Uwe Optenhögel
Berlin	Konrad Adenauer Foundation	Director of International Cooperation Department	Dr. Stephan Friedrich
Bonn	German Development Institute (DIE)	Research Fellow, Asia Division	Dr. Thomas Fues
		Research Fellow, Asia Division	Dr. Axel Berger
Brussels	German Marshall Fund of the United States	Transatlantic Relations Expert	Guillaume Xavier-Bender
		Asia Programme Assistant	Sophie Dembinski
Paris	European Union Institute for Security Studies (EUISS)	Director	Antonio Missiroli
		Analyst, Asia Affairs	Eva Pejsova
Brussels	Bruegel	Secretary-General	Matt Dann
		Senior Fellow	André Sapir
Brussels	Global Governance Institute (GGI)	Director	Joachim Koops
Leuven	KU Leuven, Centre for EU Studies	Director	Stephan Keukeleire
Bruges	University of Michigan, European Studies Programme	Director	Stephen Brooks
Bruges	NATO-related Expert; Professor at Saint Leo University	Professor	Marco Rimanelli
Bergen	University of Bergen, Department of Political Science	Head of Department	Hans Gasemyr
Stockholm	Stockholm International Peace Research Institute (SIPRI)	Head of China Research Team	Richard Ghiasy
Berlin	German Council on Foreign Relations (DGAP)	Head of Asia Economic Research	Claudia Schmucker; Bernt Berger
Brussels	Egmont – Royal Institute for International Relations	Head of European External Relations Research Team	Sven Biscop
The Hague	Clingendael Institute	Senior Research Fellow	Frans-Paul van der Putten
Amsterdam	Leiden University, Leiden Asia Centre	Senior Research Fellow	Frank Pieke; Lily Spranger

Appendix II: An Institutional Profile of the Brussels European and Global Economic Laboratory (Bruegel)

Bruegel is widely recognized as one of the most prominent independent think tanks in the field of international political economy in Europe. Since its establishment in 2005, it has steadily consolidated its position as a key actor in shaping policy debates both within Europe and in the broader global economic governance landscape. Headquartered in Brussels—the de facto administrative and political center of the European Union (EU), Bruegel is institutionally positioned at the heart of European policymaking networks. Its stated mission is "to improve the quality of economic policy decision-making in Europe through open and fact-based research, analysis, and debate," a formulation that underscores its commitment to methodological rigor, epistemic transparency, and policy relevance. Bruegel's membership structure is notably hybrid in nature, encompassing not only governments of EU member states and European-level institutions, but also a wide range of globally influential multinational corporations, thereby reflecting a governance model that integrates public and private stakeholders. In 2008, Bruegel was identified as the "fastest-growing think tank" worldwide, an early indication of its rapidly expanding influence. According to the Global Go To Think Tank Index Report 2020 released by the University of Pennsylvania, Bruegel ranked first both among "Top Think Tanks in Western Europe" and "Top Think Tanks Worldwide (Non-U.S.) in Economic Policy," and is now widely regarded as one of the most policy-influential think tanks in Europe.

I. Institutional Overview

1.1 Origins of Bruegel and the Meaning of Its Name

The name "Bruegel" carries dual significance. Firstly, it is an acronym for "Brussels

European and Global Economic Laboratory." Secondly, it stands as a tribute to the renowned 16th-century painter Pieter Bruegel the Elder. The founders of Bruegel believed that the elder Bruegel's paintings depicted the lives of ordinary Europeans, drawing inspiration from their daily economic activities—a philosophy that aligns with the think tank's emphasis on "fact-based research and analysis." Moreover, Pieter Bruegel the Elder's life story exemplifies European diversity. Born in the Netherlands, he studied painting in Belgium and Italy, and received guidance from artists in other European countries such as Germany. He died in Brussels in 1569, a city then under Spanish occupation where French was the common language. Despite the frequent wars during his lifetime, cultural exchanges among European nations flourished, and Europeans demonstrated an unprecedented openness to the world. The painter's life journey resonates with the EU principle of "Unity in Diversity," and naming the think tank after him reflects its pan-European character, transcending single-country studies.

1.2 The Founding and Development of Bruegel

The origins of Bruegel trace back to an initiative jointly proposed in the autumn of 2002 by Jean Pisani-Ferry, then Executive Chairman of the French Prime Minister's Economic Analysis Council and Senior Economic Advisor to the French Ministry of Finance, and French economist Nicolas Véron. Noting that dialogue among European economic policy researchers, practitioners, and policymakers at the time suffered from low efficiency and poor policy relevance, the pair sought to establish a European economic policy research organization modeled on leading American think tanks. This initiative subsequently gained the endorsement of French President Jacques Chirac and German Chancellor Gerhard Schröder, and was formally proposed at the intergovernmental level between France and Germany. On January 22, 2003, France and Germany issued a joint declaration commemorating the 40th anniversary of the Élysée Treaty, in which Article 30 fully articulated the vision for establishing a Bruegel-like think tank: "To strengthen Europe's position in international trade and the economy, to enable Europe to contribute fully to international debates on economic, financial and trade policies, and to enhance Europe's analytical and proposal-making capabilities in these fields, France and Germany have decided to launch a European initiative, namely the establishment of a European center for the international economy dedicated to achieving these objectives. This center could be located in Brussels and would gradually be open to the member states of all European partners, EU institutions, and private sector companies."

This important intergovernmental joint declaration reflected the value France and Germany placed on high-quality economic policy research institutes. The text of Article 30 precisely outlines many features of today's Bruegel: a focus on economic policy, a Brussels location, and the possibility of opening membership to EU member states, institutions, and private sector stakeholders. Following the Franco-German declaration, the initiative progressed in stages. First, a Franco-German project working group reached agreement on the overall concept for Bruegel, particularly its governance charter. Second, consultations were held with other EU member states within the framework of the Economic and Financial Committee, ultimately leading to confirmation of participation in March 2004 from eleven member states: Belgium, Denmark, France, Germany, Hungary, Ireland, Italy, the Netherlands, Poland, Spain, and the United Kingdom. Third, Jean Pisani-Ferry and Nicolas Véron engaged with European companies, resulting in 17 entities confirming their participation by the end of 2004. On August 10, 2004, the legal entity of Bruegel (temporarily named the "European Centre for the International Economy") was registered as a Belgian International Non-Profit Association (AISBL), and the first Board of Directors was elected in December 2004 by the founding member states and corporate members.

On January 17, 2005, the "European Centre for the International Economy" held its inaugural Board of Directors meeting. EU Competition Commissioner Mario Monti was elected Chair, Jean Pisani-Ferry was appointed Director, and the think tank's name was officially established as Bruegel. The same year, in May, Bruegel held its first seminar (on the theme of changes in productivity), and in June, its first high-level conference (on the theme "The Challenge of Regional Trade Agreements to Multilateralism"). In September 2005, Bruegel officially published its first research paper—*Globalisation and the Reform of European Social Models*, authored by André Sapir, a professor at the Free University of Brussels (ULB). Presented as a policy brief to an informal meeting of the Economic and Financial Affairs Council (ECOFIN), the paper was subsequently widely cited in European economic debates, establishing the think tank's reputation for publishing authoritative policy-oriented economic analysis.

From its inception, Bruegel has aligned itself with the trajectory of European integration. Its researchers and research topics transcend national perspectives, embody a distinctive pan-European character, and focus specifically on economic policy issues. Conducting research aimed at advancing European interests, Bruegel offers a global perspective for analyzing European affairs and a European perspective for analyzing global affairs, making significant contributions to understanding Europe's role in the evolving global political and economic order. Against this backdrop, Bruegel rapidly grew into a world-class independent think tank. In 2008, it was named the world's fastest-growing think tank, and the 2012 *Global Go To Think Tank Index Report* ranked it as the top think tank in Western Europe.

1.3 Nature, Objectives, and Core Values of Bruegel

In terms of organizational nature, Bruegel is a non-profit European think tank that is dedicated to providing independent, non-partisan, and high-quality economic policy analysis for European policymakers, while simultaneously emphasizing both the policy orientation and the professional rigor of think tank research. Its guiding mission is articulated as follows: "to improve the quality of European economic policy decision-making through open and fact-based research, analysis, and debate." The three core values to which Bruegel explicitly adheres are "independence, openness, and excellence." In May 2006, Bruegel issued a formal statement on research integrity, in which it reaffirmed its institutional independence by committing itself to avoiding any conflicts of interest related to political, national, or commercial considerations, as well as any factors that might undermine the impartiality and objectivity of its research outputs.

Given its positioning as an international economic research-oriented think tank, Bruegel's development objectives can be further specified along four principal dimensions. First, it seeks to formulate evidence-based policy recommendations, emphasizing that its research is neither constrained by any particular political ideology nor intended to represent predetermined policy positions, but rather grounded in rigorous analysis of economic developments with the aim of identifying scientifically sound policy options. Second, it conducts independent, policy-oriented research on issues rooted in European interests; while its Board and various stakeholders collectively assess policy needs and define research topics—particularly in areas such as the EU and global governance—once these topics are established, the research teams operate independently in exploring answers, and Bruegel as an institution does not adopt any official policy position. Third, it functions as a platform for interaction and exchange among researchers, policymakers, the business community, and civil society, facilitating dialogue through seminars, publications, podcasts, and other formats, thereby enhancing mutual understanding of international issues. Fourth, it places strong emphasis on the internationalization of think tank development, aiming to provide a European perspective on international economic issues and to disseminate and promote European viewpoints on issues in international political economy.

II. Internal Governance and Organizational Structure

2.1 Organizational Structure

2.1.1 Assembly of Members

The Assembly of Members is the highest governing body of Bruegel, meeting three times annually. Its primary responsibilities are threefold: 1. approving the appointment of the Board of Directors and senior officers; (2) approving the budget and financial statements; and (3) participating in the design of research programs. Bruegel's members primarily consist of three categories: state members, corporate members, and institutional members.

According to Bruegel's 2022 Annual Report, its state members included 18 European countries: Cyprus, Luxembourg, Malta, Slovakia, Austria, Denmark, Finland, Hungary, Ireland, Belgium, the Netherlands, Sweden, France, Italy, Spain, the United Kingdom, and Germany.

Corporate members included 43 large international companies such as Apple, Amazon Europe, Facebook, Google, Huawei, Microsoft, HSBC, Électricité de France (EDF), Morgan Stanley, Moody's, and Banco Santander.

Institutional members included 20 financial institutions such as the Bank of France, Bank of England, Bank of Finland, Bank of Italy, Central Bank of Luxembourg, Central Bank of Ireland, National Bank of Romania, European Investment Bank, the Finnish Pension Alliance (TELA), and the Japan Machinery Center for Trade and Investment (JMC). Bruegel's state and institutional members are predominantly European, while its corporate members are more international, encompassing renowned multinational corporations in technology, finance, the internet, and other sectors.

2.1.2 Board of Directors

The Board of Directors determines the think tank's future development strategy, research plans, and budget. However, it is not responsible for research outcomes, which remain the responsibility of the researchers under the supervision of an editorial board. The Board's main responsibilities are threefold: 1. collaborating with the management team to guide the think tank's future development strategy; 2. approving the budget and the annual research program based on broad consultation with members; and, 3. approving the admission of new members and senior officers. In 2023, the Board consists of 11 senior figures from government, business, academia, civil society, and the media, designed to reflect the diversity of Bruegel's stakeholders. The Board meets three times a year, and members exercise their voting power in a personal capacity.

The current Board of Directors is chaired by Erkki Liikanen, former EU Commissioner and former Finnish Minister of Finance. The other ten Board members include prominent individuals such as Agnès Bénassy-Quéré, Deputy Governor of the Bank of France; Simone Mori, Head of Europe for Enel S.p.A; and Caroline de Gruyter, journalist and columnist for NRC Handelsblad (Netherlands), serving a term from 2020 to 2022. The Chair of the Scientific Council, the Director, and the Deputy Director of Bruegel also attend Board meetings but without voting power.

2.1.3 Scientific Council

The Scientific Council is composed of internationally renowned economists and serves as the principal body responsible for ensuring the academic quality and scholarly rigor of Bruegel's research outputs. Members of the Scientific Council are appointed for a term of three years. Its core functions include both evaluative and advisory roles. On the one hand, it systematically assesses the quality of Bruegel's research activities; on the other hand, it provides forward-looking recommendations to both the institute and its Board regarding future research priorities and emerging policy-related topics. More specifically, the Scientific Council conducts its evaluative activities through four distinct mechanisms operating at different temporal intervals. First, it undertakes a comprehensive evaluation every three years, culminating in the publication of an Evaluation Report on Bruegel's Research Activities. Since its establishment, Bruegel has undergone multiple independent evaluations (2007, 2010, 2013, 2016, 2019, and 2022), during which each academic publication is systematically assessed and assigned a grade ranging from A to E. Second, it conducts annual evaluations, during which Council members meet with researchers, participate in Board meetings, and provide feedback on both strategic orientation and research quality. Third, quarterly evaluations are carried out to ensure ongoing monitoring of research progress. Fourth, continuous evaluation mechanisms are embedded within the pre-publication process, including internal discussions, editorial review, and peer review, thereby ensuring quality control at multiple stages of the research production cycle.

For the 2020-2022 term, the Scientific Council was chaired by Arnoud Boot, Co-Director of the Amsterdam Center for Law & Economics (ACLE). Other members included Monica de Bolle, Adjunct Lecturer at the Johns Hopkins School of Advanced International Studies (SAIS), and Meredith A. Crowley, a research fellow at the Centre for Economic Policy Research (CEPR), among other distinguished economists.

2.1.4. Executive Management

The Executive Management is responsible for the day-to-day administrative and operational management of the institute, including administrative coordination, oversight of research activities, editorial responsibilities, preparation of research programs, and organization of Board meetings. The executive team operates under the leadership of the Director, who holds ultimate responsibility for the coordination of institutional functions and the implementation of strategic decisions.

2.2 Funding, Governance, and Transparency

In order to maintain the independence and objectivity of its research, Bruegel has developed a carefully calibrated funding model designed to balance the interests of public and private stakeholders. A key institutional rule stipulates that no single member may contribute more than 5 percent of the total budget, thereby preventing disproportionate influence by any individual funding source. From a structural perspective, Bruegel's financial resources are divided into two primary categories: core funding and non-core funding.

Core funding is derived primarily from annual membership subscriptions and accounts for approximately 80 percent of the institute's total budget. These contributions are made by state members, institutional members, and corporate members. Notably, all corporate members contribute at a uniform rate of €50,000 per year, regardless of company size, thereby reinforcing the principle of equality among private-sector participants. In contrast, contributions from EU member states are determined according to a tiered system, with payment levels calibrated based on the size of the country's economy and government capacity. According to Bruegel's 2022 financial statements, state members are categorized into five tiers. France, Germany, the United Kingdom, Spain, and Italy belong to the highest tier, each contributing €209,179 annually, whereas countries such as Cyprus, Malta, and Luxembourg contribute at the lowest tier, amounting to €34,863. Institutional members are also subject to differentiated contribution levels: most national central banks contribute approximately €25,000, while larger institutions, such as the European Investment Bank (EIB), contribute €50,000.

Non-core funding consists primarily of research grants provided by EU institutions—most notably through programs such as *Horizon 2020*—as well as donations from private foundations. These externally funded research projects not only provide financial support but also facilitate interaction between Bruegel and EU policymaking bodies, thereby enhancing the policy relevance of its research and enabling it to address pressing real-world policy challenges faced by Europe.

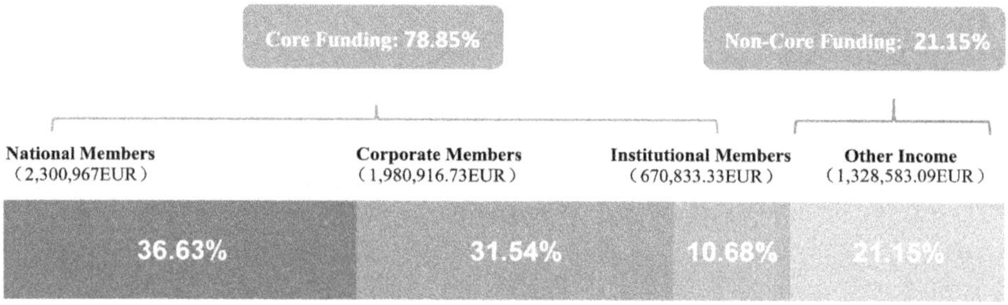

Appendix Figure 1: Funding Structure of Bruegel (2022)

Source: Compiled by the author based on Bruegel's 2022 Annual Report

Moreover, Bruegel adheres to the principle of financial transparency. Detailed income and expenditure statements are publicly disclosed in its annual reports, and member states have the right to request an audit at any time. Bruegel also follows the principle of financial sustainability, meticulously managing its funds, maintaining a cash reserve of €2 million, and refraining from using funds for financial investment. In terms of governance, Bruegel employees are required to sign statements regarding research integrity and external interests to ensure research integrity and the think tank's independence and transparency. Bruegel has received a five-star rating (out of five) from the international transparency assessment non-governmental organization Transparify, in recognition of its openness regarding financing and governance. Additionally, Bruegel implements a Gender Equality Plan (GEP) aiming for gender balance in its management and board.

III. Research Agenda and Institutional Output

3.1 Composition and Structure of Research Staff

Bruegel has established a highly internationalized and professionally diverse research team, characterized by a wide range of disciplinary backgrounds and institutional experiences, thereby enabling it to address complex issues in international political economy from multiple analytical perspectives. The institute's research personnel are organized into several distinct categories, including Senior Fellows, Research Fellows, Non-resident Fellows, Visiting Fellows, Affiliate Fellows, and Research Assistants, each category reflecting different degrees of institutional affiliation, research engagement, and professional seniority. The overall research team operates under the supervision of a Director of Research, who is responsible for coordinating research activities and ensuring the coherence of the institute's research agenda. Senior Fellows are typically based in Brussels on a full-time basis, thereby maintaining close proximity to EU institutions and policy networks. In addition to its core research staff, Bruegel provides institutional support through research assistants, administrative assistants, and interns, who contribute to both the substantive and operational dimensions of research production. According to Bruegel's publicly available annual report for 2022, the institute's research team comprises 24 Non-resident Fellows, 12 Senior Fellows, 6 Visiting Fellows, 4 Affiliate Fellows, 1 Research Fellow, and 12 Research Assistants, amounting to a total of 59 research personnel.

In summary, the Bruegel research team has three distinctive characteristics. First, it is highly international, with researchers hailing from countries such as France, Italy, Germany, the United States, China, Turkey, Poland, and Denmark. Senior Fellows and Visiting Fellows are often tenured professors at renowned universities. Second, it features diverse academic backgrounds. While most researchers hold PhDs in economics, they are typically interdisciplinary experts with backgrounds in economics, political science, history, engineering, and other fields. Third, its members possess rich professional experience. Some researchers have held key positions in government ministries, EU institutions, or international organizations, or have served as economic advisors to large multinational corporations like Shell. Consequently, they offer unique perspectives and valuable empirical insights into policymaking mechanisms, global governance, and real-world economic issues. Bruegel's research staff structure contributes both to the specialization of its academic research and the diversification of its research topics, as well as to the internationalization of the think tank and the expansion of its brand influence.

3.2 Research Areas

Bruegel seeks to maintain a dynamic balance between core economic issues and an evolving policy environment, which, in practice, entails balancing short-term policy responsiveness with long-term strategic research. To this end, the institute has developed a dual-layered research planning framework consisting of Medium-Term Research Programs and Annual Research Programs. Research topics are determined through an open and consultative process involving Bruegel scholars, members, and other stakeholders, and are subsequently subject to final approval by the Board of Directors, which determines both the three-year medium-term research agenda and the corresponding annual research plans. The medium-term program, typically spanning three years, serves as the foundational framework for governance, research, and fundraising activities, while the annual research program operationalizes this framework by focusing on specific themes. Within the annual plan, research is organized into six major policy areas, each of which is further subdivided into three thematic priorities.

3.2.1 Bruegel's Key Research Areas and Topics in Recent Years

According to Bruegel's published annual research plans for the past three years (2020-2023), its thematic areas have shown a high degree of stability, while the specific topics within these areas have been in constant flux, closely tied to the policy needs of the EU and exhibiting significant dynamism. Bruegel focuses on the following six major areas:

(1) Macroeconomic Policy and Economic Governance

The macroeconomic impact of the COVID-19 pandemic and appropriate policy responses were prioritized at the top of Bruegel's research agenda, focusing on macroeconomic regulatory measures to promote economic stability and growth, as well as pathways to enhance the fairness, legitimacy, and effectiveness of European economic governance. Following the outbreak of the Russia-Ukraine conflict, Bruegel has increasingly focused on European geoeconomic strategy, concentrating on Europe's policy framework for addressing global geoeconomic challenges amidst the Russia-Ukraine conflict and intensified Sino-American strategic competition. Key questions include how to manage rising energy prices and stagflation, and how to create fiscal space for EU investment needs in defense and migration. Specific research topics include:

European monetary, fiscal, and financial policy. Key areas include: 1. pathways for reforming European fiscal rules, specifically how to more effectively reduce fiscal risks within the EU and achieve necessary fiscal coordination; 2. enhancing European fiscal capacity, i.e., researching whether and how to establish EU-level policy tools to enhance the supply of public goods to serve green transition goals; 3. European financial governance, focusing on how to achieve a Banking Union and Capital Markets Union, how to build a more integrated financial system, and how to reconcile higher interest rates with the significant investment needs for climate transition and digitalization, while analyzing the reasons for and prospects of the slow progress in European financial integration; and, 4. euro area monetary policy, primarily studying the development trends of stagflation in Europe following the pandemic and geopolitical crises, and exploring strategies to enhance the European Central Bank's effectiveness and decision-making transparency.

Internal European governance issues. Key areas include: 1. European tax and pension policies, specifically how to reform welfare systems to protect fiscal sustainability, whether it is necessary to introduce a pan-European pension system, and issues related to funded pension schemes; 2 EU enlargement policy, studying the economic implications of the accession of candidate countries like Ukraine, and analyzing the feasibility of differentiated integration and managing divergences between euro area and non-euro area countries; 3.

European health policy, examining how the EU can coordinate health policies, exchange health information, and create a European Health Data Space (EHDS); and, 4. in monetary, fiscal, and financial governance, understanding and balancing the relationships between national sovereignty, EU institutions, and shared governance responsibilities.

Furthermore, the Next Generation EU (NGEU) recovery fund is also a key focus for Bruegel, which involves researching its economic impact at EU and global levels, monitoring the use of funds through the establishment of an NGEU database, and assessing the effectiveness and replicability of NGEU to understand how best to meet public investment financing needs for the digital and green transitions.

(2) Global Trade Policy and Governance

In this area, Bruegel primarily focuses on global economic governance, Europe's economic strategy and role, and relations between Europe and neighboring countries and other regions. Its research topics can be divided into two main threads: risk perspective and cooperation perspective.

From a risk response perspective, the research topics include: 1. the impact of the COVID-19 pandemic and the Russia-Ukraine conflict on the global economic order, such as trends in global economic structural changes, and the impact of global economic fragmentation and geoeconomic polarization on European economic policy and standing; and, 2. European geoeconomic resilience and strategic autonomy, i.e., Europe's strategic position and means in the global geoeconomy. This further includes: (a) supply chain resilience, analyzing trends and impacts of global value chain and supply chain fragmentation, and the costs and benefits of EU policy tools for managing supply chains and critical raw materials; and (b) European "open strategic autonomy," focusing on how to enhance European economic sovereignty regarding the free flow of data, goods, services, and capital, assessing the means, risks, and benefits of geoeconomic trade and industrial policies, with particular attention to how Europe can achieve the geopolitical objectives of its economic policies while minimizing efficiency costs and damage to the global free trading system.

In recent years, Bruegel has placed particular emphasis on studying China's economic issues. In its 2023 research plan, it featured specific topics such as "Understanding China's Relevance to the EU," primarily focusing on the impact of China's domestic and external economic policies on Europe and the global economy. On the one hand, Bruegel examines China's internal economic issues, such as the international implications of Chinese banking assets and debt restructuring, the utility and impact assessment of Chinese industrial subsidies, mechanisms for reforming Chinese state-owned enterprises, and whether public venture capital for Chinese start-ups and technological innovation can mitigate China's structural economic slowdown and other economic transition issues. On the other hand, Bruegel also focuses on the impact of the Russia-Ukraine conflict on the Belt and Road Initiative, its future development trends, and its implications for Europe.

From the perspective of cooperation, Bruegel's research encompasses several key areas: 1. transatlantic economic relations, which further includes: (a) transatlantic trade dispute resolution mechanisms, monitoring and analyzing negotiations regarding transatlantic steel and aluminum tariffs, a sustainable global steel and aluminum framework, and the Transatlantic Initiative for Sustainable Metal Arrangements (TISMA); (b) transatlantic climate governance cooperation, focusing on how to coordinate TISMA with the EU Carbon Border Adjustment Mechanism (CBAM) and promote global industrial decarbonization; and, (c) transatlantic trade policy coordination to facilitate economic governance in the Global South; 2. the economic development of EU member states and neighboring countries. This includes analyzing the economic, political, and institutional factors constraining regional and sub-regional economic development in Europe, and continuously monitoring the economic development of EU candidate countries, partner countries under the European Neighborhood Policy framework, Russia, and Mediterranean countries, while analyzing obstacles to and methods for improving the accession negotiations for Western Balkan countries and Turkey; and, 3. EU economic and trade cooperation with the Indo-Pacific region and the Global South. To this end, Bruegel has established collaborative relationships with think tanks in the Indo-Pacific region, such as the Centre for Policy Research in New Delhi.

(3) Banking and Capital Markets

Bruegel's research in this field focuses on financial regulation, financial stability, and global financial governance. Key topics in recent years include: the impact of the COVID-19 pandemic on the European financial system, pathways for building a mechanism for sustainable financial stability in Europe, options for expanding public and private financing for Europe's climate and digital transitions, the current state and challenges of building the European Banking Union, international coordination of green finance regulation (green bonds), trends in financial deglobalization, the digitalization of global financial markets, and potential financial risks in China, among others.

(4) Energy and Climate Policy

Within this domain, Bruegel focuses on Europe's green transition and global climate governance. Key research areas include: 1. the macroeconomic implications of decarbonization, particularly its effects on economic growth, production, consumption, and investment patterns, as well as policy measures to mitigate associated macroeconomic risks; and, 2. pathways toward decarbonization at both the European and global levels, including the potential of European green industrial policy to promote growth, industrial revitalization, and employment, as well as the social dimensions of climate policy and comparative analyses of decarbonization drivers and policies across different countries. Bruegel has also established a dedicated "European Green Deal" observatory project to track and analyze its implementation and its political and economic impacts in real time. In the field of global climate governance, Bruegel monitors developments related to the Paris Agreement and international climate negotiations (such as COP27), as well as climate policy developments in China and other Asian countries, and EU-U.S. climate cooperation. In addition, Bruegel collaborates with U.S. think tanks on joint research focusing on innovation, climate finance, and carbon border measures. Furthermore, energy security has become a central concern, particularly following the Russia-Ukraine conflict. Bruegel has devoted significant attention to analyzing policy responses to the European energy crisis and has developed data tools such as trackers for Russian crude oil exports.

(5) Digital Economy, Innovation, and Competition

Amidst intensifying Sino-American technological competition and Europe's strategic planning for digital sovereignty, Bruegel has focused on issues related to the digital economy and industrial policy. Regarding the digital economy, key research topics include: 1. the EU digital regulatory framework, such as ways to enhance the effectiveness, coordination, and efficiency of EU digital laws like the Digital Markets Act (DMA) and the General Data Protection Regulation (GDPR), and the implementation progress and economic and social impacts of digital regulations; 2 the EU digital transformation strategy, including issues like European digital infrastructure development, digital skills cultivation for European citizens, and European network and digital security; and, 3. global digital trade and data governance, such as internal and external digital trade barriers within the EU, data flows and data protection, and global digital development gaps. Regarding competition and industrial policy, Bruegel focuses on a new EU industrial policy designed to respond to global geopolitical changes and challenges, adapting it to the needs of security, climate change, and digital transformation.

(6) Inclusive Growth

As wealth inequality widens and populism becomes increasingly severe in Europe, how to promote inclusive growth that ensures equal opportunities and how to coordinate economic development with social equity have become key issues for Bruegel. To study the impact of technological progress and industrial decarbonization on workers and labor markets, and potential solutions, Bruegel has established a three-year research program titled "The Future of Work" and co-founded the Transatlantic Expert Group on the Future of Work (TEG FOW) with the German Marshall Fund of the United States (GMF). Key research topics include the effects of the digital and green twin transitions on labor skill requirements, labor market structures, worker well-being (e.g., occupational health, happiness, stress, motivation), work environments, work methods, and policy measures for labor skills education and worker transitions, among others.

3.2.2 Bruegel's New Research Topic Model

As international political and economic issues continue to proliferate, Bruegel is innovating its research topic structure to enhance the flexibility and relevance of its research. In its 2023-2024 research plan announced in August 2023, Bruegel optimized the organization of its research program by establishing a two-tier structure: Priority Projects and Additional Topics. Priority Projects focus on international political and economic issues of significant impact and urgency, where Bruegel will prioritize mobilizing resources for in-depth research. Additional Topics represent other interconnected issues or topics of somewhat lesser importance identified by researchers during their work. The key distinction is that while Bruegel will still conduct research on Additional Topics, it does not commit to producing deliverable research outputs.

Compared to the traditional model of "6 major areas + 3 sub-topics," the current research topics are more specific, detailed, measurable, and actionable. In outlining the Priority Projects, Bruegel provides a detailed list of the researchers involved, the rationale for establishing one project, the key questions to be addressed, the research methodology involved, and the planned outputs and timeline, making the purpose of the research plan highly explicit.

Appendix Table 1: Linkages between Priority Research Projects (2023–2024) and Traditional Policy Areas at Bruegel

Priority Project	Macroeconomic Policy & Governance	Banking & Capital Markets	Global Economy & Trade Policy	Digital Economy, Labor Market, Skills & Health	Energy & Climate Policy
1. Design of the Proposed EU Economic Governance Framework	√				√
2. European Public Goods and their Financing	√		√		√
3. Making the Capital Markets Union a Reality	√	√			
4. Implications of Ukraine's Accession to the EU	√		√		
5. European Economic Security	√		√		
6. The Chinese Economy and its Relevance for Europe			√		√
7. EU Digital Regulation: Achievements and Shortcomings			√	√	
8. Economic Implications of AI			√	√	
9. European Climate and Energy Governance	√		√		√
10. Decarbonization Pathways in the Global South			√		√
11. Electricity Markets: Beyond Short-Term Fixes	√				√

Note: All Priority Projects span at least two policy dimensions. The bold √ indicates the primary focus area for that Priority Project.

Source: Bruegel's official website, "Research Programme 2023-2024".[①]

① https://www.bruegel.org/sites/default/files/2023-09/RP%202023.pdf (Accessed April 5, 2026)

3.3 Research Outputs and Activities

Publications represent Bruegel's academic output on specific research topics, aiming to provide scientific economic analysis and policy recommendations. These come in various formats, including Policy Briefs, Working Papers, Analyses, Blog Posts, and External Publications. Among these, Working Papers are the longest and most academically rigorous, focusing on predetermined major academic topics, thus having a longer publication cycle. Policy Briefs focus on policy areas, are relatively lengthy, and aim to provide economic policy insights and recommendations. Analyses are shorter, timely research articles intended to succinctly outline the latest developments in economic policy.

Comments are shorter, more timely research outputs from Bruegel intended to provide commentary on real-time, hot-button political and economic issues. Additionally, First Glance articles and Newsletters are important components of the commentary section. Newsletters and First Glance articles typically use questions as titles to briefly explore the implications of hot topics for Europe, e.g., "How should Europe respond to the Inflation Reduction Act?" Commentary articles usually use declarative sentences as titles, offering commentary on current political and economic issues while providing concise policy recommendations, such as "From economic policy to economic statecraft" or "The EU needs to move faster on valuing nature."

Bruegel Datasets come in various forms, including Trackers, Dashboards, and dynamic data. As of November 2023, Bruegel had released 23 data-based research outputs, including the China Economic Database, the Russian Foreign Trade Tracker, the European Natural Gas Demand Tracker, and the Technology Adoption Dashboard.

The Sound of Economics podcast serves as a crucial channel for Bruegel's new media dissemination, aiming to expand the think tank's public influence through expert interviews in a more accessible format. The podcast content therefore addresses issues relevant to ordinary Europeans, featuring different columns annually, with episodes lasting approximately 30 to 40 minutes. In 2023, Bruegel's podcast included columns such as "Future of Work," "Read with Bruegel," and "ZhōngHuá Mundus." "Future of Work" aims to analyze the impact of technology on the nature and quantity of work, social welfare systems, and inclusive growth in Europe, discussing topics ranging from remote work to artificial intelligence, e.g., "Is technology redefining women's workplaces?" "Read with

Bruegel" invites renowned economists or Bruegel fellows to share their latest academic books and engage in open discussions on related economic issues. For instance, in July 2023, Bruegel Senior Fellow Maria Demertzis discussed her book *Backfiring: How Sanctions Hurt the US and the World* on the podcast. "ZhōngHuá Mundus" focuses on Chinese economic issues, discussing topics like China's electric vehicle industry, Sino-American technological rivalry, and China's economic situation, offering a European perspective on the Chinese economy.

Events are crucial for Bruegel to facilitate exchange and cooperation among scholars and think tanks through academic conferences, international seminars, and similar activities, while also enhancing its visibility and outreach. These events typically focus on specific economic topics, featuring invited stakeholders such as policymakers, business leaders, academics, and media for open discussions with Q&A sessions, thus allowing broader audiences to watch live streams or recordings online.

Thus, Bruegel employs diverse communication methods to balance academic rigor with accessibility in its outputs, which helps it to cultivate a wide and varied audience base. In 2022, Bruegel published 87 publications, 84 blog posts, 58 podcast episodes, and 5 datasets.

IV. Achievements and Development Experience

Specialization in economic policy and the high standard of academic research have enabled Bruegel to rapidly grow into a world-class independent think tank, earning accolades such as "Top Think Tank in Western Europe" and "Top International Economic Policy Think Tank" (non-US), and is widely recognized as one of Europe's most influential think tanks in terms of policy impact. Regarding media and public influence, Bruegel received over 50,000 media mentions globally in 2022. Its 78 organized academic events attracted 100,000 in-person and online participants. In terms of policy influence, Bruegel has frequently received research grants from the European Commission, engaging in the EU decision-making process through agenda-setting and policy progress evaluation. Its economic analyses and policy recommendations not only significantly impact the European Commission and national policy decisions within Europe but are also valued by governments and researchers worldwide, establishing it as a world-class European think tank with global influence.

Overall, the rapid development of Bruegel can be attributed to several factors. First, its forward-looking research agenda, balancing medium-term and short-term issues through a "Medium-Term Plan + Annual Plan" research model. Maintaining keen insights and incubating cutting-edge policy ideas is the lifeblood of a think tank. Bruegel has established a multi-layered research structure, with research topics that are diverse yet specific, purposeful, and actionable.

Second, its unique focus on the economic field ensures a high degree of specialization in its academic research. Since its inception, Bruegel has focused on major international political and economic issues, with its research topics and activities centered around economic issues relevant to European interests. Benefiting from a funding structure balanced between public and private sectors, Bruegel enjoys significant freedom in setting its research agenda, and its research outputs adhere to principles of independence and objectivity. Furthermore, Bruegel has established a multi-cycle, multi-layered research evaluation system; the Scientific Council responsible for monitoring research quality is independent and authoritative, effectively ensuring the academic quality of its publications.

Third, its advantageous geographic location and access to information sources. Situated in Brussels—often referred to as the "capital of the EU"—where major EU administrative institutions like the European Council, the European Commission, and the Council of the European Union are located, Bruegel benefits from such geographical proximity that facilitates timely access to the latest EU information and resources, as well as exchange and collaboration with EU institutions.

In conclusion, Bruegel is a key think tank influencing European economic policymaking and Europe's economic strategy toward China. Academically, its research agenda is grounded in real-world policy needs. Its research team is not only international, diverse, and highly specialized but also includes numerous former government or EU institution officials, as well as prominent figures from business and media with substantial economic policymaking experience. In terms of management, Bruegel focuses internally on cultivating its independence and transparency, proactively coordinating operations among its various departments. Simultaneously, it emphasizes interaction and engagement with civil society and other European think tanks, balancing academic rigor with accessibility in its outputs to cultivate a broad and diverse audience base. This solid foundation helps Bruegel continuously expand its policy and media influence, solidifying its status as a world-class European think tank with global reach.

Appendix III: An Institutional Profile of the German Institute for International and Security Affairs (SWP)

The German Institute for International and Security Affairs (German: Stiftung Wissenschaft und Politik, SWP), established in 1962, stands as one of Europe's most renowned think tanks in the field of international relations. Its primary research areas encompass European integration, Franco-German cooperation, European security policy, international security, as well as international issues pertaining to the Asia-Pacific region and Africa. As an academic think tank directly funded by the Office of the Federal Chancellor of Germany, SWP pursues, right from its foundation, the core objective of providing decision-making advice and policy recommendations to the German Parliament (Bundestag) and the Federal Government. It operates as a semi-official research institution closely affiliated with the government. Consequently, the academic research conducted by SWP exhibits a strong policy orientation, with its research agenda aligning closely with the policy priorities of the German government. Over more than six decades since its establishment, as one of the most influential research institutions in the fields of German foreign and security policy, SWP has played a pivotal role in Germany's national governance and foreign policymaking.

I. Institutional Overview

1.1 Historical Development

The origins of SWP can be traced to an initiative by Klaus Ritter, an official in the West German Federal Intelligence Service (Bundesnachrichtendienst, BND). In 1959, Ritter was dispatched to the United States on a fact-finding mission to see how political decision-making mechanisms work there. During his stay, he was profoundly impressed by the climate of debate surrounding political decision-making in the United States and the involvement of diverse think tanks, such as the RAND Corporation, in the American political decision-making process. Concurrently, during his exchanges with American foreign policy elites such as Henry Kissinger and Arnold Wolfers, they suggested to him that West Germany's foreign policymaking process then lacked the participation of non-governmental institutions, which prevented the United States from exchanging policy positions and views with the German side in the initial stages before international political issues entered the decision-making mechanisms of West German political institutions. Consequently, Ritter conceived the idea of emulating the American think tank model to establish a German institute for international relations.

Upon returning to Germany from the United States in 1960, Ritter coordinated closely with the Federal Intelligence Service to facilitate the establishment of the "Working Group on Science and Politics" (Arbeitsgemeinschaft Wissenschaft und Politik, AWP), comprising like-minded individuals from the foreign ministry, business circles, and academia. Based on the operational model of the American RAND Corporation, AWP sought to establish an independent think tank outside the governmental structure. Ultimately, leveraging start-up capital donated by companies and business associations such as the German Steel Industry Economic Association and Deutsche Bank, the German Institute for International and Security Affairs was founded in 1962 in Ebenhausen, south of Munich, with Ritter serving as its first director.

In its early years, the institute's operational funding came primarily from private donations and the budget of the Federal Intelligence Service. In January 1965, the German Bundestag decided to establish it as a foundation under the German Civil Code (Bürgerliches Gesetzbuch, BGB), granting the institute its official legal status. Subsequently, the institute has been directly funded by the Office of the Federal Chancellor, to which it also provides policy advice. In 2001, the institute's headquarters moved to Ludwigkirchplatz in Berlin. Concurrent with this relocation, researchers from the former Federal Institute for East European and International Studies (Bundesinstitut für ostwissenschaftliche und internationale Studien, BIOST) in Cologne and the Southeast Europe Institute (Südost-Institut, SOI) in Munich were integrated into its governance structure. In 2009, the institute opened a liaison office in Brussels. In the 2020 global ranking of international relations think tanks, SWP ranked 19th worldwide, establishing its reputation as a world-class European independent think tank.

1.2 Nature, Mission, and Principles of SWP

Article 2 of SWP' founding statutes stipulates that the institute's mission is "to conduct academic research in the fields of international politics, foreign policy, and security policy in consultation with the German Bundestag and the German Federal Government, with the aim of providing scientifically based, independent policy advice and making research results available to the public at the appropriate time." At the same time, 70% of SWP's funding is derived from appropriations from the Office of the Federal Chancellor. The Federal Government and the Bundestag have the right to request advisory services from the institute through commissioned studies or similar forms and may require that such results be kept confidential or their publication delayed. Consequently, the institutional nature of SWP is that of a semi-official, government-affiliated research institution. Its research topics exhibit a pronounced policy orientation, and its publications are categorized into both open and non-open forms.

Despite its official governmental background, the institute emphasizes the independence and scientific nature of its research, asserting that serving the government and maintaining scientific rigor are not mutually exclusive. Provided that the government does not interfere in its research agenda setting and research process, the think tank's ability and work to identify issues with a forward-looking academic perspective, analyze them with high-quality professionalism, and propose solutions will cause no violation of the principle of research neutrality. The direct utilization of the think tank's research findings by the government precisely embodies the societal value of the think tank, reflects the public consultative nature of political decision-making, and represents an essential aspect of democratic governance.

On this basis, the institute adheres to the following five interrelated principles: 1. Academic Rigor. As for research topics, the institute builds upon broad internal consultation and focuses on the latest developments in international politics, ensuring research quality through high-caliber research staff and robust quality control systems; 2. Independence. The institute is directly supported by public funds from the Federal Government; its policy recommendations and academic research serve the public interest rather than the particular interests of any political party, interest group, or other institution; 3. Multiple Perspectives and Diversity. The institute's researchers possess extensive specialized knowledge and conduct independent academic research from diverse perspectives. The institute does not interfere in research activities and adopts no institutional position on political issues; 4. Policy Relevance. The institute's academic research is policy-oriented, aiming to formulate actionable policy recommendations. It focuses on issues relevant, or which should be relevant, to the German Bundestag and the Federal Government, seeking to integrate researchers' expertise into the government's assessment and decision-making process, fostering joint discussions on potential policy options, impacts, and scenarios; and, 5. Confidentiality. The institute provides a space for exchange and communication between researchers and politicians, allowing decision-makers to discuss sensitive policy issues in an atmosphere of trust and confidentiality. Participants are required to adhere to the Chatham House Rule.

II. Internal Governance and Organizational Structure

2.1 Organizational Structure

The SWP Council serves as the highest supervisory and decision-making body of the institute. Its responsibilities are twofold: appointing the institute's senior management and approving the research program while ensuring the independence of academic research at SWP. The Council is composed of a Chair, two Vice-Chairs, and representatives drawn from government officials nominated by the Head of the Federal Chancellery and the parliamentary groups in the Bundestag, as well as renowned academics, business figures, and public personalities. One of the Vice-Chairs must be the Head of the Federal Chancellery. All members of the Council serve in an honorary capacity and are not involved in the institute's day-to-day administration. In 2023, the Chair of the Council is Nikolaus von Bomhard, Chairman of the Supervisory Board of Munich Re. The Vice-Chairs are respectively Angelika Niebler, a Member of the European Parliament, and Wolfgang Schmidt, Head of the Federal Chancellery. Additionally, important German government officials, such as Bundestag member Jürgen Trittin and Kirsten Scholl from the Federal Ministry for Economic Affairs and Climate Action, are also members of the Council.

The Board is responsible for the management of the institute, consisting of a Chair, a

Vice-Chair, and one other member. Any two members of the Board have the authority to represent the institute in and out of court. The three members of the Board are elected by the Council with a two-thirds majority. The Executive Chair of the Board concurrently serves as the Director of the institute and has full authority over the Executive Board. In 2023, the Executive Chair of the Board is Stefan Mair.

The Executive Board is responsible for the operational and academic management of the institute's daily activities. The head of the Executive Board is the Executive Chair of the Board. The internal structure of the Executive Board is divided into three departments: the Administration Department, the Research Department, and the Technology Department, overseen respectively by the Director, the Director of Research, and a Deputy Director. The Administration Department encompasses units such as Administration (Personnel, Finance, and Logistics), Communications and Liaison, and the Brussels Office, primarily handling the institute's daily administrative operations. The Technology Department includes units such as Information Infrastructure Services, Information Technology, Third-Party Funding Coordination, and Conference Management, responsible for technical matters like the digital library, publication of research outputs, and event organization. The Research Department constitutes the core of SWP. Supervised and guided by the Director of Research, it comprises the Research Divisions, the Centre for Applied Turkey Studies (CATS), and the Editorial Office. By different research fields, the Research Divisions are organized into seven divisions: Europe/EU; Americas; Eastern Europe and Eurasia; Middle East and Africa; Asia; International Security; and Global Issues. In 2023, the Director of Research is Barbara Lippert, a specialist in European studies, and the Deputy Director of Research is Simone Burkhart.

The Research Advisory Board is responsible for providing academic advice to the institute on matters concerning its research program and interdisciplinary issues. This Board is composed of ten university professors with high academic standing, appointed by the Council in consultation with the Executive Board. In 2023, the Chair of the Research Advisory Board is Christopher Daase, a professor at Goethe University Frankfurt. The other academic advisors are primarily full-time professors at German universities; among all ten academic advisors, only two come from universities outside of Germany.

Appendix Figure 2: Organizational Structure of the Executive Board of SWP (2023)

Source: SWP's official website, "Organizational Chart of SWP," ①

2.2 Funding Sources and Allocation

SWP gets its core operating funds from appropriations from the Office of the Federal Chancellor. In fiscal year 2022, the institute received approximately €16.1 million in government funding, of which €12.38 million was allocated to personnel costs and €3.69 million to operating costs such as office rental. To ensure that no academic research is influenced by any interest group, the government funding covers 100% of the institute's core activities. Consequently, the institute is required to manage its finances strictly in accordance with public sector regulations, such as the Federal Budget Code (Bundeshaushaltsordnung, BHO) and the public sector collective bargaining agreement (Tarifvertrag für den öffentlichen Dienst, TVöD).

① https://www.swp-berlin.org/en/swp/about-us/fundamentals/organizational-chart-of-swp. (Accessed November 11, 2023)

In addition to federal government funding, the institute may also receive third-party research funds from public entities, corporations, and other sources to support specific research projects. To safeguard the independence and scientific integrity of its research, the institute accepts third-party funding only, but does not undertake commissioned research on topics dictated by non-official third parties. Specific research projects are established by researchers in line with the principles of academic merit, independence, and relevance, aiming to conduct further in-depth research on major issues or other topics identified during the research process. In 2022, the institute received a total of €4.85 million in third-party funding. Major donors included four ministries of Germany's Federal Government: the Federal Foreign Office, the Federal Ministry for Economic Cooperation and Development, the Federal Ministry for the Environment, Nature Conservation, Nuclear Safety and Consumer Protection, and the Federal Ministry of Education and Research; six German foundations: the Alexander von Humboldt Foundation, the Robert Bosch Foundation, the German Foundation for Peace Research, and the Mercator Foundation; international organizations such as the European Commission, the Nordic Council of Ministers, and the Norwegian Institute for Defence Studies; and large corporations including Mercedes-Benz Group AG, Deutsche Bank, and BP Europe. For instance, the 2023-2024 SWP research project "German Climate Diplomacy in the Context of the European Green Deal" is funded by the European Climate Foundation (ECF).

To enhance financial transparency, the Board is required to submit an annual financial report to the Council, audited by an external auditing firm in accordance with Article 8, Paragraph 2 of the Berlin Foundation Act (Stiftungsgesetz). This report is also submitted to the Office of the Federal Chancellor for verification as documentation of government fund utilization. In 2016, the institute received the highest five-star rating for the second time from Transparify, an international non-governmental organization evaluating funding transparency, establishing SWP as one of the most financially transparent think tanks in Germany and globally.

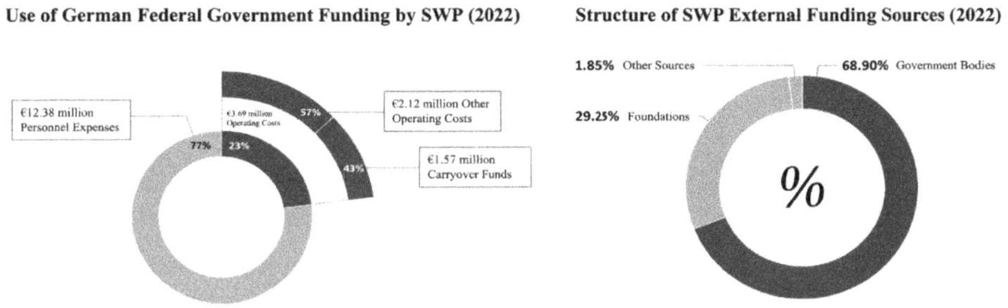

Appendix Figure 3: Allocation of Federal Government Funding and Composition of External Funding Sources of SWP (2022)

Source: SWP's official website, "Funding of SWP," ①

III. Research Agenda and Institutional Output

3.1 Research Mechanisms and Research Areas

Regarding research mechanisms, the institute has established a multi-layered matrix research structure combining Divisional Research, Project Research, and Cluster Research. This structure integrates vertical management with cross-departmental collaborative research, effectively harnessing the collective scientific creativity and dynamism of the institute's entire research staff.

Divisional Research involves the organization of specialized research divisions based on single areas defined by region or theme. There are seven such divisions: Europe/EU; Americas; Russia, Eastern Europe, and Eurasia; Middle East and Africa; Asia; International Security; and Global Issues. Funding for divisional research is derived from German government appropriations. In terms of research focus, the EU/Europe Division concentrates on the core challenges facing the EU and Europe, analyzing the internal political developments and foreign policy interests of the EU and its member states. The Americas Division primarily analyzes economic developments and foreign policies in the United States and Latin America, and their relationship with Germany and Europe. The Russia, Eastern Europe, and Eurasia Division focuses on Russia, Ukraine, the South Caucasus,

① https://www.swp-berlin.org/en/swp/about-us/fundamentals/funding. (Accessed November 11, 2023)

and Central Asian states (the former Soviet Union), examining their political structures, state-building processes, foreign and security policy developments, and their interactions with European and transatlantic institutions. The Middle East and Africa Division focuses on social and political transformation, ethnic conflicts, migration policies, and external relations in these regions. The Asia Division primarily examines the interrelationships between domestic politics, economic and social transformations, and foreign and security policy developments in South Asia and the Asia-Pacific region, as well as their global implications. The International Security Division focuses on security policy analysis, covering issues such as European and regional security, transatlantic security relations, weapons technology developments, disarmament, and the proliferation of weapons of mass destruction. The Global Issues Division addresses non-traditional security issues, including economic, financial, and climate governance, concentrating on mechanisms and methods for multilateral international cooperation.

Project Research is established by researchers based on the principles of academic merit, independence, and relevance, aiming to conduct further research on major topics or other issues identified during the research process. There is no limit on the number of researchers involved in a project; projects range from single-researcher endeavors to collaborative efforts involving researchers from other think tanks. Project funding comes from third-party sponsors. For example, the single-researcher project "Environmental Cooperation with North Korea and Conflict Resolution on the Korean Peninsula" is funded by the Korea Foundation. The "Research Network: Sustainable Global Supply Chains" is a collaborative research project involving SWP, the German Institute of Development and Sustainability (IDOS), the German Institute for Global and Area Studies (GIGA), and the Kiel Institute for the World Economy (IfW Kiel), funded by the German Federal Ministry for Economic Cooperation and Development (BMZ). As of November 2023, the institute had 14 active research projects.

Cluster Research involves working groups designed for integrated and interdisciplinary research. The research teams for these working groups are assembled by drawing researchers from various research divisions, supplemented by appropriate research assistants. The leadership of a working group is responsible for the specific implementation and management of the cluster research. Currently, the institute has established two research clusters: the Research Cluster on Cybersecurity and Digital Policy and the Research Cluster on Climate Policy and Politics. The cluster model facilitates collaboration and brainstorming among multidisciplinary experts. Using the Cybersecurity and Digital Policy cluster as an example, its members possess highly diverse academic backgrounds, originating from fields such as digital technology, European affairs, security and defense policy, global governance, and international law, thus enabling fruitful interdisciplinary research.

In terms of research areas, the institute covers a wide range of regions, including Europe, the Americas, Asia, the Middle East, and even outer space, spanning various policy domains such as security, economy, and society. This establishes es SWP as a comprehensive institute for international studies. The institute's official website lists 16 research areas. Geographically, these cover nine regions: Sub-Saharan Africa; Europe; Asia; Latin America and the Caribbean; Turkey; the Middle East and North Africa; the United States and Canada; Russia, Eastern Europe, and Central Asia. By policy domain, the seven main areas are: Digitization, Networks, and Technology; Security and Defense Policy; Energy, Climate, and Environment; Migration and Development Cooperation; United Nations, Global Governance, and International Law; Economy, Trade, and Resources; and Non-State Violence.

Despite its extensive research scope, SWP still prioritizes areas of interest to the German government, such as EU governance, climate governance, and digital governance. Ranked by the volume of published field-specific outputs in 2022, the institute's most prominent thematic areas were: EU and Europe (131 publications), Russia, Eastern Europe and Central Asia (101), Security and Defense Policy (98), Asia (92), and Economy, Trade, and Resources (69).

What is worth highlighting is the institute's particular focus on Turkish affairs. To track and analyze Turkish domestic politics and society, its bilateral relations with Europe, promote policy debates on Turkish issues at the European level, and provide information to relevant political decision-makers and the public in Germany and Europe, SWP has established the Centre for Applied Turkey Studies (CATS), funded by the Mercator Foundation and the German Federal Foreign Office. CATS's research focuses on: 1. monitoring domestic political, economic, and social developments in Turkey; 2. examining the policy framework for integrating Turkey's foreign and security policy into EU and

NATO frameworks; and, 3. tracking Turkey's regional engagement in the Middle East and North Africa, the Caucasus, Central Asia, and Africa. Additionally, CATS has set up an exchange network providing a platform for Turkish experts and scholars from Turkish think tanks, European universities, and research institutions to exchange views. CATS also offers project funding and scholarships for eligible institutions and individuals conducting research on Turkey.

3.2 Composition and Structure of Research Staff

Currently, the institute employs a total of 223 staff members, of whom 126 are full-time researchers, resulting in a researcher-to-administrative staff ratio of approximately 1:2. This indicates that the institute allocates a substantial number of research assistants and information managers to each research division, enabling researchers to dedicate themselves fully to academic work, thereby enhancing research efficiency. The research staff comprises Senior Fellows, Senior Associates, Associates, Visiting Fellows, and Research Assistants. Categorized by researchers' areas of expertise, the top eight fields are: EU/European Affairs (23 researchers), Security and Defense Policy (19), Asian Affairs (13), United Nations, International Law, and Global Governance (13), Energy, Climate, and Environment (12), Economy, Trade, and Resources (11), Russia, Eastern Europe, and Central Asia (11), and Middle East and North Africa (10).

The institute places great emphasis on internal collaboration and external exchange among its researchers, recognizing that the cross-pollination of ideas generated by such interactions helps stimulate its broad academic vitality. Internally, the institute regularly holds divisional seminars and plenary discussions involving all staff, providing platforms for researchers with diverse backgrounds to engage in in-depth dialogue on topics such as agenda setting, progress on ongoing projects, and current international affairs. Externally, the institute prioritizes external exchanges for its researchers, having established collaborative relationships with universities and research institutions in numerous countries and regions, including France, the United States, and Japan. It maintains close ties through joint research projects, co-organized conferences, visiting scholar programs, and other formats. For instance, in collaboration with the French Institute of International Relations (IFRI) under the framework of the Franco-German Research Committee (CERFA) established through a Franco-German intergovernmental initiative, the institute co-published several joint studies on the state of Franco-German cooperation, such as *France, Germany and the Quest for European Strategic Autonomy: Franco-German Defence Cooperation in a New Era*. Concurrently, the institute actively attracts visiting scholars from around the world to participate in its research projects, continually infusing fresh ideas into its research endeavor.

In summary, the research team of this institute exhibits three notable characteristics. First, it is firmly rooted in Germany, with a modest level of internationalization among its researchers. In terms of nationality distribution, the vast majority of SWP researchers are German, most having studied or worked in Germany, which fully underscores the institute's positioning as a think tank oriented towards German policymaking. Second, it possesses a diverse and highly qualified academic talent pool. SWP recruits talent through open, competitive procedures that include expert review stages. To enhance the creativity and professionalism of its research, an ad-hoc recruitment committee is formed for each hiring process to comprehensively evaluate candidates' academic backgrounds, professional qualifications, and other relevant aspects. Simultaneously, the institute maintains a rigorous performance appraisal and appointment system. Annually, the Personnel Department requires each researcher to submit a performance evaluation form summarizing their participation in projects, conferences, and other activities over the previous year. This quantitative assessment informs decisions regarding promotion, contract renewal, or termination.

3.3 Publication of Research Outputs and Academic Quality Control

The institute's primary publication formats include SWP Working Papers, SWP Research Papers, SWP Comments, Points of View, and the SWP Podcast. Publications are released in German, English, French, and Turkish. For major project outcomes, publication in both English and German versions is mandatory. With the exception of results from confidential research projects, the vast majority of its publications can be downloaded for free from the institute's website. SWP adheres to the provision in its statutes concerning "publication at the appropriate time." Full research reports are typically released to the public only three months after their submission to the Parliament and the Government, ensuring that policymakers have priority access to the policy recommendations. This practice further underscores the institute's mission to serve government decision-making needs.

Among these, SWP Working Papers represent the final outcomes of projects undertaken within the research divisions, typically authored by two or more researchers and extending to approximately 200 pages. Their content primarily offers long-term, in-depth observation and analysis of critical challenges in international politics. Distinct from Research Papers and Comments, these Working Papers are online publications within the purview of the respective research divisions and thus do not undergo the institute's formal scientific review process, though they must clearly indicate the originating research division. SWP Research Papers mainly analyze urgent major international political issues, focusing on German foreign policy areas, aiming to propose targeted policy recommendations, and typically range from 30 to 50 pages in length. SWP Comments provide brief recommendations and commentary on issues of current concern to policymakers, usually around 10 pages long. Points of View allow researchers to express their personal opinions on current hot topics, functioning similarly to political commentary. The SWP Podcast features two institute researchers in dialogue discussing current international issues, lasting about half an hour and conducted in German. This suggests that SWP primarily targets the German domestic public, seeking to enhance its influence within national media. External Publications compile articles written by SWP researchers in other newspapers, magazines, and academic journals.

To ensure the academic quality of its publications, the institute has established a rigorous academic quality assurance system comprising four main components: 1. Internal mechanisms for good academic practice. During the agenda-setting and research phases, in addition to discussions within the research divisions, the institute holds a bi-weekly colloquium (Plenum) to discuss the selection of topics for research papers and the progress of ongoing research. Furthermore, the Research Advisory Board, composed of leading academics from relevant university disciplines, advises the institute on thematic and interdisciplinary issues related to its research program; 2. A stringent internal academic review mechanism. Shorter publications, such as SWP Comments (German: SWP-Aktuell and SWP-Zeitschriftenschau), are reviewed by the Director of Research, who decides whether revisions are required and authorizes their publication. The primary review criteria include relevance to current German and European foreign and security policy, the professionalism and depth of the academic analysis, and the coherence between conclusions and policy recommendations. Longer publications, such as SWP Research

Papers, must undergo a dual review process consisting of peer review and review by the Board/Executive Board. Peer reviewers are typically colleagues from other research divisions, while the Board reviewer is generally the Director of the institute. Key criteria for this review include the policy relevance of the research question, the appropriateness of the chosen methodology, the rigor of the argumentation, and the quality and originality of the findings. Depending on the review outcome, authors may be required to revise and resubmit their work; 3. Fact-checking. As shorter SWP Comments do not include references upon release, the Information and Knowledge Management Team verifies direct and indirect quotations, temporal statements (dates, years, time spans), statistical data, and the spelling of geographical names and personal names in the text; and, 4. Editorial process. All German-language publications undergo internal editing to ensure clarity, readability, logical consistency, and coherence. Corresponding English-language texts are prepared by an external team of native English-speaking translators.

IV. Achievements and Development Experience

After more than sixty years of development, SWP has become one of the most academically prestigious international relations think tanks in Germany and Europe. In recent years, its research staff has grown considerably, expanding from approximately 50 full-time researchers in 2015 to over 120 in 2023. According to the 2020 Global Go To Think Tank Index Report published by the University of Pennsylvania, SWP ranks as the second-largest foreign policy and international relations think tank in Germany, surpassed only by the German Council on Foreign Relations (DGAP). In the global ranking of think tanks with the greatest public policy impact, SWP is positioned just behind Transparency International, making it the most policy-influential international relations think tank in Germany and one of the country's most policy-oriented research institutions. With the rise of new media, SWP has increasingly sought to expand its influence through digital platforms, establishing official accounts on Twitter, LinkedIn, and YouTube. To ensure the professional relevance of its content, the institute has also created separate official Twitter accounts for each of its research divisions, collectively amassing approximately 100,000 followers.

Overall, the development experience and salient characteristics of the German Institute for International and Security Affairs can be summarized as follows:

First, the institute embodies a distinctive synthesis of a government-serving think tank orientation and the principle of academic neutrality. As an academically oriented think tank established and funded by the Federal Chancellery, SWP was created primarily to serve governmental decision-making. Yet although the institute is, in essence, a semi-official body affiliated with the state, neither the Bundestag nor the federal government directly intervenes in its research activities. Rather, they treat the institute as a source of intellectual insight for identifying and addressing policy issues. In this sense, the fact that a think tank identifies issues through academically informed foresight, analyzes them with a high degree of professional competence, and advances policy recommendations does not run counter to the principle of scholarly neutrality. On the contrary, the direct service of research outputs to government constitutes the very social value of a think tank, while also reflecting the consultative character of political decision-making as an essential attribute of democratic politics. SWP has therefore retained a substantial degree of independence as a research institution and has, to a considerable extent, succeeded in reconciling service to government with independent inquiry.

Second, SWP has developed a multi-layered matrix research structure. The institute has established a research architecture that combines departmental research, project-based research, and cluster-based research, thereby actively seeking to balance specialized inquiry within individual fields with interdisciplinary collaboration across them. Departmental research enables the institute to concentrate the collective expertise of its researchers on precise and in-depth analysis within a given area, whereas both project-based and cluster-based studies foster intellectual exchange across perspectives and fields. More broadly, this multi-level matrix structure helps stimulate collective creativity and scholarly dynamism, and in this respect represents an especially effective organizational model for think tank research.

Third, firmly rooted in the German domestic context, SWP exhibits a comparatively weaker degree of internationalization. This is primarily reflected in several aspects: (a) its research topics are highly aligned with the priorities of the German government, focusing on issues such as EU economic and political developments relevant to German interests, and global climate governance; (b) the majority of its researchers and staff hold German nationality or are faculty members at German universities. For instance, its Research

Advisory Board is chaired by a professor at Goethe University Frankfurt, and only two of its ten academic advisors come from non-German universities; and (c) the primary language of publications is German. According to publication data publicly available on its official website as of November 2023, the institute has published 1,650 SWP-Aktuell (German Comments) and 705 SWP-Studien (German Studies). In comparison, the corresponding English-language publications—SWP Comments and Research Papers, number 973 and 231 respectively, with the volume of English-language publications thus remains markedly lower than that of its German-language output.

Appendix IV: An Institutional Profile of the Royal Institute of International Affairs (RIIA)

The Royal Institute of International Affairs (RIIA, commonly known as the Chatham House) was established in 1920 and ranks one of the world's oldest and most academically prestigious European institutions for international affairs research. As a world-leading think tank, the RIIA has, through its successful operational mechanisms and governance models, also influenced the establishment of international relations research institutions in numerous other countries. Not affiliated with the government or any political party, it is a non-governmental, non-profit independent think tank, whose mission is "to help build a sustainably secure, prosperous, and just world" by promoting the independent and objective study of international affairs through dialogue, analysis, and the development of solutions. Because it is housed within the Chatham House in London, it is more widely known as "Chatham House" , and it is the birthplace of the internationally renowned "Chatham House Rule."

I. Institutional Overview

1.1 Development History

The RIIA was born out of the wave of pacifism following World War I, representing a practical manifestation of Anglo-American idealism. During the Paris Peace Conference in 1919, British diplomat Lionel Curtis advocated for the establishment of a joint Anglo-American international affairs institute intended to foster mutual understanding among nations, work out collective solutions to global conflicts, and prevent human warfare. Ultimately, an agreement was reached between the United Kingdom and the United States to establish institutes in London and New York respectively. In July 1920, the institute based in London was established first, named the "British Institute of International Affairs." Its founding meeting was chaired by Lord Robert Cecil, one of the architects of the League of Nations, and the institute's founding declaration was drafted by former Foreign Secretary Edward Grey. The institute based in New York followed shortly thereafter, established under the name "Council on Foreign Relations."

In 1922, renowned historian Arnold Toynbee assumed the position of Director of Studies at the British Institute of International Affairs, where he pioneered the creation of a series of special reports titled *Annual Survey of International Affairs*. The same year, the institute launched the internationally renowned journal *International Affairs*, with G. M. Gathorne Hardy serving as its first editor. The journal was originally conceived as a platform for members unable to attend the institute's meetings to express their views, exchange ideas, and access meeting records.

As the number of researchers grew steadily, the institute required larger premises to accommodate seminars and other activities. In 1923, Canadian philanthropist Colonel Reuben Wells Leonard purchased Chatham House at 10 St. James's Square in London, donating this former prime ministerial residence to the institute in his own name, where it has remained to this day—hence the institute's colloquial name: "Chatham House."

In 1926, the British Institute of International Affairs was granted a Royal Charter by the British Crown, officially changing its name to the "Royal Institute of International Affairs." The 1930s marked the nascent period for the development of international organizations, with other countries also conceiving ideas for establishing international affairs research institutions. Against this backdrop, the Royal Institute of International Affairs actively disseminated its development experience, influencing the establishment of numerous other international relations think tanks worldwide, including those in Australia, Canada, Japan, and Nigeria. Following the outbreak of World War II, the institute temporarily relocated to Balliol College, Oxford. Its Foreign Research and Press Service Departments collaborated closely with the British Foreign Office, providing research reports on foreign press coverage, the historical and political background of the Empire, and related topics. Beyond its research activities, some of the institute's staff were seconded directly to government departments, making significant contributions to British wartime intelligence and post-war planning efforts.

After the Allied victory in World War II, the RIIA became deeply involved in the construction of the post-war international political and economic order. As early as 1939, the institute had established a Reconstruction Committee to study potential post-war issues. Subsequently, through the formation of study groups on international organizations, the institute participated in the preparatory work for international institutions such as the International Bank for Reconstruction and Development (IBRD), the International Monetary Fund (IMF), and the United Nations. During the Cold War, the institute organized Anglo-Soviet roundtable meetings with the Moscow Institute of World Economy and International Relations (IMEMO), seeking to establish contact with reformist elements in the Soviet Union and aiming to enhance communication and improve relations between Britain and the Soviet Union. In the 1980s, the institute demonstrated prescience by identifying global governance challenges such as climate change, becoming one of the world's first think tanks to establish energy and climate research programs. Subsequently, through activities such as hosting annual climate change conferences, strengthening research on climate and environmental issues, and promoting sustainable development in the Middle East, the institute sought to draw greater attention to environmental and developmental issues across nations.

Since its establishment, the RIIA has consistently ranked among the world's most renowned international affairs research institutions, a reputation that has also positioned it as a forum where global leaders share perspectives, engage in debate, and advocate for change. In October 1931, Mahatma Gandhi delivered a speech titled "The Future of India" at the institute, advocating for the resolution of conflict through non-violent political negotiations. Other world-renowned political figures who have visited and spoken at the institute include David Ben-Gurion, the founding father of Israel (1945); German Chancellor Konrad Adenauer (1951); King Hussein of Jordan (1969); Nelson Mandela (1996); and Chinese Minister of Foreign Affairs Yang Jiechi (2007), among many others.

1.2 Nature, Mission, Principles, and Values of RIIA

From an organizational standpoint, the RIIA is a charity registered in England and Wales (Charity No. 208223). It is institutionally independent of the government and of any political party, and is characterized as a non-profit, non-governmental, academically oriented think tank. The institute's mission is to promote independent and objective inquiry into international affairs through dialogue, analysis, and the formulation of solutions, thereby contributing to the construction of a sustainable, secure, prosperous, and just world, and equipping future generations with the capacity to advance such an order.

Entering the 21st century, the century-old institute articulated its future development aspirations as its "Second Century Goals": 1. Sustainable and Equitable Growth, focusing on research into pathways for achieving sustainable growth globally, protecting the planetary ecosystem, and reducing inequalities within and between states; 2. Peaceful and Prosperous Societies, concentrating on ways to promote the rule of law, reduce human insecurity, enhance societal resilience, and prevent large-scale violent conflicts; and, 3. Accountable and Inclusive Governance, aiming to promote political accountability and inclusive governance at global, regional, and sectoral levels, as well as examining the impacts and opportunities presented by technological innovation for international politics.

The RIIA upholds three core values: independence, inclusivity, and collaboration. First, independence. Intellectual independence, rigor, and creativity are the sources of a think tank's influence. The RIIA ensures the independence of its funding and research, adopting no institutional stance on policy issues. Second, inclusivity and diversity. It conducts academic analysis and develops solutions based on inclusive values, meaning that it explores common issues through diverse perspectives and seeks shared solutions. Furthermore, the institute strives for breadth and accessibility in its research outputs and activities, enabling people to access high-quality academic analysis and express their own views on international affairs. Third, collaboration. This entails valuing the relationships among staff within the institute as well as with members, supporters, the public, and other research institutions, developing global networks to find positive and lasting solutions to policy challenges.

To ensure the continued independence and objectivity of its research, activities, publications, and other outputs, the RIIA established its Principles for Independent Research and Convening in 2013. These include the following five principles: 1. The Principle of Mission and Public Benefit. The RIIA must be driven by its mission "to be a world-leading source of independent analysis, informed debate, and influential ideas on international affairs, working to build a sustainably secure, prosperous, and just world," insisting on conducting academic research for the public benefit; 2. The Principle of Integrity. The RIIA must avoid conflicts of interest between its funding and its mission, declining funding that would compromise its values and mission; 3. The Principle of Independence and Objectivity. The RIIA must ensure its right to conduct independent research and convene independent meetings. Simultaneously, it must maintain objectivity in its academic research, adhering to evidence-based methodologies and value neutrality; 4. The Principle of Openness and Accountability. The RIIA must publicly disclose the sources and uses of its funding. Confidential research must align with the institute's mission, and such commissioned research is permitted only if the funding amount does not exceed 5% of the institute's total annual income; and 5. The Principle of Awareness and Responsibility. Staff members of the RIIA must recognize the importance of these principles and cultivate a personal sense of responsibility for upholding them, remaining attentive to ethical considerations and potential conflicts of interest. To ensure effective implementation, the RIIA stresses during its staff induction sessions these principles, implementation criteria, and research practice code, which may be subject to annual staff discussion and review.

II. Internal Governance and Organizational Structure

2.1 Organizational Structure

The Chatham House Council serves as the highest governing body of the RIIA. Council members are elected by the institute's full membership through secret ballot. The Chair and Vice-Chairs are typically distinguished academics or political figures, serving three-year terms, renewable once. The Council's primary responsibilities include: approving the annual report, evaluating the quality and external impact of the institute's work; agreeing on annual priorities, research plans, and medium- to long-term development strategies; reviewing the institute's financial reports and fundraising plans; and ensuring that the institute makes continued progress on equality, diversity, and inclusion. To fulfill these responsibilities, the Council has established subordinate committees including the Executive Committee, the Finance Committee, and the Investment Committee, to oversee administrative, financial, and development matters respectively. In 2022, the Council established a new Remuneration Committee responsible for overseeing organizational culture, staff compensation, and related strategies. In 2023, the Chair of the Council is Sir Nigel Sheinwald, a former senior British diplomat and former British Ambassador to the United States.

The administrative structure of the RIIA primarily includes the Director's Office, the Communications and Publishing Department, the External Relations Department, and the Library. The Director's Office focuses on the institute's management, strategic direction, and engagement with key external stakeholders. In 2023, the Director is Bronwen Maddox, a Visiting Professor at King's College London. The Communications and Publishing Department is primarily responsible for the editing, publication, and dissemination of research papers, reports, and briefings, as well as for expanding brand influence and audience reach through digital channels such as press and social media. The External Relations Department manages the institute's relationships with its members and organizes the schedule of meetings and events. This department currently has 23 staff members, including a Head of Events, a Head of Donor Relations, and a Membership Events Manager. The Library team is responsible for providing specialized books, journals, and online resources in international relations, managing the institute's collections, archives, and periodicals. The library holds complete print runs of *International Affairs* and the *Bulletin of International Affairs* published by the RIIA since 1922.

Based on different research fields and content, the RIIA organizes its research departments into various programme teams. Currently, these include the Africa Programme, Asia-Pacific Programme, Europe Programme, Digital Society Initiative, Environment and Society Centre, Global Economy and Finance Programme, Global Health Programme, International Law Programme, International Security Programme, Middle East and North Africa Programme, Russia and Eurasia Programme, Sustainability Accelerator, UK in the World Programme, and US and Americas Programme. Each programme maintains its own independent research team and publishes annual departmental reports.

Additionally, the RIIA's organizational structure includes the Queen Elizabeth II Academy for Leadership in International Affairs. Officially established in 2014, the Academy aims to provide leadership skills training for current and aspiring global leaders, policymakers, and politicians, enhancing their understanding of critical issues in international affairs. Participants engage in a 10-month programme at the institute as "Academy Fellows," the core components of which are: 1. Knowledge: Participation in research projects. Under the guidance of RIIA experts, Fellows undertake individual research projects addressing major challenges in their home countries or regions, or participate in the institute's programme teams, thereby learning to understand and address policy challenges through academic research; 2. Skills: Enhancement of leadership abilities. Fellows participate in leadership development and career training, building confidence, communication, and presentation skills through one-on-one coaching, media training, and public speaking exercises; and, 3. Networks: Collaboration with leading experts in international affairs to build lasting connections.

2.2 Funding Sources and Allocation

The RIIA does not accept funding from the UK government. Its funds are derived primarily from private charitable foundations, government departments and agency contributions, membership fees, member donations, and publication revenues. According to the intended use of funds, donations are categorized as "Unrestricted Funds" (accounting for 32%) and "Research Funds" (accounting for 68%). Unrestricted Funds are primarily used for non-research expenditures such as administrative staff salaries and new media outreach, while Research Funds are entirely allocated to academic research.

Unrestricted Funds are mainly composed of membership fees, event sponsorship, and publication revenue, with membership fees representing its largest single source of funding. Currently, the RIIA has over 3,000 individual members and more than 300 corporate and institutional members. The institute operates a tiered membership structure, with Principal Members and Standard Members paying corresponding fees. Individual members come from diverse sectors including business, politics, journalism, and academia. Corporate members include private companies, government departments, universities, academic institutions, media organizations, and non-governmental organizations. Membership benefits include access to in-depth research reports on international developments, as well as opportunities to build networks with experts and decision-makers. Additionally, publication revenue comes primarily from royalties for *International Affairs* and subscription fees for *The World Today*, while event sponsorship revenue is generated from sponsorships for the institute's annual or periodic conferences.

Research Funds are primarily derived from contributions from private charitable foundations, government departments, international organizations, corporations, and non-governmental organizations. Donors may provide financial support for specific research projects or programmes, thereby enabling research on issues of concern to them. Private foundations are the institute's most significant source of funding, accounting for as much as 22%. Government department donors include the Norwegian Directorate of Health, the Dutch Ministry of Foreign Affairs, the Swiss Agency for Development and Cooperation, and the Japanese Ministry of Foreign Affairs. Non-governmental organization donors include the World Bank, the Food and Agriculture Organization of the United Nations, and the North Atlantic Treaty Organization. University and academic institution donors include the National Defense University of the United States, the National University of Singapore, and King's College London. Corporate donors include Microsoft, TotalEnergies, the BBC, Bloomberg, Boeing, Apple, and NHK. In 2022, the MAVA Foundation was the institute's largest donor, contributing over £5 million. The UK Foreign, Commonwealth and Development Office (FCDO) and Global Affairs Canada were the second and third largest donors, each contributing over £1 million. The European Commission, the IKEA Foundation, the MacArthur Foundation, the Robert Bosch Foundation, and the US Department of State each contributed over £500,000.

To safeguard the independence and objectivity of its seminar activities and academic research, the RIIA adheres to the principles of integrity, independence, objectivity, and responsible funding. Donors must align with the institute's mission, principles, and values. Currently, to promote the goal of global sustainable development, the RIIA periodically assesses whether potential donors have made credible environmental commitments consistent with the objectives of the Paris Agreement, accepting funding only from companies and institutions committed to contributing to the goal of achieving carbon neutrality by 2050. In accordance with the United Nations Tobacco Covenant, the institute does not accept any funding from the tobacco industry.

Regarding financial transparency, the RIIA lists its donors categorized by contribution thresholds (such as over £5 million, over £1 million, over £500,000) but does not publish detailed financial reports on total donations received or fund utilization. Consequently, financial transparency remains an area of improvement for the institute. In 2022, the transparency website "Who Funds You?" gave the RIIA a 'C' rating on transparency. In 2016, Transparify, which rates the financial transparency of think tanks, awarded it a four-star rating (out of a maximum of five) in the evaluation of 200 think tanks from 47 countries.

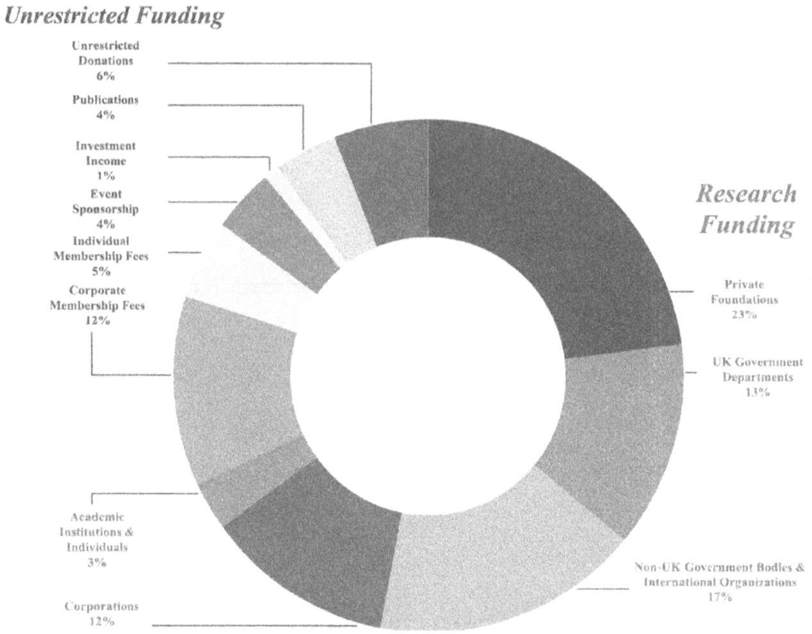

Appendix Figure 4: Funding Structure of the Royal Institute of International Affairs (2022)

Source: Official website of the RIIA, "Donors to Chatham House." ①

III. Research Agenda and Institutional Output

3.1 Composition and Structure of Research Staff

Currently, the RIIA employs a total of 449 staff members, of whom 227 are full-time researchers, giving rise to a researcher-to-administrative or research assistant staff ratio of approximately 1:1. The research team is composed of Distinguished Fellows, Senior Fellows, Research Fellows, Associate Fellows, Visiting Fellows, Advisors, Academy Associates, and Research Associates, among others. The institute's researchers predominantly hold degrees from top-tier international universities, possessing diverse professional backgrounds, excellent academic perspectives, and interdisciplinary research capabilities. Some of its researchers have held significant positions at large corporations,

① "Donors to Chatham House," https://www.chathamhouse.org/about-us/our-funding/donors-chatham-house. (Accessed November 16, 2023)

international organizations, and embassies, bringing rich practical experience and extensive professional networks to the institute's work.

By programme division, the five research programmes with the largest numbers of researchers are: the Environment and Society Centre (49 researchers), Global Health Programme (41), Middle East and North Africa Programme (37), Russia and Eurasia Programme (28), International Security Programme (27), and Africa Programme (21). Some researchers may simultaneously conduct cross-cutting research across two programmes. Each programme is overseen by a Head, supported by appropriate administrative staff.

Appendix Table 2: Distribution of RIIA Research Staff by Field and Position, 2023 (Unit: Number of People)

Programme	Distinguished Fellows	Senior Fellows	Research Fellows	Associate Fellows	Advisors	Academy Fellows	Visiting Fellows	Research/ Admin Staff	Total
Africa Programme		3		11	2		1	4	21
Asia-Pacific Programme		3		4				3	10
Digital Society Initiative		1		2				2	5
Environment and Society Centre		9	2	23	1		2	12	49
Europe Programme	1		1	7	1			1	11
Global Economy and Finance Programme	1			10	1		1	3	16
Global Health Programme	1	1	1	15	5	10		8	41
International Law Programme	1	1		7				3	12
International Security Programme		3	2	12	1			9	27
Middle East and North Africa Programme		3	2	22	2			8	37
Russia and Eurasia Programme		4		15	3			6	28
UK in the World Programme		1	2	3				1	7
US and Americas Programme		2		13	1			4	20
Total	**4**	**31**	**10**	**144**	**17**	**10**	**4**	**57**	**284**

Source: Compiled by the author based on data from the official website of the RIIA

To deepen collaboration and exchange among researchers and collectively explore new approaches to major issues, the RIIA regularly hosts seminars, discussion groups, and an annual academic conference, providing platforms for researchers to exchange ideas with experts from diverse fields. Programme teams also frequently convene their members for open discussions on specific topics. Furthermore, the institute possesses extensive networks spanning politics, business, and academia, regularly inviting external experts from business, academia, politics, civil society, and other sectors to participate in its seminar activities. Annually, the RIIA hosts hundreds of public events to foster mutual understanding among policymakers, stakeholders, and researchers.

3.2 Research Areas

The RIIA organizes its research work around specific research agendas, typically comprising six priority research domains, which are determined through open discussion and consensus-building among researchers and management, updated every three years, with the final research agenda requiring approval by the Council before taking effect. The six research agendas of the RIIA for the period 2021-2023 are as follows:

(1) The Future of Conflict. Research focuses on approaches to mitigate and limit the negative impacts of conflict on social stability and the international order, such as large-scale armed conflict between states and the impact of technological advancements on the conduct of warfare. Key research areas include: disruptive technologies; the Russia-Ukraine conflict; issues pertaining to Afghanistan; issues pertaining to Iraq; domestic political protests in Iran; and effective approaches to humanitarian and development assistance provision.

(2) The Geopolitics of China-U.S. Competition. Research is concerned with analysis of how systemic competition between China and the United States shapes different regions and policy domains, so as to help governments, the private sector, and civil society understand and respond. Key research areas include: domestic political developments in China; the impact of the Sino-American technology and trade wars on other countries and potential response strategies; and how to manage the rise of China.

(3) The UK in the World. Research focuses on ways to advance and protect British national interests, as well as the UK's priorities, partners, and policy options for building a stable, secure, and sustainable world. The goal of this agenda is to analyze the foreign

policy decisions and trade-offs Britain is likely to face over the next five to ten years and to formulate recommendations ahead of the next general election.

(4) Achieving Sustainable Development. Emphasis is placed on assessing the political and economic risks of climate change and exploring policy pathways for achieving a sustainable transition in energy, land use, forests, and food systems, while balancing global economic development with low-carbon environmental protection. Key research areas include: carbon neutrality; global forest governance; provision of a platform for the African green transition; and climate change challenges.

(5) Revitalizing Multilateralism. Research focuses on how international institutions can reform their purposes, inclusivity, legitimacy, and institutional mechanisms to enable effective global governance in health, economics, digital technology, and human rights. Key research areas include: cybercrime; health; income inequality; gender equality; and the development of international law in cyberspace.

(6) Enhancing Democracy. Research is concentrated on re-evaluation of the relationships and responsibilities between the state, markets, and people, and specific policy options for renewing social contracts in Europe, the Middle East, and Africa. Key research areas include: enhancing the democratic resilience of democratic states; promoting responsible social governance in Africa and Latin America; and policy pathways for improving global human rights conditions.

The six priority areas outlined in the research agenda provide directional guidance for the RIIA's research activities. Under the research agenda set by the Chatham House Council, individual programmes have the autonomy to define their own research priorities and objectives and to secure third-party funding at the programme level. In terms of scope, the institute extensively covers various thematic areas of international relations, including security, economics, global governance, and international law, providing independent analysis of global, regional, and country-specific issues. Regional studies are particularly prominent, encompassing all major global regions such as Africa, Asia, Europe, the Americas, the Middle East, and Eurasia. In terms of focus, the RIIA places special emphasis on global governance issues, with the Environment and Society Centre and the Global Health Programme together comprising over 80 staff members. Given the considerable degree of autonomy enjoyed by each programme, the research foci of the different programmes are briefly summarized below:

(1) The Africa Programme. This programme primarily focuses on international relations issues affecting African states and regions, with the aim of providing intellectual leadership on political and socio-economic transformations in Africa. The programme's five key research areas for 2023 are: elections and political systems in African states; inclusive economic growth, governance, and technology; sustainable resource governance; regional peace and security; and the foreign policies of African states and their roles in international relations.

(2) The Asia-Pacific Programme. This programme is primarily concerned with political, economic, and social developments in the Asia-Pacific region, providing objective analysis of key issues affecting the region to foster understanding of fundamental questions arising from its rise, informing policy decisions and generating impact. The programme's five key research areas are: geopolitics and governance; trade, investment, and economy; conflict, peace, and stability; technology and society; and demographics, population, and migration.

(3) The Digital Society Initiative (DSI). This initiative primarily focuses on technology policy and the construction of inclusive digital societies, especially the opportunities, challenges, and responses posed by technology to domestic and international politics. The programme's research objectives are: to develop solution-driven policy recommendations; and to maximize the potential of technology to help build a sustainably secure, prosperous, and just world.

(4) The Environment and Society Centre. This Centre is primarily focused on the systemic impacts of major environmental challenges on international geopolitics and local communities, developing solutions and providing governments, businesses, and society with information, networks, and tools to enhance global resilience in the face of climate change and natural resource depletion. The Centre's research outputs are internationally recognized and widely used by decision-makers in the public, private, and non-profit sectors. Its key research areas include: climate and energy transition; solutions for sustainable food, land, and natural resources; and accelerating and financing the sustainability transition.

(5) The Sustainability Accelerator. Originally the Hoffmann Centre for Sustainable Resource Economy, the Sustainability Accelerator project was launched in 2021, managed under the Environment and Society Centre and sharing its researchers. It focuses on

overlooked technologies, actors, and frameworks, collaborating with innovators, investors, entrepreneurs, policymakers, and other stakeholders to shorten the cycle between policy design and implementation, aiming to speed up the global sustainability transition. Its key areas of focus include: regenerative land economy and circular built environment; the enabling role of finance and technology in the sustainability transition; and consumption-driven economic models. The MAVA Foundation provided £10 million in funding for this project.

(6) The Europe Programme. This programe primarily focuses on European democracy and political economy, European security, UK foreign policy after Brexit, and the future of transatlantic relations.

(7) The Global Economy and Finance Programme. This programme conducts policy-oriented research and analysis on frontier issues in the global economy and finance. Through activities such as high-level seminars that bring together leading academics, policymakers, business leaders, and policy officials, it ensures that its independent analysis yields practical and timely policy insights and recommendations Recent research priorities include: the COVID-19 pandemic and the global economic crisis; international economic cooperation; global economic governance and the role of the G7 and G20; the economics of climate change; international trade and investment; debt issues in developing country; corporate purpose and responsibility; and the evolution of the international monetary system.

(8) The International Security Programme. This programme is primarily concerned with frontier issues in international security and defense, examining emerging technology security, conflict prevention, and global security policy with the aim of achieving human security, peace, and prosperity. The programme's three recent research themes are: international security, defense, and governance; science, technology, and security; and society and security.

(9) The International Law Programme. This programme is dedicated to examining global governance issues through the lens of international law, with the overarching research objectives of influencing policy and legislative change, promoting the development of international law, and protecting international human rights. Recent research priorities include: understanding institutional changes in international law during the global order transition; solutions for new technologies and the global commons governance deficit;

revitalizing the international human rights system; and promoting inclusive global governance.

(10) The Global Health Programme. This programme primarily focuses on international public health governance, with the aim of fostering dialogue between the international relations and public health communities, and advising governments on health sector reform and its political economy. Recent research priorities include: universal health coverage; global health security; and healthy societies.

(11) The Middle East and North Africa Programme. This programme primarily studies the economic, political, and social trends in the Middle East and North Africa, and publishes research, commentary, and analysis in both English and Arabic. Recent research priorities include: the rise of hybrid actors in regional power dynamics and their challenges to state power; interconnected political economy networks and their impact on regional conflicts; the central role of state-building in regional conflicts and their resolution; the role of regional actors in regional conflicts and geopolitics; and citizen mobilization and its intersection with state institutions and elite stakeholders.

(12) The Russia and Eurasia Programme. Established in 1986 as the Soviet Foreign Policy Programme, this programme focuses on the domestic and foreign politics of Russia and the Commonwealth of Independent States (CIS) states, as well as the dynamics of power competition in the Eurasian region. The programme's four recent research themes are: the Russia-Ukraine war; the impact of the war on Russian domestic politics; internal political developments in Ukraine; and geopolitical competition in the Eurasian region.

(13) The UK in the World Programme. Primarily focuses on the UK's geopolitical, diplomatic, and security position and strategy in a changing world, this programme seeks to identify priorities, partners, and pathways for Britain in the global scene in the coming years. Its research objective is to examine UK foreign policy through roundtables, academic research, and extensive networks, making recommendations to improve British standing in the world.

(14) The US and Americas Programme. This programme primarily focuses on political, economic, and security issues in North, Central, and South America and their global implications. Recent research priorities include: U.S. domestic politics and its role as a global power; the international and regional roles of middle powers such as Canada and Mexico;

the role of regional states in trade, finance, climate change, and migration governance; evolving democracy; and major economic, political, and cultural transformations.

3.3 Research Outputs

The RIIA publishes its research outputs in various formats, including books, research reports, journals, and magazines. Digital publications released online primarily include Research Papers, Briefings, and Expert Comments. Research Papers represent the academic outcomes and policy recommendations resulting from in-depth research by full-time RIIA researchers on major issues. These are typically the final reports of research programmes, often exceeding 50 pages in length. Chatham House Briefings constitute interim outputs from programme researchers, focusing on relatively narrower topics but characterized by clear research questions, conclusions, and citations. These are scholarly publications typically around 15 pages long. Expert Comments are short, timely analyses written by RIIA researchers on current political events.

Books published by the institute generally address major international political issues and propose original foreign policy ideas, focusing on topical policy issues such as security, economy, environment, and international law. They aim to offer new perspectives on an increasingly complex, uncertain, and interconnected world. Most books are published through the "Insights" series co-published with the Brookings Institution. Published books include *The Justice Laboratory: International Law in Africa* and *Tectonic Politics: Global Political Risk in an Age of Transformation*, among others.

The journals and magazines published by the RIIA include *International Affairs*, the *Journal of Cyber Policy*, and *The World Today*. The bimonthly academic journal *International Affairs*, founded in 1922, is the institute's oldest and most prestigious publication. It remains one of the most authoritative journals in the field of international relations globally, primarily analyzing cutting-edge and major theoretical issues in current international affairs. The *Journal of Cyber Policy*, founded in 2016 and published three times a year, focuses on issues related to cybercrime, cybersecurity, cyber policy, and emerging technology governance. As an emerging academic journal in the field of cyber policy, it has achieved over 210,000 downloads of its published articles in the eight years since its inception. *The World Today* is a bimonthly magazine focusing on analysis and commentary on current international political issues. It is less academic in nature but offers high timeliness and has great appeals to a broader audience.

Beyond publications, the RIIA also engages with its members and the public through television, online platforms, podcasts, email, and other new media channels. For example, it launched a weekly podcast called "Independent Thinking." Hosted by the Director of Chatham House, the podcast features dialogues with policymakers, journalists, and RIIA experts on current political issues, providing insights into the latest international affairs. Additionally, the institute has established a "daily media briefing" system to promptly disseminate its policy insights to the media.

The institute places great importance on external engagement, regularly inviting experts and scholars to participate in hundreds of public and private international conferences, seminars, roundtables, and other events annually. Most events are open to the public, who can also participate via live online streaming or access meeting summaries and recordings for free on the official website of the RIIA. Furthermore, the institute hosts approximately 120 events annually exclusively for individual members, featuring speeches by heads of government, government officials, and other prominent figures, as well as specialized lectures by renowned experts and scholars in international politics. Corporate member activities primarily focus on networking, such as business leader breakfasts.

IV. Institutional Achievements

First, as a research institution with over a century of accumulated history and academic prestige, the RIIA has become one of the largest in the United Kingdom and one of the world's most renowned think tanks on international issues. Because its researchers frequently raise major international political issues that shape global debate, *Foreign Policy* magazine once characterized it as the top non-U.S. think tank. The 2020 *Global Go To Think Tank Index Report* published by the University of Pennsylvania ranked it as the sixth-best think tank globally and the fifth-best in Western Europe. Moreover, given its extensive networks with the UK government, business community, media, and academia, and because "The UK in the World" is a priority on its research agenda, the RIIA wields considerable influence over the foreign policy of the UK government.

Second, the institute's researchers and its journal *International Affairs* have played a significant role in advancing the development of international politics and international political economy as independent academic disciplines. For instance, Susan Strange, a pioneer of international political economy, served as a full-time researcher at the RIIA from 1964 to 1978, focusing on topics such as the sterling crisis, the politics of monetary relations, and transnational relations. In 1970, she published the article *International Economics and International Relations: A Case of Mutual Neglect* in *International Affairs*. This article profoundly revealed the differences between the disciplines of international economics and international relations, articulating the necessity of establishing international political economy as an independent field of study. It is widely regarded by scholars as a foundational text marking the birth of international political economy as a separate discipline. In 1971, Strange founded and led the International Political Economy study group at the institute, where she completed works such as *Sterling and British Policy* and *International Monetary Relations*. Building on this cumulative research expertise, Strange ultimately developed the influential theory of "Structural Power" in international relations, catalyzing significant advances in the discipline of international relations.

Third, the RIIA established the information confidentiality rule designed to facilitate free discussions at meetings, known as the "Chatham House Rule," which has now become a widely accepted principle for seminars and conferences around the world and within international organizations. The Rule was first formulated in 1927 and subsequently revised in 1992 and 2002. Its core principle is sharing content without revealing the source. It stipulates that participants are free to use information gathered during a meeting or discussion in their own work, with proper attribution, but must not reveal the identity or affiliation of the speaker concerned; nor may the meeting organizers record the speaker's comments without consent. The Rule allows participants to discuss sensitive or contentious issues, enhancing the inclusivity of discussions on public policy and current political affairs, and has contributed significantly to fostering open debate on international relations issues.

Index

0-9

17+1 / 16+1 cooperation, 25, 38, 143, 151–152, 157

2011 Greek debt crisis, 22, 80

2014–2015 Ukraine crisis, 2, 14, 130, 149, 164

A

advocacy coalition framework, 72, 195, 228

agenda-setting, 17, 37, 41, 49, 63, 75–76, 79, 84, 90, 92, 97, 107, 111, 167, 196–197, 200, 203–204, 236, 253, 330, 334, 344

Allio, Lorenzo, 37, 165–167, 171–172

anti-dumping measures, 27, 81, 83–84, 127, 132, 142–143, 150, 153, 157

anti-subsidy measures, 81, 83–84, 142–143, 157

Arab Spring, 2, 14, 149

Asia-Pacific, 1, 136–139, 149, 157, 187, 198, 222–223, 250, 253–257, 259–261, 360

B

Barroso, José Manuel, 144, 189–190

Belt and Road Initiative (Silk Road Economic Belt), 7, 25–26, 38, 143–152, 157, 325

Blum, Sonja, 202–203, 205, 270

Borrell, Josep, 30, 32

Boucher, Stephen, 161–165, 170–171, 196, 201

Bourdieu, Pierre, 45, 54–56, 70, 187, 224

Brexit, 4, 29, 47, 82, 122, 124, 129, 225, 230, 235, 237, 242, 251, 361

Brookings Institution, 15, 52, 64, 198, 226, 363

Bruegel, 14, 18–19, 32, 47, 49, 89, 153, 160–162, 169–181, 184–192, 194, 196–198, 216, 247, 250–251, 259, 261–262, 273–277, 312–331

  funding structure, 178, 180, 184, 191, 250, 319–321, 324, 327, 331

  governance and organization, 162, 172, 174, 177, 184, 186, 188, 190–191, 312, 315–318, 321–330

  media presence, 171, 177, 184, 247, 259, 261, 318, 329–331

  Policy Contribution series, 173–174

Brussels, 11, 17, 21–22, 27, 29–30, 32, 35–37, 39, 43–44, 46–47, 81, 89, 92, 110–117, 133, 143, 151, 153–154, 160, 162, 165–169, 171–173, 178, 184, 190–191, 194, 214, 216, 219, 224–225, 230, 233, 235–236, 247, 253, 269, 272, 274, 311–313, 315, 321, 331, 333

Brussels Route, 46–47, 110–115, 117, 194, 214, 224, 230, 233, 235, 272

C

Carnegie Endowment for International Peace, 6–7, 40, 105, 219, 311

Central and Eastern Europe, 25, 120, 148, 151, 339, 341

Central Asia, 26, 147–150, 340–342

Centre for European Policy Studies (CEPS), 92, 162, 171–173, 188, 198, 219, 311

Chatham House (Royal Institute of International Affairs), 41–42, 47, 49, 61, 92–93, 95, 115, 123, 145–149, 198, 226–227, 230, 235–244, 247–254, 256–257, 259–264, 273–277, 335, 348–359, 363–365

China, passim

perceptions of, as threat or rival, 6–8, 10, 14, 28–32, 84, 94, 140, 152, 206, 330

investment from, 10, 25, 30, 118, 140, 142, 145, 150, 152, 157, 174, 178, 189, 195, 214, 238–239, 242–243, 250, 252, 276

China-EU relations, 2, 8, 26–30, 38, 149, 155, 159, 208, 213–214, 250–252

China-U.S. strategic competition / rivalry, 6, 8, 14, 28

Clingendael Institute, 26, 28, 93, 312

Cold War, 2–5, 13, 20, 205, 226, 350

Coman, Ramona, 161–162, 169–170, 172

connectivity strategy, 32, 150

Council of the European Union, 1, 33, 68, 79, 97, 108, 111–113, 117, 155, 174, 189, 216, 233, 237, 257, 331

Council Conclusions, 209

COVID-19 pandemic, 9, 11, 30, 32, 323–325, 361

Coxall, Bill, 36, 201, 228–229, 272

critical raw materials, 158, 324

D

Denham, Andrew, 37, 39, 164, 170–171, 202–204

DG Trade, 81, 185, 189

E

economic security, 24–25, 180

Egmont Institute, 26, 83, 142, 162, 312

epistemic community, 8, 37, 43, 64, 71, 166, 173, 178, 195, 226, 228, 251

EU Global Strategy (2016), 7, 137–138, 200, 236

EU-China 2020 Strategic Agenda, 150, 157

EU-China Summit, 1, 10, 30, 143, 145–146, 150, 156, 252

"EU-China: A Strategic Outlook" (2019), 10, 28, 30, 32, 84, 118

Euro area crisis, 3, 14, 21, 24, 38, 47

European Central Bank, 108, 184–185, 189–190, 194, 237, 251–252, 257, 323

European Commission, 1, 5, 7–8, 10–11, 13–14, 17, 19, 25, 27–30, 33, 43, 48, 68, 79, 81–83, 97, 108, 111, 113, 117, 132, 142–144, 150, 153–157, 161–162, 165–166, 168, 174–177, 180–181, 185, 189–190, 194, 207–208, 214–215, 217–219, 221, 233, 237, 239–241, 244, 247, 249–254, 257, 273–274, 330–331, 338, 355

communications and strategy papers, 1, 5, 7, 11, 14, 17, 19, 28–30, 83, 142, 157, 162, 189

Staff Working Document, 27, 83, 153, 155

trade defense role, 27, 48, 81, 83, 132, 142–143, 150, 153, 155, 180, 207, 252

European Community Studies Association,

167

European Council, 5, 33, 79, 108, 111–112, 143–146, 155–156, 174–177, 189–190, 208–210, 216, 233, 239–241, 331

European Council on Foreign Relations (ECFR), 18–19, 32, 44, 92, 145–147, 150, 160, 236

European External Action Service (EEAS), 79, 108, 113, 138, 198, 215, 217–219, 251–252

European Investment Bank, 184–185, 317, 320

European Parliament, 1, 7, 10, 19, 27, 30, 33–34, 79, 81, 83, 92, 97, 108–109, 117, 124, 137, 142–143, 155, 157–158, 168, 171, 174–177, 189, 192, 208–210, 219, 221–222, 237, 239–241, 252, 254, 257, 335

European Policy Centre (EPC), 40, 92, 113, 162, 172–173, 198, 269, 311

European Think-tank Network on China (ETNC), 236, 251–252

European Union Institute for Security Studies (EUISS), 89, 137–138, 145–147, 149–150, 201, 312

expertise, role of, 39, 51–54, 58, 64, 71–72, 74, 79, 89–90, 93, 164, 166–169, 195, 202, 204, 214, 228, 236, 253, 266, 268–269, 276–277, 335, 342, 346, 365

F

Fischer, Frank, 49, 60, 62, 76, 196, 228, 270

Flinders, Matthew, 231

foreign direct investment (FDI), 27, 29–30, 48

framing, 14, 54, 206, 276

France, 48, 55, 83, 120, 122, 124, 129, 131–132, 134–135, 142, 161, 191, 238–239, 243, 261, 314–315, 317, 320, 342–343

French Institute of International Relations (IFRI), 93, 219, 251, 342

Friedrich Ebert Stiftung, 91, 202, 204–205, 215, 269, 312

G

García-Herrero, Alicia, 10, 14, 32, 174

geoeconomics, 150, 169, 323–324

German Institute for International and Security Affairs, see *Stiftung Wissenschaft und Politik*

Germany, 8–10, 15, 19, 22, 29, 36, 38, 42, 44, 47–49, 75, 83, 90–92, 94, 115, 120, 122, 124, 128–132, 134–136, 142, 150, 167, 187–188, 198–207, 212, 214–216, 219, 221–222, 224–225, 229, 243, 251, 254–255, 261, 265–269, 274, 311–312, 314–315, 327, 332–336, 338–341, 343–347

global financial crisis (2008), 2–3, 8, 14, 17–19, 21, 24, 119, 134–136, 236, 238

Global Go To Think Tank Index, 39, 47, 160, 199–200, 227, 261, 270, 313, 316, 345, 364

Greenwood, Justin, 43, 85, 272

H

High Representative of the Union for Foreign Affairs, 30, 32, 134, 144–146

Huawei and 5G, 9, 250

I

industrial policy, 9, 11, 15, 18–19, 23, 32–33, 45, 48, 81, 133, 158, 177–179, 209–212, 241–242, 263, 277, 326–327

interdependence, 12, 16, 220

interest groups, 8, 10–11, 35–36, 43, 45, 57, 59, 62–64, 67–69, 71, 73, 79, 85, 90–91,

107, 109, 111, 114, 144, 167–169, 185, 190, 193, 204, 228–233, 235, 248, 253, 255, 258, 266, 269, 272–274, 334, 337

investment screening, 7, 29–30, 48, 83–84, 142–143, 150, 153, 157, 180

issue networks, 73–74

Italy, 48, 83, 120, 122–125, 135, 138, 142, 215, 242, 251, 317, 320

J

Jacques Delors Institute (Notre Europe), 160–164, 166, 170–171, 196, 201, 215, 219, 251

James, Simon, 96, 195, 229, 260–261, 269

Japan, 15, 17, 28, 31, 90, 127–128, 135–136, 150, 157, 219, 254–256

Jochem, Sven, 202–203, 205, 269

Joint Communication (EU-China), 33, 157

Juncker, Jean-Claude, 5, 11, 14, 29, 31, 83, 144, 154, 190

K

knowledge regime, 56–57

L

level playing field, 27, 127, 156, 158

von der Leyen, Ursula, 5, 8, 11, 14, 17, 19, 29–31, 83, 162

lobbying, 40, 43, 57–58, 62–63, 67–68, 72, 79, 90–91, 109, 167, 169, 203, 228–229, 235, 248, 253, 269, 272–274

M

market economy status, 27, 48, 82, 140, 152, 156

McGann, James, 39, 47, 49, 52, 74, 97, 160, 199, 202, 226–227, 269–270

Medvetz, Thomas, 42, 57, 70–71, 171, 224

member states, 5, 11, 18, 21–22, 29–30, 36, 46, 79, 85–86, 91, 109–111, 114, 117, 120, 129–130, 132, 134–135, 142, 144–145, 157, 161–164, 167–169, 180, 182, 184–185, 188, 191, 194, 197–198, 200–201, 224, 230, 233, 242, 253–254, 262, 266–267, 274, 313, 315, 320, 339

mercantilism, 20, 125, 139

Mercator Institute for China Studies (MERICS), 95, 174, 251

Merkel, Angela, 128–130, 133–134

Middle East and North Africa, 2, 26, 44, 149, 164, 340–342, 350, 353, 357, 359, 362

Missiroli, Antonio, 138, 162, 165, 171, 196, 201, 312

N

National Route, 46–47, 110–111, 113–114, 117, 194, 214, 216, 224, 230, 233–235, 254

network capital, 166–169

normative power, 3, 13, 133

North Atlantic Treaty Organization (NATO), 129–130, 254, 312, 342

Notre Europe, see *Jacques Delors Institute*

P

Peterson Institute for International Economics, 13, 67–68

Pisani-Ferry, Jean, 174, 314–315

policy networks, 37, 45, 71, 228, 321

policy paradigms, 37, 43, 72
Polish Institute of International Affairs (PISM), 137, 146, 148, 200, 215
pressure groups, 35–36, 43–44, 71, 85, 228–229, 272–273
protectionism, 6, 15, 20, 23, 27, 81, 118, 125–127, 130–131, 139, 141, 154

R

RAND Corporation, 41, 226, 333
reciprocity, 27, 156, 158, 274
revolving door, 191–192, 194, 197, 220, 224, 230, 252–253, 259, 274
Rodrik, Dani, 4–5, 20–21
Royal Institute of International Affairs, see *Chatham House*
Russia, 10, 130, 148–149, 323–326, 339, 341, 357, 362
Russia–Ukraine war, 323, 325–326

S

Schubert, Klaus, 202–203, 205, 270
Shanghai, 54–56, 147, 202, 205
Sherrington, Philippa, 160–161, 163, 166–168, 170–171
Silk Road Economic Belt, see *Belt and Road Initiative*
Smith, James Allen, 39, 42, 62, 96, 229, 261, 269
social learning, 72, 201, 228, 261
soft power, 13, 196
South Korea, 138, 187, 215, 219, 256
sovereignty (economic and technological), 3, 5–6, 8, 10–14, 16–17, 19, 21–22, 29, 31–32, 126, 324, 326
state-owned enterprises (SOEs), 26, 127, 152, 174, 180, 325
Stiftung Wissenschaft und Politik (SWP), 8, 14, 47, 49, 83, 92–93, 105–106, 142, 145–146, 150, 198–201, 206–210, 212–220, 222–225, 247, 257, 259–262, 273–277, 311, 332–341, 343–347
  research projects, 212–214, 216, 338, 343–344, 346
  revolving door at, 220, 222, 224, 259, 261
  SWP Comments, 207, 343–345, 347
  SWP Research Paper, 8, 14, 207, 343–344
Stone, Diane, 37, 39, 49, 69, 164, 170–171, 195–196, 202–204, 270
strategic autonomy, 6, 14, 32, 324
Summers, Tim, 147–149, 174, 239
systemic rival, see *"EU-China: A Strategic Outlook"*

T

technology transfer, 27, 118, 158
think tanks (European), passim
  agenda-setting by, 37–38, 41, 44, 48–49, 62, 64, 75, 87, 90, 92, 99, 107, 167, 172, 196, 203–204, 236, 243, 253, 331, 334
  conferences, 48, 98–99, 101–102, 161, 163–164, 166–171, 180, 184, 186–189, 197, 217, 219–220, 243, 251, 330, 350
  funding of, 40, 74, 87, 112, 140, 202, 205, 212, 233, 248, 252–253, 256, 265–266, 269, 320, 332, 338, 340, 342, 346, 351–352, 356
  lobbying by, 43, 57–58, 60, 62–63, 68, 72,

79, 86, 90, 109–110, 167, 169, 203, 228–229, 235, 269, 272
publications, 44, 74, 98–100, 103–104, 154, 217, 227, 251
revolving door, 48, 191–192, 220–222, 224, 252, 259
Thunert, Martin, 202–205, 269
trade defense instruments, 23, 27, 48, 81, 83, 157, 207, 252
Trump, Donald, 4–5, 8–10, 20, 118–119, 122, 124–134, 139–141, 165

U

Ullrich, Heidi, 37–38, 164, 170–171
United Kingdom, 36, 44, 49, 52, 72, 75, 89–90, 92, 94, 96–97, 115, 122, 124, 129, 135, 144–145, 165, 199, 201–202, 204–205, 226–231, 233–237, 242, 247–249, 254–257, 259–263, 265–269, 274, 320, 348–349, 358, 362, 364–365
Brexit and, 129, 200, 235, 237, 242
United Nations, 254, 341–342, 350, 355
United States, 3–10, 13–15, 17, 19, 28–29, 31, 36, 38–41, 44, 52, 59–60, 63, 68, 71, 97, 106, 119, 125–133, 135–136, 140–142, 149, 160, 198, 205, 215, 220, 260, 265–269, 271–273, 332–333, 339, 348, 358
China policy and trade war, 1, 6–8, 10, 14, 28–29, 31–32, 95, 127, 130–131, 135, 140–141, 149, 206, 215, 239, 322, 358

W

Wacker, Gudrun, 150, 206–207
Western Europe, 13–14, 17, 25, 120, 123, 151, 199–200, 266
Wolff, Guntram, 19, 174, 192
World Trade Organization (WTO), 2, 9, 48, 125–126, 128, 133, 136, 139, 141, 156–158

X

Xi Jinping, 143–144

www.ingramcontent.com/pod-product-compliance
Lightning Source LLC
LaVergne TN
LVHW070524061126
851857LV00024B/2139
* 9 7 8 1 9 7 0 3 1 6 1 4 8 *